Folk Psychological Narratives

Folk Psychological Narratives

The Sociocultural Basis of Understanding Reasons

Daniel D. Hutto

A Bradford Book
The MIT Press
Cambridge, Massachusetts
London, England

MIT Press books may be purchased at special quantity discounts for business or sales promotional use. For information, please e-mail special_sales@mitpress.mit.edu or write to Special Sales Department, The MIT Press, 55 Hayward Street, Cambridge, MA 02142.

This book was set in Stone sans and Stone serif by SNP Best-set Typesetter Ltd., Hong Kong, and was printed and bound in the United States.

Library of Congress Cataloging-in-Publication Data

Hutto, Daniel D.
 Folk psychological narratives : the sociocultural basis of understanding reasons / Daniel D. Hutto.
   p. cm.
 "A Bradford book."
 Includes bibliographical references and index.
 ISBN 978-0-262-08367-6 (hardcover : alk. paper)
 1. Attribution (Social psychology) 2. Cognition. 3. Cognition in children. 4. Social perception in children. 5. Philosophy of mind. 6. Social psychology. I. Title.
 HM1076.H88   2007
 150.1—dc22   2007005539

10 9 8 7 6 5 4 3 2 1

For my son Justin Rais,
desipere in loco

Contents

Preface

The Cognitive Revolution . . . was intended to bring "mind" back into the human sciences after a long cold winter of objectivism. . . . Some critics, perhaps unkindly, argue that the new cognitive science, the child of the revolution, has gained its technical advantages at the price of de-humanising the very concept of mind it had sought to re-establish in psychology, and that it has thereby estranged much of psychology from the other human sciences and the humanities.

—Bruner, *Acts of Meaning*

Folk psychology is a philosopher's label for the practice of making sense of intentional actions, minimally, by appeal to an agent's motivating beliefs and desires.[1] It is the sort of thing one does, for example, when digesting Jane's explanation of her late arrival at a meeting because she *mistakenly thought* it was being held in a different room. Taking our friend at her word (i.e., if we assume that she had genuinely *wanted* to attend the meeting on time), we will blame the content of her beliefs for the confusion on this occasion. This is something we do, and have the standing capacity to do, unthinkingly. We rely on it constantly.

Established wisdom has it that this workaday ability is something we inherited from our ancient ancestors. Proponents of the hotly debated dominant offerings for understanding folk psychology—known as *theory theory* and *simulation theory*—typically hold that our ancient cognitive endowment takes one of three forms. It is (1) a very special kind of subpersonal mechanism that literally contains the relevant mentalistic theory, (2) a basic starter theory that is modified by theory-formation mechanisms that fashion a mature theory of mind during ontogeny, or (3) a series of subpersonal mindreading mechanisms that enable direct manipulation of the relevant mental states themselves. To accept any of these views (or some hybrid combination of them) is to accept that our folk psychological abilities are essentially (or at least in important respects) a kind of biological inheritance.

That some such account must be true is encouraged by the apparent fact that, after a fairly stable pattern of staged development—though one that can be subject to specific delays—all normal human children of all cultures come to understand actions in terms of reasons using the same basic mentalistic framework and its conceptual ingredients. In other words, many believe that the human capacity to use mature folk psychology is a universal trait of our species. An important exception is those individuals who have autism. They exhibit a distinctive set of impairments—impairments that, inter alia, severely restrict their capacity to develop a folk psychological understanding, to the extent that they are able to do so at all. These considerations fuel the idea that such abilities must be written into the very fabric of our being: a gift from our evolutionary ancestors.

Against this idea, this book provides an elaborate defence of the claim that our capacity to understand intentional actions in terms of reasons has a decidedly sociocultural basis. It advances and explicates the hypothesis that children only come by the requisite framework for such understanding and master its practical application by being exposed to and engaging in a distinctive kind of narrative practice. I call this the Narrative Practice Hypothesis (NPH). Its core claim is that direct encounters with stories about persons who act for reasons—those supplied in interactive contexts by responsive caregivers—is the normal route through which children become familiar with both (1) the basic structure of folk psychology and (2) the norm-governed possibilities for wielding it in practice, thus learning both how and when to use it.

The overarching aim of this book is to introduce this possibility into the mix, thus breaking some new ground. My purpose is to make as strong case as is possible for the underexamined idea that our interpretative abilities may well be socioculturally grounded. This requires not only spelling out the positive contours of the NPH, which is the task of chapter 2, but also challenging certain widely held assumptions that might otherwise make it look like a less-than-serious contender for explaining the basis and origin of our mature folk psychological abilities. Consequently, apart from extolling the virtues of the NPH, a fair bit of space is given over to putting its dominant rivals under appropriate pressure. I make no apologies for this since overturning assumptions that prevent us from thinking clearly about important issues is a legitimate, indeed unavoidable, philosophical activity.

Equally, however, I want to engender a positive understanding of our capacities and practices. It helps to be clear about the status of the NPH in this regard. As I said, it marks out a section of, as yet, underexplored conceptual space. It is inspired by the fact that certain types of narratives have precisely the right form and content to introduce children to folk psychology and explain their understanding of it over time. As a philosopher I do not see it as my job to fashion and supply straightforward empirical hypotheses. I regard the NPH not so much as conjecture but as a product of a kind of observational philosophy. Like its counterpart observational comedy, which can be funny or unfunny, this kind of philosophy too can be illuminating or unilluminating. My hope is, obviously, that the NPH is the former.

That said, the NPH has interesting empirical implications that deserve investigation. But marshaling such data and putting it to the full test (that is, by attempting to falsify the proposal) is not the purpose of this book. My aim is rather to prepare the ground for its acceptance mainly by revealing the limitations and bankruptcy of its rivals and discrediting certain popular suppositions that might stand in the way of taking it seriously.

For example, in chapter 1, I set the stage for the appearance of the NPH by challenging the all-too-common assumption that the primary function of folk psychology is to enable us to carry off third-person predictions of the behaviors of others by adopting a speculative stance. Undeniably, the actions of others sometimes cry out for explanation, but in all such cases, when making sense of these, what we are seeking is a narrative that fills in or fleshes out the relevant details of that person's story. This is the very heart and soul of folk psychological understanding. Hence, I call the narratives that do this kind of work *folk psychological narratives*. The practice of supplying or constructing them *just is* that of explicating and explaining action in terms of reasons. Folk psychology is, by my lights, in essence, a distinctive kind of narrative practice.

The crucial point is that folk psychological narratives come in both third-person and second-person varieties. Moreover, the success or otherwise of such explanations depends, in the main, on who is doing the telling—that is, who produces the account. Although we often attempt to generate such accounts on behalf of others "at a remove," by calling on simulative or theoretical heuristics, the fact is that even when this speculative activity is well supported it is quite unlikely to succeed in hitting on the right explanation. The likelihood of success in such endeavors is more or less inversely proportional to need.

In contrast, although not foolproof, by far the best and most reliable means of obtaining a true understanding of why another acted is to get the relevant story directly from the horse's mouth. The activity is familiar enough. Such accounts are typically delivered—indeed, fashioned—in the course of ordinary dialogue and conversation. It is because of this that they are usually sensitive to a questioner's precise explanatory needs and requirements. The nature of such engagements is complex and deserves greater attention than it has received to date, but that too is not my focus in this work. A primary ambition of the first chapter is to draw attention to the banal truism that second-person deliveries of these folk psychological narratives are not only commonplace but they also do much of the heavy lifting in enabling us to make sense of the actions of others in daily life—that is, when there is a genuine need to do so.

After supplying reasons for thinking that our sophisticated folk psychological understanding is essentially narrative, I introduce the NPH in chapter 2. The basic claim is a developmental one: that we acquire our capacity to understand intentional actions using a framework incorporating the central propositional attitudes of belief and desire through participating in a unique kind of narrative practice as children—that of engaging with stories about protagonists who act for reasons. It is through scaffolded encounters with stories of the appropriate kind that children learn how the core propositional attitudes behave with respect to one another and other standard mental partners.

Serving as exemplars and complex objects of joint attention, these folk psychological narratives familiarize children with the normal settings and standard consequences of taking specific actions. But deriving an understanding of folk psychology from these is nothing like learning a rigid set of rules about what rational agents tend to do in various circumstances. Learning how to deploy the framework of everyday psychology requires the development of a very special and flexible kind of skill, one that can only be acquired by seeing reasons in action against a rich backdrop of possibilities. Folk psychological narratives provide precisely the right sort of training set for this. For in such stories the core mentalistic framework—consisting of the rules for the interaction of the various attitudes—remains constant. However, other important features vary. Thus children learn the important differences that the content of the attitudes make to understanding action, as well as the contributions made by a person's character, history, and larger projects. In this way, encounters with stories of the appropriate kind foster an understanding of the subtleties and nuances needed for making sense of intentional actions in terms of a person's reasons. By repeated exposure to such narratives, children become familiar with both the forms and norms of folk psychology.

This is not a passive process. Children must be guided through it by caregivers. Moreover, to reap the benefits just described, they must call on a range of basic interpersonal skills and exercise their imaginations in relevant ways. And even this is not enough. They must also have a prior and independent (even if somewhat tentative) grasp of the core propositional attitudes. There is good evidence that younger children have just this kind of practical understanding and this raft of abilities. But having all this does not presuppose or constitute having "theory of mind" or any equivalent mindreading capacity.

Establishing all of this is the burden of chapters 3 to 7. Achieving it requires a rather long detour in which prenarrative, and indeed, prelinguistic modes of social understanding and response are examined and explicated. I begin this in chapter 3, by supplying reasons for thinking that nonverbal responding, quite generally, only involves the having of intentional—but not propositional—attitudes. Distinguishing these two types of attitudes is absolutely vital, but this is not often done in the existing literature. I therefore provide a detailed account of intentional attitudes in terms of a thoroughly noncognitivist, nonrepresentationalist understanding intentionality—one that regards embodied, enactive modes of responding as basic and sees symbolic thinking as the preserve of those beings that have appropriately mastered certain sophisticated linguistic constructions and practices. This matters because only those that have achieved the latter are in a position to have and to understand bona fide propositional attitudes.

With respect to those in the former class, which includes nonverbal animals and preverbal infants, I argue that they are intentionally directed at aspects of their environment in ways that neither involve nor implicate truth-conditional content. As such, basic intentionality is neither to be modeled in semantic terms nor understood as a property of content-bearing mental states or representations.

This position is motivated by a rejection of the standard naturalized theories of content on offer—a rejection prompted by an exposé of misguided thinking about the nature of informational content and how it is (allegedly) acquired. Thus in what may appear to be a deflationary maneuver I argue that the nature of basic intentional directedness is best understood in biosemiotic terms. (Crudely, biosemiotics is what you get when you subtract the semantics from biosemantics.) In essence, accordingly, although organisms must be informationally sensitive to specific worldly offerings, this sensitivity does not involve the acquisition or manipulation of encoded informational content as, for example, modularist accounts of perception would have it.

Chapter 4 takes this idea a step further, showing that a minimalist understanding of nonverbal thinking—that is, one that does not posit the existence of propositional attitudes but only intentional attitudes—can account for even the most sophisticated of nonlinguistic activities. This chapter therefore sets out to meet a recent challenge laid down by Bermúdez. Ultimately, the minimalist proposal is put to the test by giving due consideration to what would have been required in order to fuel the kind of consequent-sensitive instrumental thinking exhibited by our hominid forebearers—that is, protological reasoning capacities of the sort that they would have needed in order to fashion the kinds of complex tools that populated the middle Palaeolithic. I argue that imaginatively extended but nevertheless perceptually based modes of responding would have sufficed for this and that despite their sophistication, these feats of our ancient ancestors do not imply that they were capable of propositional thinking.

Chapter 5 builds on this conclusion and rejects the proposal that, at root, cognition depends on having an in-built, symbolic "language of thought." Against this, I defend the idea that the only true language of propositional thought is natural language. Concomitantly, possessing genuine content-involving propositional attitudes requires mastery of complex linguistic forms and practices.

With all this in hand, I return in chapter 6 to the question of how best to understand our primary nonverbal interactions. It is proposed that such engagements, as typified by emotional interactions, involve a special kind of sensitivity and responsiveness to one another's intentional attitudes, as expressed in bodily ways. This involves neither the manipulation of propositional attitudes nor any understanding of them. It is not rightly characterized as a form of "mind" or even "body" reading. Embodied responsiveness of this kind, which is in some cases extended by imitative and imaginative abilities, better explains what fuels our unprincipled inter-personal engagements than does the postulation of mindreading abilities involving propositional attitudes. This verdict applies, I argue, even to rudimentary forms of nonverbal joint attention.

Chapter 7 is devoted to saying how, in the human case, our natural responsiveness to other minds develops in stages as we master language. This process, which depends on children exercising their abilities in specific kinds of socially scaffolded activities, provides them with their first, tentative practical grasp of desires and beliefs as propositional attitudes. In this way children come into possession of all the pieces needed for playing the understanding-action-in-terms-of-reasons game before they can actually play it. What they are missing in their early years, prior to the relevant narrative encounters, is not the components needed to play this game: they lack knowledge of the basic rules for doing so.

This brings the reader full circle. For in order to continue the story, something like the NPH is needed. Therefore what might at first appear to be an abrupt and unexpected departure into discussions about the root nature of intentionality and basic social responsiveness for several chapters turns out to have great tactical importance.

This labor is worthwhile for another reason since it deals with the likely background worry that the NPH may be circular. We can call this the "narrative competency objection." At its core is the thought that if children are only able to acquire folk psychological skills by being exposed to "stories involving characters who act for reasons," then this must surely presuppose the very capacity that participating in such narrative practices is meant to explain—that is, "theory of mind" abilities. After all, it is not as if the narrative competence in question is of a *general* variety. Thus it would seem that in order to engage fruitfully with such stories at all, children must already have precisely the sort of understanding that such encounters are conjectured to engender. I deny this: a basic competency with the relevant narratives rests on having a range of abilities, including sophisticated imaginative and cocognitive abilities and a practical grasp of the attitudes, but, even taken together, these do not add up to having a "theory of mind." Young children come to the table with some basic practical knowledge and a range of intersubjective capacities and skills that fall just short of genuine folk psychological understanding.

After introducing the NPH and demonstrating its logical and empirical adequacy, I put its prominent rivals to the test and find them wanting. In chapters 8 and 9, I critically examine the existing alternatives, which can be divided into two main types. On the one hand, there are theories that posit the existence of native mindreading capacities or devices. (These come in both theory theory (TT) or simulation theory (ST) varieties.) On the other hand, there is the hypothesis that each child constructs his or her mentalistic theory by engaging in scientific activity during ontogeny. On close scrutiny it turns out that none of these proposals has the credible resources for explaining the basis of our folk psychological abilities since none of them can account for our acquisition of the concept of belief. This being the case they all fail a fundamental test of adequacy. Worse still, in lacking such an account, they are unable to explain the source or basis of the mature folk psychological *structure*. Certainly, they have nothing to offer on this front that is remotely as satisfying as the explanation espoused by the NPH. If my arguments in these chapters prove sound, they provide compelling abductive grounds for favoring the latter over its current competitors.

To remove other potential barriers to the acceptance of the NPH, in chapter 10, I consider and discredit three standard but ill-considered motivating considerations that are often cited as reasons for believing that folk psychology must be some kind of ancient endowment rather than a late-developing socioculturally acquired skill. These are that (1) the normal learning environments of children are too impoverished to explain how they could possibly acquire their folk psychological skills and understanding, (2) folk psychology appears to be universal in our species (and hence must be built in), and (3) the best explanation of the failure of certain autistic individuals on "false-belief" tasks is that they suffer from "mindblindness" brought on by malfunctions in biologically inherited metarepresentational mechanisms.

After showing that these claims are either straightforwardly false or harmless (once properly modified), I turn to one final challenge. In the final two chapters, I say something about what our true phylogenetic inheritance—our ancient endowment—might really amount to. In reviewing the evidence from primatology and cognitive archaeology, I cast serious doubt on the familiar claim that our immediate ancestors must have had mature "theory of mind" abilities—a view that is given credence by the popular but mistaken thought that their remarkable technical and social achievements would have been impossible otherwise.

Recent evidence strongly suggests that our closest living cousins, the chimpanzees, lack metarepresentational mindreading abilities. Despite this, they are capable of entering into quite sophisticated intersubjective engagements with one another. As a consequence, some researchers have postulated that these great apes must have "theory of behavior," a "weak" theory of mind, or unprincipled "mindreading" abilities. I doubt that any of these conjectures are true. If I am right, chimpanzees are not making contentful predictions or explanations of any kind.

Whether or not one accepts this, the limits of chimpanzee intersubjective abilities are now well established, and they fall a long way short of full-fledged "theory of mind" abilities. Hence, those abilities and any putative mechanisms that might sponsor them must have been selected for at a later point in human prehistory—at some time during the Pleistocene, when the hominids reigned.

Yet, despite its popularity, this hypothesis turns out to be not very plausible when reviewed closely in light of the evidence of cognitive archaeology. A much more promising and parsimonious explanation of the relevant capacities of our hominid forerunners is that they had powerful mimetic abilities; these best account for their unique forms of interpersonal engagement, including those norm-engendering activities that paved the way for the development of language.

This is good news for my account, for if true, not only does this Mimetic Ability Hypothesis (MAH) show that there is simply no *need* to postulate ancient mindreading abilities, it also utterly defuses the "narrative competency" objection mentioned earlier. It provides an alternative and credible explanation of how and why modern humans come equipped with the basic abilities needed for engaging with and appreciating folk psychological narratives.

In all, there is good reason to think that our true biological endowment does not include native mindreading mechanisms of any "folk psychological" variety. We have little choice but to look to sociocultural practices in order to understand how we acquire our sophisticated skills in making sense of the intentional actions of persons—actions that are performed for reasons of their own. As chapter 12 emphasizes, the development of this sort of understanding would have been late-emerging in our prehistory and intersubjectively grounded in certain complex and very public narrative practices.

Acknowledgments

First and foremost, I offer sincere apologies to my wife, Farah, and three boys—Alex, Rais, and Emerson—for lost family time, unhealthy levels of household stress, and the general distractedness of their husband and father. I fear, like Victor Frankenstein, "Study had before secluded me from the intercourse of my fellow creatures and rendered me unsocial" (Shelley, *Frankenstein*, 2003/1817, 55). Equally, my parents, Margaret and William Hutto, deserve special mention. They have been absolute pillars of moral support not only during this project but in everything leading up to it. I owe them far more than I can possibly express.

I am especially grateful to the Edwards family for supplying me with a ticket to an abundance of sustaining caffeine—and to the staff in Caffé Nero, Chesham, for providing me with a place where I could think in peace away from builders (and make free use of electricity) during the early stages of the work. Our research assistants, Michael Paulin, Kim van Gennip, and especially Hanne De Jaegher, provided invaluable support, copyediting and supplying comments on the manuscript in ways that enabled me to get the final version of it in good order. I am extremely grateful to them for this.

Intellectually speaking, I am grateful to the following researchers either for invigorating discussions or for comments on material relating to this project: Fred Adams, Jens Allwood, Kristin Andrews, Sherry Asgill, Ignar Brinck, Filip Buekens, Mark Cain, Ron Chrisley, Tim Crane, Gregory Currie, Adrian Cussins, Hans Dooremalen, Ralph Ellis, Shaun Gallagher, Vittorio Gallese, Peter Goldie, Alvin Goldman, Bob Gordon, Peter Hobson, Tomasz Komendziński, Heidi Maibom, Bertram Malle, Victoria McGeer, Richard Menary, Danièle Moyal-Sharrock, Erik Myin, Keld Stehr Nielsen, Matthew Ratcliffe, Mark Rowlands, Anthony Rudd, Chris Sinha, Barry Stocker, Marc Stors, Karsten Stueber, Penny Vinden, Bill Wringe, Dan Zahavi and Jordan Zlatev.

The correspondence I had with Donald Davidson and Ruth Millikan has had and continues to have a profound influence on my thinking. Although they would probably be aghast at my attempted fusion of their approaches, I remain deeply indebted to both of them for their generous advice and formative comments.

More generally, I thank my colleagues at Hertfordshire and the staff at the following departments who allowed me to make preliminary trials of my ideas: Leeds (February 2002), Lund (September 2002), New Hampshire (December 2003), Durham (February 2004), Reading (February 2004), Sussex (October and November 2004), Tilburg (November 2005), Gothenburg (December 2005), Lund (December 2005), and Copenhagen (October 2006).

In a similar vein, I thank the organizers and audiences of the following workshops and conferences: European Society for Philosophy and Psychology (ESPP) (Salzburg 2001); Philosophy, Phenomenology and Psychiatry (Gothenburg 2003); Joint Session of the Mind/Aristotelian Society (Kent 2004); Joint Conference of the Society for Philosophy and Psychology (SPP)/ESPP (Barcelona 2004); "Phenomenology, Intersubjectivity and Theory of Mind" (Orlando 2005); The Royal Institute of Philosophy "Narrative and Understanding Persons" conference (Hertfordshire 2005); ESPP (Lund 2005); "Examining Folk Psychology" (Toronto 2005); "Theory of Mind, Representation and Action" (Antwerp 2005); Philosophy, Psychiatry and the Neurosciences (Leiden 2006); "Situated Cognition" (Durham 2006); ESPP (Belfast 2006); "Embodied and Situated Cognition" (Torun 2006).

I am grateful to the editors and publishers of the following journals/ anthologies for allowing me to reuse material (often reworked) in this book: "Folk Psychological Explanations: Narratives and the Case of Autism," *Philosophical Papers* 32, no. 3 (2003), 345–361; "The Limits of Spectatorial Folk Psychology," *Mind and Language* 19, no. 5. (2004): 548–573; "Knowing What? Radical versus Conservative Enactivism," *Phenomenology and the Cognitive Sciences* 4 (2005): 389–405; "Starting without Theory," in B. Malle and S. Hodges, eds., *Other Minds: How Humans Bridge the Divide between Self and Others*, 56–72 (New York: Guilford, 2005); "Unprincipled Engagements: Emotional Experience, Expression and Response," in R. Menary, ed., *Consciousness and Emotion: Special issue on Radical Enactivism* (Philadelphia: John Benjamins, 2006) (I have also used elements from the following replies made to commentaries on that target paper: "Against Passive Intellectualism: Reply to Crane"; "Embodied Expectations and Extended Possibilities: Reply to Goldie"; "Four Herculean

Labours: Reply to Hobson"; "Narrative Practice and Understanding Reasons: Reply to Gallagher"); "Folk Psychology without Theory or Simulation," in D. Hutto and M. Ratcliffe, eds., *Folk Psychology Reassessed* (Dordrecht: Springer, 2007); "The Narrative Practice Hypothesis: Origins and Applications of Folk Psychology," in D. Hutto, ed., *Narrative and Understanding Persons*, Royal Institute of Philosophy Supplement (Cambridge: Cambridge University Press, 2007); "First Communions: Mimetic Sharing without Theory of Mind" and "Understanding others through Primary Interaction and Narrative Practice" (the latter coauthored with S. Gallagher), in J. Zlatev, T. Racine, C. Sinha, and E. Itkonen, eds., *The Shared Mind: Perspectives on Intersubjectivity* (Philadelphia: John Benjamins, 2007).

Financial support for this project has come from a range of sources. The National Endowment for the Humanities provided a stipend enabling me to attend the NEH summer seminar on theory theory and simulation theory in June and July 1999. My thinking was strongly influenced by discussions with my fellow seminarians and by the fine series of talks organised by Bob Gordon. Both the Mind Association and the Arts and Humanities Research Board awarded me grants and fellowships that provided me with relief from normal duties, enabling me to complete this book. The University of Hertfordshire matched that leave. My Dean, Graham Holderness, and Head of School, Andrew Clutterbuck, supported a short period of much needed leave to allow me to recover from a lack of a summer holiday (our home was under siege by builders during the crucial phase of research). Both have also generously supported my research in other ways. I thank them both.

Finally, I want to express my gratitude to Tom Stone, my editor at The MIT Press, for his patience and extreme tolerance concerning the delayed submission of the final draft. His flexibility about deadlines and his insistence that I should "write the book I needed to write" helped me get through a difficult patch.

Abbreviations

ADT   Asymmetric Dependency Theory
BAA   Basic Architectural Assumption
CTM   Computational Theory of Mind
CSSH   Core Syllabic-Syntax Hypothesis
EMS   Early Mindreading System
FP   Folk Psychology
IBS   Information Based Semantics
IMDs   Inherited Mindreading Devices
IRR   Intensional Representation Requirement
LAD   Language Acquisition Device
LIGs   Local Indexical Guides
LoT   Language of Thought
MAH   Mimetic Ability Hypothesis
MoP   Mode of Presentation
MSH   Mirror System Hypothesis
NPH   Narrative Practice Hypothesis
PDP   Parallel Distributed Processing
PIH   Pre-Narrative Intelligence Hypothesis
PoSA   Poverty of Stimulus Argument
RIH   Re-Interpretation Hypothesis
RMH   Restricted Mindblindness Hypothesis
RTM   Representational Theory of Mind
SAM   Shared Attention Module

SIA   Supplemented Informational Atomism
SIH   Social Intelligence Hypothesis
ST/IST   Simulation Theory/Inherited Simulation Theory
STT   Scientific Theory Theory
SVT   Supralaryngeal Vocal Tract
ToB   Theory of Behavior
ToM   Theory of Mind
ToMM   Theory of Mind Module
TNLH   Thinking in Natural Language Hypothesis
TT/ITT   Theory Theory/Inherited Theory Theory
UCA   Universal Convergence Assumption
UG   Universal Grammar

1 The Limits of Spectatorial Folk Psychology

It is a datum that psychologically normal, adult humans often act for reasons. Equally, they often make sense of intentional actions by seeking the reasons motivating such performances.[1] I took off to London for a break because I was at my wit's end. She canceled her trip because she no longer loved him. The giving and receiving of reasons is a prominent and distinctive aspect of much familiar social commerce. The context in which we do this, the form this takes, and how we come by this ability are the central topics of this book.

In speaking of "reasons" I mean what philosophers have traditionally understood to be the products of discrete episodes of means-end practical reasoning—that is, intentions to act. These constitute what might be called a person's "motivating" reasons.[2] When speaking of reasons in this sense philosophers typically focus on beliefs and desires (sometimes exclusively) and their special properties, the former being cognitive attitudes that aim at truly representing how things stand with the world and the latter being motivational attitudes that specify goals for action. When appropriately united these are held responsible for the formation of intentions.

When conjoined in the right way, in virtue of their contents, beliefs and desires are minimally what is required in order to motivate us to act for a reason. In the right combination these attitudes are the essential components of reasons—and they can be appropriately tied together because they are not just psychological attitudes; they are *propositional* attitudes. As such, they exhibit a special kind of intentionality—a directness or aboutness toward possible situations. In having such attitudes we are psychologically related in special ways to propositional contents: "X believes that P" and "X desires that Q," where P and Q are propositions with intelligible semantic content, such as "The boys get home at 4:00 p.m.," "Ashridge is a fine place for a picnic," "There are only forty pounds left in my current account," and so forth. One can adopt beliefs and desires about any of these situations (and other propositional attitudes, too, such as fear, hope, and so on). It is debatable whether desires must always take a propositional complement; some hold that we can have desires for intentional objects—such as desiring a Ming vase or our neighbor's singing ability—and not just situations. But with respect to beliefs—which aim at truths—this is not an option. One can only believe propositions, not objects.

We need not decide if it is possible that the intentional objects of desires can be nonpropositional. It is enough to note that when desires are partnered with beliefs (thus constituting reasons), the content of such desires must be of a kind that permits them to enter into appropriate logical relations with the content of believed propositions. This requires that they have appropriate logical form and content. Without this the attitudes would not be able to bind together to form reasons, for this requires that their constitutive contents overlap at significant points—that is, they must be linked in virtue of having certain contentful components in common.

But is it always true that if an action is executed for a reason then it must be possible to explicate it, minimally, by appeal to a particular belief/desire pairing? This thought is deeply rooted and seldom challenged in Anglophone philosophy of action.[3] Some, however, argue that insisting on the rule that there can be no reason for acting without motivating beliefs and desires fails to accommodate our ordinary understanding of what it is to act for a reason, which includes a much wider class of psychological motivations (see Goldie 2007; Ratcliffe 2007a, 2007b). For example, we often explain action by appeal to other kinds of relevant propositional attitudes (hopes, fears, and so on) and other more basic kinds of psychological attitudes, such as perceptions and emotions. And we do this in more or less refined ways. More than this, to fully come to terms with the reason why someone acted, we frequently need to know about the person's character, situation, and history—in short, we need to know the unique details of his or her "story." This is true and important, and I will have more to say about all of this in the next chapter, but it should not obscure the fact that at least some of our actions are performed for reasons in the restricted sense (understood as belief/desire pairings) and that our capacity to make sense of intentional actions in such terms is commonplace.

Thus even if we think that folk psychology includes more than the practice of making sense of actions in terms of beliefs and desires, it should at least include this ability as well.[4] To keep things straight, when I talk of folk psychology I am concerned with the practice of predicting, explaining, and explicating intentional actions by appeal to reasons in a way that must include understanding a person's motivating reasons as restrictively defined above. *Folk psychology* stricto sensu—the target phenomenon of interest here—incorporates the practice of making sense of a person's actions using belief/desire propositional attitude psychology.[5]

Defining folk psychology in this way distinguishes it from a much looser rendering equating it to the way or ways—whatever these turn out to be—that social beings manage to conduct their interpersonal relations.[6] As a working definition of folk psychology, the latter is far too encompassing; indeed nothing concrete could answer to it (see Morton 2007). To define commonsense psychology in this way would make it ubiquitous. Yet even with the tighter definition in mind, many of its so-called friends have overstated and misunderstood its role in social cognition; typically they see it as more basic and as far more pervasive than it actually is. Unless we assume that folk psychology is deployed tacitly without our noticing—and we should not (for reasons I supply in subsequent chapters)—it is surely not fundamental to social engagements, not even exclusively human ones.

We have many other, more basic means of coordinating with one another in our social interactions. Our primary modes of interpersonal engagement are not driven by mentalistic predictions or explanations, rather they are characterized by the possession of embodied expectations. Such expectations are not intellectual products; arguably they are not the outcomes of the manipulation of representations by inferential operations at all—but, certainly, they do not involve the manipulation or representation of propositional attitudes. Like most creatures, our basic dealings with others are more visceral; we get by with scriptlike patterns of recognition-response, some of which can be quite sophisticated and complex. Typically, these are initiated and guided by indexical signs that take the form of the expressive behavior of others. However, in some creatures anticipatory responding operates in a more off-line way, thanks to the added resources of their recreative imaginations. As I will argue in later chapters, in all such cases well-calibrated social activity only involves a capacity to selectively respond to end-directed intentional attitudes that are revealed in the expressions of others; these expressive attitudes are unlike those of the propositional variety. For this reason, among others, these primary modes of interacting with others should not be classified as a species of mindreading. In "normal" contexts, such methods are a highly effective—indeed, arguably the best—means of navigating social dynamics.

It is therefore false to say that without folk psychology we would be bereft of any reliable means of interacting with others. Nor do we call on it that often. Many of our routine encounters with others take place in situations in which the social roles and rules are well established, so much so that unless we behave in a deviant manner we typically have no need to understand one another by means of the belief/desire schema. More often than not we neither predict nor seek to explain the actions of others in terms of their unique beliefs and desires at all.

That said, sometimes the actions of others cry out for explanation— sometimes they violate norms (or appear to do so) in ways that we can only make sense of by understanding them in a wider context, by acquiring the narrative that fills in or fleshes out the particular details of that person's story. Any account that has as its subject matter the reason why a person acted on a particular occasion (in line with the inclusive criterion detailed above) I will call a *folk psychological narrative*. The practice of supplying such narratives *just is* that of explicating and explaining action in terms of reasons. Folk psychology is thus, in essence, a distinctive kind of narrative practice.

As such, it is a unique specialty of linguistically competent human beings (*Homo sapiens sapiens*), which is not to say that all humans are capable of using it, or that they in fact do so. There are notable exceptions, the most prominent being the class of persons with extreme autism. And, if I am right in thinking that the basis for this skill is sociocultural, we cannot be sure that folk psychology (stricto sensu) is deployed in every contemporary human society. What is clear, going by the available evidence, is that neither our closest living cousins—the chimpanzees—use it, nor did our Pleistocene ancestors, as I will argue.

For several decades the dominant view has been that folk psychology is either a kind of low-level theory about the propositional attitudes or a simulative ability involving their direct manipulation (today many hold it to be a mix of both). That is, many imagine it to be, first, a specialized theory, understood as a systematically organized body of knowledge detailing the links between typical perceptual inputs, intentional states, and behaviors; second, procedures of simulative imagining that directly manipulate the relevant intentional states themselves, without using any principles about such states (for example, this might be achieved by using "shared circuits" or by running practical reasoning and other subpersonal mechanisms off-line); or third, some hybrid combination of these processes. Theorists are divided on the question of whether these heuristics are deployed tacitly or explicitly.

In the place of these conjectures I defend the idea that folk psychology is a unique kind of narrative practice and that viewing it as such is the best way to account for its ultimate origins and everyday applications. The Narrative Practice Hypothesis (NPH) claims that the normal route through which children become familiar with the core structure of folk psychology and the norm-governed possibilities for its practical application is through direct encounters with stories about people who act for reasons. The topic of childhood acquisition is the focus of the next chapter; in this one I provide reasons for thinking that neither theory nor simulation could be the true basis of our everyday folk psychological understanding. To clarify, I do not deny that these heuristics often come into play when we speculate about why another may have acted or how they might act. What I reject is the thought that theory and simulation are ultimately responsible for folk psychological understanding or that they drive the practice; they are simply supplementary methods that we are sometimes forced to call on when we attempt to construct, understand, or ascribe folk psychological narratives. Theory and simulation only come into play in those cases in which we lack direct and reliable access to the narratives of others.

It is crucially important to recognize that folk psychological narratives come in both third-person and second-person varieties. This matters since the success or otherwise of reason explanations depends mainly on who is doing the telling—that is, on who produces the account. Although we often attempt to generate such accounts on behalf of others, even when this speculative activity is well supported—say, by simulative or theoretical heuristics—it is quite unlikely that such attempts will succeed in hitting on the "right" explanation.

To add appropriate force to these observations, the rest of this chapter is devoted to making the case for rejecting the widely held assumption that the *primary* business of folk psychology is to provide third-person predictions and explanations.[7]

The Primacy of Second-Person Applications

It is almost universally assumed that the main business of commonsense psychology is to provide generally reliable predictions and explanations of the actions of others. The main focus for the past two decades has been to decide whether these feats are achieved by the deployment of some kind of theory of mind or by a process of simulative imagining. Yet, in the rush to enter into the debate about how folk psychology is carried off, philosophers and psychologists have tended to make a number of questionable assumptions about the context in which we regularly deploy it. Chief among these is that we are normally at a theoretical remove from others. The attitude we adopt toward others is thus on a par with that deployed when understanding "foreign bodies" quite generally: we ascribe causally efficacious inner "mental states" to them for the purpose of prediction, explanation, and control. As a consequence, this fosters the idea that our initial stance with respect to others is essentially estranged. Bogdan (1997, 104) conveniently labels this the "spectatorial view of interpretation," because it portrays "the subject as a remote object of observation and prediction."

This idea has no legitimacy when it comes to understanding how we interactively engage with others in basic encounters as we traverse the landscape of action. I say more about this in later chapters. But we also have reason to doubt that adopting a detached stance is the primary way we understand intentional actions performed for reasons. We must reconsider the received views about the kind of context in which folk psychology normally operates, taking seriously the idea that our starting point is second-personal. In abandoning the idea that contexts in which we make sense of others are, at root, spectatorial, we can recast and reorient our thinking about the nature of our everyday social expectations and about how folk psychological explanations are ordinarily achieved. It turns out that explaining and predicting actions from a third-person stance is not only late developing, it is relatively infrequent and far less reliable than our normal intersubjective means of coming to understand others through dialogue and conversation.

Expectations and Explanations in Second-Person Contexts

I advance what might at first seem a radical claim—that even in understanding the reasons for which others act, including adults, we often do not make any attribution of beliefs and desires at all. However, my reason for thinking this is the case is utterly banal: we simply do not need to make such ascriptions in most everyday, second-person contexts. An ordinary example from adult life will hopefully illustrate this.

Imagine that you see a man approaching the closed door of a shop while struggling with bags of groceries. We would hardly be surprised to see him put these down in order to open it or for him to wait until someone came to his aid. Should we suppose that our lack of surprise indicates that we were predicting, albeit tacitly, that this man might do either of these things?[8] We might suppose that a tacit mentalistic prediction is unnecessary precisely because we already know what to expect from others and they know what to expect from us in such familiar social circumstances. To anticpate this set of actions I need know or assume nothing about the particular mindset of this individual. Rather, the thought is that if we make ourselves more readable to one another by conforming to shared norms of readability, it follows that much of the work of understanding one another in day-to-day interactions is not really done by us at all, explicitly or implicitly. The work is done and carried by the world, embedded in the norms and routines that structure such interactions. (McGeer 2001, 119)

In McGeer's words, it is through a common social training that we gain an "insider's view" on what to expect from others in everyday situations; it is not by relying on a set of innate principles or absorbing any explicit ones.[9] Being brought into "the fold"—learning what to expect of others and vice versa—amounts to gaining a second nature or a common sense.[10] With this observation in hand, we can begin to see the quite sophisticated practices of giving and understanding reasons in a new light.

Folk psychology just is the practice of making sense of intentional action by means of a special kind of narrative, those that are about or feature a person's reasons. These narratives play two vital roles in commonsense psychology, one developmental and the other practical. First and foremost, they help to shape our expectations about the reasons for which actions are likely to be taken and the appropriateness of doing so. More importantly and more fundamentally, they are the very medium through which we acquire our basic understanding of what it is to act for a reason. Saying how this is achieved is the topic of the next chapter. For now, I want to highlight a different role played by the practice of supplying and interpreting folk psychological narratives—the application of commonsense psychology. Such narratives are used to mediate in cases in which an action deviates from our expectations. They do this by helping us to tame the extraordinary. By using narratives to explicate why an action was taken we are able to forge "links between the exceptional and the ordinary" (Bruner 1990, 47). That is, folk psychological narratives function as normalizing explanations, allowing us to cope with unusual or eccentric actions, by putting them into contexts that make them intelligible, where possible. Getting the relevant details of another's story enables us to see if their action falls within the fold of the normal. Alternatively, such stories can also—at least sometimes—serve to extend the bounds of what is regarded as normal. If, however, they fail to do either of these things, then we simply will have failed to make sense of why the action was performed.[11]

For example, I could, in a very unilluminating way, explain why I swallowed an acorn by appeal to the fact that I believed it to be an acorn, while avowing my desire to consume acorns. Assuming that this explanation correctly identifies my reason for action, such a project is not irrational. There is no conflict between my stated beliefs and desires, yet it remains utterly puzzling. This shows that at least in some cases the mere citing of the appropriate belief/desire, even when it fits appropriately with the other relevant beliefs and desires and even assuming it is causally responsible for the action in question, does not suffice to explain an action in the strong sense of making it intelligible. A larger narrative that further contextualizes the reason, either in terms of different cultural norms or the peculiarities of a particular person's history or values, is required for that (that is, if anything can achieve this end). A richer narrative serves to explain the action, by enabling us to understand its rationale when this is not immediately obvious.

In this way, narratives make the explanation or domestication of eccentric, exotic, or otherwise extraordinary actions possible. They do this either by helping us to see that the reasons behind such actions are in fact already familiar or by making them so. This is achieved either by supplying missing details that reveal an action to be already within the fold of the ordinary (despite appearances) or by fleshing out a larger context such that we extend our understanding of what is acceptable, which entails rethinking the bounds of what we take to be "normal." Thus it goes without saying that this sort of negotiation requires a prior fluency with the normal. In Bruner's words, in such cases "the function of the story is to find an intentional state that mitigates or at least makes comprehensible a deviation from a canonical cultural pattern" (Bruner 1990, 49–50; entire sentence emphasized in original).

Narratives can explain by smoothing our understanding of others in cases where their actions (or their accounts of why these actions were taken) do not initially make sense. Crucially, such explanations are only needed in the sorts of cases in which we are surprised or perplexed by another's actions. For "When things 'are as they should be,' the narratives of folk psychology are unnecessary" (Bruner 1990, 40). With this in mind, we might reconsider the implications of Fodor's (1987, 3) claim that commonsense psychology "works so well it disappears." For Fodor this highlights the fact that much folk psychological theorizing goes unnoticed, but for me it points to the fact that for the great bulk of social interactions it is not used at all.

Of course, making sense of an apparent action is not always possible. Sometimes the behavior of others is so erratic that we have no option but to regard those individuals in the same light as we do objects. Stich (1983, 163), who once observed that folk psychology is best regarded as a kind of domestic anthropology, provided us with a plethora of such cases involving exotic subjects, such as children, animals, and confused or demented folk, in which it necessarily fails. Faced with these subjects we may have to resort to the postulation of theoretical inner states to explain their behavior, but these will not be of the folk psychological variety. It must be stressed however that this only occurs when our normal way of understanding others breaks down—that is, when no mediating narratives can be brought to bear or are of any use (see Gallagher 2001, 95).

Understanding folk psychology as a kind of narrative practice flies in the face of the prevalent view that reason explanations are merely a subspecies of theoretical explanations, the logic of which is structurally identical to the kind of explanations found in and throughout the natural sciences. Fodor (1987, 7) describes this tradition, telling us that when folk psychological explanations are made explicit, "They are frequently seen to exhibit the "deductive structure" that is so characteristic of explanation in real science. There are two parts to this: the theory's underlying generalizations are defined over unobservables, and they lead to its predictions by iterating and interacting rather than by being directly instantiated." This is to adopt a broadly Hempelian approach, according to which the explanation for a particular action requires that we subsume it under a general law that reveals the relation between the events in question. It is a feature of this way of thinking that, despite facing in different directions, predictions and explanations are regarded as having the same structure. Ideally, a reliable theory based on information about past cases, known regularities, and recurring patterns enables us to work backward from known effects to the causes of specific happenings, in just the way that we work forward from known, or presupposed, causes in order to predict future effects.[12]

As long as we believe that our basic relations to others are of a detached nature, this idea can seem almost irresistible. In the abstract, how else ought we to characterize and, indeed, rank the assumptions needed for predicting and explaining such "mental events" as the occurrence of specific thoughts and desires? How else would someone who had no knowledge of others get by? Yet a little reflection shows that everyday practical application of folk psychology should not be modeled on the way explanations are advanced in the purely theoretical, abstract sciences. For it is not just that folk psychology would have to have its own special set of laws or generalizations, it must invoke the slippery notion of rationality. This sets folk psychology apart from all other theoretical sciences. Commonsense psychological explanations come with built-in reference to rational agents, such that its laws take the form: "In a situation of type C, any rational agent will do x" (Kölger and Stueber 2000b, 13–15).

Proponents of this sort of claim are notoriously vague when it comes to spelling out exactly what *rationality* means in this context. For example, Dennett (1987, 98) writes that "the concept of rationality is systematically pre-theoretical.... When one leans on our pre-theoretical concept of rationality one relies on our shared intuitions."[13] Yet, however this everyday notion of rationality is unpacked, the fact that it is a nonnegotiable feature of folk psychology means that we cannot have a closed system for propositional attitude ascriptions. Folk psychology neither is nor can be suitably reduced to a tractable lawlike science. Understanding actions in terms of reasons is irredeemably disanalogous to the way we understand the behavior of "mindless" entities (Davidson 1991, 162–163; see also Davidson 1996). One can accept this while allowing that in some sense reasons do in fact cause actions and that reason explanations are a type of causal explanation (see Davidson 1980). To put it mildly, folk psychology has special constitutive features that make it unique among theories because of the "normative character of mental concepts" (Davidson 1987, 46). But this is putting it too mildly for my taste. If we challenge a few additional assumptions about the primary function of folk psychology we can take this thought further; there is no reason to think of folk psychology as any kind of theory at all.[14]

Moreover, abstract theories only ever constitute *general* knowledge. This makes them fundamentally incapable of providing the sort of explanations needed in applied or forensic sciences (and in other areas such as history and psychoanalysis). This is made evident by the fact that explanations in applied domains are always more than mere chronicles of what has happened during a particular time frame. They involve discriminating and selecting which specific event—under a particular description—is the important one for the purposes of explanation. Hence, explanations of particular happenings take the form of

1. Selecting the appropriate events
2. Ordering them within a temporal series
3. Isolating their relevant properties with a view to making them intelligible within a particular idiom

It is with this in mind that we should regard such explanations as having an essentially narrative form. For, as Roth (1991, 178) observes, "Narratives give [events] a connection which is not merely chronological. The process of presenting a narrative about one's past [or the historical past] requires identifying which events are significant and why."

This requirement is common to all singular causal explanations. They are contextual in a way that distinguishes them from purely theoretical explanations. Consequently, what constitutes a sound abstract explanation of the general causes of carburetor failure differs altogether from what is required from a singular causal explanation that identifies why a particular carburetor actually failed to work on a specific occasion. Although general theories are no doubt useful in framing such specific investigations, it is clear that even in the natural sciences the two types of explanation must not be conflated.

In this light, we would be well advised to adopt Woodward's (1984, 232) approach to singular causal explanations (or some close cousin), accepting that these constitute "a distinct genre of explanation, which does not possess anything remotely like a covering-law structure." He maintains that what they seek to explain "is simply the occurrence of a particular event . . . rather than some more complicated *explanandum*" (p. 232).[15] Thus, at best, the covering-law model is appropriate for all-inclusive, purely theoretical forms of prediction and explanation. Explanations of that kind are quite unlike those in which we deliberately avoid mentioning certain features in tune with the context of inquiry, since these can be taken for granted or regarded as idle or irrelevant. This last point is worthy of note, for if everyday explanations function by supplying *only* relevant information, then exactly which details will be significant will vary from context to context.

The standard picture that reason explanations operate in abstract, theoretical contexts must be rejected. For it is not as if we offer such explanations to complete outsiders or newcomers to our world or practices—that is, to someone who lacks all information and shares no background understanding with us. In many cases, background details go without saying. I hold that it is just as plausible that they go without thinking. Although we can imagine abstractly reconstructing what would have had to be the case for such psychological explanations to work (by detailing all of the nomologically sufficient conditions), there is no justification for reading all of this back into the minds of those doing such explaining or those receiving such explanations.[16] If we insist on this where exactly would one stop? In ordinary contexts in which we can reliably take most things for granted, good explanations stop precisely when enough has been said to make the particular action intelligible. The context determines just how much of this structure and the peculiar character of the target individual's psychology or history we will need to reveal in order to make sense of the actions or to fine-tune our predictions. We are normally only interested in tips, not whole icebergs.

In general our practical, everyday explanations are not designed to fully account for why something happened. It is only the citing of relevant details in a particular context that does the explaining. In this light, far from being mere supplementary or peripheral information to be situated in a larger theory, in everyday contexts the narratives we supply about our reasons for acting—those that home in on the relevant details—just are the explanans.

Most importantly, a restorative narrative need not issue from the person seeking the explanation. In attempting to discover why someone acted we do not always occupy an estranged, spectatorial point of view. In many ordinary cases the other is not beyond our reach. The fact is that we often engage directly with others in order to determine their reasons. This is quite unlike other forensic investigations that attempt to delve into the causes of other kinds of happenings. To establish with any confidence why an action was performed we simply cannot approach the issue using the same sort of method as we would when trying to determine, say, the cause of a plane crash. Our best chance, by far, is to rely on the revelations of the other: the authors of actions are uniquely well placed to explain their reasons for themselves. Of course, their admissions are defeasible; often people lie or are self-deceived about why they act. Nevertheless, we have fairly robust methods for testing, questioning, and challenging such testimony when it is important to do so, as in legal cases. For example, we compare the person's avowals about relevant public events with the accounts given by others; this uncovers lies or internal contradictions in the agent's story that will invalidate either the details of the account or the person's overall credibility. Countless everyday conversations involving the explanation of actions in terms of reasons mimic this process to a greater or lesser degree. Also, when directly engaging with others in "normal" contexts there are a wealth of telltale cues, expressions, and responses of a more embodied variety that provide fairly reliable guidance and feedback when deciding if we can place our trust in what another says.

The Unreliability of Third-Personal Folk Psychology

Understanding others in normal contexts of interaction is not a spectator sport. This is not to claim that we never adopt a spectatorial stance—but doing so is the exception, not the rule. As Gallagher (2001, 92) observes,

Even in cases where we know (or think we know) a person very well, we may express puzzlement about their behaviour. In discussing a friend's behaviour with someone who doesn't know her well, we may come to devise a theory about why she is acting in a certain way. It seems very possible to describe such cases in terms of a theory of mind.

Gallagher also notes that "in the situation of talking with someone else about a third person, it seems possible to describe our attitude toward the person under discussion as theoretical or as involving a simulation of the other person's mental states" (p. 93). Even so, these heuristics remain at the periphery—coming into play only in special cases, such as those in which we do not accept the other's account of his or her reasons. Driven by suspicion we may be left with nothing but speculation and supposition about their motives. That is, we may be forced to make third-party predictions and explanations of actions precisely in the sorts of cases in which we do not know what to expect from others or when we cannot engage with them directly. But, for this very reason, these sorts of approaches are bound to be, on the whole, much less reliable than our second-person modes of interaction.

Consider that most third-person predictions operate with framing information about the other's background beliefs and desires already in hand, as in the following paradigm case: "Suppose I wish to predict what John will think of the new jacket; will he think it garish? Suppose further that I know that John believes the jacket to be scarlet and he thinks all bright colours to be garish. I will, of course, expect him to think the jacket garish" (Heal 1995, 39).[17]

Heal (1998b, 86) is quite clear that this heuristic, at least on its own, cannot account for how we succeed in "interpreting and explaining behaviour." But if simulation procedures were used to enable us to understand reasons for action, folk psychology would either be a very dull business or a very uncertain one indeed.[18] For the cost of having reliable predictions is inversely proportional to the need to make them at all. To come back to Bruner's point about our expectations, if a situation is familiar there will be no question about what another will do and no need to make any predictions. In contrast, in third-person cases, we are faced with two extremes. At one pole, we already have framing information that is good enough for us to deduce logically what another will think or do—in which case it is unclear what need such predictions might serve. At the other pole, to the degree that we lack such information the need to make predictions will be clearer but they will be less reliable.

Consider how folk psychological predictions are allegedly achieved on Goldman's account of the simulation process of manipulating the mindreader's own stock of mental states, putting them through their paces, as it were.[19] This is achieved by modifying the normal routine of mechanisms that support practical reasoning in particular, and others that support psychological responding more generally. Goldman, for example, proposes that simulation is fueled by subpersonal mechanisms. He presents this claim as a straightforward empirical hypothesis: the very same mechanism that permits the manipulation of beliefs and desires in the course of practical reasoning is also our stable but flexible basis for "high-level" mindreading. Normally, the outcome of practical reasoning is the formation of an intention to act on the part of the reasoner. But on this account when we make sense of another's action our practical reasoning mechanism—although functioning properly in one sense—is being put to a different end. It continues to process beliefs and desires as usual but because it is fed with pretend beliefs and desires as "input," the resulting "output" takes the form of predictions or explanations (rather than issuing intentions to act, as it would normally). It is, to coin a phrase, being run off-line.[20] On this basis, successful mindreading exploits the similarities in the reasoning processes of individuals. Or rather, it succeeds if appropriate allowances are made for differences in the other's psychological set and the right believed and desired contents are used (that is, those that in fact motivated the target).

In taking my practical reasoning mechanism off-line, I shelve certain of my beliefs and desires and allow others—which I do not genuinely harbor—to go "live." To get any interesting results, I need to make a number of fine-tuned adjustments. Clearly, the more I know about my target the better my chances of successful prediction. Precisely the same challenge attends the generation of retrodictive explanations from a third-person perspective. If X is to simulate Y, X cannot simply imagine what it would be like to be in Y's position; one must take into account the relevant differences between the simulator and the target.

An illustration makes the point better than a description, and the annals of Sherlock Holmes prove a useful sourcebook. Holmes avows that he frequently imaginatively reenacts the thought processes of criminals when making predictions about their next moves or explaining their past steps. In *The Musgrave Ritual*, Conan Doyle (1892–1893/1986, 343) provides a tidy account of how the basic simulation heuristic is supposed to work:

You know my methods in such cases, Watson: I put myself in the man's place, and having first gauged his intelligence, I try to imagine how I should myself have proceeded under the same circumstances. In this case the matter was simplified by Brunston's intelligence being quite first rate, so that it was unnecessary to make any allowance for the personal equation, as the astronomers have dubbed it. He knew something valuable was concealed. He had spotted the place. He found that the stone was too heavy for a man to move unaided. What would he do next?

Many describe this process of simulation as one of "placing oneself, figuratively speaking, into the shoes of the other"; it is to enact, emulate, or otherwise get an imaginative handle on how things look, looked, or will look from the other's perspective. Predicting or explaining their actions is then improved by fine-tuning such projections. This, in any case, is the driving insight. And in the very first paper to introduce the idea of simulation, Gordon stressed that the procedure

is not the same as deciding what I myself would do. One tries to make adjustments for *relevant differences*. In chess, for example, a player would make not only the imaginative shifts required for predicting "what I would do in his shoes," but the further shifts required for predicting what he will do in his shoes. To this purpose the player might, e.g., simulate a lower level of play, trade one set of idiosyncrasies for another, and above all pretend ignorance of his own (actual) intentions. Army generals, salespeople, and detectives claim to do this sort of thing. (Gordon 1986, 162; emphasis added)

The point is that when simulating I focus on the situation as it might be for the other, not on what I would do in such a situation if I were the other. But if I am in a position to determine, without further ado, in what respects the other's perspective is relevantly different from mine, this obviates the need for the explanation. Yet without such information the simulation procedure leaves us with nothing more than *possible* explanations. And this reminds us that unless this activity is constrained in some further way it is unlikely to yield accurate results. There are simply too many possibilities about how someone might act in any situation, all of which fall within the rational spectrum. One is faced with an embarrassment of riches. Because of this, at best, we are left with mere hypotheses about what the other will do. Once again, unless we already know (or can safely assume) enough about the other's background beliefs, desires, and psychological attitudes, there is a good chance that our simulated predictions will go astray. The problem is that, unlike ordinary conversations, on its own the simulation heuristic has very meagre resources for determining which psychological states to put aside and which to keep in play.

The point can be illustrated graphically if we examine Goldman's schematic, as presented in figure 1.1. Although an appropriate box is set aside to perform the function of generating pretend propositional attitudes, it is interesting that it alone stands free of input. Since everything is clearly labeled, it is easy to see what is left crucially unexplained: the means by which particular beliefs and desires are selected to act as pretend inputs.

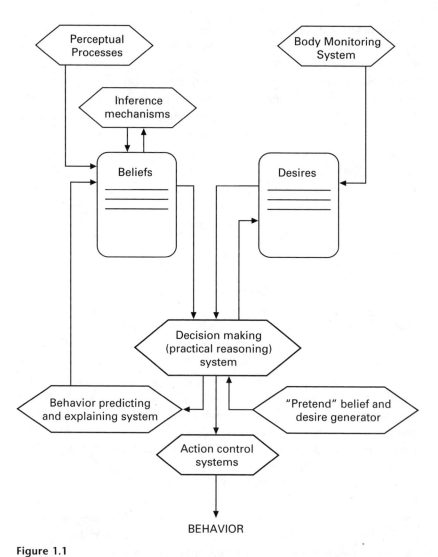

Figure 1.1
Practical Reasoning Mechanism (adapted from S. Stich and S. Nichols 1995, 92;
S. Nichols et al. 1996, 40; and reprinted from D. D. Hutto, "The Limits of
Spectatorial Folk Psychology," *Mind and Language* 19, no. 5 (2004): 548–573. Used
with permission from the editors, *Mind and Language*).

These criticisms of simulation theory are well rehearsed and have led some to hold that when interpretation gets tough, simulators need to get a theory. Indeed, for over two decades, the dominant theory, in both philosophical and psychological circles, has been that at some level folk psychological predictions and explanations are achieved by making use of a set of principles about how we humans (and disputably certain other primates) navigate our everyday social affairs. Fodor once neatly illustrated the character of folk psychology's core principles with an example from *Midsummer Night's Dream*. He traced the elaborate path of Hermia's reasoning that drove her to suppose (wrongly, as it happens) that Demetrius had harmed Lysander. Ultimately, her conclusion was reached, inter alia, on the basis of her knowledge that "if x wants that P, and x believes that not-P unless Q, and x believes that x can bring it about that Q, then (*ceteris paribus*) x tries to bring it about that Q" (Fodor 1987, 2). Within the space of a page, Fodor cast this account of what is clearly recognizable as the skeleton of the practical syllogism in the form of an "implicit theory." This was understood as constituting the central pillar of a body of knowledge that regularly takes up the "burden of predicting behaviour—of bridging the gap between utterances and actions" (Fodor 1987, 3). Apart from enabling us to enjoy Shakespearean comedies, it is claimed that tacit knowledge of such abstract principles is what permits our more mundane mentalistic predictions. The core of folk psychology is, on this conception, a kind of schematic that details the ways the core propositional attitudes must interrelate if they are to generate action: a "theory of mind" (or ToM).[21]

Whether on its own or as part of a hybrid, it is generally thought that somehow a theory of mind could reliably provide causal explanations that designate another's reason for acting.[22] Allegedly, it is because theories employ subsuming causal laws that "the mechanism posited by the theory-theory is supposed to underpin the giving of robust psychological explanations of behaviour by the folk" (Arkway 2000, 135). But, as suggestive as this thought may be, theories are in no position to deliver where simulation procedures cannot. They fare no better when it comes to dealing with difficult cases.

This should not be surprising since internal resources of theories of mind—understood as a set of core principles about the behavior of the attitudes—are just as limited as those of simulation heuristics. In different ways, both regard folk psychology as grounded in our shared rationality.

It might be thought that we can build on this base by adding some auxiliary hypotheses—a kind of *Homo sapiens* psychology with some local variations—to support the self-contained folk psychological theory. The core mentalistic principles only detail the appropriate interrelations between the central propositional attitudes (beliefs and desires) and nothing more. To get any interesting predictive or explanatory results it is recognized that this theory would need to be augmented with other more specific laws or generalizations, for as Botterill (1996, 115) observes, "if that was all we knew of other people, we wouldn't know what to expect of them."[23]

Holmes provides an example of one such generalization when explaining his deductive methods to Watson in "A Scandal in Bohemia":

When a woman thinks that her house is on fire, her instinct is to rush to the thing which she values most. It is a perfectly overpowering impulse, and I have more than once taken advantage of it. In the case of the Darlington Substitution Scandal it was of use to me, and also in the Arnsorth Castle business. A married woman grabs at her baby—an unmarried one reaches for her jewel box. (Doyle 1891/1986, 108)

The Baker Street detective is here supplementing the core principles of folk psychology with a specific "empirical" generalization about human (indeed, specifically female) psychology. In other words, he factors in what he knows (or thinks he knows) about the general proclivities of this special class of human beings and makes adjustments based on the subject's marital status (which he takes to be relevant). The result, if we believe the story, is an accurate prediction of Irene Adler's very next action.

But really this is not enough. A less fanciful example helps to make this clear. As I was preparing for a long visit to St. Louis, I asked my wife to arrange for my car to be serviced and kept in my local garage while I was abroad. I supplied her with the appropriate telephone number and she kindly made the booking for me. On the morning of my flight, she agreed to drive me to Heathrow after I had first dropped off my car at the garage. So, we set off in our separate cars and she took the lead, her trunk laden with my luggage. As we came to the relevant intersection, she stopped at a set of red traffic lights but uncharacteristically failed to signal. This surprised me because my wife is a stickler for such things. But then something even odder happened. To my amazement when the lights changed she did not turn, but began driving toward the town center, straight past the garage at which she herself had made the booking! As time was against us, this alarmed me. I raced to make sense of her action, assuming that her mind must have been elsewhere. At first, I flashed my lights with my signal light blinking, expecting her to realize that I was no longer following in the hope that she would notice her mistake. Things went from bad to worse when I saw her cast a glance in her rearview mirror without stopping. At this point, I was faced with a rather tricky interpretative problem. Given that my wife is very competent and reliable, lacking any malicious streak or any known reason to treat me badly, I was at an utter loss to make sense of her actions. Although a number of possible explanations sprang to mind, knowing my wife, none of these looked plausible. I was unable to make any sense of her actions. Assuming my wife had not become irrational, I could not begin to narrow the field of possibilities enough to yield a plausible explanation even though I had a detailed knowledge of the circumstances as well as her history and character. No supplement to a core theory of mind would have been any use.

And this is the moral. Achieving the requisite explanation would not have been made possible by means of a graft—that is, if my (alleged) core theory of mind was reinforced by a clutch of auxiliary hypotheses, even if these took the form of minitheories about the dispositions and traits of the person in question. Certainly, we often explicitly call on such information when speculating about others. It might even be thought that if we are prepared to take a *very* relaxed view of what constitutes a theory, then person-specific theories could be formed on the basis of regular encounters and prolonged experience with particular individuals. No doubt this would help in weeding out some explanations. For example, Stich and Nichols (1992) consider a case in which such detailed information about a person's character could be used in order to evaluate the suggestion that he was speaking in a foreign language for purposes of comic effect. They write that "some belief/desire pairs will be easy to exclude. Perhaps the agent is a dour fellow; he never wants to make anyone laugh. If we believe this to be the case then [this proposal] won't be very plausible" (p. 43).

Although such knowledge of a person's character certainly helps enable us to make refined guesses about why someone might have acted, in most cases these guesses will still fall short of providing the explanation for an action. Or rather, nothing ensures in any given instance that an action, even if it is not irrational, stems from a fixed set of dispositions that define one's character or personality traits: it is always possible that the person is, in fact, acting "out of character" or is spurred on by an unpredictable emotion. Moreover, many situations have novel features that we just cannot guess accurately.[24]

Luckily, on learning the history of my wife's actions it was possible to rationally explain her otherwise disturbing behavior. After the incident, she explained that although it was true that she had phoned the garage to make the appointment herself, and she had used the number I had given her, she believed it was the number for our old garage, which is located in the next village.

The point is that neither core theory theory nor simulation theory, nor the two in concert, could have reliably generated this explanation. This matters because it is explanations of just this sort that we require—and regularly get—in our everyday affairs. Third-person methods therefore lack the resources to enable us to reliably and successfully deal with many ordinary cases that cry out for explanation. Put otherwise, given that successful reason explanations require us to designate *the* reason for acting—as opposed to simply offering a *possible* reason for acting—all such third-person approaches are of limited use (see Hutto 1999b). Ironically, if we accept the idea that folk psychology is central to our practice of accurately explaining actions in terms of reasons, and reliably so, then it cannot be conducted in the way most theorists suppose. In most everyday cases it is the narratives of others—those they relate to us directly—that explicate and explain why an action was performed.

To reiterate, the greatest chance of obtaining a successful explanation—of deciding for which reason an action was performed—depends on the authors of actions identifying and explicating their reasons for themselves. Other conditions must hold too—that is, the person must not be confabulating, must not be engaging in post hoc rationalization, must not be self-deceived, and so on. Nevertheless, by way of comparison, asking the other for their reasons is vastly more reliable than trying to determine why they in fact acted as they did from the distance of a third-party spectator—and the likelihood of accuracy decreases in direct proportion to our explanatory need. By way of contrast, it is only in second-person contexts that we confidently obtain true folk psychological explanations (to the extent that we do at all), as opposed to merely speculating about possible ones. When in doubt, it is best to find out why someone acted from the "horse's mouth." Even though in some cases we will have legitimate reasons to doubt the other's word, the explanations that we generate on their behalf rarely rise above the status of mere supposition (at least in those cases where there is any interesting question about why they acted as they did in the first place). This should give us pause for thought about what the primary function (or functions) of folk psychological explanations really is. I return to this in the final chapter.

The stories others tell about their reasons are typically delivered, and indeed, often fashioned, in the course of online interactive dialogue and conversation—dialogue of the sort that is, with luck, sensitive to the questioner's precise explanatory needs and requirements. The nature of such engagements is complex and deserves more attention than it has received to date. That is not my focus here. The crucial point to recognize is that it is what is conveyed in these second-person deliveries—the narratives narrated—that do the heavy lifting in enabling us to understand and make sense of others with confidence. As before, I call narratives of the kind that explicate actions in terms of reasons (as understood above) *folk psychological narratives*.[25] Providing these is the primary work of folk psychology stricto sensu, which is—at root—a distinctive kind of narrative practice. It just is the practice of providing (or generating) narratives about reasons.

Folk psychological narratives can, of course, be constructed and used for third-person speculation—as in those cases in which we wonder why another may have acted in a certain way on a particular occasion. But such attempted explanations are unlikely to hit the mark in any case of real need.

Yet even if this claim about the nature and source of folk psychological explanations is accepted, it might still be thought the only way we can makes sense of these narratives—the only way to digest them—is by means of operating "theory of mind" machinery of some kind or other (of either the TT or ST varieties). Surely, such machinery must be at work in enabling our folk psychological understanding. I think it is only a familiar habit of thought that encourages this view. To break it I devote the next chapter to considering how children might acquire their basic folk psychological understanding and skills through narratives themselves.

2 The Narrative Practice Hypothesis

What Does It Take to Be a Folk Psychologist?

Not everyone has what it takes to be a folk psychologist. The birds and the bees don't do it; chimps don't do it. Even little kids don't do it! This should not surprise us. Folk psychology is not easy—it is a quite sophisticated skill. Mastery of it rests on having met a number of prerequisites. At the very least, one has to have

1. A practical understanding of the propositional attitudes
2. A capacity to represent the objects that these take—propositional contents as specified by *that*-clauses
3. An understanding of the "principles" governing the interaction of the attitudes, both with one another and with other key psychological players (such as perception and emotion)
4. An ability to apply all of the above sensitively (that is, adjusting for relevant differences in particular cases by making allowance for a range of variables, such as the person's character, circumstances, etc.)

Any interesting explication of folk psychology should not only say what having this rich set of abilities entails, it should also say how it is acquired. On the assumption that these abilities do not come as a "package deal," this chapter focuses on providing an acquisitional account of (3) and (4) in terms of the Narrative Practice Hypothesis (NPH). I will, therefore, be working, as it were, from the top down. I postpone discussion of what I take to be the right acquisitional account of (1) and (2) until the next chapter.

The rival offerings—theory theory and simulation theory—are uninspiring in this respect. For, as later chapters will reveal, they do not provide any deep understanding of (3). All the existing theories presuppose some kind of commerce with the principles of intentional psychology, whether

this is imagined to take the form of a tacit or explicit theoretical understanding or a practical capacity to manipulate one's own mental states in
accord with them (thus, quite literally, embodying them). But presupposing the existence of such abilities is not the same as adequately *explaining*
how they first came to be in place. Eventually, I aim to show that the existing theories do not meet this explanatory demand. More than this, as far
as I can see, they do not trouble themselves with giving an account of (4)
at all.

Before getting started, it is worth saying a few words about what distinguishes having an understanding of desires or beliefs (and even desires *and*
beliefs) from having an understanding of reasons. Doing so will help us to
properly characterize our true quarry. It is empirically well established that
children make propositional attitude ascriptions before they learn to explicate, explain, or predict actions in terms of reasons. For example, at around
two years of age, children are in secure possession of "an early intentional
understanding of persons having internal goals and wants that differ from
person to person" (Wellman and Phillips 2001, 130; Bartsch and Wellman
1995, chap. 4).[1] The two-year-old understanding of desires can be rather
sophisticated: children understand, for instance, how desires relate to emotions and perceptions and what would relevantly and consistently satisfy
specific desires—thus they exhibit some fluency with counterfactual thinking of a limited sort.

As impressive as this is, it goes without saying that these abilities do not
amount to an understanding of beliefs. Nor would an understanding of
desires and beliefs conjunctively equal an understanding of reasons. These
are all logically distinct abilities. We can see the main point at issue if we
consider that for a great many coordinating purposes it is often enough to
know simply what it is that McX likes or wants. Young children are certainly capable of noting this sort of thing and making good use of it—it is
what enables them to make certain low-level, inductively driven predictions about what others are likely to do. But this capacity in itself is quite
different from understanding why McX might have acted for a reason.
More is needed for that—in particular, the child would have to be able to
understand that McX's action issued from a complex "state of mind," one
having a particular kind of implicit structure. Said structure is what one
alludes to when one says McX not only likes, say, yogurt but is eating it
for breakfast because he believes it will make him healthy—implying, of
course, that good health is also something he seeks.

I mention this because while it is quite unlikely that anyone would
confuse the ability to understand and attribute desires with that of being

able to understand and attribute beliefs, there is a fairly widespread tendency to conflate the latter sort of ability with a capacity to understand and attribute reasons. This mistake stems from assuming, as is commonly done, that children are already in the possession of the bulk of their theory of mind at the point at which they begin to pass false-belief tests. Hence, success on these tests is taken to be the mark of their having acquired the final piece of the theory of mind puzzle. Having mastered the core concept of belief, it is supposed that they have mastered the full set of folk psychological principles.

But if we give due consideration to what false-belief tests actually test, there is reason to doubt this. In the original version of the false-belief test, of which there are now many well-known variants, children were introduced to a puppet, Maxi.[2] The test was conducted in a room in which a pile of cookies was the main attraction. In the course of events, Maxi, like the children, observes as the cookies are put in one of two cupboards. The puppet subsequently leaves the room, and during his absence the children watch as an experimenter moves the cookies into the other cupboard. The question they are asked is, where will Maxi think the cookies are on his return? For anyone with a sound grasp of the concept of belief, and how perception fixes belief, answering this ought to be straightforward. But, famously, for some—children below a certain age and those with specific impairments—it is not.

Such children have difficulty ascribing to the Maxi puppet a belief that differs from their own belief about the location of the cookies. They are unable to ascribe to the puppet a false belief, or so it seems. The reason for this is, it has been plausibly suggested, that they are unable to understand that the puppet (or anyone) has a cognitive take on the facts that diverges from their own. Younger children and those with infantile autism cannot simultaneously represent how they take things to stand with the world (from their point of view) and also how things stand from another cognitive vantage point. Thus, in lacking an ability to ascribe false beliefs they demonstrate a lack of an understanding of belief, if we suppose, as we ought, that grasping that concept requires having a metarepresentational ability.

If we stick to the evidence and put aside any attachment to theory theory for a moment, it is quite clear that merely having demonstrable metarepresentational abilities—that is, showing command of the concept of belief—is not equivalent to understanding reasons per se. It is easy to be misled on this score due to the great emphasis that developmental psychologists place on the moment when children begin to pass false-belief tasks. These are often called theory of mind tests for the reasons given above. I say more about what is involved in passing such tests in chapter 6, but for now it is enough to note that they do precisely what their name suggests *and nothing more*—that is, they test for an explicit understanding of false belief.[3] To call them theory of mind tests therefore gives a quite erroneous impression, which trades on the assumption that folk psychological abilities simply fall into place automatically once children master the application of the concept of belief. This is simply untrue. Knowing that children manage to pass false-belief tests, reliably enough, at a certain age under very particular experimental conditions, gives no insight into the extent of their understanding of that concept in other contexts. This being the case, such tests certainly do not tell us about the general abilities of children when it comes to ascribing or understanding reasons, per se.

The myopia associated with conducting and analyzing false-belief tests has tended to blind researchers to the fact that children's nuanced folk psychological skills only develop securely after ages four and five. Thus, "Proponents of the dominant theories have been notably quiet about what happens in development after the child's fifth birthday. However research that explores whether 5-year-olds can use simple false belief knowledge to make inferences about their own and others' perspectives finds that they singularly fail to do so" (Carpendale and Lewis 2004, 91).[4] Apparently, it takes some time for them to incorporate their newfound understanding of belief within wider explanatory strategies.

The simple truth is that having an understanding of belief is logically distinct from having an understanding of what it is to act for a reason. One can ascribe beliefs using a simple inference rule of the following sort: if X says (or sincerely asserts) that P then X believes that P (ceteris paribus). Knowing that X believes that P is useful for at least some social coordination purposes—for example, it enables one to predict what else X might believe. This might be achieved by focusing on what X *ought* to conclude from thinking that P (on the assumption that X observes standard norms of rationality). Very well, but this does not equate to ascribing to X a reason: that would require ascribing to X a complex state of mind, minimally consisting of a belief/desire pair with interlocking contents. Reasons are not to be confused with isolated thoughts or desires. To think of an action as performed for a reason, it is not enough to imagine it as being sponsored by a singular kind of propositional attitude; one must also ascribe other kinds of attitudes that act as relevant and necessary partners in motivational crime.

This is not always evident given the way reason explanations are often presented. He left the party because he *believed* the host had insulted him. She will head for the cabin in the woods because she *wants* peace and quiet. These are quotidian examples of truncated reason explanations, one backward looking and the other future facing. Both imply more than they say. To leave a party because of a suspected insult suggests that one desires not to be insulted, or at least that the desire to avoid insult is stronger than that for some other good on offer. Similarly, to seek tranquillity in an isolated cabin implies that one believes that it can be found there, or at least more so than elsewhere. Although still woefully underdescribed, these "fuller" explanations demonstrate that an understanding of what it is to act for a reason always ultimately rests on a quiet understanding of the way propositional attitudes interrelate. This is why having *discrete* understanding of the core propositional attitudes is only a necessary but not a sufficient condition for being a practicing folk psychologist. These observations will be important again in the next chapter and are a reminder of the challenges that must be met in this one. With them out of the way, we can now turn to the main event.

Acquiring Folk Psychology in Ontogeny

How do we come by our familiar understanding of folk psychology and our ability to deploy it so successfully during childhood? The process is not simple. This familiar achievement rests on a complex series of foundations—that is, children must already have a number of more basic imaginative abilities and interpersonal skills in order to learn how to make sense of actions in terms of reasons successfully. Long before they are able to do this, they are at home in navigating their social worlds in embodied and imaginative ways: they get by in the earliest stages of their interpersonal careers without ever attributing desires, beliefs, or reasons to anyone. In time, they get a practical grasp on the different kinds of propositional attitudes—learning about each in discrete stages, as their command of language and its syntactic constructions grows. The kinds of capacities this involves and how this happens are the topics of the next four chapters. For now it is enough to note that children come into the possession of all the pieces needed for playing the understanding-action-in-terms-of-reasons game before they can actually play it. What they are missing in their early years is not the necessary components, but knowledge of the basic rules.

As noted in the previous section, proficiency in making isolated propositional attitude ascriptions—attributing certain goals, desires, thoughts, and beliefs—is not the same as *knowing how* these combine to form reasons. This stronger condition must be satisfied if one is to be a folk psychologist. This requires mastery of the norms governing the interplay between these attitudes. What children are missing, on acquiring a practical grasp of the concept of belief, is not therefore another ingredient needed for baking the folk psychological cake—rather it is the instructions for mixing all the ingredients properly in the making of many such cakes. But if such instructions are not built into their minds, how are they acquired?

The NPH claims that the normal route is through direct encounters with stories about people who act for reasons. I call these folk psychological narratives. We might also call them "people narratives," for they are "narratives in which people feature as people (and not, for example, as objects for scientific investigation)" (Goldie 2004, 115). In addition, "The narrative should . . . present what happened in a way that enables the audience or the reader to make sense of the thoughts, feelings, and actions of those people who are internal to the narrative" (p. 115). Hereafter, for expositional variety, I will use these terms interchangeably.

The important thing is that stories of this kind provide a crucial training set needed for understanding reasons—and they do this by serving as exemplars, having precisely the right features to foster an explicit understanding of the forms and norms of folk psychology. By engaging with stories of this kind children come into possession of a direct insight into the way propositional attitudes, including belief and desire, behave with respect to each other and their familiar partners, emotions, perceptions, and so on. More than this, in such stories a person's reasons are shown in situ, against appropriate backdrops and settings. For example, children learn how a person's reasons can be influenced by such things as their character, history, current circumstances, and larger projects.

Children are repeatedly exposed to stories detailing the reasons why characters act, as related by caregivers and others who support them in this activity. I discuss the characteristic kind of support given to children in this particular kind of storytelling practice in more detail in chapter 10. An appropriate characterization of this process is crucial for making a full case for the NPH, but it gains prima facie credibility from the fact that this special kind of interpersonal activity takes place at the right point in children's development, making it plausible that it could form the basis of their sophisticated folk psychological training. People-focused conversations of the right sort are introduced fairly early on and storytelling activities are, in general, usually well under way by the ages of four or five. This is no accident, as will become clear in the next chapter, since it is only around this point that children can begin to appreciate stories that incorporate the familiar mental terms and predicates.

Although it will be important to say more about this, for now I want to stress that folk psychological narratives can play this crucial role because they are complex representations that are also public objects of mutual attention. As such, the stories in question serve as exemplars and teaching tools: In their guided encounters with such stories children come to see the relations that hold between the various psychological attitudes—crucially, but not exclusively, the focus is on beliefs and desires. This is important because, as stressed above, not only must children have an understanding of the core propositional attitudes, they must also learn how these interrelate. Thus the way beliefs and desires conspire to motivate actions—which, in abstracto, we might think of as the folk psychological schema—is a constant feature of these narratives. But this requires knowing not only how they interrelate with one another, but also how they do so with other standard players in psychological dramas. In sum, these comprise what we might think of as the "core principles" of intentional psychology.

According to the NPH these "principles" are revealed to children not as a series of rules but by showing them in action, through narratives, in their normal contexts of operation. In this way, narratives not only show which features are constant to folk psychological explanation but also, importantly, what can vary in such accounts—such as the particulars of what a person believes and desires, how these attitudes can change over time and why, and also how character, history, and other commitments might impinge on why a person acts as they do. All of this is put on show. In this way children learn which kinds of factors must be taken into account and adjusted for when it comes to making sense of the stories that others tell about the reasons why they acted, as well as learning what needs mentioning when providing their own accounts. It is in this way and in this sense that children acquire an understanding of the core structure of folk psychology, its governing norms, and guidance on its practical application. This is not a process through which children distill a set of general rules.

To understand the NPH correctly, two senses of *narrative* must be distinguished—that is, the narratives that are the third-person objects of focus, and the narratives through which these are presented and shared—that is, the acts of narration that constitute the second-person storytellings.

As an object, a narrative—the story itself—might be spontaneous production, an autobiographical account, a bit of gossip, or an established cultural artifact. Many of the latter are texts of which there may be multiple versions—such as Perrault's "Little Red Riding Hood" or its Grimm Brothers variant "Little Red Cap." Indeed, this is one of the best-known folk psychological narratives:

Little Red Riding Hood *learns* from the woodcutter that her grandmother is sick. She *wants* to make her grandmother feel better [she is a nice, caring child], and she *thinks* that a basket of treats will help, so she brings such a basket through the woods to her grandmother's house [beliefs and desires lead to actions]. When she arrives there, she *sees* the wolf in her grandmother's bed, but she *falsely believes* that the wolf is her grandmother [appearances can be deceiving]. When she *realizes* it is a wolf, she is *frightened* and runs away, because she *knows* wolves can hurt people. The wolf, who indeed *wants* to eat her, leaps out of the bed and runs after her trying to catch her. (Lillard 1997, 268; emphases mine)

Tales of this sort are legion. This is, I take it, not in doubt, yet I have no precise data on how many of these stories children encounter in the normal course of their development. I leave it to the reader to speculate about this. What matters is that they are the best means of revealing how propositional attitudes work together in motivating actions and indicating which other factors might make a difference. Given their content and structure, they have precisely the right properties for this work. Well-crafted fairy tales are a secure medium for introducing folk psychology. They are among the earliest forms of published fiction, typically deriving from orally preserved folk tales. Yet any story that describes reasons for action, even those related through casual conversations, also has the potential to do so—at least to some degree. This is despite the fact that the latter are not as regimented or structured as the canonical texts used in much preschool storytelling. This is important because such narratives are frequently traded in run-of-the-mill conversations.[5] And it is through listening to and participating in conversations about people and why they act that children first hear propositional attitudes being discussed and described, and they learn about the kind of objects these attitudes take—complex linguistic constructions embedded in *that*-clauses.[6]

Folk psychology exhibits precisely the sorts of features that led philosophers, such as Lewis (1970, 1972), to mark it out as being theorylike—that is, it has characteristics that makes the "theory theory" a compelling hypothesis. Nevertheless, despite having an identifiable framework at its core, folk psychology is not, in fact, theoretical in its origins or principal applications.

It is worth saying a bit more about this. Many philosophers who are attracted to theory theory are of the view that the contents of theoretical concepts are determined by the role they play in a network of principles—principles that, when working in unison, enable the prediction and explanation of action. It is also commonly held that the "meanings" of mental predicates, those that form the basis of such principles, are fixed in the same way—that is, terms such as *belief, desire*, and *hope* are defined by the way they systematically interrelate with one another and with other terms.

However, the claim that the meaning of mental predicates depends wholly on their lawful relations is apparently undermined by the fact that children develop a practical understanding of the different propositional attitudes at distinct stages in their early careers. Thus they have a grasp of the concept of desire, quite independently of and prior to having an understanding of belief. And an understanding of both of these attitudes appears to precede an understanding of the roles they play in making sense of a person's reasons for action. At best, then, it seems that children significantly extend their understanding of the core propositional attitudes when they learn how these cooperate with one another (and others of their ilk) in the context of reason explanations. It is not that the latter ability constitutes their understanding of mental predicates. Nevertheless, one might hold that it is getting to grips with the roles played by the attitudes in this context that is, minimally, what is required to be capable of understanding what it is to act for a reason.

To be a practicing folk psychologist rests on having an understanding of the roles that mentalistic concepts play in the specific sort of framework described above. Some have concluded, because of this, that the framework in question is a theoretical one and mental predicates thus have a theoretical status. But that is a mistake. It may be an essential feature of all theories that they have complex network structures—and it may even be that the meanings of theoretical terms are determined entirely by the roles they play within such networks (well, maybe). All of this could be true without it being the case that folk psychology is a theory. Clearly, the mere fact that something has a framework structure does not entail that it is a theory or that the meaning of its concepts is holistically constituted. Ordinary games, such as cricket or chess, have rules, but these activities are not theoretically but conventionally grounded; they are well-established, regulated social practices. Folk psychology, too, has a framework structure, but it is neither a game nor a theory.

So, it looks like we should agree with holistically minded theory theorists only up to a point: in order to understand what it is to act for a reason we must understand the roles played by the mental predicates. But this gives us absolutely no reason to think of such concepts as theoretical constructs—similar to electrons, atoms, or gravity. To be sure, understanding the distinct roles that such concepts play in folk psychology requires having an understanding of their place in a network of possibilities. But, at most, this means that, in this context, mentalistic terms may be similar in this one respect to certain theoretical terms (on the disputable assumption that this is the best way to make sense of the meaning of theoretical constructs). The point is that even if we should wish to acknowledge this it should be remembered that folk psychology need be like a theory in no other interesting aspect, and certainly not in its origins or its primary applications.

For all these reasons, using the label theory of mind as a byword for folk psychological practice is highly misleading. The practice should be shunned in light of the bad effects it has had (and continues to have) on the imaginations of many philosophers, psychologists, and others working on this topic.

Norms of Practical Applicability

Successful application of folk psychology involves more than merely coming to grips with its core structure, it requires skilful know-how. One must be able to use it, sensitively, occasion by occasion. Encounters with folk psychological narratives help foster this practical ability as well. For, although the structure of intentional psychology is a constant in narratives of the relevant kind, they vary in other aspects. Through them children also learn that many nonmentalistic factors are pertinent to why someone has acted or might act. For example, they learn that what a person believes or desires matters to the actions they take, but they also learn how their character, unique history, and circumstances might affect their motivational set. These are the sorts of features, inter alia, that differ from story to story, within a single story over time—and often from protagonist to protagonist within the same story. They are prominent in nearly all interesting stories even if only in the background. Knowing how to make relevant adjustments to accommodate just such factors is necessary for the skilled application of folk psychology. The simplest person narratives engender this kind of practical knowledge by introducing children to distinct characters and their specific background beliefs and desires, particular agendas, unique histories, personality traits, and so on. Although the stories in which they figure are at first quite simple, they become more sophisticated over time.

The main point, again, is that these stories have precisely the right properties for familiarizing children, not only with the core mentalistic framework, but also with the rudimentary norms governing its practical application. By putting examples of people acting for reasons on display, they show how the items in the mentalistic toolkit can be used together to understand reasons in general, as it were, and also how and when these tools might be used—that is, what to adjust for—in specific cases. They not only teach children this but they also give some hints about how to make the relevant adjustments (for example, a character with suspicious tendencies is likely to form certain beliefs in such and such a situation, and so on). Encounters with such stories look ideally suited to providing children with the requisite specialized know-how—that is, to teaching them how to apply folk psychology, with sensitivity, in everyday contexts.

The NPH therefore has the potential to explain something its rivals do not; it offers insight into how we might acquire our workaday skills in wielding folk psychology. This matters, for if an effective use of folk psychology requires coming to grips with the sorts of factors mentioned above, there is little to recommend the thought that such practical worries can be shunted to one side and dismissed when it comes to understanding folk psychological abilities. Surprisingly, this is the standard strategy. Thus, it is widely supposed that questions about day-to-day "application" can be relegated to the sideline and dealt with by a liberal invocation of ceteris paribus clauses. Consequently, although everyone acknowledges that there are many factors—psychological and nonpsychological—that are relevant to any particular attempt to make sense of an action in terms of reasons, our ability to cope with these factors in practice is treated as if it is outside the scope of folk psychology per se. The mainstream offerings, TT and ST, are conspicuously silent on the question of what grounds this aspect of folk psychological practice. In my view, this is a serious lacuna.

Most theorists do not accept that there is a need to give an account of such practical knowledge because they imagine, quite wrongly in my opinion, that folk psychology is just the name of a theory or procedure, one that can be understood quite independently from its practical application. I take the opposite view: although folk psychology has a core framework—which can be abstractly described as a set of principles—it is first and foremost a practical enterprise. Its business is just the application of a special narrative framework in specific cases of making sense of actions.

Any theory of folk psychology that fails to recognize and to account for this will ultimately fail to satisfy. And this, I fear, is true of all existing accounts.

Take TT as an example. Here the sole focus is on explaining the nature of the basic rules of folk psychology—understood in vacuo—those that define its core mentalistic framework. Little attention is given to the question of how children learn to apply these rules in practice. We are told instead that we rely on a tacit understanding of "idealized rational agents" when making mentalistic predictions and explanations (see Dennett 1985, 16–22; Dennett 1987, chap. 4; Stich 1990, chaps. 2, 3). Mentalistic attributions imply such an understanding. Thus, if I know that McX is thirsty for a glass of water, and I know that he believes he could get one by going downstairs to the refrigerator, I will probably predict that he will do just this (all else being equal and assuming he has the right sort of background beliefs and desires, and so on). But, as mentioned in the previous chapter, I will only expect this of McX if I think he will behave as any rational agent would. For if McX is irrational, interpreting or predicting his behavior in terms of his reasons is a nonstarter.[7]

In one sense this is surely right. But knowing this is hardly sufficient for being a practicing folk psychologist; our everyday skill involves much, much more than knowing in some thin, attenuated sense that a person has acted or might act thus and so because they have a certain belief/desire pairing and that they are not irrational. Alone, knowing all this would not be of much help in making a person's actions intelligible. In those interesting cases in which we might need to make sense of McX's action we would need a much thicker description not just of his psychological set, but of his character, his history, and his circumstances. In effect, we need to know his particular story.

Sustained experience with folk psychological narratives primes us for this richer practical understanding by giving us an initial sense of which kinds of background factors can matter, why they do so, and how they do so in particular cases. Stories can do this because they are not bare descriptions of the current beliefs and desires of idealized rational agents. They are snapshots of the adventures of situated persons, presented in the kinds of settings in which all of the important factors needed for understanding reasons are described—that is, those that are relevant to making sense of what is done and why.

The various personae dramatis in such tales, even the not-very-interesting ones, each have their own unique psychological profile consisting not only of occurrent psychological attitudes but also of habitual tendencies or other personality traits (which may conflict in various ways). They depict reasoners to be sure, but not ideal ones. The principal players in narratives have substantial attributes; these may make them admirable, pitiful, or deeply or tragically flawed. It is the knowledge that people too have such attributes—learning what to watch out for and how to recognize these attributes—that, in large part, fuels the activity of making sense of their actions (and indeed our own). This is a far cry from making generalizations about what we can expect that any rational "someone" might do or might have done in specified circumstances.

Once again, this works because story characters, like their real-life counterparts, do not pursue their projects in a vacuum. Often their reason for taking a particular course of action is influenced by their character, larger projects, past choices, existing commitments, ruling passions, or unique circumstances and history. My claim is that our ability to make sense of intentional action in practice—and our proficiency at doing so—rests on our knowing, in general, which details might be relevant and knowing how and when to make the appropriate adjustments in particular cases. Folk psychological narratives are uniquely well suited to fostering this kind of understanding because they provide examples of people acting for reasons in appropriately rich settings.

It is, of course, true that we do not always supply pertinent details of a person's history and character when making sense of their reasons for acting. Saying why someone has acted normally only requires telling quite short stories. But this does not alter the fact that our potential for this kind of sense-making requires a sophisticated capacity—specifically, it requires knowing which kinds of background factors might matter and the ability to accommodate these factors, case by case.

To see this, it is important not to conflate issues about what our folk psychological ability requires with issues concerning the pragmatics of explanation. That we usually do not supply full details when making sense of intentional actions is a fact about the latter; it tells us nothing at all about what lies at the heart of our capacity for understanding actions in terms of reasons. As noted earlier, many reason explanations—even those that only make appeal to a person's propositional attitudes—are truncated. Thus in most contexts it is possible to explain why someone acted, for example, by citing a relevant belief, without bothering to mention its partner desire. But, of course, for anyone who understands such an explanation, the latter is clearly implied. Thus, if asked why Ms. Y was late for the 3:00 p.m. meeting we might simply report that she believed that it was going to start at 4:00 p.m. In accounting for her tardiness, it is not usually necessary to add that she must also have desired to attend it. That can be taken as read, as it were. And the same holds true of countless of her other background beliefs and desires that are, for want of a better phrase, lurking in the background. For example, if the above explanation is to succeed then it must also be assumed that Ms. Y believed that attendance at the relevant meeting required her physical presence, and that the meeting was to be held today (not tomorrow, or next Tuesday, or on some other day), and so on. Had she not believed such things, we would have to explain the reason for absence differently. The same applies to other potentially mitigating propositional attitudes.

The point is that in giving everyday explanations we only supply details on a need-to-know basis, as dictated by the requirements of the audience or questioner. We assume that they share a common knowledge with us on most points—and we are usually quite justified in assuming this. Initially, this is what determines just how much or how little we make explicit. But if their ignorance demands it, we are capable of telling a longer story. Sometimes this requires saying more about the person's core propositional attitudes and how they interrelate. As the above example involving Ms. Y makes clear, this implies that the storyteller knows the details. But the fact he or she can supply these on demand reveals that the storyteller also has knowledge that background beliefs and desires can make a difference. The same holds true of the kind of know-how needed for making the relevant adjustments concerning an individual's personality, character, history, or circumstances. Early engagements with people narratives impart practical skills and knowledge of both varieties.

Admittedly, a full and properly nuanced awareness of what is involved in acting for a reason requires acquaintance with narratives of a much more sophisticated kind than those that figure in preschool dialogues and simple fairy tales. And there is much more on offer in adult conversations and grander literary offerings. The characters that populate children's stories would struggle even to pass muster as what E. M. Forster called "flat characters"—those that "can be summed up in a single sentence" (Goldie 2004, 3). Typically, storybook characters and the situations in which they find themselves are not very complex. Little Red Riding Hood is no Madame Bovary, to be sure. But this does not change the fact that such early narrative encounters supply the basics needed for acquiring a first understanding of reasons. This is folk psychology 101, after all, not grad school.

These kinds of narratives also play a part in teaching us when we need to use folk psychology—for we do not use it constantly or indiscriminately.

It is only brought to bear in the sorts of cases in which we are surprised or perplexed by another's actions. The fact is that "when things 'are as they should be,' the narratives of folk psychology are unnecessary" (Bruner 1990, 40). Folk psychological narratives only come into play—they are only sought and supplied—when our culturally based expectations are violated (or it is thought that they might be). Mostly, well-rehearsed patterns of behavior and coordination dominate and we have no need to make sense of what others are doing. By and large, we manage without having to make or seek any folk psychological explications at all. In most everyday social interactions we generally do not need to interpret what others are doing or why by asking about their reasons. Occasionally, what someone does deviates from our expectations (or we have reason to suspect that it will) in ways that require special attention.

Folk psychological narratives are used to make sense of these seemingly aberrant actions. Typically—or at least when they work—they help us to understand why someone has acted in a way that has strayed from our normal expectations (on the assumption that they have acted for a reason nonetheless).

This was discussed in the previous chapter; I raise it again in this context because I want to suggest that our early narrative encounters may also help us to know when folk psychological explanations are required. I suggest that they are likely to be a major source for establishing what is culturally normal—what is to be expected. Quite generally, stories—real or fictional—teach us what others can expect from us, but just as importantly, what we can expect from others in specific contexts and situations. They teach us at the same time what we and others ought to do (and thus what "we" are likely to do). And they often teach us what "we" ought to think and feel in particular circumstances.

Stories therefore help to shape our common cultural expectations, making us familiar with the norms governing actions in "ordinary" situations. They are an important source of guidance about the boundaries between what is acceptable and what is not. Through them we learn, for example, about the social roles that pervade our everyday environments—shops, restaurants, post offices. Such encounters help fund our common sociocultural activities; they make much unreflective social navigation possible. Bruner (1990, 40) is right that rather than merely providing a framework for disinterested prediction and behavior, narratives—and especially folk psychological narratives—work to regulate our actions; as such they are "instruments of culture": they summarize "not simply how things are but (often implicitly) how they should be."

Narratives are a potent means for establishing local standards about which actions are acceptable, which kinds of events are important and noteworthy, and even what constitutes having a good reason for acting. Just as some actions are not in good taste, so too are some reasons for taking action ignoble or dishonorable—they may fail to live up to local standards. Absorbing such standards gives us our first ground for judging a reason's appropriateness, though, of course, in time, these standards are typically questioned and overturned. It seems hard to deny that stories are at least one important medium through which initiates become familiar with the preestablished ethical norms of their local cultures. Apart from enabling us to make sense of actions, folk psychological narratives help to instill this kind of evaluative framework in the young. They also contribute to the development of a common sense of the obvious, the significant, and the ethical on which that understanding rests.

I opened this chapter by saying that it is a test of adequacy for any good theory of folk psychology that it should be capable of explaining (at least potentially) not just how we acquire an understanding of the core mentalistic framework but also how we acquire our normal capacity to apply it sensitively in practice. This is integral to what we most want to understand about the distinctive but everyday phenomenon of making sense of intentional actions; it is not an optional extra. The importance of this can be best seen if one considers that it is possible to learn about the core folk psychological principles without knowing how or when to apply them (or at least not with the same fluency that ordinary practitioners of intentional psychology exhibit). One could learn how the core mentalistic predicates relate to one another in conceptual space without knowing, for example, how they function in a richer setting—that is, without having any idea of how or when they should be attributed as might happen if one learned such principles by means other than by engaging with folk psychological narratives in early childhood. Pretty clearly, on its own, such an understanding would be of limited value.

Let me be clear about one other aspect of the central claim of the NPH. Although exposure to person narratives is the normal route for learning the forms and norms of folk psychology, it is possible to achieve this (or something approximating it) by other means. Apparently, it is possible to learn the basic rules of intentional psychology by heart, as some individuals, initially diagnosed with infantile autism, have seemingly managed to do. The process is described as a purely logical one, using observation to fashion a set of usable generalizations that are then committed to memory, as are the principles for their application. On this basis, autistic individuals have been described as being able to "compute" and "calculate" what others are thinking and feeling based on available evidence, as if they were using a set of algorithms (Bowler 1991; Gallagher 2004). This is achieved in later life, perhaps thanks to their strong general intelligence and powerful rote memories, in order to compensate for their lack of insight into the reasons why others act. This is the most likely explanation for how such individuals eventually become capable of passing false-belief tasks.

Picking up the relevant folk psychological principles and rules for their application as sets of explicit regulations is quite unlike the training I suggest is imparted through storytelling practice. And the effects of this alternative kind of training regime are transparent. Those who acquire their folk psychology skills in this way remain quite awkward in their dealings with others; they never fully develop a capacity to make sense of actions in the easy and familiar way that most of us do (Eisenmajer and Prior 1991; Happé 1995). The phenomenological differences are also salient (Zahavi and Parnas 2003). For example, Temple Grandin, an autistic individual who has, by her own account, succeeded in fashioning rules for understanding others in this way, still "describes herself as like an anthropologist on Mars" (Kennett 2002, 347).

Of course, such feelings of estrangement have deeper roots, but the point is that these persist even after autistic individuals learn to master false-belief tasks.[8] This suggests that they never quite achieve the kind of understanding of others that is the norm for most people. If nothing else, consideration of such cases should discourage the tendency to think that folk psychology is nothing more than the name for a theory or set of rules as opposed to a special sort of rule-based know-how.[9] This is a salient reminder that our true explanandum, our real quarry, is a highly nuanced and skilled practice—albeit one that makes use of the core mentalistic framework.

Extracting this schema and becoming familiar with the norms for its application through experience with a certain class of discursive narratives is the culminating, nonnegotiable requirement for a *basic* mastery of our everyday folk psychological abilities. Engaging in the relevant kind of storytelling practice is the normal route through which this practical knowledge and understanding are procured.[10]

I opened this chapter by observing that the NPH requires for its truth that children must have a basic grasp of the propositional attitudes in order to begin to engage in the relevant FP-engendering narrative practices; this must be in place *in advance* of their basic folk psychological training. In chapter 7, I will say how this is possible without postulating hardwired modules that already somehow contain such concepts or theory-formation mechanisms that allow for their construction. In advance of supplying that developmental story, it is crucial to make some important distinctions in order to better understand the nature of nonverbal responding and different kinds of attitudes that can be adopted. This will occupy us for the next three chapters.

3 Intentional Attitudes

I don't think the issue whether animals have beliefs is in itself of any importance—one can use words as one pleases. But if you want to talk about pre-linguistic thought, you need to explain precisely what you have in mind.
—Donald Davidson, personal communication, November 1991

MoPs and Props

Without question, much nonverbal responding takes the form of highly sophisticated patterns of activity. In one sense, these patterns are well suited for interpretation using folk psychological apparatus. Watching cat-and-mouse antics offers a spectacle of high-level anticipatory predator/prey interactions in which the participants exhibit knowledge of their legendary opponents (that is, knowledge of the sorts of things that cats and mice are, in general, likely to do). Moreover, such interplay involves more than general understanding; each animal must also form expectations about what their *current* adversary, as a token of a more general type, is doing or is about to do in light of the particular circumstances (that is, "Jerry is about to scurry behind that obstacle," "Tom is giving me space to run," and so on).

It is quite compelling—almost irresistible—for us to say that such creatures are acting out of beliefs and desires. Many feel compelled to ascribe these mental states—propositional attitudes—to Tom and Jerry even if the consensus is that we stop short of supposing that cats and mice (and other nonverbals) can ascribe such states of mind to one another. It is natural for us to interpret at least the more sophisticated kinds of animals as regularly weighing possible courses of action, comparing these against others and assessing such strategies in light of their strongest desires, and so on (presumably, all of this occurs at an unreflective suborganismic level). Minimally, it seems that many nonverbals reason practically about what to do next—and the end product of such acts of reasoning is the formation of "intentions to act," which take the form of some sort of internal motivating imperative (for example, "Leap to the right," "Make a run for it").

The relevant processes of reasoning are described in full-fledged mentalistic terms—Tom *wants* to catch Jerry and he *thinks* that Jerry will appear from his hiding spot just here and right about now. And if Jerry fails to do so, it is Tom's false belief that putatively explains his ineffective mouse-catching behavior on this occasion. Against this backdrop, it is common to hear claims like the following:

A cat is conscious, I assume, and it *has the sort of consciousness whose content can be put into words* only with the help of the first person pronoun. A cat *could never* catch a mouse if it couldn't have thoughts representing the world from its own egocentric perspective, thoughts with the English-language equivalents such as "I'm gaining on it" or "I've got it." (Velleman 2004, 2; emphasis added)[1]

I object to such ascriptions, if they are construed as anything other than theoretically innocent *façon de parler*. As serious attributions about the mental life of animals, such content-based ascriptions are unwarranted, however tempting they may be. Accepting this is not easy. The waters here are muddied because our command of the folk psychology enables us to make crude generalizations, which work in predicting the behavior of a wide range of things—even those to which we clearly would not want to seriously ascribe beliefs and desires.

So, to make headway, we must distinguish the quite uninteresting sense in which the mentalistic predicates can be legitimately applied to non-verbals. Animals might be regarded as believers in the sense that they are the sorts of things whose behavior can be usefully predicted by adopting the "intentional stance." That is surely true, but this fact alone should not encourage anyone to suppose that such creatures *in fact*—really, really—harbor propositional attitudes or that they are genuinely capable of reasoning about means to ends by making calculations concerning the contents of their beliefs and desires when "deciding" on a course of action.[2]

The mere fact that folk psychology can be fruitfully applied to some system is not an adequate test of whether it acts on the basis of manipulating propositional beliefs and desires. By appeal to this lenient criterion almost anything can be *treated* as—and therefore would *be*—a genuine practical reasoner, or as Dennett says, a "true believer." If so, the class of true believers would include thermostats, rivers, lightning bolts, animals, and people, and we would have to assume that there was no interesting mentalistic difference between any of the entities in this category.[3]

I am not proposing that we should draw a Dennettian moral from these observations; quite the opposite. We should insist on a more stringent test, not a purely operational one, when it comes to deciding which systems are or are not "true believers." The mere fact that many nonverbal animals execute intelligent performances that can be usefully described by the folk psychological idiom, and that seeing them in such terms gives some predictive grip, is entirely consistent with the possibility that the animals in question do not harbor any propositional attitudes at all. If so, they cannot be rightly thought of as engaging in practical reasoning involving such attitudes either.

It helps to remember that the crude predictive uses of folk psychology are quite distinct from those in which we call on it to seriously explain behavior. Only in the latter cases are we committed to the existence of a belief/desire pair that was causally responsible (in some sense) for a particular action. Notoriously, when it comes to specifying the content of the beliefs and desires of nonverbals, folk psychology comes "under stress" (Godfrey-Smith 2003). This is not merely because of interpretative difficulties that arise in deciding just how nonverbals think about the world (though these are serious enough). Rather, it is because engaging in bona fide practical reasoning is a content-involving process, one in which the contents in question must have an appropriate internal structure. The elements of complex contents (that is, the "propositions" that are believed and desired) must interrelate in systematic ways if reasoning of the sort needed to form intentions is to be at all possible. ·

Consider our cat again. Tom can only form an intention to act in the way described above if we assume that he apprehends the state of affairs concerning Jerry's location in a particular way. Contents can therefore be understood as ways of grasping or apprehending complex states of affairs that enable organisms to represent and reason about them in truth-evaluable ways. To think a thought in a content-involving way is to think about a relevant state of affairs intensionally—that is, under a particular "description" or Mode of Presentation (MoP). In using such terminology I intend to be utterly neutral with respect to the various proposals about the nature of MoPs, such as Frege's.[4] I use the term only to distinguish those intentional attitudes that are content-involving from those that are not.

Recognizing this is important. To think that (1) "Peter Parker is Peter Parker" is not to think that (2) "Peter Parker is Spiderman," although these thoughts have the same extension. If we want to understand a thought's cognitive value, its potential to enter into nondemonstrative inferential liaisons, we must individuate it in terms of its *content*. Since the material inferences one can draw are determined by "the way in which one grasps the proposition in question," it is MoPs—and not just the unmediated having of attitudes directed at situations (or, for some, "propositions")—that do the work that makes reasoning possible, including practical reasoning. To see this, one has but to imagine J. Jonah Jameson's reaction on discovering (2) as opposed to (1). We can expect an excitingly different reaction precisely because there is no immediate basis for inferring (2) from (1).

So, if Tom and Jerry are engaged in practical reasoning, then the MoPs that characterize their thoughts must be appropriately structured; their MoPs must, in some sense, "contain" recurring semantic elements that can occur in other "graspable" MoPs toward which these animals also adopt different kinds of psychological attitudes (at least desires). This is, for example, how Tom's belief about Jerry's location gets tied at significant points with the MoP under which he apprehends the relevant desired state of affairs (that is, his apprehension of his opponent). Quite simply, his propositional attitudes—or more precisely, the content of his beliefs and desires—must have internal forms that share common elements; this allows them to interrelate logically. Ultimately, although these elements will have semantic properties, it is generally held that reasoning is conducted in virtue of their formal properties alone.

But the point is that only in combining resources in this way can propositional attitudes conspire to form intentions—only in this way can they be *motivating* reasons. The same goes for us. My desire to retrieve a particular book by Davidson will be satisfied if my belief that "*Actions and Events* is kept on the third shelf to the right" is true—if the book is in fact located where I represent it as being. If this state of affairs obtains, if my belief is true, it ensures my successful action (all else being equal).

Fregean thoughts, "senses" (*Sinn*) or their equivalent—that is, contents—are required in order to reason (practically or theoretically). These might be intellectually "graspable" objective entities existing in public space.[5] If so, acts of reasoning involve grasping and regrasping numerically identical thought contents by the same individual, whereas communication involves the mutual grasping of the same thought content by several individuals.

Alternatively, as is the wont of proponents of classical approaches to cognitive science, "thought contents" might be construed as private, inner mental representations instead of as publicly graspable, abstract objects. For example, Fodor, who embraces an industrial-strength intentional realism, rearranges the Fregean idea so that contents are understood as internal-to-the-cranium representations in the Language of Thought (or LoT) (see Fodor 2003, 143–144). More precisely, MoPs are individuated in a rather complex and roundabout way, first by appeal to what one's thoughts are about (externally designated) but also by appeal to internal *structures* of the representational tokens that specify the narrow content of such thoughts. Hence, "modes of presentation are sentences (of Mentalese), and sentences are individuated not just by their propositional content but also by their syntax" (Fodor 1994, 97). In this idiom, talk of grasping and regrasping one and the same thought content is converted into talk of harboring numerically distinct token representations of the same type in one's head on different occasions. Again, this is important because it is the syntactic properties of Mentalese sentences that, in line with the Computational Theory of Mind, drive logical operations and transformations.[6]

The upshot is that if nonverbals really are practical reasoners then they make use of structured contents, MoPs, of some kind (whether public or private). In principle, these would be needed to individuate and specify their propositional attitudes. Many in philosophy and the cognitive sciences hold that intelligent nonverbal responding does in fact involve a kind of relatedness to—indeed a manipulation of—contents. I deny this. I have been neutral with respect to the Fregean and Fodorian proposals about the nature of content by talking of content-involving mental states (as opposed to speaking only of content-bearing states), precisely because I reject both pictures; basic embodied responding is not content-involving.

Content: The Very Idea

To have a content-involving thought it is not enough that an organism is merely intentionally directed at a possible situation or state of affairs, for the latter might be understood in purely extensional terms. I therefore distinguish intentional attitudes from propositional attitudes, reserving the latter title for those attitudes that are content-involving. This is not just a terminological stipulation, though I recognize that some would claim that attitudes of both sorts are directed at propositions, albeit in different ways. In my view intentional attitudes are not directed at propositions (only possible situations), yet they exhibit intentional directedness all the same. I hope it will be clear shortly why I draw the distinction in this way. Until then the reader is free to assume that my use of terms is decided by fiat. The main point is that within the class of intentionally directed attitudes, we can distinguish between those of the extensional and intensional varieties.

Usefully, this way of carving things up respects the fact that propositional attitudes can be individuated by their MoPs (or narrow contents) as well as by their truth conditions (or by their broad contents). And this explains why they, like quotations, have the property of being opaque: coreferential substitution in intensional contexts is not automatically permitted. As we have just seen, specifying what a thinker thinks when they reason requires more than specifying which extensional state of affairs is being thought about. If contents are to do their required logical work they must have a significant structure. They must have subparts with determinate referential or denotational content. These elements are also thought to exhibit a kind of directedness; they are *about* things (for example, objects, places, behaviors, mental states, and so on). They are thought to have referential properties in just the way names do. As traditionally understood, I deny this. Nonverbal responding is not contentful, and it does not segment into elements with freestanding referential or semantic properties.

Let me clarify more precisely the clutch of ideas that I am rejecting. For analytical philosophers, the modern locus classicus of the claim that basic perceptual acts are content-involving can be found in Evans's *Varieties of Reference*:

In general, we may regard a perceptual experience as an informational state of the subject: it *has a certain content*—the world is represented a certain way—and hence it permits of a *nonderivative classification as true or false*. For an internal state to be so regarded, it must have *appropriate connections with behaviour*—it must have *a certain motive force* upon the actions of the subject.... The informational states which a subject *acquires through perception* are nonconceptual, or nonconceptualised. Judgements based upon such states necessarily involve conceptualization. (Evans 1982, 226–227; emphases added)

When it comes to understanding "content" as described in the passage above, we should not be distracted by the fact that it (apparently) comes in both conceptual and nonconceptual varieties. This distinction does not mark two different *types* of content, but only two different *ways* of "having" it. The difference relates to an organism's expressive capacities. Thus nonconceptual content is generally thought to be had by organisms that are unable to specify, verbally or otherwise, how they think about the world. Nevertheless, they can be in mental states with a kind of content that is potentially expressible—in a very strong sense of *potential*—without loss of meaning in conceptual terms. As such, the content of nonverbal mental states can be accurately characterized using canonical concepts (in principle) even though the creature itself may lack the concepts or capacity to specify these (see Cussins 1990).[7] Thus the claim is that there are unique "terms of reference" that could be used to express such contents in words.[8] This holds true whether the content in question is propositional, to be expressed using complement *that*-clauses, or merely referential. The received view is that nonverbals have content-involving mental states (states that can be individuated—in theory—in terms of their contents) and that these are to be understood and, ideally, specified in semantic terms.

All of this is very much in line with the spirit of Evans's view, though his terminology would need some adjustment to be acceptable today. For example, he speaks of perceptual experiences as being a species of truth-evaluable "informational state" with representational content. It is now recognized however that informational content, which is grounded in mere covariance relations, is not any form of representational content. Pure informational content is neither referential nor truth-evaluable. Even those who endorse psychosemantic theories in which informational content plays a foundational role accept that further conditions must be met before it can be regarded as representational.

For example, according to teleofunctionalists, informational content becomes representational if it is used to indicate or represent something for an organism. If and only if information-carrying states are assigned dedicated work in guiding organismic responses (that is, once they have specified work to do) are semantic relations instantiated; these relations are typically thought to hold between contentful inner vehicles and the specific external state of affairs that is represented.[9]

But this is a mistake. Natural signs (or signals) only serve to "represent" anything at all if they are used in a very particular way—that is, as "entities which stand for something else" (Grush 2003, 350). And although nonverbal organisms certainly respond to natural signs in coordinating their behavior, neither animals nor their subparts use such signs or inner proxies of them to stand for anything else. Perceptual devices do not interpret such signs; they do not take them to denote anything. Thus they are not forming veridical or even referential mental representations in the process.

What successful responding depends on is the existence of a correlation between specific natural signs and distal states of affairs. These hold good often enough, at least in the historically normal environments of organisms. But the signs themselves do no declarative work, nor are they interpreted as doing such by organisms or their perceptual mechanisms when they respond to them appropriately in discharging their proper functions. It is not as if one part of the system in any sense *tells* another that "this is how things stand" in the process.

What matters to the success of organismic actions is whether or not, in fact, such correlations hold. In responding appropriately organisms do not know, believe, or represent that such facts hold. Getting by in the world does not depend on cognitively registering that such correspondences hold, at any level. Nor do the signs (or signals) to which organisms are sensitive "have" contents of their own. They do not "naturally indicate"— that is, they do not silently "say how things stand." They do not quietly "refer to" other worldly items. Nor are such contents "picked up" and "ported into" organisms to be borne by internal vehicles, in the way royal personages are carried on litters (an image inspired by the metaphor of written and spoken linguistic signs "carrying meanings").

After all, it is not as if animals (or their subsystems) need to decode or decipher the natural signs to which they are sensitive in order to act. Basic responding does not require knowing anything about the state or composition of the external world. To speak of information "being carried" by a signal from a source to a receiver—for example, from the world to a sensory buffer—introduces a notion that goes beyond anything legitimately found in the idea that informational relations should be understood in covariational terms.

It is easy to be misled on this score by free and easy talk of information "being carried" by signals and states. Such talk is equivocal. The notion can either be understood in terms of mere "covariance" or "containment." Let me say a word about this. On the one hand, we can say that s's being F "carries information about" t's being H iff it has the property of standing in a covariance relation to that other state of affairs (and vice versa).

Philosophers quibble about the scope and strength of the covariance relations needed to engender a true "information relation"—pushing for stronger or more relaxed criteria (see Dretske 1981; Millikan 2004). I favor the latter when speaking about the informational sensitivities of biological organisms, but in this context that is a side issue.[10] Importantly, on any such account, covariance relations, however strong, are always symmetrical. Thus if the first state of affairs "carries information" about the second then equally the second "carries information" about the first (that is, from the point of view of the universe—or, better, from no point of view at all). Hence, the mere fact that two states of affairs reliably covary in and of itself in no way implies the existence of a natural relation of indication, reference, or truth. If it did, the world would be everywhere silently refer-ring or marking truths about itself (a strange metaphysics indeed). This point will be important again soon.

Talk of information being encoded in a signal, in contrast, relates to how signals can uniquely designate a particular state of affairs. Engineers and information scientists encode information by pairing down the possibili-ties for characterizing a source so that signals can be given an unequivo-cal specification. Thus the quantity of information carried by any given signal will be a direct function of the number of possibilities to be dealt with (that and any background knowledge that can be taken for granted on the part of the receiver). A well-known example of such a code would be the famous use of church-tower lanterns that signaled "one by land, two by sea." Because Paul Revere was properly primed, on spotting the signal, he was spurred to make his famous midnight ride and the Ameri-can revolutionaries were alerted to the British military tactics. In a similar way, some use talk of "contained information" to refer to the specific content that is conveyed or encoded "in" a signal (information that would be revealed when it is properly decoded). But in the case of basic organis-mic responding no such decoding ever occurs: we can think of Paul Revere as a mechanism that is primed to act and initiate others to act without anyone in this play knowing or needing to know what his cry "The British are coming" means. As a triggering mechanism, even if that utterance did "mean" something, this property would be superfluous. The very idea that that content must be encoded in perceptual signals and eventually decoded in order for such signals to initate successful action guidance is deeply suspect.

In any case, talk of encoded sensory content is an *additional* theoretical move—and one that wants both explication and justification. It is my contention that when it comes to understanding our primary modes of engagement, content-based accounts are in any case utterly surplus to requirements. Under the sway of what might be called the "containment metaphor," some theorists have been led to think that sensory inputs contain information that is extracted and further modified.[11] Surviving such processing, the content originally contained in signals is transformed, thus becoming genuinely representational. But for this to be the case per-ceptual signals would need to already possess encoded information about how things stand with some external state of affairs. And someone or something will have had to have set up the code. Perhaps one could attempt to defend such a view, but I doubt they could do so convincingly and there is surely no need.

Before sketching the alternative, it is worth observing that this "encoding" idea resonates with certain philosophical imaginations because it is practically built into talk of "data" and "the given." It is enshrined in the ancient thought that the mind is "informed" by the world—something that literally receives "contentful" impressions from it, those that are stamped on it. It is perhaps therefore not surprising that those attracted to this sort of view are also typically inclined to talk of "presentations to subject" and "the reception of perceptual givens" that are supplied by the senses.[12] Although Sellars and others have subjected the myth of "the given" to scathing critique, it continues to walk abroad in the minds of many philosophers today.[13] It is the beating heart of classical cognitive science.

Equally, traditional philosophical thinking about the functions of sense perception wrongly promotes the idea that our primary contact with the world is intellectually mediated: the data to be digested and processed comes in the form of deliverances of the senses and it is through such deliverances that inner mental states are imagined to acquire their content. Indeed for some the primary job of sensory responding is to supply contents that mental states "pick up." Sensory stimulation is thought to deliver "inputs"—inputs typically thought to contain contents already. Thus a sensory encounter might tell a subsystem that "t is G" because "s is F." That's what the signal says and what it will say to the appropriate subsystem, once it has been decoded. Special procedures are used to extract and re-present the content so as to make it amenable for cognitive use by organisms. There is a sense in which organisms are only able to refer to and think about worldly offerings in determinate ways if they do so in contenful ways. But we need not think that their basic ways of responding to worldly offerings involve reference or content-involving thoughts.

Biosemiotics (or: Why I Am Not a Biosemanticist)

There is a simpler, and more attractive, way of understanding nonverbal cognition and its form of intentionality. Organisms of all kinds are informationally sensitive to select worldly offerings—sometimes in complex ways. These built-in sensitivities permit them to identify and track certain environmental particulars of importance (to them); detection of these particulars initiates responses that enable the coordination of successful actions in certain environments. This package will have been selectively forged in the service of meeting the end-directed needs of specific creatures.

Still, the basic worldly engagements of animals (including ourselves) are not content-involving; they do not involve conceiving of, categorizing, classifying, or otherwise "representing" that which is the focus of such responding, and certainly not representing it as such. Perceptual sensitivities to specific natural signs prompt action in a quite immediate way and inherited mechanisms drive characteristic responses. Such online informational responsiveness comes in degrees of graded complexity. Some creatures are only sensitive to single cues, others to a whole variety of them, and they may have sophisticated checks and balances, learned or inherited, that constrain just how they respond to a given occasion. Just which strategies are adopted and how robust they are depends on the degree of environmental "hostility" as indexed to the history of the organism, its home environments, and the particular needs in question (see Sterelny 2003, chaps. 2, 3). Thus some organisms get by with simple detection-response systems, while others make use of more baroque tracking strategies because they face greater environmental challenges (for example, from mimics, parasites, or cunning predators).

The nature of such responsiveness can be best understood in terms of indexically inspired Action Coordination Routines (ACRs). Organismic sensitivities to certain natural signs prompt responses in cooperating mechanisms; these initiate characteristic patterns of organismic response that can be characterized as scripted patterns of action and reaction. They have the following sort of structure:

Step 1: Paradigmatic recognitional element involved in X
Step 2: Paradigmatic outward expression of X
Step 3: Paradigmatic bodily changes and feeling of those changes
Step 4: Paradigmatic motivational response involved in X
Step 5: Paradigmatic action out of X[14]

These sorts of response routines may be hardwired or learned—but in all cases the informational sensitivity that drives such organisms is indexical and "contentless": no contents are perceptually acquired or decoded. Despite this, the possibility of misalignment forever attends; we can speak of "success" and "error" in such cases, but the *kind* of error in question is nothing like that which is sometimes a consequence of the application of concepts or the formation of judgments. Our primary worldly engagements are nonrepresentational and do not take the form of intellectual activity.[15]

All organisms have been fashioned by selective pressures so as to target and respond appropriately to relatively stable, reidentifiable environmental kinds. This is what grounds primary forms of intentional directedness and its determinacy of focus. If we rid ourselves of the implausible idea that conceptual understanding is required in order to make basic identifications, it becomes a relatively straightforward matter to account for nonverbal recognitional abilities by appeal to mechanisms honed by natural selection. Quite simply, we could understand the natural responsiveness of nonverbals to specific features and worldly phenomena in terms of biological proper functions. When thinking about intentional directedness we must look at what an organism is supposed to do, not merely at what it is disposed to do. Existing organisms are informationally sensitive to certain triggers because this benefited their forebears in coordinating their actions with respect to specific worldly offerings—and by implication this enabled their perception-response systems to proliferate for the benefit of future generations.

The distinction between what a creature does and what it "ought" to do is important. Although detection systems will have been formed in historical environments in order to meet the needs of specific kinds of end users, they are not optimally "designed"—they do not always and only detect what they ought to. Or, putting things the other way around, although such systems will de facto be triggered by many things, they exist as they do because they were sensitive to a subset of these things.[16]

The phase-locked character of the FM neuron in the auditory cortex of bats is a good example. Such neurons fire in the presence of certain auditory stimuli, the signature sound of the beating wings of a certain kind of insect. These stimuli reliably enough correlate with the presence of specific types of insects that are the standard prey of the bats in question. Nothing, of course, guarantees that the correspondence will *always* hold. Other qualitatively similar stimuli generated by other sources, natural or artificial, could and would elicit the same pattern of response. Thus Batesian mimics of the bats' usual prey might come to populate their home niches, thereby degrading the correspondence by which they make their living. That said, we can be confident that such correspondences must have held well enough in the past since the bats and their sensory mechanisms are with us today.

Indeed, it will have taken a long time to forge such sensory systems. Bat antics, honed over eons, will have established the relevant indicative relationships; these relationships were not lying about ready-made to be pressed into service for their purposes. The very fact that these sorts of correspondences exist is therefore no accident, but neither can it be explained by the existence of ahistorical natural laws. Selectional forces will have been responsible for many of the covariances we find in nature.

It is tempting to say that if the channel conditions between source and receiver are historically normal, then the bats' neural and perceptual states carry information. But, as I stressed above, if unregulated, such talk can mislead. For the *only* sense in which information is carried by or contained in the bats' "inner states" is in the sense in which a well-informed interloper, one *au fait* with the activity of the bats, would be able to make reasonable if imperfect predictions about the presence of the insects by knowing what neural state a bat was in (and vice versa). This would require explicitly knowing, inter alia, about the purpose and mechanics of FMFM neurons, the natural history of the bats in question, and so on. And this is the crux; knowing that the inner states of the bats carry information in this way implies nothing at all about how the bats respond to natural signs. The bats do not decode or interpret these signs when responding. So, their inner states only carry unexploited information in the same way that a tree's age carries information about the number of its rings (and vice versa).[17]

Once again, in responding to telltale stimuli the perceptual subsystems of organisms neither extract nor decode it for further use. When conditions are normal, creatures are hooked up to the world in the right sorts of ways and their actions succeed (mostly). This only requires that the appropriate correspondences do *in fact* hold: it does not require the manipulation of internal contents that *say that* they hold. There need be no cognitive registering of the fact that insects are present. Signs, of the strong but silent type, those that really "say nothing" at all, will do for the required work.

Usually when philosophers appeal to such biological considerations they do so in order to develop and defend theories of representational content (McGinn 1989; Papineau 1987; Millikan 1984, 1993, 2004). For example, Millikan's Pushmi-Pullyu (or P-P) representations are what she calls "intentional icons" of the very simplest variety. They are inventively called such because they have twofold interrelated proper functions: that of mapping onto specific states of affairs and that of prompting a certain response in relation to said state of affairs. They have indicative and imperative aspects. According to Millikan, PP icons are representations but in the same way that "zero is thought of as a number"—that is, she thinks of them as representations primarily because they can be, quite literally, misleading (albeit in a special way). There are other conditions for something to be a representation other than simply having a proper function. But it is because they have proper functions that such responding admits of the possibility of "going wrong." Thus because they exhibit normativity in this very minimal sense, Millikan (2004, 158) is prepared to regard her PP icons as representations.[18]

This is, at best, misleading. Although natural signs guide (and misguide) end-direct responding and this can be assessed normatively in just the way Millikan proposes, I see no reason to think that they have or carry content of any kind at all. Nor do I think that the signs that guide a system are found in the heads of organisms, although the perceptual and guidance mechanisms surely are.[19] To emphasize this, I talk of Local Indexical Guides (LIGs) instead of P-P representations. LIGs are *not representations*—not even of a very basic variety. As the term implies, LIGs coordinate actions with respect to specific worldly offerings. They are like Sherpas in that they have the right local connections to safely direct others through specific domains. Yet, unlike their human counterparts, LIGs have no mediating practical knowledge of their own.

Bee dances provide a very clear, if rather overworked, example of LIGs in action. They have the proper function of generating characteristic responses in cooperating consumer mechanisms—the watching bee or bees—initiating patterned flight responses that will take them to the location of nectar. Bees use various types of dances to achieve this (see figure 3.1). Round dances—the simplest—are used when nectar is located within 50 meters of the hive. They prompt general foraging behavior in their consumers, who initiate searches in the relevant area. Waggle dances, of the more interesting adagio variety, are used when nectar is more than 150 meters away. These more complex dances have two distinct aspects: one

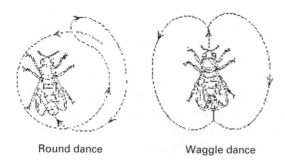

Round dance   Waggle dance

Figure 3.1
Two Types of Bee Dance (reprinted from Karl von Frisch, *Bees: Their Vision, Chemical Senses, & Language*, rev. ed. Copyright © 1950, 1971, by Cornell University. Used with permission of the publishers, Cornell University Press).

carries information about the distance of the nectar from the hive and the other carries information about the direction in which it is located. When performing dances of this kind, bees shake their abdomens for extended sequences, giving off a low-frequency buzzing noise. The length of these performances corresponds directly to the distance of the nectar, as a direct mathematical function. The direction of the nectar, on the other hand, is indicated by the way the bees position themselves along the vertical axis, relative to the sun and the hive. For example, if the bees dance straight upward this corresponds to the nectar's being located in the same direction as the sun; if they dance downward it is to be found directly away from the sun. Dancing at varying degrees along the vertical axis is used to indicate other locations. All being well, consumer bees respond to these imperative, directive signals by bringing about a certain state of affairs—ideally, by making their way to the nectar.

To respond appropriately the bees must be informationally sensitive and responsive to the relations that hold between the sun, hive, and nectar. This can make it seem as if their successful action depends on "extracting" information contained in the dances—information about such complex relations. But this is not so.

These natural signs do not *say* how things stand in order to guide action; they guide it directly. Thus, while true, it can nevertheless be misleading to say—without qualification—that they "function to indicate the direction and distance of nectar," since the way this they achieve is precisely not by saying that nectar is "20 meters in that direction at an angle of 45 degrees relative to the sun," in the way a propositional assertion might. Such responding involves no such content. Nor is there any sense in which the imagined content of an LIG could be segmented into its meaningful freestanding subparts. Modifying the response patterns of the consumers, in this case other bees, requires making transformations to aspects of the size and shape of the whole dance.

LIGs therefore guide action in an online and thoroughly context-bound way: this is evident from the fact that if the context alters they too must be appropriately modified, if the appropriate correlations are to be maintained. If not, they will almost certainly fail to guide action successfully (unless by accident). For example, because waggle dances only correlate with direction and distance, but not time or place, bees must dance differently—adopting different physical configurations—at different times of day, as the sun moves from east to west. Without such adjustments, their dances will fail to yield the usual results.[20] LIGs are therefore even less stable than the reference-shifting demonstratives of natural languages such as "Here" or "Now," since often they must change their syntactic form in order to do their work.

Despite admitting of specific kinds of significant transformations, LIGs are incapable of entering into even the most basic logical operations, such as negation. For example, modifying the angle of a bee dance systematically affects the direction in which watching bees will fly. But it is not possible to "reverse" a bee dance or to transform it in any other way so as to negate the imagined content of its "message"; reversing bee dances only has directional implications. We can safely conclude from this that, in successfully directing their compatriots, bees are not using their dances to *say* anything at all.

Being contentless it follows, a fortiori, that we cannot capture the putative "contents" of such responding using natural-language translations. There is no content to translate into words—*pace* Crane—not even potentially. This spares us from having to try to specify such imagined contents. This is a good thing, since the results of such attempts are usually awkward and unconvincing; moreover, they typically reveal that the alleged content of interest is really nothing other than an action-guiding imperative in any case.[21] If LIGs say nothing, this is not only unnecessary, it is simply impossible.

This takes us to the heart of the matter—for although they are not representations, LIGs give us everything we need in order to understand the determinate *intentional directedness* and *normativity* of basic forms of perceptual responding. LIGs prompt ACRs of varied complexity. When in historically normal environments, they successfully guide organismic actions (or will have often enough), directing creature responses to specific worldly offerings.

Of course, this goes against the grain of much current thinking, which holds that some kind of content is necessary in order to explain how sophisticated worldly alignments are maintained. As noted above, this received wisdom is sponsored by a number of assumptions that have a venerable pedigree—ancient views about the function of the senses, the nature of what they supply, and how what they supply (their informational content) is further processed. Yet once it is realized that the only legitimate notion of carried information that applies to basic sensory states is that which can be explicated in terms of covariance relations—and that these must not to be confused with referential or truth relations—it becomes clear that nonverbal responses only exhibit sensitivity to purely indexical signs. We can easily explain the nature of responding without introducing contents into the equation. Sensitivity to natural signs, whether by means of single or multiple channels—which prompt response routines, whether fixed or plastic—is sufficient to explain how most nonverbal organisms succeed in getting around their worlds (when the appropriate conditions hold).

Although biosemantics is the most popular strategy for making use of biology in the philosophy of psychology, there is also a less ambitious option. We can attempt to understand basic forms of *determinate intentional directedness* in nonsemantic terms.[22] I call this approach *biosemiotics*. Organisms are informationally sensitive *to* and selectively end-directed *at* certain worldly features, objects, and states of affairs in a way that explains their success and failure on certain tasks. The intentionality they exhibit is an attitude of the whole organism expressed in their behavior; it is neither a property of the signs themselves nor of organismic inner states.[23]

These responses are not content-involving in the way the intellectualist tradition seeks to understand them. To avoid confusion a few reminders are in order. Covariance relations are information relations; they must not be confused with truth or reference relations. The holding of specific covariance relations is what matters to successful action in basic cases (in contrast to noting or registering that such relations hold). The fact that a creature can "go wrong" in the sense of being extensionally misaligned does not establish that they are responsive to things in ways that somehow establishes a representational relation involving truth. Nonverbals are not responding to signs in the right sort of way for that. Nor are the signs they are using of the right kind for that.

What then of the standard story about nonconceptual content? Of course, you or I could *say* what conditions would have to hold if a bat is to succeed in its insect-gobbling actions. That is not in dispute. You or I can also make true claims about the age of trees based on what we know about the number of their rings. The question is whether in either of these cases we would be putting into words preexisting content that is already there in the world or in the mind of the creature. Are we articulating, making explicit, the content of the animal's mental state or the content inherent in the informational relation? The point of asking this is not to excite familiar interpretative worries about whether we are in a position to *specify* such content correctly; my concern is more fundamental—I find the very idea that parts of the world or parts of organisms might *be* content-involving simply incoherent. To my eye, the cases of the bat and the tree are equivalent in this respect.

We can, of course, *say* what a given nonverbal ought to think (if it only could think) if its action were to succeed. It does not follow, of course, that the success of its action depends on its thinking the thought we ascribe to it in such circumstances or—and this is important—on its thinking anything at all. To use folk psychology to predict its behaviors, it is enough for us to say how things would have to stand with the world in order for its action to succeed. But this is consistent with two quite different possibilities. The creature in question might grasp the relevant state of affairs under some MoP, or it might not grasp the situation in an intensional way at all. I see absolutely no reason to think that the first alternative is true.

Certainly, we are not entitled to infer anything about a creature's cognitive abilities simply by observing that it is capable of engaging in complex world-directed behavior. For what outwardly looks like rationality in action may not, in fact, involve any propositional attitude-based reasoning at all. If nonverbal responding is not content-involving, then no truth relations are instantiated at this level. But how then *should* we understand what goes on when we say what would have to be the case in order for the nonverbal action to succeed? Here I advise adopting a Jamesian approach. Instead of positing existing but unexpressed content, we can talk of virtual truth—that is, truths that would be expressed if someone were to express them. For, like James (1909, 205), I hold that "the truth with no one thinking it, is like the coat that fits tho no one has ever tried it on."

On this matter it pays to remember that there is literally no sense in talking about the instantiation of truth relations without presupposing the existence of propositional contents as one of the key relata. After all, "P" is true (in L) if and only if "P." However, if we ultimately decide to unpack this platitude, it is surely only those creatures that are capable of having attitudes that aim at truths in appropriately structured and content-involving ways—that is, those capable of believing propositions—that instantiate truth relations. Quite simply, "If there is to be truth . . . both realities and beliefs about them must conspire to make it" (James 1909, 197).[24] Put otherwise, it is only when beliefs are formed about worldly states of affairs that truth relations arise.

Against this, it might be argued that truth is a property of propositions (not a relation) and that propositions (the objects of thought and potential thoughts) are the bedrock of the world—that is, one might identify facts with *true* propositions, as Russell once did.[25] The idea of a reality composed of true thoughts or propositions commits itself to a very odd worldview indeed. For surely, "Realities are not true, they are: and beliefs are true of them" (James 1909, 196). James puts confusion on this score down to what he describes as the "vulgar" tendency to confuse "truths" with "facts" (pp. 78, 144, 223). I think he is right.

An obvious and nontrivial advantage of adopting the biosemiotic approach is that it relieves us of the burden of having to explain the nature and source of representational content associated with nonverbal responding, since a fortiori such responding, though exhibiting intentionality, would be contentless. A number of important results follow from this: nonverbal reactions are purposeful and end-directed, despite the fact that they are not content-involving. Basic intentionality is not a property of inner "mental states," rather it is a directedness of whole organisms to specific worldly offerings. Creatures that only get about by using indexical guides are prone to extensional misalignments; they are incapable of making intensionally based errors of judgment.

Tom and Jerry Revisited

I contend that the world-directed actions of Tom and Jerry—indeed, all nonverbal responding including ours (which, by the way, constitutes a fair percentage of what we do)—are best explained in terms of intentional rather than propositional attitudes; that is, in terms of attitudes that are extensionally directed but intensionally unmediated in anything like a semantic manner.[26]

Since nonverbals do not speak—nor do they express themselves in equivalently refined nonlinguistic ways—it is not possible to chart the patterns of their response so as to specify the content of their alleged thoughts. Some regard this as nothing more than an epistemic problem. Defenders of the view that nonverbals are true believers claim that the problem we face in this regard is really *our* problem, as interpreters; that this difficulty abounds supplies precisely no reason to doubt that animals do in fact harbor propositional attitudes. Thus we are told that "since the common-sense assumption that cats do have thoughts works pretty well there had better be some powerful independent argument if we are to give it up. But in fact there is none" (Botterill and Carruthers 1999, 142).

This, as I hope to have shown above, is a serious misappraisal. When it comes to interpreting animals—especially other mammals—we must be very wary; the bugbear of anthropomorphic overinterpretation lurks forever nearby. The truth is that "our minds are very good at automatically construing certain behaviours in terms of mental states" (Povinelli and Vonk 2004, 16; see also Currie and Sterelny 2000, 155). This is no accident. In light of our natural predilections, it is not enough to appeal to commonplace "intuitions" when arguing that nonverbals are, in fact, bona fide believers and practical reasoners. One should at least reserve judgment on this until it can be demonstrated that there really is no other, or no better way, to explain nonverbal intentional, world-directed behavior. Because I think there is a better way, I am inclined to think nonverbals are not "true believers."

For the record, I am not motivated to withhold mentalistic ascriptions to animals solely because we lack the appropriate means of determining the precise content of their mental states with any confidence or justification. My motivation is more complex. It is driven by this fact in conjunction with another—that our best explanations of the basis of nonverbal "thinking" reveal that such thinking is not content-involving. Putting this together we get the result that making *serious* folk psychological attributions to nonverbals is neither needed nor warranted. Nonverbals are only capable of harboring intentional attitudes, not propositional ones. The two must not be confused.

Thoughts, understood as the affirmation or negation of some proposition, and desires, which are concerned with the pursuit or avoidance of some object, need to share a common logical structure in order to be brought together in reasoning. This is a fundamental requirement according to received philosophical wisdom. Yet if I am right, the informationally sensitive online responding of most organisms lacks the relevant structure. When organisms get about by using local indexical guides, their scripted response patterns are such that the indicative/imperative aspects are built in; there is no process of "cognitive integration." They do not have separate representational components—believed and desired contents—in their cognitive architecture.[27] For this reason, nonverbal intelligent action is not grounded in the adopting of attitudes toward contentful mental representations and the bringing together of these representations in order to form plans and intentions. Thus, with respect to nonverbal responding, I reject the Basic Architectural Assumption (BAA), according to which "the mind contains two quite different kinds of representational states, beliefs and desires" (Nichols and Stich 2003, 15).

It is a major step up, cognitively speaking, to be able to think using detached representations, as opposed to merely getting by in the world by responding sensitively to indexical guides (see Millikan 2004, 212–216). Representing states of affairs using structured propositions with recombinant elements of the kind that allow for voluntary planning, practical reasoning, and decision making is a late-developing capacity and requires using special environmental props. Specifically, I hold that it is an achievement that requires mastery of the tools provided by natural language. If I am right, practical reasoning abilities and propositional beliefs and desires are not as ancient or ubiquitous as some have supposed.[28]

Still, it might be thought that even if my biosemiotic approach could explain the kinds of online worldly engagements of many creatures, something is needed to explain nonverbal cognitive acts of greater sophistication. In particular, some of these might be thought to require cognitive architectures utilizing "decoupled representation and goal-based rather than drive-based motivation" (Sterelny 2003, 57). I balk at talk of representation (unless it is heavily qualified). But if we do not insist that representations must have determinate semantic content, then I agree that some languageless creatures must be making use of detached representations that are, as it were, at least belieflike. The interesting question that needs answering is just how belieflike should we imagine these representations to be? I will address this question in the next chapter before saying more about the nature of propositional attitudes in the one after that.

Postscript: No More Modules

Some ACRs have attributes that might suggest that they are subserved by Fodorian modules (Fodor 1983). After all, they involve responses that are mandatory, involuntary, and operate below the level of access consciousness. They are normally subserved by mechanisms that have a relatively fixed neural architecture, which is prone to specific forms of malfunction. These are the characteristics that Fodor ascribes to his modules, verbatim.

But, if I am right, such responding cannot be understood in modular terms. I reject Fodor's model of the mind based on a "trichotomous functional taxonomy" of transducers, input systems/analyzers (that is, modules), and central cognitive mechanisms (see Fodor 1983, 41–42). Perceptual signals do not have any informational content contained in them to be acquired and then manipulated in the way that his theory supposes. Indeed, because there is no contentful input, it is—strictly speaking—a mistake to speak of input devices, even purely perceptual ones. Of course, this is not to deny that organisms are complex mechanisms that respond selectively and sensitively to certain natural signs (signs that covary reliably enough with certain worldly items); many organisms robustly track particulars and kinds (sometimes using multiple sensory channels, and sometimes even using multiple channels within a single sensory modality; see Sterelny 2003, chap. 2). Nevertheless, if we think of these tracking abilities in terms of informational sensitivity instead of in terms of the acquisition of informational content, the standard implications of talk of "information processing" must be reinterpreted.

Crucially, according to my deflationary proposal, "informational content" is not first received via the senses and then further manipulated and formatted by specialized mechanisms (a process by which it is thought that much content is lost and only some retained). I do not deny that something like this process occurs, but I do deny that it should be understood in terms of the processing of acquired contents. Nor, for this reason, is the product of the process the creation of representations—representations that preserve the same basic content acquired via the senses, only recasting it in a form that is "accessible to thought" (see Fodor 1983, 40). This is simply not possible if no contents are received to be processed in the first place.

Those who endorse the modular approach (or approaches) make the traditional mistake of confusing legitimate talk of carrying information that can be explicated in terms of covariance, with talk of carrying information in which contents are imagined to be somehow contained in a signal. We can see the two ideas at work in Fodor's thought when he first introduces his construct of a module: "*Any* mechanism whose states covary with environmental ones can be thought of as *registering information about the world*; and given the satisfaction of certain further conditions, the *output* of such systems can be reasonably thought of as *representations* of the environmental states with which they covary" (Fodor 1983, 39; second and third emphases added).

According to Fodor, two intervening steps take place when informational content is reformatted so as to be used in inferential forms of cognition. The first step involves the transduction of low-level proximal stimulations (presumably, as Dretske would have it, this involves a reformatting of information from analogue to digital form). The second step involves transformations of the content that are posttransductive and inferencelike but that are, despite this, not conducted by central cognitive mechanisms. Making transformations of the second kind is the dedicated work of modules. Thus, "The inferences at issue have as their 'premises' transduced representations of proximal stimulus configurations, and as their 'conclusions' representations of the character and distribution of distal objects" (Fodor 1983, 42). Hence, modules are interface devices that take in relatively shallow inputs, those having low-level informational content, and yield full-fledged representations as output.[29]

Let us imagine, for the sake of argument, that each ACR has a dedicated mechanism that supports it and that the domain-specific responding of these mechanisms exhibit all of the characteristic features that Fodor associates with his modules. Even so, these supporting devices (should any exist) are not modules. They *cannot* be if there are no such things as acquired contents to serve as modular inputs. It follows that there will be no contents to convert into representations—and hence no modular outputs. If there are no content-bearing mental representations at this level, then it is a serious mistake to think of basic perceptual acts in traditional input and output terms (Hurley 1998). We must retire the thought that, in basic cases, perception and action are in the first instance disintegrated (at least in the ways standardly proposed).

ACRs do, however, operate quite independently of central cognition: in predating language-mediated forms of thinking and believing, they would have to. They were scripted to enable organisms to respond to specific environmental prompts. Since the organisms in question had no beliefs—and a fortiori no background beliefs—these basic modes of responding are not in their raw form belief-sensitive. This follows from the fact that the mechanisms that drive such responding will have been fashioned to function in creatures, our immediate ancestors included, that lacked contentful mental representations of the sort that could have been penetrated in any case. This follows automatically if the creatures that relied on them were simply incapable of harboring propositional attitudes. I take it therefore that indexically inspired response routines are *naturally* cognitively impenetrable: they are in essence nonrepresentational, lacking the kinds of forms and contents that would allow them to enter into bona fide inferential liaisons.

ACRs kick in without any background thought. And, surely, this is a good thing. If creatures had to wait for the top-down verdicts of central cognition before responding in the simplest cases they would be effectively crippled. Indeed, without some such bottom-up responding to get a grip on worldly offerings, there would be no way for "central cognition" to judge, on reflection, *which* considerations are relevant to particular cases.

This does not mean that the ACRs are impervious to influence by higher-level judgments—for it is at least possible that, in some cases, the patterns of response initiated can be controlled, overridden, or overcome, albeit indirectly. In a significant number of cases, despite being directly unresponsive to reason, many of our unprincipled modes of response are open to education and training. This is true in our case and seems equally true to some extent of other species as well: with effort at least some perception-response links of some ACRs might be retied.

4 Imaginative Extensions

Natura non facit saltum
(Nature makes no leaps)

The Challenge to Minimalism

It might be conceded without too much contest that indexically inspired ACRs are sufficient for explaining the online behavioral antics of simple organisms, such as ants and bees. Still, it might be doubted that the same explanatory strategy can be extended successfully to more sophisticated nonverbal responding. Picking up on this thought, Bermúdez lays down an important challenge to supporters of what he calls "minimalist" approaches. Minimalists—like myself—hold that

> nonlinguistic thinking does not involve propositional attitudes—and, *a fortiori*, psychological explanation at the nonlinguistic level is not a variant of belief-desire psychology.... It is not, according to the minimalist view, appropriate to describe nonlinguistic thoughts as having determinate contents. Nor should the types of reasoning engaged in at the nonlinguistic level be modelled on those at the linguistic level. (Bermúdez 2003b, 21)

So defined, I am a minimalist. Other minimalists seek to explain the sophisticated abilities of nonverbals by appeal to their capacity to see "affordances"—that is, their capacity to exploit locally perceived opportunities in the ambient features of an environment. These are reacted to in fixed ways or more flexibly by appeal to motor memories grounded in trial-and-error learning. I hold that such nonverbal responding is best characterized in terms of indexically inspired ACRs, as I argued in the previous chapter. It is a kind of embedded, embodied, and enactive *know-how*, not a form of thinking *that*. It should be clear that I am a fully paid up supporter of "Three E" approaches. Accordingly, nonverbal responding appears to be a form of context-bound, pragmatic, and dynamic mode of "thought."

While Bermúdez accepts that some basic forms of nonverbal responding are amenable to such explanations, he holds, nonetheless, that some non-linguistic responding is too plastic and flexible to be explained without appeal to propositional attitudes—that is, some of it has all the marks of being content-involving. Obviously, it is vital to assess this argument for explanatory need, keeping this separate from proposals about how that need might be met if it should turn out to be genuine. I will argue that it is not. But before turning to this task I digress to say a quick word about Bermúdez's positive proposal about how we ought to make sense of non-linguistic thought.

The Failure of Success Semantics

Bermúdez's work on this topic is of special interest, in part because he rejects the LoT hypothesis, primarily for its epistemic shortcomings.[1] Most importantly, he does not go in for causal-informational or biosemantic theories of content. Instead he advocates a version of success semantics, endorsing Ramsey's principle, which construes truth and success as internally related with respect to actions in the following way: true believing suffices to bring about successful action by satisfying desires (Ramsey 1926/1990; Whyte 1990).

Drawing on this guiding idea, Bermúdez (2003b, 190, 11) claims that "the requirements of successful action fix the content of belief in such a way that what a creature believes can be worked out from how it behaves and what it wants to achieve." Yet working back from behavior to the underlying propositional attitudes that generate it, even in seemingly straightforward cases, is not easy. Since beliefs and desires interrelate in complex ways that are not open to view, trying to determine what someone believes by scrutinizing their outward behavior alone brings one face to face with well-known problems of interpretative holism and inde-terminacy of content.

In the case of competent language users it is possible, at least in princi-ple, to get a fix on the intensional content of another's beliefs (or, what amounts to the same thing, the meaning of their utterances) by charting their patterns of assent and dissent. These reveal the ways a person's thought is resistant to truth-preserving coreferential substitution and, as a result, we are given insight into how they think about a particular subject. That is, intensions can be fixed if we can, in effect, chart the pattern of their judgments (Davidson 1984, 138–139, 225). By this process we discover precisely *how* someone thinks about a particular subject by establishing which properties they would and would not be prepared to predicate of it, which inferences they are prepared to make, and so on. We begin to learn *how* Ms. X thinks about "next Tuesday" when we discover that she accepts (1) and (3) as true but draws a blank when asked about (2):

1. "Next Tuesday is the first day of April."
2. "Next Tuesday is April Fools' Day."
3. "Next Tuesday is the first day of the month in the Julian calendar named after Aphrodite."

Such intensional cartography is achieved by getting sincere answers from Ms. X to the right questions or, more arduously, if the radical interpreter's thought experiment could be actualized, by tracking the patterns of her utterances over time, and by bringing various principles of charity to bear (see Hutto 1999b, chap. 5).

Radical interpretation, should anyone really attempt it, would be hard enough when dealing with cooperative linguistic subjects but—everyone knows—things always get much worse when you are working with children and animals.[2] Obviously, without modification, the interpretative method just described is hopeless for determining the putative content of nonverbal thoughts. Even if some of their responses could be construed as "assents" or "dissents" (which is already begging the question), without language there would be no reliable way to chart the intrastructural connections in such responses. Thus, for those hoping to prosecute this task, some other method must be used if we are to determine with confidence how they apprehend particular predicates and states of affairs at the level of sense.

Bermúdez has risen to the challenge. Taking his lead from the thought experiments of Quine and Davidson, he proposes to adapt their general approach to the practical explication of nonverbal thought. Essentially, he proposes a twofold general strategy for specifying the content of putative nonverbal propositional attitudes. It is (1) to make some initial assumptions about what the creatures in question desire, and (2) to try to establish a fix on what they would have to believe by considering their characteristic patterns of response, taking stock of their relevant discriminatory capacities, procedures, and expectations, and especially the success or otherwise of their actions.

Rats are used to illustrate how this proposed method is meant to work. They are a good choice since it can be reasonably assumed, with little argument, that they are driven by an overarching object-focused desire for food. This desire is, of course, satisfied when food is found in particular locations. Or—to use the jargon of success semanticists—that food is located at such-and-such place is the utility condition of the belief that relates to satisfaction of the relevant desire. This is why the obtaining of this fact, which makes the relevant belief true, also guarantees the success of the animal's action.

Furthermore, rats also display the kinds of cognitive capacities that make ascribing beliefs to them at least prima facie plausible. For example, when scouring for food, instead of merely engaging in random searches they use past knowledge of their surroundings. This knowledge will have been acquired from previous reconnoitering adventures in which they will have traced and retraced their paths, again and again, in order to gain a detailed sense of their local environment. Their powerful memories allow them to keep tabs on the places they have previously visited.

This last point is important for it indicates that the navigational behavior of rats is marked out by their ability to reidentify specific landmarks. Mapping out their local terrain as they do entails that they have more cognitive sophistication than that of creatures only capable of mere feature-based responding. Famously, the latter is found in frogs; they slavishly lash out their tongues whenever their retinas are stimulated by small-dark-moving-things of the appropriate size and speed. While this works well enough for getting food into their stomachs (in the right conditions) it is clear that frogs do not think of these dots as food sources (or as anything else). They do not even recognize particular dots as being the same or different again. In other words, such feature-based responding does not imply a capacity for reidentifying individuals.[3] Rats, but not frogs, seem eminently capable of the latter.

All this is grist to Bermúdez's mill. But noting all this does not show how we might specify the exact content of nonverbal beliefs and desires. Casual observation of rat food-seeking behavior is inadequate for determining the canonical description of how they predicate "the location of food" in thought. Without a more refined characterization, their antics are consistent with any number of ways of so doing. Bermúdez considers four possibilities, each yielding four candidate thought contents, correspondingly. Initially, it seems that any of the following are equally good ways of specifying the MoPs of rats:

1. Food is located at the end-point of movements $M_{1...n}$ (using rules based on a series of bodily movements).

2. Food is located at coordinates (x, y) in egocentric space (using subject-relative predicates—"to my right," "in front of me").

3. Food is located at coordinates (x', y') in maze space (using allocentric reference points internal to the maze).

4. Food is located at coordinates (x", y") in environmental space (using allocentric reference points external to the maze).

However, by looking more closely at what rats do, Bermúdez proposes to discredit all but one of these candidate interpretations. He calls on the wealth of data detailing how trained rats run mazes of different configurations.[4] Because this procedure is meant to illustrate his general method for uncovering the intensional thought contents of nonlinguistic creatures, it is worth reviewing the example in some detail.

We must elicit additional salient behaviors from the rats if we are to decide between the alternative interpretations set out above. This can be done by putting them through their paces, quite literally, looking for constants in their performances as their environments are significantly altered. In this way, as with Ms. X, we can chart their responses over time and in specific conditions so as to eliminate certain candidate content ascriptions. In the case of rats, the relevant patterns are uncovered by carefully observing their maze-running tendencies when the location of the food is kept constant.

Bermúdez uses such data to rule out the idea that rats might entertain the first two candidate beliefs. For it turns out they are able to navigate *directly* to food, even when they (unknowingly) begin their searches from the opposite end of the mazes they usually run, as revealed by "reversed-start" experiments. The point is that the rats would be unable to do so if they were thinking about the food in the ways suggested by interpretation (1) or (2). In other words, if they thought about the location of the food under an MoP detailing specific movement sequences or egocentric instructions, then under the stated conditions, their actions should fail— that is, they ought to wind up in the spot precisely opposite the location of food in such cases.

This is all very well, but it still leaves two seemingly equally good ways of understanding the content of the rats' beliefs. Yet the fourth possibility can also be eliminated by watching how the rats perform when the position of the maze as a whole (as opposed to their position within it) is modified by turning it 180 degrees. This proves decisive, for even in such circumstances rats still manage to get at the food reliably. Such performances would not be possible if they were thinking about the location of food under an MoP that characterized the location in allocentric terms. On these grounds, Bermúdez (2003b, 103) concludes that (3) is the only "way of spelling out the mode of presentation under which the rat is apprehending the target place." This result is meant to vindicate the viability of a general strategy—that is, showing that it is possible in practice to determine the precise frames of reference used by nonverbals, by giving appropriate critical attention to their behaviors.

The strategy described above is designed to show that success semanticists can meet the challenge of saying which intensional contents nonverbals operate with. But it rests on the as-yet-untested assumption that this is something we ought to try to do—and this in turn rests on the assumption that ascribing propositional attitudes to rats is the best way to explain their behavior. I want to retreat and question the grounds for taking this for granted. On reflection, I hold, there is simply no *need* to even try to make sense of the rats' performances, their successes and failures, on such tasks by ascribing content-involving food thoughts to them at all. We can accommodate all of this evidence in a simpler way. If my skepticism is justified, the same conclusion will apply, mutatis mutandis, to any creature exhibiting their level of reidentificational abilities.

Before proceeding, it is worth mentioning two observations that ought already to raise some suspicions about the motivations behind Bermúdez's project in any case. First, it is surely peculiar to think that propositional attitude psychology is needed in order to understand and explain specieswide behaviors. For the assumption we have been working with is that all rats are motivated by the same general desire for food and that they share the same beliefs about its location. We should remember that much of the power and interest in folk psychological ascriptions derives from the fact that they track differences in the contents of the attitudes of individuals (and the changes in the mindset of such individuals across time). While it is theoretically possible that all members of a given species have the same content-involving beliefs and desires, the mere fact that we are being asked to suppose this suggests from the outset that there is probably a simpler explanation for their behavior.

Second, psychological experimentation on the categories has revealed that humans, at least, privilege intermediate levels of conceptual abstraction—thus we are quicker at identifying something as a cat, as opposed to identifying a particular breed of cats, such as Siamese (subordinate level), or as being a kind of animal (superordinate level) (Rosch 1973, 1975; Prinz 2002, 10). By comparison, the very idea that rats are capable of entertaining thoughts that can be specified with predicates such as "coordinates (x," y") in maze space" looks by contrast—well, surprising to say the least. The concept of a graphic coordinate is fairly abstract. Perhaps rats have a native facility with more abstract concepts than do humans; the latter appear to form concepts, in the first instance, relating to concrete, middle-sized entities of everyday perceptual encounter. Again, while this does not prove anything, it provides a further motive for wanting to find a different explanation for the rat abilities, if at all possible.

In this light, it is a happy fact that ascribing propositional attitudes to such creatures is neither necessary nor even the best option. Let us start with the rats' alleged general desire for food. Apparently we are entitled to make the ascription of this antecedent desire to all rats because it has been consistently observed that they cease searching behavior upon locating and devouring food. Thus they frequently seek out food in preference to other goods and, moreover, they initiate these search behaviors without even the promise of a reward. This suggests that they are motivated by a goal that is not perceptible in their immediate environment. Although these patterns of action are counterfactually robust, we might equally well understand their "motivation" as an operational imperative to relieve hunger—one to be explained by simple mechanisms rather than their attempt to satisfy a general desire for food. If so, there is no need to ascribe to them a desire understood as a motivating propositional or pro-attitude.

In line with this thought, it is surely plausible that *as a species* they have inherited a standing disposition to map out and retrace their past steps in the absence of any internally encoded desires. Engaging in such search and re-search strategies is likely to have had adaptive value for their forerunners. Such behavior surely does not need to be understood in terms of being motivated by goal-based desires for some good that is not currently in sight—a contentful desire that is common to each and every rat.

A similarly deflationary story can be told about alleged rat beliefs. Let us suppose, for the sake of argument, that the way rats locate food is by fixing on certain allocentric coordinates internal to maze space. Bermúdez has convinced me that this is so. Yet it is easy enough to understand this capacity without calling on the apparatus of content-involving thoughts at all. Indeed, the more natural interpretation of the cited experimental results is that they reveal which types of landmarks rats remember when retracing their steps, not under which MoP they are thinking about food. In other words, paying attention to the way they run mazes shows us what rats focus on in extension, not how they grasp things in intension. Of course, if we take this view the interesting question is: By what means do they reidentify these specific signposts?

Millikan has provided a detailed account of what is involved in the reidentification of individuals, stuffs, and kinds within circumscribed historical domains (she uses the umbrella term *substances* to cover all the items so tracked). Essentially, this is to have the ability to keep track of what is the same through differences—a capacity to reidentify some thing or things as being the "same again" by imperfect but reliable enough identification procedures (Millikan 2000). This is to exhibit a kind of basic embodied know-how. Properly explicating the nature of this practical knowledge would require explaining how organisms systematically mark a given substance as being the same despite using disparate, multiple means of identifying it. Millikan illustrates the abstract functional profile of this process graphically: in effect, in order to mark sameness we use a distinct "Strawsonian dot" for each distinct substance identified. Thus each of the various methods we have of identifying a substance can be thought of as causing that same dot to light up.

This rules out the possibility that sameness marking might be achieved just by repeatedly having the same passive representation tokened in one's "mind" (such as thinking that x is F over and over again). Indeed, her analysis reveals that it is a mistake to try to explicate reidentification in terms of the making of identity judgments. In recognizing that some item is the same again, we are not ascribing a property to a thing. Reidentification neither requires nor involves being able to classify or categorize substances *as such*: it is not predicated on a prior capacity for classification or categorization at all.

In this light, there is absolutely no reason to think that creatures capable of reidentifying particulars (such as rats) must be making referential use of proprietary concepts or intensional predicates during this process. All the relevant cognitive action takes place well below the level of, and prior to, the formation of intensional beliefs and judgments. The reidentificational abilities just described only require that certain individuals and environmental kinds are detectable by means of their telltale or signature properties—for example, a characteristic trajectory, manner of movement, unique composition, and so on. The biosemiotic account of the previous chapter is well placed to explain just such nonconceptual capacities.

Consider that in some cases—at least, relative to certain contexts—spotting and tracking substances can be achieved by being sensitive to quite simple identifiers, such as specific colors, shapes, or odors associated with particular things or kinds of things. If you are the only person who carries a full-length umbrella to class, this can be used as an easy way of picking you out (even if it is not utterly foolproof). Or consider the ways I reidentify the milkman, again fallibly, by hearing the distinctive sounds he makes when opening the gate and clinking the milk bottles at a particular time each morning. In my usual setting, these are reliable enough indicators for my needs. The point is that the ability to reidentify substances in this way is the basis for, not the product of, judgments of the sort "There's the milkman" or "It's the milkman again." In my own case, but not that of rats, this can tie in with desires to do certain things, such as ensuring that I get my weekly payment out to him.

Identifying movements, sounds, looks, smells, or feels are not the target of one's attention or concern during acts of reidentification. They are merely pointers—mediating indicators—of the presence of something else. We must not conflate what is being responded to with the methods of response. This is why Millikan frequently insists that "ways of identifying" something do not equate with "ways of thinking" about it.

The point is that the mere fact that rats navigate by reidentifying particular places (as opposed to responding in a purely feature-responsive way) is not evidence that they are grasping possibilities in content-involving ways. The experimental results cited above are entirely consistent with a much simpler explanation of their intelligent food-acquiring navigational abilities just sketched. We should not be tempted by a neo-Fregean analysis of their acts of reidentification. We can explain the behavior of these nonverbal animals without supposing that they represent worldly affairs by adopting *propositional* attitudes toward them. The objects and states of affairs to which they are informationally sensitive, and at which they are end-directed, are not presented to or apprehended by them under intensional MoPs, descriptions, or the like.

And it is not just that we need not understand nonverbal reidentification abilities in content-involving terms; the fact is, we can't. There is reason to reject the idea that the nonverbals have the requisite cognitive apparatus to apprehend the worldly affairs under specific MoPs. All along, in imagining what they might be doing we have been modeling nonlinguistic thought directly on linguistically mediated acts of thinking. It is no accident that intension, Fregean "sense," MoPs, and the like are invoked when we want to explain the kinds of errors that arise with the use of core-ferring names—that is, in explaining the kinds of mistakes that ensue if, for example, one is unaware that the author of *Animal Farm* is known both as George Orwell and as Eric Blair. Such trouble arises because, in general, language users have two distinct ways of type-individuating such names. The first distinguishes them as distinct linguistic signs, signs that are, thanks to certain conventions, meant to look and sound different. Thus even though the sound profiles associated with the name "Eric Blair" will vary considerably from speech act to speech act, each occurrence can be recognized as a token of the same linguistic type—that is, as being the same name in this sense. By this criterion "George Orwell" is classed as a quite different name. Yet, functionally classified, these names are both tokens of the same type. They do precisely the same denotational work—not just in the global sense that both serve to name things, but in the quite specific sense that both serve to name the very same thing—in this case, the very same person.

If nonverbal responses are content-involving, then something must play exactly the same role that names play in public languages—presumably that of mental symbols of some sort. But, unless it is somehow shored up, the analogy with public language surely breaks down at this point. For since there are no private conventions to fix the individuation of names in the first sense described above, it looks as if there is exactly one way of individuating names at the nonlinguistic level—that is, in purely functional terms. Thus anything that serves to denote the same thing in one's mental lexicon just is the same "mental name." Without a conventional mode of alternative individuation at this level, different mental symbols cannot function as coreferring names. Ultimately, this is because "for mental representations there is no distinction between public convention and private response. Whatever the individual mind/brain treats as the same mental word IS the same word again" (Millikan 2000, 166).[5] Of course, the very idea of nonverbal MoPs has it origins in the practice of modeling thought contents on what is expressed by public sentences, but, as often happens with metaphorical extensions, the idea has been used without explaining how the necessary adjustments are to be made (or explaining why they are not required).

It looks therefore as if the minimalist approach is not only an adequate approach but is the right one to adopt when it comes to understanding the nonverbal responding of organisms as sophisticated as bees and rats. However, the game is not over. For although Bermúdez has focused on the abilities of rats in order to explicate his proposed success semantics strategy for characterizing nonlinguistic thought, he has argued that the clearest evidence that such thought exists derives from considerations about the decision-making and tool-making abilities of chimpanzees and hominids. Thus, it is to these that I now turn.

Nonlinguistic Instrumental Thinking

There has been recent speculation that decoupled belieflike structures may have been the by-product of "the demands of social complexity [which] select for a cognitive structure something like that depicted by folk psychology" (Sterelny 2003, 57). Without doubt, a capacity to monitor and track third-party relationships and how these evolve over time—which apparently grounds the complex social interplay of primates—entails a capacity for off-line responding of a kind that, to use Sterelny's terminology, is both broadbanded, in that it is sensitive to multiple cues, and has a long breadth of response, in that relevant actions do not follow immediately. To be sure, this aspect of primate social intelligence requires having strong memories and a capacity for reidentifying not only patterns but particulars—in the latter case, this includes noting the tendencies of various individuals in the group and how these stand with respect to others and oneself. Such abilities would have been needed to keep track of the traits of specific group members, established within-the-group statuses and particular alliances. This would constitute a variant of the Social Intelligence Hypothesis.[6] However, although it is natural to want to interpret such abilities as belief-based, the same observations about the navigational abilities of rats in complex physical environments apply to those of primates when it comes to navigating their complex social world. As far as the tasks of keeping tabs on the social space go, there are other methods of doing this than by fashioning and maintaining a set of beliefs.

A more plausible story about the ontogenesis of belieflike mental representation focuses on the distinctive capacities of apes to use and fashion tools by modifying natural materials for certain purposes. This, along with the need to meet the cognitive demands of dealing with what for such large animals would have been dangerous arboreal environments, may have been responsible for forging the capacities for "remembering organised programmes of manual actions, and for understanding the actions of others and so learning from them" (Byrne 1999, 81). Some apes have these abilities in a way that impressively distinguishes them from other animals.

Wild chimpanzees, for example, are known to modify leafy stems to create two different types of wands, each type having distinctively shaped tips and other special properties. One type is effective for obtaining ants, the other for termites—but neither is useful for both tasks. What is of interest is not just that these chimps are capable of remembering complex motor sequences, but that these wands are crafted long in advance of need and far away from the sites where they are employed. Thus, not only does their creation indicate both purposeful design and thoughtful end-directed preparation, but manufacturing these wands is not perceptually driven by current events and needs. This suggests capacities for some kind of instrumental thinking.

The tools manufactured by our hominid ancestors provide even more striking evidence of this. Accommodating the complex fractural dynamics of stone knapping, as would have been required for the fashioning of even the simplest of Oldowan hand axes, is likely to have required these ancient toolmakers to "keep in mind" a specific goal and a plan for achieving it throughout this complex process. For example, the fact that some stones flake and break in specific ways is the sort of thing one must be sensitive to while directing and controlling the force of one's blows—at least, this would have to be the case if one is to fashion a usable end product, reliably. Equally, since the craft requires special materials it requires a good deal of advanced planning. Again, putting all of this together there can be little doubt that hominid toolmakers must have had a capacity for "complicated instrumental reasoning about possible consequences of different courses of action" (Bermúdez 2003b, 51, 127; see also Carruthers 2004, 267).

At the very least, this implies that our forerunners had a capacity for some kind of mental rehearsal. It seems likely that they would have to have had a developed ability to initiate, interrupt, and modify "rehearsal loops" relating to the relevant ACRs. This would have involved rehearsing an ACR in a repetitive sequence, observing its consequences—then deliberately altering the form of the original ACR, by varying one or more of its parameters to see what new consequences are thrown up, and so on. Such activity would have taken the form of practical experimentation. The process of elaboration appears to be fueled by memories of previous patterns of activity and driven by an idealized image of the expected outcome (see Donald 1999, 141). This implies not only strong and flexible imaginative abilities but also a capacity for voluntary recall. Thus, as Donald (1999, 143) stresses, "Hominids had to gain access to the contents of their own memories. You cannot rehearse what you cannot recall." Importantly, such imaginative abilities are needed for practicing and honing any complex skill that is not built in; indeed we know that regular practice results in a firm degree of control, as would have been required for sophisticated tool manufacture.

Early hominid toolmakers were apparently possessed of these gifts, and they look to have been steadily strengthened with successive generations. This proposal is surely at home with the fact that modern humans have a "highly developed kinematic imagination," whereas, in contrast, living apes show only very weak signs of this. This may be one reason why "it often takes thousands of trials to establish a reliable signing response in a chimpanzee" (Donald 1999, 143). This is probably the best explanation for the fact that while chimpanzees can fashion and use tools to a very limited degree, they do not practice or develop these crafts.

We can be reasonably sure, in light of the above, that the early humans of the Middle Paleolithic, those capable of fashioning the Levallois flake, will have been able to engage in imaginative rehearsals. This surely would have been required in order for them to fashion such flakes since these were made-to-order components to be incorporated into more complex tools (for example, spears). Hence, not only would their manufacture have required a more refined set of technical skills than those displayed by earlier hominids, the planning that would have gone into the making of such flakes would have been impossible "without the explicit representation of contingencies" (Bermúdez 2003b, 128).

All of these activities imply a capacity for consequence-sensitive planning that is a feature in practical reasoning more generally—planning of a sort that involves not just the mere representation of an action or perceived course of action, but the capacity to decide on a course of action based on its perceived outcomes. Such thinking is distinguished by its sensitivity to various means of achieving an anticipated end; it is not merely seeing and exploiting immediate possibilities for action. At the very least, it requires a capacity to distinguish different possibilities for action in a way that allows for the evaluation of their likelihood to achieve the intended outcomes. Minimally, this requires being able to think something like: If A then B; if C then D. Thus unlike instrumental conditioning, which leads to actions being performed because of their consequences, what we have here is instrumental thinking in actions that are being performed in light of their perceived consequences. Still, such basic forms of consequence-sensitive reasoning fall far short of utility-based assessments of the decision-theoretic variety.

But what enables such mediated thinking? Bermúdez (2003b) insists that it demands the manipulation of instrumental beliefs. Following a long tradition, he holds that in prosecuting these basic acts of planning and decision making the "creature is representing the outcomes of particular courses of action in a manner that we would most naturally model in terms of a sequence of instrumental statements" (p. 55). Consequently, nonlinguistic thinking implies the capacity to reason with and calculate over atomic propositions.

Bermúdez suggests that the nature of such reasoning is very basic indeed. Effectively, nonlinguistic thinking is protological, essentially taking the form of reasoning in predicate calculus, sans the quantifiers, such as *some*, *all*, and *every*. This being so, it appears that our ancient ancestors would have only been able to reason about "particulars," not generalities. Thus, they would have been unable to "represent any general information of the form 'All As are Bs,' or generic causal information to the effect that 'As cause Bs,' or even conditional information about present circumstances like 'If A were to occur, then so will B'" (Papineau 2003, 93).[7] This is, of course, a considerable limitation.

Indeed, thinking at this level cannot be correctly characterized by appeal to operations using the basic logical constants such as conjunction, negation, disjunction, and material inference (Bermúdez 2003b, 140). Despite this, Bermúdez argues, nonlinguistic thought might be understood in *proto*inferential terms; it is a lesser kind of reasoning that has its own special ways of dealing with laws of the excluded middle, modus ponens, and modus tollens. As a characterization of the requisite *level* of logical ability of the hominids this is surely right.

According to Bermúdez, protological thinking is similar to truly logical thinking, apart from exhibiting the differences just noted, in being belief-based—that is, languageless thinkers capable of it must be able to manipulate fully determinate and appropriately structured propositional contents. Yet, if one denies the existence of a LoT, it is not at all clear in what medium nonlinguistic creatures are imagined to entertain their beliefs or conduct their thinking.

Matters are not helped by the fact that Bermúdez (2003b, 134) chooses to "prescind from questions that have to do with the vehicle of nonlinguistic thinking." This is because, in his view, "Protoinferences at the nonlinguistic level are *not made in virtue of their form*. Creatures who engage in, for example, proto-*modus tollens* need not have any grasp of the form of an inferential transition as truth-preserving" (pp. 148–149; first emphasis added). But it is one thing to say that protological thinking does not require a grasp of purely formal principles and quite another to say that such reasoning is not conducted by means of the formal properties of thought contents. Presumably, the alternative idea is that it only depends on being sensitive to the *semantic* properties of thought. But it seems impossible to think in a structured way at all (even protologically) without a sensitivity to recurring semantic atoms, and presumably these will only be recognized by means of some formal property. Thus, it is difficult even to imagine what it is to be directly sensitive to semantic structures if one does not posit "a structured medium of thought" (Frankish 2004, 198).[8]

Now, it could be argued that this structured medium need not be in the head; perhaps it is in the world. Maybe nonverbals use environmental features—that is, what their thoughts are about—to effect basic acts of reasoning. The idea here would be that the world and its features have enough structure to enable them to think systematically by using stable and reencounterable kinds as "external vehicles"; this might allow languageless creatures to reason and respond in appropriately complex ways (see Rowlands 2003). While I have no objection to this proposal in general, in this context the reasons to be suspicious of it are twofold. First, it is not at all clear that the environmental resources to which nonverbals respond are structured in the right sorts of ways to support even protoinferential operations. Specifically, the worldly offerings to which they selectively respond are not carved up into discrete, meaningful elements in the way basic linguistic components are. Thus if, as Bermúdez insists, nonlinguistic thoughts must be based in *propositional* attitudes, then it looks as if the world, unless somehow interpreted in a structured way, is not enough to provide these in the right format for reasoning, as argued in the previous chapter. Second, on the face of it, it looks as if this proposal would make nonverbal thinking insufficiently off-line and detached to meet Bermúdez's other requirements.

As a result, if we assume that protological thinking is conducted by means of manipulating propositional attitudes, then it looks like the only structured medium that could plausibly explain its occurrence is a sentential one. Therefore, if our languageless ancestors were true believers and protological thinkers, they would have had to have made use of linguaform *mental* representations—that is, they must have had some kind of Mentalese. If this line of reasoning is sound, far from providing a viable alternative to the LoT hypothesis, Bermúdez would have provided important grounds for wanting to believe in its truth.

But there is an alternative. For nonlinguistic, protological reasoning need not be content-involving. While we should be persuaded that at least the toolmaking and planning abilities of our hominid forerunners had a level of sophistication that would be hard to explain if they were not instrumentally mediated, it does not follow that such thinking was dependent on having instrumental beliefs per se. Can there be instrumental thinking that is not mediated by propositional attitudes? I hope to show that there can.

Recreative Imaginings

The instrumental components in protological thinking are likely to be perceptually based imaginings—those generated by perceptual reenactments (Currie and Ravenscroft 2003; Prinz 2002, 128). Such recreative imaginings have been understood to be a kind of simulation in that they are produced when the mechanisms responsible for generating perceptual experiences are operating in an off-line mode. When Currie (1995b, 29) first proposed this idea, focusing then on the relations between visual experience and imagery, he suggested that in essence the claim was that (1) these share substantial parts of the same processing system, while having different inputs and outputs; (2) the outputs are similar in structure and function; and (3) the imagery is evolutionarily parasitic on vision. For example, an imagining as opposed to an episode of visual experience might occur if, instead of receiving the usual retinal stimulations, the visual system is prompted by a verbal command to produce such-and-such an image or by an associative memory, or the like. The basic formula is that different inputs yield different outputs (happily, the inputs and outputs in this case are not representations with determinate semantic content).

In recent writings, this basic proposal has been expanded so as to encompass all other modes of perception, including the perception of motor actions (Currie and Ravenscroft 2003).[9] This thesis is attractive because it promises to explain why imaginings are similar in key respects to acts of perceiving since both are sponsored, substantially, by the very same mechanisms. The outputs of perceptual reenactments, the imaginings that Currie and Ravenscroft call *counterparts*, are similar in certain central respects to prior acts of perceiving but they do not replicate them exactly. This is due not only to the different inputs, but also to the fact that there is only a partial overlap in the processing paths (Rollins 1994, 355; see also Podgorny and Shepard 1978; Segal and Fusella 1970; Farah 1985). Of course, this is a good thing for the theory since perceivings and imaginings are, barring hallucinations and other psychopathologies, qualitatively distinguishable.[10]

This hypothesis about recreative imagining can be easily enlisted in order to explain how nonverbal thinking, of the kind restricted to using only perceptually based images and similarity-based cognitive processes, could be importantly extended in such a way that it transcends the limitations of online reactions to what is offered by the immediate here-and-now environment. But, crucially, such imaginative extensions would not involve holding beliefs or having mental states with (or relating to) determinate semantic contents. Having a capacity for recreative imagination would allow organisms to respond in flexible ways to that which is not perceptually present but without the need to mentally represent (narrowly, construed) or to harbor any propositional attitudes. If so, nonpropositional imaginings could be the instrumental components that Bermúdez insists are needed to fuel protological, off-line thinking.

In evaluating this proposal, it is important to be clear why instrumental beliefs per se are imagined to be an absolute must when it comes to explaining the nature of such thought. At the very heart of the argument against minimalism we find the claim that

> instrumental beliefs really only enter the picture when two conditions are met. The first is that the goal of the action should not be immediately perceptible and the second is that there should be no immediately perceptible instrumental properties (that is to say, the creature should not be capable of seeing that a certain course of action will lead to a desired result). (Bermúdez 2003b, 129)

And, so the argument goes, the "instrumental component of intentional action cannot always be understood at the level of perceptual content" (Bermúdez 2003b, 51). Acknowledging in passing that perceptual content is not a species of propositional content, it is concluded that the instrumental pivot needed for off-line protological thinking must take the form of a belief—that it is an attitude directed at a coherently structured proposition with determinate content. These must play the mediating role in thinking when neither the goal nor the means of obtaining it are immediately perceptible.

This argument clearly depends on the way the minimalist's arsenal is characterized, and the fact is that Bermúdez seriously underestimates it in two key respects. For it does not follow from the fact that cognition is perceptually grounded that (1) it is tied to the "here-and-now" of the cognizer's current environment or that (2) its "vehicles" are wholly unstructured. Bermúdez's characterization of minimalism is, well, just *too* minimalist. Once we make appropriate adjustments for these oversights it becomes clear that minimalist accounts can satisfy both requirements; thus they can satisfactorily explain the character of the instrumental component and the capacity to think at a distance without presupposing the existence of nonlinguistic propositional attitudes. It can do so by appeal to imaginings and the forms of thinking they sponsor.

There is a consequence of taking this line. Notoriously, imagistic thinking is not strictly speaking logical. This is because images are not composed of discrete individually referring parts. Indeed, images resemble, they do not refer (or at least not intrinsically).[11] They lack determinate content because, as is well known, they resemble too many things in too many ways to serve as adequate media for reference or representation. Resemblance theories of semantic content flounder precisely because they rely on similarity metrics. It is possible for one thing to look like another without standing in a referential relation to it. Identical twins look alike but they do not corefer. Because images and pictures fail to meet this requirement, they are incapable of doing the work of propositions; they do not have complex semantic contents, nor are they composed of discrete meaningful parts. Note that it makes no sense to talk of believing an image, only believing propositions will do.

Furthermore, images cannot be combined in the way that logical symbols can. Some have held that because of this they must lack genuine generative power or combinatorial properties. But this is a non sequitur. Images have combinatorial capacities; they are just not of the strictly logical sort. Prinz has done more than most to show just how closely similarity-based modes of cognition can approximate to propositional modes of thinking. He has attempted to draw on the best insights of traditional empiricism, updating and augmenting these using the resources of exemplar and prototype theories. He refits and revamps some rather timeworn ideas in modern dress.[12] Thus he shows that while connectionist-based thinking cannot fund true negation, it can manage what he calls *simnegation* (Prinz 2002, 288–289). For instance, a system could not have a prototype with the combined weighted features of all items that did *not* fall into a particular class—for example, there is no prototype that captures what is common to all noncats, no prototype for being "not a cat"—but something softer is possible. In simnegation one does not form a negative prototype, rather one operates in characteristic ways on an existing prototype. Thus simnegation is what you get when "similarity to a negated prototype is inversely related to similarity to a prototype. Something far below the threshold for being a cat will be far above the threshold for being a noncat . . . negation introduces a different similarity function. An instance will be judged to be a noncat if it fails to possess a sufficient number of cat features" (Prinz 2002, 289).

In a similarly sloppy or fuzzy way, prototypes can merge to form combinations that can give rise to certain emergent features, and these underpin specific kinds of expectations about novel situations. Again, to borrow from Prinz, although we are unlikely to have seen "concrete hamburgers" (or even to have thought about them before—unless you have read Prinz's book already), it is easy enough for us to imagine what would follow from trying to ingest one. Such an expectation, while not achieved by standard deductive inference, could be sponsored by combining the two prototypes in thought. Pretty obviously, such imaginative combinations would not be properly systematic. Indeed, we can anticipate just the kinds of psychological inequalities that would occur if thinking about such possibilities involved the use of images as opposed to operations with purely logical symbols. For example, as a matter of psychological fact, it is easier to imagine a person eating an apple than it is to imagine an apple eating a person (Prinz 2002, 300).[13]

In their infamous attack on connectionist architectures, Fodor and Pylyshyn (1995, 116) argued that since such networks do not employ structured context-invariant symbols they could never support the kind of systematicity required for genuine thought. Even the best of associative engines are only capable of responding to situations in a distributed, context-sensitive fashion. This is commonly illustrated by Smolensky's coffee cup, which is a paradigm example of what Clark (1993, 22) calls a "blended" response. As far as a PDP network is concerned, coffee-in-a-cup, coffee-spilled-on-the-table, and coffee-in-the-form-of-granules-in-a-jar are all greeted by distinct activation patterns with no structural components in common. Hence, there can be no stable inference across cases. Purely associative networks are incapable of recognizing the object-property and subject-predicate distinctions.

In this light, the proposal that nonverbal instrumental thinking might be imagistically grounded might be met with the appraisal: close, but no cigar. Even if imagistic thinking admits of a respectable architectural explanation, and even if such cognizing falls within the spectrum of the broadly rational, it remains nonlogical, noninferential, and noncomputational strictu dictu (Fodor 2000a, 43).[14] It is true that because images only admit of limited types of combination, permitting only quasi-logical operations and combinations, they cannot be regarded as bona fide inferences. They clearly do not have the right logical form to sponsor the kinds of inferential relations of the sort amodal symbols permit (Barsalou 1999, 2003).

But that should not bother us. Our concern is not whether they can support full-fledged, truly abstract thought, but only whether they can support the kind of concrete nonlogical instrumental thinking in which (perhaps) apes engage and that it seems that hominids engaged in. Surely, images are good enough to enable this. It has been said that "we don't need association because Turing showed us how to replace it with computation" (Fodor 2003, 115). Perhaps linguistically competent humans do not need association (or perhaps they do not need it exclusively), but—if I am right—nonverbal apes do and hominids certainly did.[15]

Similarity-based psychotectonics offer a powerfully updated vision of how imagistic, nonlinguistic thinking could be carried off in its own special way. When combined with the recreative imagination hypothesis, such processing stories look ideally well placed to explain how what is, in essence, perceptually based responding might be extended beyond the confines of an immediate here-and-now. If so, off-line imaginings can serve as the instrumental components for the kind of nonverbal thinking that Bermúdez has argued can only be achieved if we assume nonverbals have propositional attitudes.

Off-line images can be thought of as the counterparts to local indexical guides (LIGs); they would be local iconic guides. Extended nonverbal cognition can therefore be thought of as being iconically guided. Importantly, iconic thinking could influence behavior "at a distance," enabling quite kinky links to associated remembrances. Surely the empiricists were right about this much.

Yet because they resemble perceivings, imaginings—like their perceptual counterparts—inherit the properties of being tied to certain proprietary domains: they too are in a sense local *in their intentional directedness*. And in this explanatory context, this fact turns out to be a virtue, not a vice. For it would neatly explain why even the most sophisticated feats that nonlinguistic thinking exhibit are importantly limited. The means-end reasoning of our ancestors was apparently limited in scope, only being applicable in certain domains and with respect to certain tasks. Nonverbals, quite generally, seem incapable of reasoning in an open-ended way that characterizes true inferential, conceptual thought. Their thinking is best understood as being restricted to islands of practical rationality, as opposed to operating in the continuous, unfettered space of reasons (Hurley 2003a).

The kind of cognition that relates to hominid tool manufacture certainly bears this stamp. It looks likely to have been achieved through mental rehearsals involving acts of visual-motoric perceptual reenactments. Images and icons—not propositions—could serve as the links in the chains of such nonlogical thinking. Let us consider the stone knapper again. What is needed is a powerful capacity for haptic and visual imaginings: picturing the "right look" of the tools and implements; remembering where to find the right stones by recalling "the spot" where something that looks like "one of those" can be found; "getting a feel" for how to aim one's strikes; remembering the proper sequence of iterated movements; recollecting how hard to hit a stone and when and where to place one's blows; and so on. Fashioning or sculpting a tool is just the sort of activity that is best explained by imaginative capacities and sensitivity to visual or tactile feedback. It is no accident that, even today, learning such a skill requires hands-on training and practice. And while the preparatory activity would have demanded a kind of forethought, there is no reason to think it must have been or indeed was that of a propositional variety.

Assuming Bermúdez is right about the level of hominid thinking, he is surely wrong about its basis. Positing a capacity for recreative imagination supplies much-needed details of the intentional directedness, vehicles, and processes that serve to enable extended, off-line nonlinguistic thinking. Thus although some nonverbal responding may involve "belief-like" representations, we should not suppose that it involves beliefs. Minimalism is the right approach. Nonverbal responding is not content-involving; even when it is iconically extended it only involves intentional attitudes, not propositional attitudes. Even when it comes to explicating the basis of the most sophisticated kinds of nonverbal cognition, we are driven toward an account of protoreasoning that breaks faith with the Basic Architectural Assumption.

What then is required for being a true believer and bona fide reasoner? That is the topic of the next chapter.

5   Linguistic Transformations

The Virtues of Sententialism

For a creature to have an attitude directed at a proposition (and not just a worldly offering)—for it to apprehend a state of affairs intensionally, so to speak—it must have the capacity to direct its attention at that state of affairs via structured vehicles of thought of some appropriate sort. Paradigmatically, the public sentences of natural language or those of a *lingua mentis* are such vehicles.

Traditionally, the having of propositional attitudes is analyzed as instantiating a three-place relation; thinkers stand in relation to sentences of some kind and this, in turn, is what allows them to adopt various psychological attitudes toward the complex contents that those sentences express. Sentences have the right form and content to be truth-evaluable; they are true or false depending on how things stand with the world. If the world obliges, if the relevant state of affairs obtains, then the proposition expressed by a given sentence will be true. If not, the believed proposition is false. It is no accident that the relevant state of affairs must be picked out disquotationally. Also, in line with traditional analyses, the meaningful subparts of a sentence denote worldly objects such that the content expressed by a whole sentence is thought to be fixed by these subparts and their arrangement, inter alia.

Philosophers like to bicker about such things (me too). However, it is not necessary, for our current purposes, to pass judgment on the nature or ontological status of contents or propositions—nor to decide how best to understand truth-conditional semantics.[1] Here my interest is only in the idea that in order to have a content-involving propositional attitude one must have facility with complex linguistic forms—sentences of some kind or other. Only sentences have the right syntactic and semantic properties for expressing propositional contents. If so, sentences are the required medium for thinking and speaking truths (or falsehoods, for that matter).

More than this, because they have complex structures, sentences are purpose-built for doing logical work; they can be parsed at their meaningful joints and this kind of internal organization makes them ideally suited to fund computationally tractable inferential operations. This is a good thing. For we know that propositional attitudes, especially beliefs, are bound by standard logical rules (within certain limits). Thus, if we know that "X believes that P and Q," it can be safely assumed that "X believes that P." And propositional attitudes can be generatively combined in acts of reasoning and inference. Thus it is possible to produce an indefinite number of new beliefs by manipulating those one already has. The creation of new attitudes happens in a small way with every act of practical reasoning, when new intentions are formed. All of this is easy to account for if we suppose that beliefs and desires involve sentential mediation— and seemingly impossible to account for otherwise. As we have seen in the previous chapter, an appeal to nonlinguaform representations falls short of what is required to support classical logical operations.[2] If we think of contents in terms of a facility with sentential structures, this has the added virtue of explaining how the appropriate manipulations are possible since, being spatiotemporal particulars, sentences are the kinds of thing to which one can be causally related. As Dennett (1998, 290) observes, unlike abstract entities, sentences are *manipulanda*.

Reasons for Doing without the LoT

There are really only two varieties of sentientialism on the market. One popular view is that the objects of propositional attitudes are appropriately structured, nonlinguistic linguaform representations—they are items in a subpersonal Language of Thought (LoT), a mental code with its own syntax and semantics. The LoT hypothesis is a computationally based, representational theory of mind. Its advocates claim that all intelligent behavior is best explained by cognitive transformations made over internal formulas, the units of which have both syntactic properties (which link coded symbols mechanically to other physical states) and semantic properties (which link the coded symbols, denotationally, to the external environment).[3] The basic idea is that mental processes are orderly causal sequences of mental representation tokens that are computed thanks to their having appropriate internal structures that enable them to interrelate in rule-governed ways.

The motto of these classical cognitivists is: no intelligent action without symbol manipulation. Or to make the claim more precise: "Insofar as behaviour is properly traced to propositional attitudes, it results from sententially driven computational processes" (Mahoney 1989, 109). According to this version of sententialism, it is claimed that in order for a subject to have a propositional attitude they must stand in a subpersonal psychological relation to a complex, occurrent mental symbol—a mental sentence—tokened in one's head. Apart from their syntactic properties, such symbols also relate in a contentful way to specific worldly items or states of affairs (Fodor 1987, 17; 1975, 198; 1994).[4]

The important thing to note is that although the LoT is composed of sentences it is unlike any natural language in that it alone is intrinsically meaningful. In contrast, the ordinary sentences that we utter have only derived meanings at best; these are provided by their transduction into and out of Mentalese sentences. In this respect, the defenders of the LoT hypothesis endorse a Priority of Thought Thesis (Fodor 2001b; Davies 1998).[5] Mentalese representations exist independently and are ontologically prior to those of natural language. It is therefore at least theoretically possible that they also emerged temporally prior to the arrival of natural-language expressions.[6] If they did, then Mentalese sentences could have served as the medium for content-involving acts of nonverbal cognition.

Some are sanguine about the truth of these claims. And why not? After all, Fodor has supplied several grounds for thinking that we really cannot get by without a LoT. His arguments tend to be short ones. For example, he proclaims that the LoT hypothesis is the only remotely plausible theory that could possibly explain such important phenomena as perception, nonverbal decision making, and concept and language learning. Of course, his hypothesis has this special status—of unique explanatory virtues— because it rests on the assumption that in order to explain such phenomena we must necessarily invoke content-involving mental representations. The thought is that in each case all of these cognitive activities implicate a capacity to reason with or think in terms of propositional attitudes. If nonverbal responding involves having thoughts with fully determinate (if inexpressible) contents and acts of genuine inferential reasoning (for example, of the sort that are imagined to take place even in low-level perceptual modules), then it looks as if Mentalese is not only a plausible theory, it is really nonnegotiable.

This strategy backfires, however, once we realize that we have no reason to think that basic perceptual acts are "modular"—in that they involve the inferential manipulation of contents and representations—and that there is no evidence that nonverbal thinking takes the form of truly logical reasoning involving the manipulation of internal symbols. For once we realize this, we have no reason at all for believing in the LoT. The arguments of the preceding chapters should therefore lead us to reject the claim that "some nonneglible amount of what many animals do, admits of explanation drawing on propositional attitudes" (Mahoney 1989, 109).

Let me be clear. Nonverbal responding often outwardly appears to warrant explanation in terms of practical reasoning—and it is easy enough to describe it as such. But this fact alone provides no ground for believing that mental representations are responsible for such behaviors. The unprincipled approach I have been developing in previous chapters provides an alternative understanding of nonlinguistic thinking. It provides an adequate and parsimonious way of explaining what underlies such intelligent responses—one that easily accounts for its natural limitations—without invoking propositional attitudes at all. With respect to the putative evidence of nonverbal practical reasoning I can but say: one person's modens tollens is another's modens pollens.

Thus we have already dealt with two of the major reasons for wanting to believe in a LoT. The other two, those concerning the explanation of concept and language learning, cannot be dealt with so speedily—but they can be dealt with all the same. For example, Fodor (1975, 61) advanced a notorious *ur*-argument about what is required in order to learn our first concepts and words. He claims that we must postulate preexisting linguaform representations with precisely the same expressive power as any conceptual system or language to be learned. This is necessary in order to explain how we form the hypotheses needed to fuel the learning processes in such cases. To learn a concept (or local linguistic label for one), one must *already* be able to think about what is to be learned as such. This, apparently, requires having a LoT in which to couch one's hypotheses.[7]

Of course, this argument only works if we are prepared to accept certain assumptions—specifically intellectualist assumptions about how such "learning" takes place. The key premise is that new learners must form full-fledged belief-based hypotheses about the meaning of the words or concepts and that these are tested out with feedback from teachers and caregivers. Since formation of such hypotheses must precede the learning of public language, they cannot be based in public-language sentences; hence a LoT is required. To be conclusive, defenders of this argument must rule out the possibility of any other serious proposal about how word learning takes place, one that avoids this questionable intellectualist assumption. Unfortunately for LoT theorists, there are other credible accounts. I will say more about this in chapter 10.

Apart from having these weak supports, the LoT hypothesis is *in essence* not a very credible proposal. Although it is beyond the scope of this book to provide a full-dress refutation of it, I will quickly supply some other—pretty compelling—reasons for disbelieving it. The first thing to note is that the core features of Mentalese, its syntax and semantics, are modeled on those of public-language sentences. The analogy is not perfect. On the one hand, Mentalese lacks some properties that natural languages have—for example, its sentences lack phonological properties. Mental sentences are therefore only envisioned to have formal properties akin to *written* linguistic signs. Yet, unlike the inscriptions of public language, the manipulation of LoT sentences leaves no physical trail, trace, or record in the world—not even at the neurological level. On the other hand, these sentences are imagined to have additional features that natural languages lack; they are utterly well formed, perfectly unambiguous constructions: the LoT is an ideal language. Its sentences are therefore only partially modeled on natural-language sentences. The ways in which they are, and those in which they are not, are provided by the attendant "commentary" on the "model" (Sellars 1956/1997, 103–104). In this case, theory development has been driven by particular explanatory needs—these drive decisions about what is to be kept and what is to be disregarded in unpacking the analogy. The LoT is a well-tailored product designed to meet those needs precisely (one might think too precisely).

It is common scientific practice to begin theorizing by using metaphors and modifying and developing them until the core constructs can be explicated in other terms (McMullin 1984, 33; Brown 1986, 295). The trouble is that this has not happened with the LoT hypothesis. For example, we are never told how the LoT came to be or how it came to have its special properties. Yet, one thing is quite clear: the account given of its peculiar syntax and semantics must be entirely different from that which we would give of public-language sentences. This follows from the fact that according to LoT theorists public languages derive their compositional and meaningful properties from Mentalese. Very well, but that just makes the question of how its mental symbols came by their structure and content all the more urgent. The spotlight worry is that credible answers to these questions will not be forthcoming. Certainly, the offerings to date have not been encouraging.

The truth is that, as things stand, the defenders of the LoT hypothesis have no workable theory of content that could support the claims of semantic and compositional supremacy that they make on behalf of Mentalese. There are intractable difficulties in providing a workable psychosemantics along causal-informational lines. Nor is the gravity of the situation lost on the theory's most prominent supporters. It is admitted that "the hardness of understanding intentionality and thought isn't, these days, as widely advertised as the hardness of understanding consciousness, but it's quite hard enough to be getting on with" (Fodor 2003, 22). Surely, however, it would be unreasonable to reject the theory on these grounds alone. It is, we are told, still developing. Rather than supplying a reason for condemning it, its worrying lack of a theory of psychosemantics should be noted as a major agenda item for its board of directors and an important demand of its shareholders. The hope is that an explanation will come, in time. We must reserve final judgment until one is developed.

Still, even if we are prepared to accept this, the above considerations help us to correctly understand the true status of the theory. After all, it is not as if there is an existing theory of content that is in good basic order, only requiring some further adjustments. On the contrary, the naturalistic theories of semantic content that have been offered to date have been beset by difficulties of such a fundamental nature that this fact ought to inspire doubts that any psychosemantic theory will work (Hutto 1999b, chaps, 2, 3; Putnam 1990, 1988). The root problem is that the very idea of content—as something "given" in perceptual encounters, "acquired by" mental states, and "manipulated" in subpersonal cognitive processing—is deeply problematic if not incoherent. And, as I argued in chapter 3, attempts to legitimize our understanding of content by appeal to an information-based semantics are sponsored by confusions about what can be legitimately derived from the carrying-information metaphor.

And the situation is even worse (and more obviously so) when it comes to questions about the ontogenesis of Mentalese syntax. As yet, there has been no attempt to explain how the LoT came to be structured as it is—not even inadequate ones. This is just presupposed. However, to see why this is important, it helps to make a comparison with natural-language inscriptions. If I write the sentence "I will not speak ill of the Language of Thought" a hundred times on a chalkboard, the words in the first and the hundredth sentences will no doubt look considerably different (if for no other reason, this will be due to a tired hand). But, in truth, on close inspection none of the resulting token linguistic signs comprising any of the other sentences will look exactly the same. Still, they are easily recognizable as being composed of the same words and letters—written out over and over again. We can see this because each letter and word adheres to its own common template (making allowances for illegibility). These linguistic signs are produced in line with common normative standards for their formation: years of painstaking training will have paid off. The same would be true if I wrote the sentences in an alien alphabet; the marks in question should be recognizable as having the same shapes, even to a nonnative speaker who knows nothing of their meaning. What such an onlooker would see would be the commonality in the repeating forms.

The point is that the shapes and sounds of linguistic signs are themselves grounded in certain public conventions that relate to their formation and combination. Part of our linguistic training is to get competent language users to recognize and follow such rules. Recognizing and implementing such norms would have been instrumental to the original forging of symbols and their subsequent maintenance. Linguistic symbols are cultural artifacts; they are not natural kinds. It is possible to tell the story of the origins of their formal and meaningful features, though it is likely to be quite complex and will require making an appeal, at least in part, to the emergence of certain public practices and conventions (Arbib 2005; Hutto 2006g; Sinha 2004).

What equivalent story can LoT theorists tell about the ontogenesis of the structural properties of Mentalese symbols? How and when did LoT symbols emerge? How did they each acquire their unique syntactic shapes—the shapes that putatively enable them to play the role of MoPs in private mental languages? Obviously, there can be no appeal to public conventions in this context and the idea of private conventions is oxymoronic. Perhaps there is a naturalistic explanation in the offing, but for the moment this looks, on the face of it, like another very serious lacuna for LoT theorists.

Yet even if we withhold final judgment on the fate of the LoT hypothesis and ignore these concerns, what this discussion makes clear is that the hypothesis currently gets all of its theoretical strength from the analogy with the known properties of public language sentences. Any greater explanatory virtues it might have, potentially, stem entirely from the fact that its proponents are prepared to write bold promissory notes on its behalf. I take this to be a major weakness.

To be sure, philosophers, in general, do not assess a theory's worth in such terms. But such evaluation is the norm in scientific circles. And since the LoT hypothesis is presented as a straightforward empirical hypothesis it is surely a fit target for such appraisal. The reason it survives it is that it looks (to some) as if it is the only possible way to explain certain otherwise perplexing phenomena—such as our capacities to learn a language, to reason logically, to communicate with sense, and so on. This is why, when push comes to shove, the theory is never seriously defended on empirical grounds.[8]

In sum, there are many good reasons to be suspicious of the LoT hypothesis. It is seriously lacking in important respects and it has made little progress in paying back its theoretical debts since its inception. Collectively, these deficiencies ought to convince us that it should only be entertained as a last-ditch option. In this light it is interesting that appeal to inference to the best explanation is cited as the best reason for believing in the LoT. In fact, if we accept that it has no rivals, it earns the accolade of being the best explanation by default. For, as Fodor (2003, 102) acknowledges, "Arguments to the best explanation can be pretty persuasive, especially when the explanation that they claim is best is, *de facto*, the only one that anybody has been able to think of." Masquerading as an "argument from an inference to the best explanation," what we really have here is an "argument from an inference to the *only* explanation": the truth of the LoT hypothesis is guaranteed (at least as things stand, for presumably even if as contingent matter of fact no other explanations exist they are surely logically possible). And so the logic goes, "Remotely plausible theories are better than no theories at all" (Fodor 1975, 27). So if it were true that core cognitive phenomena mentioned earlier could *only* be explained by postulating a built-in linguaform system of representation, "The cost of not having a Language of Thought is not having a theory of thinking" (Fodor 1987, 147). But, rhetoric aside, the situation is not this desperate.

The fact is that there is another possibility, which I will describe in the next section. Perhaps Fodor's style of argument is therefore better described as "inference from lack of imagination." Before looking at the challenger theory of thinking, it is worth noting that if the LoT hypothesis turns out to be false or incoherent, this would radically reduce the possibilities for understanding the relation between natural language and propositional thought (see Carruthers and Boucher 1998 for a detailed discussion of these possibilities). For example, its fall would undermine the claim that language is nothing more than a public medium for sharing preformed private thoughts, a view associated with the more reductive versions of the communicative view of language. Equally, it would undermine Carruthers's modest variant of the cognitive conception of language. He claims that prelinguistic, fully conceptual thinking takes place *within* mental modules, although such thinking is clearly restricted in specified ways. For him, natural language significantly augments and extends these native modes of reasoning in two important respects. First, it makes possible certain types of inference, such as subjunctive and conditional variety, by providing additional nontrivial representational resources; it alone enables free-wheeling hypothetical and counterfactual thinking. Natural language literally would have provided a means for re-representing preexisting thoughts, by minting new cognitive coin using public-language vehicles or inner proxies thereof (in the form of "inner speech"). In this way, the natural-language faculty would have provided the means for free inter-modular representational trade. This would explain why humans, and humans alone, exhibit a capacity to "reason conjunctively, disjunctively, to and from universal or existential claims, and so forth" (Carruthers 2004, 263). For modular thinking is by comparison hobbled (Carruthers 1998, 110; Pinker 2003, 27).

As Carruthers puts it, it is *"naturally necessary* that *some* of our thoughts should constitutively involve natural language" (Carruthers 1998, 94; original emphasis). The use of the scope quantifier is important; his claim is not that all inferential cognition is made possible by language, only some. Of course, this rests on the assumption that intramodular cognition would have taken place using a linguaform or quasi-linguistic representational medium, such as Mentalese. Obviously, without a LoT there would be no content-bearing mental representations to play this role. There would have been exactly no instances of cognition of a properly logical variety prior to the advent of language—none whatsoever—not even those confined to imagined special-purpose modules.

The Supermentalists

There is a much more credible version of sententialism: it is that the sentences of natural language *are* the vehicles that enable propositional thought. In learning how to interpret and use the complex symbols of natural languages, members of the species *Homo sapiens sapiens* get into a position to adopt propositional attitudes, not just intentional attitudes. And, in getting an appropriate handle on the compositional semantics of language, they are able to engage in genuine, content-involving practical reasoning. Thus true believers are able to apprehend propositions by manipulating complex public forms, those provided by natural language (or inner-speech surrogates derived from them).

In light of the above considerations, we have good reason to favor what has been called the "Thinking in Natural Language Hypothesis" (TNL hypothesis) (Davies 1998, 226). Its central claim is captured in the memorable slogan: "The language of thought is natural language" (Frankish

2004, 197). Supporters of this view assume that linguistic symbols are required for properly logical, honest-to-God systematic and productive modes of reasoning. In its strongest form, which I endorse, the public symbol systems of natural languages make bona fide inferential thinking possible because they have a compositional semantics.[9] Learning to think using the unique resources of natural language, by explicitly manipulating sentences and their internal parts, is learning to think and reason propositionally. The relation between thinking and natural language—between having propositional thoughts and beliefs—is constitutive (see Hutto 1999b, chap. 5). Propositionally based, inferential reasoning only comes into being when the external symbol systems of complex natural languages are used in certain appropriate ways. Consequently, entering into the realm of language is to take the first step in crossing a major cognitive Rubicon.

In explicating this idea it helps to call on Frankish's (2004) handy distinction between the basic mind and the supermind.[10] Accordingly, the latter types of mind use the public vehicles of language to radically extend our cognitive abilities. Thus they are understood as being built on top of, or as supervening on, more basic modes of cognition. In my view, the latter decidedly cannot be legitimately understood in sentential terms. Basic or nondiscursive modes of cognition are nonlinguaform and, to the extent that we ought to think of them as involving "belieflike representations," rudimentary forms of cognition should not be understood as implicating propositional attitudes or even representations with determinate semantic content.

In a famous incarnation, Dennett (1991) modeled the conscious mind as having a serial, stream-of-consciousness, or Joycean character. But this underrates it. I follow Frankish in casting the supermind in a more dynamic role, treating it as a kind of "premising machine." Accordingly, the tools provided by language are used in deliberative acts of explicit practical or theoretical reasoning—those of the classical deductive, inductive, and abductive variety. The job of the supermind is therefore not simply to enable us "to speak as if the proposition were true but to reason as if it were—to take it as a premise" (Frankish 2004, 91). As a consequence supermental thinking involves "consciously and deliberatively calculating some of the consequences of one's premises. And acceptance—that is, having a policy of premising—involves committing oneself to doing this, on appropriate occasions, in appropriate contexts" (Frankish 2004, 91).

Supermental thinking is thus based on adopting linguistically mediated attitudes toward propositions; it rests on the ability to use and understand complex linguistic constructions. The relevant activity takes the form of making certain conscious commitments—that is, adopting and maintaining specific premising policies. These are active commitments made concerning the use of propositions that are explicitly taken as premises in truth-seeking and means-end reasoning. The meaningful components of natural-language sentences provide the necessary structures needed for open-ended, context-invariant, and systematic modes of thought. Nonaccidentally, linguistically mediated thought bears all the hallmarks of truly logical thinking and planning. And since the mastery of the complex linguistic forms needed to effect such thinking only arrived late in our prehistory—beyond the date that it could have been hardwired into our brains—I take it that the supermind is a kind of softwired virtual machine, one that establishes new regularities of thought, substantively altering and enhancing more basic reasoning habits and dispositions in interesting new ways. Yet since supermental thinking is consciously accessible, indeed transparent to us, I agree with Clark (1998, 180–182) that this may—at least in part—account for the mistaken tendency to see its likeness in *all* acts of cognition, even those of the decidedly more basic variety.

Supporters of the TNL hypothesis typically hold that it is only after we achieve facility with the external symbolic forms of natural language—after we are practiced in "public thinking"—that we eventually learn to "think in our heads," using inner speech as a medium. This is an achievement, not a given (Dennett 1998, 284). Private thinking requires replicating auditory and visual images of the structures used in overt speech acts and linguistic forms. Apparently schoolchildren do something similar when they first learn how to manipulate mathematical symbols publicly before being able to perform feats of "mental mathematics." Perhaps the most remarkable example of this is the proficiency certain well-trained Japanese children have for calculating enormously large sums using only a "mental abacus." But this should not distract from the important point, which is that, on the TNL account, either public natural-language sentences or their internal surrogates serve as mediums for conducting propositional reasoning and as the basis for having propositional attitudes.[11]

The Grooves of Thought

As discussed in the previous chapter, iconically based thinking has inherent limitations of applicability (derived from the perceptual-based responses that it resembles). Linguistically based cognition does not suffer in this way. Casting thoughts into a sentential format is precisely what is required if one is to engage in topic-neutral, domain-general reasoning.[12]

This being so, it should come as no surprise that cross-domain thinking only showed its face after the development of complex natural languages and the capacity to deploy their resources. We can expect that linguistically based superminds would have taken over some of the important "reasoning" work already familiar to basic protological minds, significantly upgrading the range and quality of such thinking.

Augmenting our cognitive toolkit with a premising machine that makes use of linguaform structures would have constituted a major addition—one with truly transforming effects, not just a modest extension but a radical transformation of the cognitive possibilities. Clark (1998, 177, 179–180) is right to suppose that the acquisition of language allows for the "ultimate upgrade." Humans have powerful recreative imaginations, likely inherited from our hominid forerunners. But even off-line iconic thinking is still embodied and visceral because of its re-enactive character; it is therefore quite unlike the kind of reflective or neutral responding afforded by the manipulation of abstract amodal symbols. The capacity for such thought is something humans have to a degree that, indisputably, no other species does. The TNL hypothesis regards this as a consequence of the capacity to represent objects and situations using complex linguistic signs.

We can illustrate this kind of transforming effect by reviewing the plight of Sheba, a chimpanzee, who after years of intensive training eventually learned to use some basic symbols in order to represent different quantities of food. A series of experiments revealed that it was only by deploying these symbols as intermediaries that she was able to override her otherwise irresistible natural predisposition, shared with others of her kind, to reach for larger amounts of food whenever these were available. This proved important since in the test conditions doing this consistently resulted in her getting a lesser amount. Much to her manifest frustration, Sheba could not overcome this tendency even after she apparently grasped the experimenter's rule (indeed, the experiments were designed to see if she could master it). Yet after she was trained in the use of simple conventional symbols a new possibility in her behavioral repertoire emerged: she became able to curb her base tendencies. Representing the object of her desire in a more abstract way gave her a new means of achieving an old end. She was able to use the symbol as a go-between—as a detached representation of the food quantity—and this freed her from her "more natural," nonsymbolic embodied mode of responding.

It is important not to overstate Sheba's abilities. To count as a truly autonomous act of symbolic thinking, one that meets the generality constraint, she would have had to be capable of using the symbol in question freely in a wider system of signs and across multiple contexts. Learning a handful of individual symbols falls far short of mastering a stable system of complex signs, ones with recurring subunits—that is, natural-language sentences. This is what is required for a more sophisticated representation and properly logical reasoning about ends and means of the sort that permit reflective evaluation and freedom of choice of the highest order. This looks to be beyond the cognitive reserve of wild chimpanzees, for only those that have been enculturated exhibit any capacity for limited symbol use—a fact that is brought home by tracing the painstaking and round-about route through which Sheba came to be in a position to solve her problem. Her training required an extremely long regime in order to estab-lish the relatively simple associative link between different quantities of food and symbols for these quantities.[13] Nor did she reach a new decision about how to act based on a series of inferential steps calling on her pre-existing instrumental beliefs. Still, it is easy to imagine the greater freedom and flexibility of response she would have had if she could have engaged in linguistically mediated practical reasoning. Her mastery of even this basic symbol, although of limited use, was a hard-won but important achievement for this chimpanzee.[14] We humans, of course, have the capac-ity in spades. For this reason we are capable of widely divergent reactions when faced with emotionally charged situations; we are uniquely capable of responding to situations on a variety of levels.

It is therefore important to stress that even in the human case, super-mental thinking does not wholly usurp our more basic nonlinguistic modes of thinking—it is not as if the acquisition of a "premising machine" involves a complete cognitive refit. Indeed, our older ways are likely to dominate in many—perhaps even the majority of—circumstances, with supermental capacities only being called on a fraction of the time. Basic minds, which come in different varieties, are good enough for getting most organisms through most situations, provided they are in their home envi-ronments. In the human case, they often allow us to navigate by autopi-lot as it were, but sometimes they are thwarted. Tackling problems that the basic mind cannot handle is a job for the supermind. However, contrary to what might be expected, going over to "manual control" is to switch into low-gear thinking. It is a shift to a slow, careful deliberative mode that is serial, sequential, and fragile. This suggestion is in line with dual-process theories of reasoning that have been advanced in order to make sense of the independent empirical data showing that although sometimes people reason logically, "sometimes they do not" (Gigerenzer 1997, 282; Over 2002, 201–204).[15]

Moreover, the exercise of the recreative imagination would have prepared the grooves for and oiled the wheels of instrumental thinking using only nonsentential vehicles. This suggests a plausible explanation of how the wetware of the ancestral brain—which is not ready-made for logical reasoning but only imagistically grounded protological thought—so easily accommodates supermental thinking. This deals neatly with an otherwise serious objection that has been raised against the supermentalist hypothesis. It is that the appearance of complex natural-language forms on their own is simply insufficient for explaining the ontogenesis of logical reasoning abilities. As Carruthers observes, it is "quite obscure how the evolution of a grammar-faculty could, by itself, confer capacities for *nondemonstrative* social, causal, or explanatory reasoning" (Carruthers 1998, 108; original emphasis).[16] As we have seen, there are good reasons for believing that even the pinnacle of hominid thinking was not of a truly logical variety, but it approximates to such reasoning to some degree. Thus if the *basic* moves of reasoning were already somewhat familiar to at least certain nonverbal minds, it becomes easier to see how the use of new items of thought, public symbols with stable forms and contents as opposed to images, would build on more basic believing capacities. This is consistent with the claim that public-language vehicles would have constituted a new, elevated mode of reasoning. It is therefore not surprising that the capacity to engage in supermental tasks of reasoning comes automatically or naturally; humans only gain such abilities over time and after training, once they have mastered the use of public-language symbols.

We can conclude that only those capable of using linguaform vehicles in the appropriate way can engage in bona fide practical reasoning; only they can act for reasons (some nonverbal animals give the appearance of doing so, but this is just an appearance: they are not "true believers," still less "true reasoners"). There is a real difference between acting on the basis of propositional attitudes and merely appearing to do so (for example, acting on the basis of intentional attitudes or even reflexively). Hence, there is a way of agreeing with Davidson over Dennett, but without becoming Fodor. There are "facts of the matter" about whether one has acted for a reason or not.

With these observations in hand, we can now return to the important question: How do young children come by their first understanding of the propositional attitudes of others?

6 Unprincipled Embodied Engagements

Dealing with the Developmental "Paradox"

The detour taken in the past three chapters was necessary in order to clarify the important distinction between intentional attitudes and propositional attitudes. With it in hand, it will be possible to say how children eventually acquire their first understanding of propositional attitude terms and what form it takes. My claim is that this must wait for the mastery of certain complex linguistic forms and that it builds on a natural sensitivity to the intentional attitudes of others as well as on a growing capacity to respond to these attitudes in complex ways in face-to-face encounters. It is therefore important to say more about the nature of such primary engagements in order to make explicit in what way they act as the platform for such developments. That is the job of this chapter.

Human infants identify, attend, and respond to the intentional attitudes expressed in the goal-directed behavior of others in reliably expectant ways. They are naturally attuned and appropriately sensitive to the expressed attitudes of certain others, at least in certain types of circumstance. Uniquely human forms of intersubjective responding are more sophisticated than the responses found elsewhere in the animal kingdom, and they become ever more refined in the early, formative years, unfolding along a stable and fixed trajectory.

During the first two years of life, prior to being able to produce and use even basic sentences, infants exhibit impressive responsiveness to a class of phenomena that fall under the umbrella "intentions-in-action." They begin life by selectively attending to their caregivers and only at a later stage, at around the age of five months, do they begin to attend to physical objects. Moreover, the feedback they receive from others has particular importance for them; thus even two-month-olds react negatively if their face-to-face encounters with significant others are disrupted (see Hobson

2007). Over time, they show still more focused capacities to distinguish between goal-directed agency and animacy (circa three months). Slightly older children distinguish between human actors as opposed to mechanical "agents," as well as between object-directed actions (and the paths taken to them) and mere movements. This occurs around the ages of six to nine months. Also at about this time, children begin to alternate their attention between objects of interest and the gaze of others. This eventuates in the activities of declarative pointing and "checking back" to ensure that the other's gaze is properly directed at the relevant object (this is a more advanced kind of social referencing than that which occurs early on). These latter abilities are associated with the basic forms of joint attention; they begin to emerge around ten to twelve months and are securely in place by eighteen months or thereabouts. During an overlapping time frame, children also gain the ability to segment complex behavior streams meaningfully (at about ten to fifteen months) and to distinguish and imitate intentional actions as opposed to incomplete/unintentional behaviors (at about eighteen months).

That young children have such capacities at roughly these times is empirically well established and beyond dispute (Meltzoff 1995; Baldwin et al. 2001; Baird and Baldwin 2001; Eilan 2005; Woodward 2005). What is not settled is how best to characterize what underlies such responsiveness. This chapter is devoted to making the case for an unprincipled embodied account of what this involves. Before turning to that project, it is important to stress that all sides agree that these infantile abilities do not rest on the kind of folk psychological understanding of reasons that I discussed in chapters 1 and 2. We know this because, to reiterate an earlier lesson, understanding what it is to act for a reason minimally requires not only an understanding of the core propositional attitudes but also how they interrelate. There is no prospect of younger children acquiring this if they only get a handle on what it is to have a belief at around age four.[1]

This verdict is in line with the standard interpretation of the evidence provided by "false-belief" tests. Interestingly, there have been disputes about whether such tests are good indicators of the true timing of the onset of this conceptual competence. A range of individual and situational factors have been shown to make a difference in enabling some children to display "false-belief" understanding prior to four years of age—in some cases such understanding manifests itself up to six months or a year earlier. Among the prominent variables that matter are number of siblings, levels of family discourse, parenting styles, and test settings (that is, whether they are conducted in normal social environments as opposed to under laboratory conditions) (Dunn 1991; Surian and Leslie 1999). Yet even if we make the relevant adjustments for such factors, the emergence of an understanding of belief still considerably postdates the child's responsiveness to intentions-in-action. This has been identified as a source of tension in the way we characterize infantile abilities. It has been observed that

there is something paradoxical about intentional attribution. Though it is true that motivational states are more obvious and more frequently inferred than beliefs, the attribution of intention—in a precise and complete sense—is not simpler, and may indeed be harder, than the attribution of belief. The paradox might lie in the fact that, although children seem to have some command over some aspects of the concept of intention early on, not until later years do they seem to have command over other aspects. (Astington 2001, 86)

As Astington's concluding sentence implies, one will only see a problem here if one imagines that the concept of intention at play in the child's initial economy *necessarily* implies an understanding of the mentalistic concepts of belief and desire. Clearly, that is not possible if children only acquire a grasp of these concepts later.

This raises the question of how best to characterize the kind of "understanding" that young children have of intentions (and their understanding related phenomena such as "perspectives," "attending," and so on). A spectrum of possibilities exists—at one extreme we find the idea that young children have a kind of theoretical understanding, at the other we find the claim that their modes of response are entirely nonintellectual and embodied. I defend the latter view. But before doing so, it is worth saying a word about what motivates cognitivist interpretations and why they should be avoided.

The Principled Approach

A common response to Astington's paradox is to conclude that "although very young children have considerable insights into intention-relevant matters, they do not yet possess a concept of intention that is consummate with that of adults" (Moses 2001, 70). This implies that children are still operating with their own concept of intention, one having its own special features and content. This view is sponsored by the orthodox assumption that infantile interpersonal engagements must be conceptually grounded in rules and representations of some sort.[2] Or, as I will say, the core intersubjective competence of children is thought to have a principled basis. For those persuaded by this approach, the interesting and difficult questions center around specifying the form and content of the principles that children or their subpersonal mechanisms are using, for it

is these that inform children's peculiar way of understanding and struc-
turing their social world and navigating that space.

This sort of cognitivism is buoyed up by a particular interpretation of
the data concerning nonverbal cognition—data provided by experimental
paradigms involving the use of "stimulus habituation/dishabituation" and
"violation of expectation" methodologies. These methodologies have
become industry standards. Developmental psychologists devised these
techniques in order to challenge the once orthodox view that young
infants are incapable of objective thought and hence do not start life with
a structured understanding of things (Baillargeon 1987, 1995; Spelke 1990,
1994; Spelke and Van de Walle 1993). The strongest evidence in support
of that view is the apparent fact that infants only appear to recognize that
objects continue to exist unperceived at around the age of nine months—
when they achieve the stage of what Piaget would call "object permanence." Prior to this point, if an object of interest is removed from an
infant's sight they make no further attempt to engage with it or to search
for it, giving the impression that, as far as they are aware, these objects no
longer exist. If so, this would indicate that they do not even understand
objects qua objects, which is a minimal requirement for carving up or representing the world in structurally distinct ways.

Against this, new experimental methods were devised to test the conjecture that, perhaps, the reason young infants do not seek out objects that
they can no longer perceive is simply because they lack the requisite motor
skills and abilities for making such attempts. Their relative immobility, it
was thought, might have a direct impact on their exploratory motivations.

Putting this to the test required focusing on those infantile reactions that
were not related to the direct physical manipulation of objects of their
interest. This led to the development of the dishabituation/habituation
and preferential-looking techniques. The former involves regularly expos-
ing infants to specific stimuli that initially evoke measurable patterns of
interest and response, such as longer looking times or increased sucking
activity. In the familiarization stage, this process is repeated until the
infant's interest in the stimuli begins to wane; this is known as habitua-
tion. In the second phase, subjects are then presented with a novel class
of stimuli. If the new stimuli provoke renewed levels of interest and
response—that is, if complacency disappears—then subjects are said to
have been dishabituated.

Coupled with more easily discernible telltale patterns of differential
response, such as straightforward displays of preference, this data has been
used to build up a picture of nonverbal predispositions of human infants

and nonhuman animals.[3] Unquestionably, these experiments achieve this. Significantly, they show infants do not share the same worldly expectations with adults; many of their sensitivities and reactive tendencies are quite unique.

To take a nonpsychological example, this shows up in the way they respond when keeping track of moving objects. Adults anticipate that if an object is moving along a stable trajectory and suddenly disappears out of sight, say because it is occluded by another object, it will reappear at an appropriate point in space and time (if its progress is not otherwise interrupted). Using the paradigms mentioned above, this is shown by the fact that they exhibit surprise if under the stated conditions the object in question fails to make an appropriate spatiotemporal appearance. Interestingly, infants do not share this expectation, or at least not precisely. That is, when witnessing the same kind of event they react differentially if *nothing* appears at the appropriate point, but they remain unmoved as long as *something* does—that is, even if what appears is not the same object or even one of a quite different sort from the original. To be precise about the data, infants will look longer in these circumstances only if nothing appears at the right place in space-time (Brower, Broughton, and Moore 1971; Brower 1982). Generalizing from this sort of case, the focus of many recent studies has been to chart the differences in adult and infantile expectations in more and more refined ways.[4]

I have no wish to question the value of this work, but I want to challenge the standard assumption that nonverbal minds are in essence just like those of linguistically competent adults in being content-involving— that is, that the real difference between them lies only in the particular concepts and principles with which they operate. This idea is promoted by the way we interpret the nature of their responding. It looks as if because infants and adults both show signs of surprise when expectations are violated, we can safely suppose that both are making belief-based predictions; the reason they react in the characteristic ways they do is that they have discovered their beliefs to be false. This sort of interpretation is encouraged by the fact that "surprise requires that I be aware of a contrast between what I did believe and what I come to believe. Such awareness, however, is a belief about belief; if I am surprised, then amongst other things, I come to believe my original belief was false" (Davidson 1985, 479).

Actually, this is far too strong. For if nonverbals were exhibiting surprise of this sort, it would imply not only that they harbor propositional attitudes such as belief, but that they are capable of second-order metacognitive capacities! While few would endorse the latter idea, most researchers are prepared to convert questions about nonverbal expectations into questions about the content of nonverbal beliefs, without qualification. Murphy, tellingly, puts his finger on the pivotal assumption that lies behind and (apparently) also justifies these interpretations: "*If the only way* to distinguish situations X and Y is *via* a particular fact or belief then even a very coarse measure that shows discrimination of these situations will *a fortiori* show the presence of the belief" (Murphy 2002, 273; first emphasis added).

Those who adopt principled approaches hold that nonverbals hold coherently organized sets of beliefs about the world—that is, they are not just responsive to selected features of a structured world. Like adults, they understand or represent it (or aspects of it) in their own special way, using unique sets of principles and concepts that inform their distinctive patterns of judgment. This is at least a logically possible way of explaining the internal coherence exhibited in the patterns of infantile response to intentions-in-action, and how these interface with the child's own emotions and their abilities to attend to those of others.

Principled approaches come in various strengths. In extreme versions, even neonates are thought of as operating with knowledge structures that "are rich enough and abstract enough to merit the name of theories" (Gopnik and Meltzoff 1997, 82).[5] Thus it is imagined that "infants, like older learners, formulate rules or hypotheses ... and elaborate these hypotheses in light of additional input" (Aguiar and Baillargeon 2002, 329). Although this variant of theory theory has some followers, even some die-hard cognitivists find such claims hard to swallow, at least in this unadulterated form. Thus it has been observed that in order "to have theoretical status, knowledge must be encoded in a format useable outside normal input/output relations" (Karmiloff-Smith 1995, 78). Yet none of the experimental data concerning the violation of infantile expectations suggests that infants can reason about these topics off-line (see also Prinz 2002, 214). There is also no evidence that infants can apply their putative "conceptual understanding" in different contexts.

Quite unlike the application of laws and concepts that typifies scientific theorizing, nonverbal responding appears to be highly task bound; the selective responsiveness of infants and animals to certain types of stimuli bears none of the characterizing marks of abstract, cross-domain thinking. In this light, it is surely overkill to explain their abilities and how they develop over time by presupposing they are operating with detailed theoretical knowledge at this stage.[6] The old adage about sledgehammers and nuts springs to mind. Or, more simply, we are not compelled to adopt the theory-theory interpretation based on the existing evidence.

There is a softer option. For it is possible to deny that infants are "theorists" as such, while defending the idea that they operate with domain-specific bodies of knowledge nonetheless (Carey 1988; Carey and Spelke 1996). The knowledge in question can still be imagined as taking the form of a coherently organized set of rules and representations.

Proponents of this sort of view face a major challenge when it comes to specifying the precise content of these putative nonverbal beliefs. This, as we have seen, is not merely a matter of saying what they are "about," extensionally speaking. My reasons for skepticism about Bermúdez's project, discussed in chapter 4, are also reasons for thinking this cannot be done.

And such theorists carry an even heavier burden. Ultimately, if claims about nonverbal believing are to be credible, we are owed an account of the source and basis of the contents and concepts that inform such thinking.[7] Since these cannot come from language, the most straightforward way to make sense of nonverbal acts of believing is to place a positive bet on the truth of the Language of Thought (or LoT) hypothesis (in fact, as I have already argued in chapters 4 and 5, I think this is the only way to proceed, but I also think it is doomed to failure).

In this light, it is somewhat ironic that proponents of principled approaches do not, in general, embrace sententialism when it comes to thinking about the vehicles of nonverbal thought. They allow that such thinking is conducted by a variety of means, including "schemas, scripts, lists, prototypes and other representations that arise and change during cognitive development" (Carey and Spelke 1996, 516; Karmiloff-Smith 1995, 77–78). Although it is true that these cognitive models allow for entailment relations of some kind, if one adopts this sort of liberal view about the nature of cognitive processes, the claim that nonverbal expectations are to be understood as involving belief-based inferences is put under pressure immediately. Even if we allow that cognitive *processes* are one thing and their *products* are another, unless the former are thought to mimic classical logical operations involving appropriately structured mental representations, it becomes very hard to explain how they could support truth-preserving inference. Or, to put it another way, the fact that they do would begin to look more than a bit miraculous.

It should be clear that one cannot push too far in this direction without undermining the very idea that nonverbals are believers in any case. For example, persuaded of the need to rethink the nature of cognitive processing, eliminativists have long argued for a fundamental reform in our understanding of the nature of mental representations. Churchland (1989, 130–131) therefore proposed a model of cognition that contrasts "sharply with the kinds of representational and processing strategies that analytic philosophers, cognitive psychologists, and AI workers have traditionally ascribed to us (namely, sentence-like representations)." The trouble is that this account of representation is chased out in terms of a kind of state-space semantics, one that ultimately fails to honor the traditional distinction between representational content and its vehicle. The result is that the notions of representation and knowledge involved are, to say the least, highly unorthodox. A creature will represent an item as falling in a given category if it is deemed sufficiently similar to a standard-setting prototype or exemplar. While this may be a true account of the nature of such processing, it is inadequate as a basis for a classical account of representations in terms of determinate, truth-conditional content. It is no accident, for example, that Churchland's approach openly eliminates the very possibility of misrepresentation in this sense. Lots of things that do not belong to a concept's extension will exhibit enough similarity to be counted as so doing, and many items that belong in the concept's extension will exhibit features that make it appear as if they do not. Whether a system classifies them "correctly" will vary according to circumstance. Yet, that is an entirely misleading way of putting things. For to talk of "correctness" at all presupposes the bounds of true category membership is fixed in some way other than in terms of perceived similarity. If not, the result is—disastrously enough—that there is no chance of "concepts" being misapplied. We need more than a system's processing tendencies to establish such a standard. For this reason, in their unadulterated forms, prototype and exemplar theories are, at best, well placed to explain the *procedures*, or *means*, by which creatures identify, categorize, and respond to phenomena—particularly those of the sensory variety (Osherson and Smith 1981; Rey 1996/2000). Without supplement, they are an inadequate basis for a theory of concepts and incapable of explicating the semantics of mental representations (traditionally conceived).

There has been a recent attempt to occupy the middle ground on this issue by combining nonclassical models of cognitive structure and processing with informational theories of content. Prinz (2002, 238), for example, has developed a kind of dual-factor theory, according to which "concepts are proxytypes. Proxytypes are perceptually derived representations used in category detection ... [thus] proxytype theory identifies concepts with structured detection mechanisms, not with atomic indicators." This theory might be thought to provide a nonsententialist way of making sense of nonverbal beliefs. As a result, nonverbal thinking would not be properly inferential (strictly speaking). This would fit with the ecumenical proposals about the vehicles of content mentioned earlier. But the more serious issue relates to Prinz's preferred theory of content and his account of its acquisition, for as far as I can see, it requires us to take seriously the idea that content is contained and encoded in perceptual signals—an idea that was discussed and rejected in chapter 3.

Because that notion of content is deeply problematic, we have good reason to think that neither Prinz's nor any other naturalistic theory will be successful. And since I know of no other viable way of accounting for subpersonal content-bearing mental states, I am inclined to deny the existence of nonverbal beliefs. This leads me to conclude that "believing propositions," in the sense of apprehending them under intensional modes of presentation, is not the *fundamental* way in which we or other animals relate to worldly offerings. This being so, we can be certain that the infantile expectations that are violated in the kinds of experiments described above are not of the propositional sort; they are neither theoretically nor even conceptually grounded. These considerations supply a strong motive for preferring more modest interpretations and explanations of the relevant nonverbal data, wherever these are available.

Embodied Expectations

Nothing can be automatically inferred about what underwrites nonverbal expectations merely by establishing that they exist and determining their character.[8] There is a quite toothless, formalist, way of understanding nonverbal sensitivities to "domain-specific principles," one that carries no interesting implications about their psychosemantics or psychotectonics. For these principles may be nothing more than rules that nonverbals can be externally characterized as following. Their patterns of behavior may be predictively tractable (at least when they are operating in their normal environments), but this does not imply that such behavior is generated by manipulating rules and representations that incorporate the relevant norms (see Hutto 2005b). Their natural predispositions and developing tendencies, habits, biases, or preferences need not tell us anything interesting about the organism's underlying mental architecture or inner wiring.[9]

Neither whole organisms nor their lower-level devices follow rules in performing their duties—such rules are not internally or externally represented, consulted, mastered, or obeyed. It is rather that skillful activity is interpreted by us in such a way that makes it hard to resist thinking that certain organisms are following such rules. Once again, to borrow a thought from Dennett, the systematic responses of creatures cut wakes in the world. But if we say that these "real patterns" result from organisms obeying certain principles, then this is something that we do from our point of view and for our convenience. We should not make the mistake of supposing that, because of this, such creatures are in fact reasoning by means of the principles so described.[10]

At the very least it should be clear that representationalists and formalists have vastly different explanatory burdens and commitments. The representationalist needs to explain (1) how the principles in question get their constitutive contents; (2) how they are explicitly represented, albeit subpersonally; and (3) how they are consulted and applied. These are tall tasks—ones that are best avoided if at all possible. Achieving a manageable explanatory load directs us to use Ockham's razor as liberally as we can when it comes to interpreting the evidence of developmental and comparative psychology concerning nonverbal cognition.

Bearing this in mind, we can accept that animals and human infants do not come into the world empty-headed without assuming that their heads are full of theories or propositional knowledge. Although I reject his commitment to conceptualism, Prinz (2002, 218–219) is surely right in thinking that

it seems more likely that we have an innate similarity space that succeeds in carving things up at many of nature's joints, and that theoretical beliefs appear later to explain and refine these divisions. . . . Rather than say the mind is prepartitioned into theories, we can say it is prepartitioned into senses, which are attracted to particular kinds of stimuli. . . . The world is not a booming, buzzing confusion; it is an orderly network of entities interacting in systematic ways.

This insight lends itself to a nonconceptualist construal. Certainly, it is easy to see how sensory-based responding might go "all the way down" (but not all the way up) whereas, by way of contrast, it is not at all clear where to draw the line with respect to those nonverbal responses that are based on theory or knowledge and those that are not. Advocates of conceptualism are faced with a slippery-slope argument. After all, why shouldn't we suppose that even very simple creatures—such as humble marine snails (*Aplysia*)—harbor beliefs and conceptually based expectations? Despite being resistant to operant conditioning, they are apt test subjects for the habituation/dishabituation paradigm. They curl inward when first poked but cease to do so after a while if this is kept up. Yet a differential response can be elicited from them again if they are subjected to certain kinds of new stimuli, such as electric shocks. I am presuming that this kind of reaction is not something that anyone would be tempted to explain in terms of knowledge and belief. Why shouldn't the same verdict apply to other forms of online nonverbal responding, despite the fact that the patterns of response are sometimes much more sophisticated than those of sea snails?

Focusing on the case in point, there are good explanations of infantile sensitivities and expectant responding to intentional phenomena afoot that do not suppose it to be belief-based. Mirror neurons it seems are an adequate mechanism for initiating simple intentional recognition and response. They, unlike their cousins of the purely canonical variety, have a dual functionality; they fire when the goal-related actions of conspecifics are perceived (visually or audibly) and when the observer performs actions of the same type (Gallese et al. 1996; Gallese and Goldman 1998, 495). Famously, they were first discovered in macaque monkeys, for whom they enable the detection and strict matching of actions (in terms of both a goal—for example, grasping—and method for achieving it—for instance, precision grip). Their discovery provides an important insight into the mechanics behind the activity described by the old saying "monkey see, monkey do."

In nonhuman primates, these capacities have limited application. For example, the capacity to recognize an action in this way does not automatically confer a capacity to repeat or copy the action. The evolutionary pressures that wrought imitation systems from more basic mirror systems, it seems, were not operative in the ancestors we shared with these primates (Arbib 2005). Subsequent research has shown that there are mirror matching systems of various kinds; it has been speculated that these allow for a kind of shared manifold for acting and responding to the goal-directed actions of others that is present in the great apes and humans. But even in these cases the detection and response processes do not involve either inference or interpretation of any sort; they remain "immediate, automatic, and almost reflexlike" (Gallese 2005, 101). Although our primary modes of detection and response have this form, they can fuel complex, in some cases even recursively iterated, action coordination routines. Those of the inherited variety will have been tailored to serve specific needs of particular species. Those that are developed through learning and enculturation will be particular to individuals and communities.

For our purposes, what matters is that all these response systems are thoroughly embodied; they neither yield nor call on any conceptual understanding. They do not depend on having a capacity to represent the mental states of others, but only sponsor a reliable enough responsiveness to them. And the rub is that the neural systems that make this possible only take a special interest in those actions that are expected to be completed successfully. For example, a class of parietal mirror neurons have been discovered that fire during observation in a way that is "conditioned by the type of not yet observed subsequent act (for example, bringing the object to the mouth)" (Gallese 2006, 4). In specific contexts and in relation to specific actions these neurons are primed to discharge before the full motor sequence involved in completing an action is finished. We can conclude from this that although the response systems that enable primates to attend and respond to the intentional attitudes of others are relatively simple, they qualify as a kind of an "anticipatory mechanism" nonetheless.

Before saying more about the positive features of this proposal it will prove useful to distinguish it from certain other unprincipled accounts on the market. Nichols and Stich have postulated the existence of an Early Mindreading System (EMS), which is driven by the direct manipulation of mental-state representations and powered centrally by a practical reasoning mechanism that is supported by a crew of other specialized subpersonal mechanisms, such as a planner and updater (see figure 6.1).

This trio of mechanisms is assumed to be built into our cognitive hardware, having been put in place long before full-fledged or high-level mindreading capacities appeared on the scene.[11] Basic mindreading, on this account, is thought only to require the most minimal of conceptual understanding. Although early mindreaders are assumed to have beliefs, they are not thought to have mastered the concept of belief. It is the special kind of beliefs that they have and what they do with them that constitute their practical understanding of the concept of a goal.[12] For the EMS makes important use of second-order beliefs about the desires of others—that is, those that take the form of "X believes that Y wants P" (this is thought of as "Y wants P" occupying a place in X's belief box).[13]

The trouble with this proposal is that there are no representational contents of the right kind to make this account work, if we accept that nonverbal responding is not content-involving. As we saw in chapter 4, despite strong evidence that apes may be and hominids would have been capable of a kind of protological instrumental thinking, there are good reasons to suppose that this is driven by recreative imaginative abilities as opposed to the manipulation of propositional attitudes in practical reasoning. At

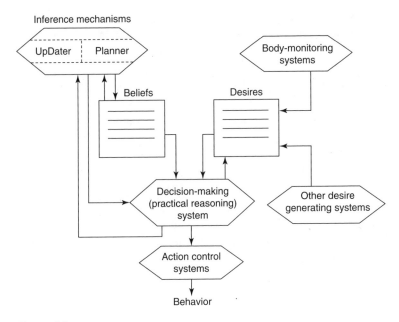

Figure 6.1
Basic Cognitive Architecture, including Updater and Planner (reprinted from S. Nichols and S. Stich, *Mindreading*, Oxford University Press, 61. Copyright © 2003. Used with permission from the editor of Oxford University Press).

best, basic mindreading might involve imagining nonpropositional goals, as expressed in the intentional attitudes of others. The Achilles' heel of the EMS is its commitment to intentional realism of the Basic Architectural Assumption.

Ultimately, the same verdict applies to Gordon's recent account of our basic capacity to recognize certain others as "agents like ourselves." His account is weaker in some ways than the EMS proposal, but it is still stronger than the sort of embodied proposal I have been promoting. It is particularly useful to compare the two accounts, since Gordon (2005) developed his precisely in order to clarify the "embodiment talk" of Gallese and others. His proposal is distinctive because he does not think basic engagements with others are a species of mindreading. For him, such processes occur without enlisting any mentalistic concepts at all (like me, he holds that such responsiveness is developmentally fundamental to the acquisition of such concepts).

Nevertheless, he talks of "interpreting" the behavior of others under the "same scheme" that makes his own behavior "intelligible" to him. This involves having practical, not declarative, knowledge of the "intentional scheme of reasons and purposes"—one that directly engages "productive processes such as practical reasoning, emotion formation and decision making" (p. 101). And this kind of understanding is meant to play a vital developmental role, for "this implicit recognition is crucial to understanding how we bootstrap ourselves into an explicit folk psychology. Bootstrapping is possible because intentional explanations in terms of reasons, purposes, and objects are at least implicitly mental" (p. 105). I am not entirely clear on what Gordon means by a nonconceptual but intelligible schema, but insofar as his account buys into the idea that implicit grasp of it rests on the manipulation of content-involving propositional attitudes, it suffers from precisely the same problem as the EMS proposal.[14]

In light of this we have reason to prefer Gallese's (2006) account of mutual intentional attunement, at least when it comes to understanding some of the basic mechanisms involved in the process of basic intersubjective responding. Confusingly, Gallese describes his account as a kind of embodied simulation. But this is surely a misnomer for at least two reasons. The process is not thought to involve a "conscious subject" that engages in any form of pretense. Neither the organisms nor their subsystems make any "as if" judgments about the contrasting mental states of self and other. Indeed, such responding is not voluntary. Thus if a defining characteristic of simulation is that it is a process in which one explicitly uses one's mental states as a model of those of the other, then it is clear that what happens at the neuronal level is not a *process* of this kind (see Gallagher 2007a; Gallagher and Hutto 2007). While this is not in dispute, it has been argued that there is a more generic understanding of simulation that would encompass the activity of resonance systems.[15] This may be so, but it does not touch the important point, which is that "embodied simulation" and simulation involving the manipulation of propositional attitudes are entirely different phenomena—so much so that embodied simulation cannot be thought of as an implicit form of the latter.

What matters is that in substance, if not in name, the account offered by Gallese and others looks to be along the right lines when it comes to understanding the mechanisms that underpin the nature of unprincipled, embodied infantile responding.[16] At base, it is always what others do that affects and moves us and vice versa. Importantly, this gets the direction of affection, characteristic of such interplays, the right way around—unlike projective varieties of simulation. Our primary reactions to others are not the result of our having first mentally projected ourselves in their minds or situations. Interpersonal responding is more direct and immediate than that. It should be understood in hot terms. Engaging with others brings about transformations that directly "exploit one's own motivational and emotional resources" (Gordon 1996, 11). This is most easily seen in cases of subliminal emotional contagion, motor mimicry, and goal emulation in which onlookers are literally altered in physiognomic and bodily ways.

To be so moved by another does not involve making any inferences or assumptions of analogy (not even implicit ones). My claim is that facts about our natural history ultimately account for these primitive ways of engaging with others; they explain why we are calibrated to them and vice versa.[17] In this light, incautious use of the "mindreading" metaphor, as is the habit of many of today's behavioral ecologists and developmental psychologists, is unfortunate on several levels.[18]

Nonverbal acts of intersubjective responding are not prosecuted by the deployment of theory, inferential reasoning, or projective simulation. We can be sure of this because no ascriptions are made to others on the basis of their observed behavior—there is no need to bridge an imagined gap between self and other; indeed the very idea of such a gap existing at this level is problematic (see Hutto 2002, 2006b). Emotional interplay, imitation, motor mimicry, and even more sophisticated contrastive forms of emotional responding are better explained in terms of unprincipled, embodied reactions.[19] Indeed, they had better be if nonverbal responding is not grounded in inferential thought, of the theoretical or practical varieties.

Basic one-to-one intersubjective interactions of social animals (including much normal adult interaction) are not accomplished by bringing any psychological or behavioral principles to bear. Such encounters are not rightly characterized as involving analogical comparisons with others or the neutral observation of outward behavior followed by cold inferences that the other is in such-and-such an inner mental state. Rather we react directly to the attitudes of others as expressed bodily and we do so because of our natural predispositions, some of which get reformed by experience and enculturation. It cannot be stressed enough that on this model the intervening cognition that makes this possible is not fueled by representations of the behavioral or mental states of others.

Those sympathetic to this sort of view are inclined to claim that what is being read in such cases is the expressions of others, not their minds. Thus in explicating his own account of such embodied practices Gallagher (2001, 90) has encouraged use of the lingo of "body reading." While this is a step in the right direction, it is misleading in two respects. First, continued use of the "reading" metaphor is unfortunate. It retains intellectual connotations that misrepresent what goes on in basic intersubjective responding, which involves no interpretative processes at any level. Second, although sensitivity to the bodily expressions of others initiates our reactions, we must not forget that these are, in normal circumstances, direct reactions to the distress, growing anger, or sexual interest and intentional attitudes of others. Although they are not *reading* minds, participants in intersubjective encounters are immediately *responsive* to "other minds" nonetheless.

In such encounters natural signs—the expressions of others—serve as reliable enough guides to "other minds," at least in historically normal conditions. Given this feature of my account, Goldie (2006) has queried if my proposal about unprincipled engagements is not best construed in terms of direct noninferential perceptual knowledge, because this might be a way of avoiding use of the metaphor of transformation altogether. Yet it is not just intentional directedness and informational sensitivity that matter; we must also always consider the other half of the equation—that is, the way such signs are consumed by organisms. We must give appropriate attention to the imperative as well as the indicative aspects—in other words, to the organism's appropriate response patterns. With this in mind, it is more correct to say that we are directly moved by another's psychological situation rather than that we directly perceive it (or at least where the latter is heard in the way supporters of a model of passive perception hear it). This view is, of course, perfectly consistent with the fact that some social animals can learn to control their emotional expressions by inhibiting them or even sending false signals. It is just that these are secondary developments. As Wittgenstein (1992, 35e) observed, "One can say 'He is hiding his feelings.' But that means that it is not a priori they are always hidden."

Basic organismic capacities for recognition and response to agency, emotions, and goals can be best, and most parsimoniously, explained sans theory, sans principles, sans propositional attitudes. We can be certain that folk psychological abilities operating tacitly do not feature in our ground-floor acts of interpersonal navigation and social coordination.[20] In interacting with others by attending to their intentional and affective attitudes, neither organisms nor their internal parts are engaging in "acts of interpretation." During such engagements there is no processing of contentful informational inputs that are manipulated by inferencelike processes and thus transformed to yield representations in the form of mentalistic predictions and explanations as output.

Such encounters only foster embodied expectations, expectations that are cued by the perception of the other's expressive behavior. The visceral patterns of response to which these expectations give rise are best understood as affect programs of the sort discussed in chapter 3.[21] Unprincipled intersubjective engagements are in this way based on sensitivity to a special class of natural signs that engender interaction routines constituting other-directed responding. These recognition and response patterns can be understood in terms of biosemiotic proper functions, obviating the need to think of them as dependent on the manipulation of any content-involving inner representations or subpersonal processes of inferential thought.

Intersubjective Interaction without Mindreading

The essential idea of my proposal is that both infants and adults are directly responsive to the psychological situation of others because they are informationally sensitive to a special class of natural signs—the expressions of intentional and affective attitudes, as revealed in another's gaze, gesture, facial comportment, and so on. In one-to-one encounters of this sort participants embody intentional attitudes that are directed toward the intentional attitudes of others. To understand this proposal, it is important to recall that intentionality is not a property of functionally specified internal or inner "mental states"; only whole organisms and their coordinated efforts exhibit it. Intentionality and affect are therefore expressed by the way organisms carry themselves. As Gómez (1998, 89–90) once proposed, "The perception of X attending to O is almost the prototype or skeleton of a propositional attitude, except that there is no proposition (just a physical agent) and the attitude may, literally, be a position of the body or a direction of the eyes, accompanied or not by facial and vocal expressions."

Building on the observations about intentionality discussed in chapter 3, let us call the response patterns to which intersubjective engagements give rise Interaction Coordination Routines (ICRs). These can be thought of as a subspecies of action coordination routines, ones having the proper functions of exploiting particular kinds of social affordance (see Costall 1995).

My claim is that the basic routines and mechanisms for intersubjective engagement have been fashioned in evolutionary time, through extended bouts of tinkering and adjustment. Thus we can expect that those of any existing species will have been shaped in response to their quite specific needs. Such developments will have been vital for creatures whose chances for reproductive success depended in important ways on their methods and style of dealing with others.[22] Social skills matter, not just for obtaining basic resources, as in predator/prey battles, but also for mastering the art of group living and deciding the outcomes of sexual competitions.

Certainly, some great-ape species have interesting intersubjective abilities. Chimpanzees, for example, are not only adept at gaze monitoring, but they have also shown a limited sensitivity to the visual access of conspecifics, at least in certain circumstances. For example, in one experimental setup chimps were confronted with a human experimenter whose gaze was fixed in a specific direction but whose line of sight was blocked by an opaque barrier that was located between the human and the chimp (Povinelli and Eddy 1996a). Under these conditions chimps reliably move forward to check behind the barrier, apparently in order to discover what it is that the experimenter is looking at. This suggests they have some understanding of visual access.

That they do has been confirmed, more dramatically, in a series of experiments designed to achieve ecological validity that have been conducted by Call, Hare, and Tomasello (see Hare, Call, and Tomasello 2001; Tomasello, Call, and Hare 2003a, 2003b). The basic structure of the experiments was simple. Two apes, a subordinate and a dominant, were placed in opposite but facing rooms that adjoined a third. Food was baited in the central chamber and doors were used to control the chimps' access, visual and otherwise, to it (see figure 6.2). During the food contests involved in the tests, the subordinate was given certain advantages over the dominant in order to better reveal if they had some native grasp of what another can

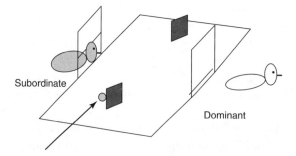

Figure 6.2
Experimental Setup in Food Competition Experiments (reprinted from J. Call, "Chimpanzee Social Cognition," *Trends in Cognitive Science*, 5, no. 9; 388–393. Copyright © 2001. Used with permission from Elsevier).

and cannot see. This was done by allowing subordinates to see that food had been placed on their side of opaque barriers.

Perhaps unsurprisingly, subordinates showed a significant preference for those pieces of food that were shielded from the dominant's sight, but this tendency vanished when transparent barriers were used. Given that these animals had no previous experience with the proprieties of transparent objects, the results seem to confirm those of the other study—that the apes have some implicit grasp of what can and cannot be seen.[23]

At most, these performances only reveal a limited ability to respond to the psychological attitudes of others. Chimp performances fall decidedly short of a full grasp of attention, visual perspective, prior intentions, communicative intentions, and beliefs. The fact is that these animals are only sensitive to the intentional attitudes of their conspecifics *under certain conditions*. The emphasized qualification is important. The empirical findings concerning their intersubjective skills are "decidedly mixed" (Call and Tomasello 2005, 61).

Another series of controlled tests, replicated by various laboratories, has revealed that chimpanzees have no natural proclivity to use the direction of gaze of cooperative human experimenters to aid them in food-location tasks. In one such study, not a single chimpanzee exploited the fact that a human was staring continuously at the place in which food was hidden as a means of acquiring it (Call, Hare, and Tomasello 1998).[24] Over a dozen other experiments have revealed even more fundamental limitations in chimpanzee responsiveness to the perceptual access of others (see Povinelli and Eddy 1996b). In the test conditions two human experimenters, both with access to food rewards, were placed behind Plexiglas sheets. These had suitably positioned holes to allow the chimpanzees to insert their arms so as to make begging gestures for the receipt of food. However, matters were complicated by the fact that only some of the humans were in a position to see and thus honor these requests. In the trials, some humans had their eyes covered by their hands, while others wore blindfolds or buckets over their heads. Initially, the chimps employed their begging gestures quite indiscriminately. And although they quickly modified their routines, it was successfully shown that this was the result of trial-and-error learning as opposed to any inherent grasp of the concept of seeing per se.[25] In this respect, chimpanzee performances compared poorly with those of human children between the ages of two and four years.

In all, chimpanzees exhibit a limited responsiveness to the perceptual access of certain others based on their sensitivity to what those certain others can and cannot see. These intersubjective abilities are most clearly exhibited when they are dealing with conspecifics in particular competitive situations—that is, those that mimic ecologically familiar contests over food or other resources.[26] Not only are their capacities in this regard significantly circumscribed, it appears they do not travel well. They cannot readily extend their "understanding" of seeing to apply to just any targets in any old context.[27]

A plausible explanation of these findings is that the mentalistic responsiveness of chimpanzees breaks down, partially or completely, in predictable ways when they are faced with tasks that require them to respond in ways that vary from the sort of engagements that would have been typical of those characteristic of their ancestral environments. And to the extent that they manage to cope with these at all, it is because of significant supplementary trial-and-error learning.

For biosemioticists, this is not at all surprising. Naturally evolved systems of detection and response are only effective in particular contexts—that is, ecologically normal conditions. This is a consequence of the design constraints placed on Mother Nature: she seeks workable solutions to pressing local problems as opposed to all-purpose ways of dealing with quite general ones. And it is not just that creatures are well adapted to operate in particular environments, these environments are themselves often a crucial resource that makes the successful exercise of their cognitive abilities possible (Clark 1989). It should be expected that creatures that rely on inherited response systems perform poorly when in abnormal surroundings. In such circumstances, their abilities will be incapacitated, partially if not entirely. They can be expected to do poorly when they "play away from home"—for example, in those cases when they attempt to apply their stereotypical patterns of response in the face of novel challenges or challengers.

Here again, we should resist the familiar tendency to assume that chimps must be operating with *some* unique concept of seeing, albeit one quite unlike those used by human infants and adults (see Andrews 2005, 2007). It might be imagined, for example, that the chimpanzee concept only applies to some extent at some times and with respect to some targets. I have already given my reasons for wanting to resist this familiar move. Certainly, any concept with the profile described above would be in violation of the generality constraint—which is normally taken to be a minimal requirement for concept possession *tout court*. This alone provides grounds for thinking that basic responsiveness to the seeing of others is not likely to be conceptually based or to constitute a manifestation of conceptual understanding.

Rather than watering down what it is to have a truly conceptual under-standing by making adjustments, in an ad hoc way, in order to accommo-date certain ill-motivated cognitivist tendencies, I hold that there is more mileage (and ultimately less confusion) if we recognize that nonverbal intersubjective sensitivities are not content-involving. They are nontheo-retical, unprincipled, downright nonconceptual, and embodied. Chimps are neither making judgments about nor representing the states of mind of others. A fortiori they are not representing and reasoning about such things using behavioral or weak mentalistic concepts and theories. Instead, they are—in an extremely prescribed way—directly responsive to the intentional attitudes expressed in embodied ways by means of telltale signs. Close scrutiny of the chimpanzee behavioral repertoire reveals nothing to per-suade us that these animals are mindreaders of any kind at all.

It will be correctly observed that human beings are not great apes. It cannot be assumed that the way our closest living relatives get by in their interactions with others provides any direct insight into our ways of doing the same. It must be remembered that "members of other species are not, after all, immature adult humans" (Povinelli and Vonk 2004, 19). Indeed, the performances of chimpanzees and preverbal human infants, in this regard, suggest that there have been significant downstream evolutionary adjustments and additions to the primary modes of human social respond-ing during the six million years or so that separated our lineage from that of the simians.

Nevertheless, the same general verdicts hold about the nonconceptual, embodied nature of intersubjective responding in both cases. Humans too come equipped as standard with a battery of mechanisms and routines that dictate our sensitivities and constrain the basic form of our initial unprin-cipled interpersonal engagements. A crucial difference is that the native forms of human responding are not just more sophisticated, they are much more open-ended and flexible. This is best explained by the fact that we have benefited from a hominid capacity for recreative imagination, as dis-cussed in chapter 4. This will have served as the fount of powerful mimetic skills, a topic that will be addressed further in chapter 11. For now, it suf-fices to note the plausibility of the claim that "by 'parachuting' a domain-general device of this power on top of the primate motor hierarchy, previously stereotyped emotional expressions would have become rehearsable, refinable, and employable in intentional communication" (Donald 1999, 147).

Increased imaginative and imitative abilities would have yielded vastly more flexible and malleable modes of intersubjective interaction than witnessed in any other species—indeed this looks like the best explanation of the wide range and variety of response forms we find elaborated in modern humans. This will have opened up the range of possibilities for expression and response enormously, complicating everyday social dynamics no end.

Because much human interpersonal responding calls so heavily on imitative capacities it is, by its very nature, reciprocal. Although individual patterns of interpersonal responding are largely shaped by unique learning histories, an infant's tendencies in this regard are open to strong influence by others. To understand this process, we must not underestimate the importance of the support given by caregivers, who act as "parental scaffolds" (see Bruner 1983). Young infants are powerfully influenced by such encounters not only, for example, because they are natively predisposed to focusing selectively on human faces, voices, and gestures of the sort that make possible their first protoconversational exchanges, they also imitate these gestures. And their caregivers, in turn, imitate the infants' attempts at imitation (often in exaggerated ways), and so on. Normally developing children are thus naturally receptive to being molded in the manner of their responses in line with unspoken local habits. It is through such repeated acts of mutual imitation that children begin to take on a norm-governed second nature, one initially imparted by their caregivers, peers, and local communities (see McGeer 2007). This is, of course, counterbalanced by the strength of their personalities and preferences, which continue to shine through in their one-to-one interactions. The point is that despite this elaborated complexity, the general principle holds; these basic social interactions remain unprincipled and embodied.

Let me be clear about the scope of this claim. In their later years, children start to find their own voices about how they should respond to others. This occurs only after they have mastered the capacity to reflect on and make explicit judgments about such matters (if they are given the opportunity to do so). Such reflection can result in a deliberate modification of their interpersonal styles and strategies, either in general or those used with particular others. Human beings are uniquely privileged in being able to achieve this kind of self-control, for we alone can treat our own and others' patterns of intersubjective responding as objects of attention and mature reflection in their own right. Doing so makes it possible to rescript our response tendencies (or at least some of them) in important ways (see Hutto 2006d).

Hence, although I have argued against the idea that inferential reasoning processes are involved in primary nonverbal intersubjective engagements, I do not deny that it is possible for linguistically competent children and adults to acquire and use propositional knowledge about such patterns of interaction to reshape them. For adult human beings these ways of engaging with others exist side by side with our more native modes of embodied engagement. For this reason, there is no straightforward or clear-cut way of deciding which strategy is being deployed in any particular case. Yet, acknowledging this is wholly consistent with the claim that basic intersubjective engagements, even those of linguistically accomplished humans, are not grounded in propositional judgments. Such interactions do not yield declarative knowledge (at least not in any direct or automatic way since this is not their biological proper function). For these reasons, we should be careful that unguarded talk of "perceptual knowledge" does not mislead on this score. And the same applies, mutatis mutandis, to talk of knowing communications when it comes to understanding basic expressive acts (see Hutto 2006f).

Our embodied routines and habits kick in without any background thought. This would explain why, unless we rein ourselves in, we are irresistibly moved to react to agency, animacy, and emotional expression—even when we are in possession of the knowledge that no agency is present. In such cases, we cannot help but "see" it as being there. For example, experiments have shown that if a series of illuminated dots or suitably animated geometric figures are made to move in a certain manner this provokes characteristic responses from us—responses that, at a basic level, are of the same sort as those evoked in encounters with genuine agents (Heider and Simmel 1944; for a related discussion see McGeer 2007). The way we respond to such things is on a par with the way we react to certain perceptual illusions, the Müller-Lyer illusion being perhaps the most famous (a version of it is reproduced in figure 6.3). When confronted with this

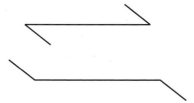

Figure 6.3
A Version of the Müller-Lyer Illusion (from D. D. Hutto, *The Presence of Mind*, John Benjamins. Copyright © 1999. Used with kind permission from John Benjamins Publishing Company, Amsterdam/Philadelphia, www.benjamins.com).

visual illusion, what we see is that the lines look to be different lengths, but in fact they are the same length. And as with our perception of agency, the effect persists even after we know this—that is, one of the lines still looks longer.

Recognition of these parallels has prompted some to posit the existence of non–folk psychological Social Intelligence Modules (Currie and Sterelny 2000). These are imagined to be second-order modules that take in representational inputs from other modules of a more basic perceptual variety. They are thought to specifically target social scenes, yielding "intentional markers," which are understood to be representations carrying informational content of the kind required to govern basic social coordination. Examples of such markers are "means me harm," "is friendly," or "is angry." Although I deny the existence of modules, for reasons discussed in chapter 3, I am prepared to accept that some embodied responding may be driven by hardwired mechanisms that function somewhat like modules. What I resist is the idea that such mechanisms would trade in informational contents or that they would produce subdoxastic representations. Rather, they would be indexically prompted, inspiring interactions with others of the sort that would be appropriate if the other "means me harm," "is friendly," or "is angry" (these reactions would be initiated because they would have been selected for in the historically normal environments of the organisms in question).

The fact that some basic intersubjective responses have this characteristic is surely a good thing. Karmiloff-Smith's assessment, although originally supplied to emphasize a key virtue of modules, applies equally well to such fixed modes of embodied responding. We can think of these hard-to-resist tendencies as "the stupidity in the machine": "They are just what a young organism might need to get initial cognition off the ground speedily and efficiently" (Karmiloff-Smith 1995, 3). That said, while *some* rudimentary responses may be reflexlike in this way, the emerging patterns of individual one-to-one engagements are not rigidly preprogrammed. The right way to understand this is to note that even the most baroque forms of interpersonal responding found in humans depend on our having a fixed set of sensitivities to target the intentional attitudes and goal-related behavior of others.

The most important thing to note, for our purposes, is that such responding is not content-involving; it is not an intellectually governed activity involving rules and representations. No matter how complex such interactions become, we must not lose sight of the fact that they are based on reactions to the intentional and affective attitudes as perceived via their expressions and responses. Thus although the study of chimpanzees may at best tell us only very little about the human case, it seems safe to conclude that simian intersubjective capacities are on the same general level as that of preverbal human infants—that is, both have an unprincipled, embodied basis.

The profiles of infantile interpersonal responsiveness bear all the hallmarks of being nonconceptual. They are highly focused and limited in crucial respects. For example, six-month-old infants can attend to and remember an actor's goals, but not the means used when trying to achieve them (Woodward, Sommerville, and Guajardo 2001; see also Wellman and Phillips 2001). And these responses are only prompted by certain kinds of triggers—for example, the signature actions of humans as opposed to the qualitatively different movements of mechanical artifacts (or certain kinds of action in certain kinds of contexts, such as grasping but not other types of self-propelled motion). Arguably, even low-level detection mechanisms with robust tracking functions could fulfill the purposes of detecting and initiating the appropriate response routines to the outward signs of goal-directed actions (Baird and Baldwin 2001).

Similarly, there is no need to posit any conceptual understanding on the part of infants in order to explain how they successfully parse the behavior stream at its mentalistic joints. Furthermore, infantile reactions like those of chimpanzees do not extend into a wider conceptual space. Although they prompt complex responding they do not imply the infants are making any inference about other minds using concepts such as "goals," "desires," "emotions," and so on. Indeed, the way infantile sensitivity to goal-related actions unfolds and augments over time lends itself to an explanation in terms of a series of mechanical upgrades that give the impression of ontogeny recapitulating phylogeny. This is to be expected if their basic detection mechanisms are in fact well-worn hand-me-downs. We should not conclude from this that embodied responding is simply mechanical or reflexive for, in line with the biosemiotic proposal, these mechanisms have been forged with the purpose of targeting specific kinds of psychological phenomena.[28]

Nonlinguistic Joint Attention

With these lessons in hand, in closing I want to focus on the most sophisticated form of nonverbal intersubjective engagement—the capacity of human infants of around one year to attend jointly with others. This involves participants not only attending to the same objects at the same time; it also requires that they mutually recognize that their attending has a common focus—that they both attend to one another's attending to one another and some worldly point of interest. Intersubjective interactions of this kind are thus of a quite different order from more mirror-like forms of reciprocal imitation. The capacity builds on the uniquely human capacities for declarative pointing, social referencing, and, as will become clear momentarily, imaginative perspective shifting.[29]

Typically the scene is set for such engagements when one or another of the participants draws attention to some object or feature in the local environment, using the sort of strategies familiar to children once they have learnt to point declaratively, at around nine to twelve months (Tomasello 2003). Gaze monitoring, "checking back," and other social-referencing techniques are then used to ensure that the communicative triangle has been established and that it is maintained. In this way, joint attention involves attending not just to the object of the other's interest but also to "the intention behind the behavior (yet without entertaining higher order thoughts about it)" (Brinck 2004, 196).

If we focus on this aspect of the phenomenon it might be assumed that it requires making some kind of simulative leap. Simulation is often presented as a kind of imaginative attempt to adopt another's perspective on events, a coming to see how the world looks from the other's perspective. It is as if I had climbed in behind your eyes, while at the same time recognizing that I am not you. But there are problems even for defenders of simulation theory, such as Gordon, who only invoke a first-person "transformational" as opposed to a "projective" version of the theory. For, unless such acts of simulation are assumed to take place within a context in which the simulators are somehow already independently aware that the other in question has a different point of view, the heuristic would be an utterly hopeless means of getting to grips with the perspective of others; at best it would be a means of becoming the other while losing one's sense of self (see also Gallagher 2007a). Joint attention requires both identification and recognition of difference (Hobson 2007); it involves having the experience of acting in and attending to a shared world, alongside others—in response to public objects. This is quite different from the experience of identifying with others or of merely acting on the world in response to objects.

In such nonverbal engagements I see what the other is attending to, I see that they are attending to it, and I see that they are attending to my attending to both the object and to my attending. Only in this way is the object recognized as a common focal point. The mechanisms that underpin the mutual connectedness that enables identification and common focus are likely best explained by the mirror-system hypothesis. Interestingly, key elements of the human mirror neuron system for grasping are found in Broca's area—an area of the brain that relates to language comprehension. This has inspired researchers to speculate that there may be interesting, possibly quite tight, connections between this kind of intentional attunement and basic lexicon-forming abilities (Rizolatti and Arbib 1998; Billard and Arbib 2002; Arbib 2005). For example, Arbib (2005) suggests that this part of the brain evolved on top of those implicated in more basic modes of intersubjective engagement precisely because it once subserved a manual, gesture-based form of communication that he calls "protosign." It is plausible that resonance systems of this kind may have played a pivotal role in enabling humans to enjoy a shared world and develop a common language for describing it. Ultimately, the intentional attunements they subserve may be the basis for the "parity" between speakers and hearers that enable first communions (Arbib 2003, 2005; Heiser, et al. 2003).[30] These lines of research are especially attractive given the important link between joint attention and word learning. I say more about this in chapter 11.

Yet, as noted above, to jointly attend requires more than mere identification. It also requires being able to see the other as other. This fact can make it look as if such triangulation must be in debt to the services of some kind of inference-based ToM abilities, of the TT or ST sort. To attend to the other's perceptual take in the appropriate way can certainly seem to require a capacity for conceptually distinguishing between self and other, and indeed for making "inferences from me to you" based on assumptions of similarity by some means. Characterized in this way, joint attention might be thought to implicate full-fledged mindreading abilities involving propositional attitudes. But it ain't necessarily so. As always, there are richer and leaner interpretations, even when it comes to making sense of what is perhaps the most sophisticated form of nonverbal intersubjectivity (Carpendale and Lewis 2004).

There is little doubt that joint attention depends on having a multitasking ability to shift one's perspective across distinct axes—focusing, at different moments, on the common focal point; on the other's attention to the same; and also on the other's attending to one's own attending. It is quite plausible that such interactions therefore call on recreative imaginative perspective-shifting capacities. But these should not be confused with mindreading activity of the folk psychological sort. As those who have done the most to explicate their nature make clear, they are nonpropositional and nonsimulative (Currie and Ravenscroft 2003, 96). Seeing another's seeing (whether directed at the world or at my own seeing) does not involve representing the other's *cognitive* take on things, it only involves imagining their *perceptual* ones. If this is right even the most sophisticated form of nonverbal intersubjective engagement does not involve the manipulation or attribution of propositional attitudes.

Although much more needs to be said to make sense of this phenomenon, it should be clear that we need appeal to nothing more than capacities for intentional attunement and recreative imagination in order to explain prelinguistic joint attention. Most importantly, such acts do not require their participants to make full-fledged propositional attitude ascriptions. Indeed, for the reasons cited in the opening section of this chapter, this could not be the case. Infantile forms of attending to the attending of others cannot be explicated in terms of metarepresentational understanding, if the requisite understanding is only operative at a later stage. We have little choice but to conclude that nonverbal acts of joint attention are only based in responsiveness to intentional attitudes—not propositional ones. Infantile capacities to identify and respond to enacted intentions are quite distinct from the understanding of intentions that rests on having mastered the concepts of desire and belief (and how these propositional attitudes interrelate in explaining intentional actions).

Understanding our primary modes of intersubjective engagement in nonconceptual and embodied ways has important advantages. If we start from this base it is possible to explain, in a rather straightforward manner, how it is that children get a first handle on genuine, content-involving, propositional attitudes. The next chapter will seek to make good on this claim.

7 Getting a Grip on the Attitudes

There is no sense in being anything but practical.
—Ernest Hemingway, *The Old Man and the Sea*

Ability Profiling

Having a grasp of the core propositional attitudes is indisputably a non-negotiable attribute of practicing folk psychologists. The NPH makes no offer to explain how children come into possession of such understanding prior to their acquisition of folk psychological skills. It simply assumes that the basic components needed for playing the understanding-reasons game are mastered in advance. This claim is surely in good empirical standing; the evidence suggests that knowledge of the attitudes is acquired in a punctuated way during early childhood. Three major moments have been identified:

Children's understanding progresses through at least three phases: an early desire psychology, based on non-representational mental state constructs such as simple desires; a transitional desire-belief psychology, in which desires continue to dominate causal-explanatory reasoning despite the existence of an auxiliary concept of belief; and a belief-desire psychology akin to adult understanding. (Bartsch and Wellman 1995, 206)

Typically, these sorts of developments are characterized by talk of the child's growing mastery of "mentalistic concepts." This is, however, less than helpful, because the standard models of what this involves are less than adequate. I say why in greater detail in chapters 8 and 9. In this chapter I try to provide my own account of the form such understanding takes and the stages of its development. Before doing so it is important for me to say what I take it that concepts—at least the mentalistic ones—are *not*. They are not symbols-in-the-head acquired by a kind of "locking-on" process. Nor are they scientific constructs, fashioned through dynamic—but rationally constrained—theory development. Nor are they objects of introspective attention, distinguished by their distinctive qualitative features.

In the place of these favorites I do not offer an alternative theory of concepts or of concept possession, but a general recommendation: to understand what it is to "have" a concept one must ask what kind of abilities someone would have to have in order to satisfy the criteria for practical mastery of said concept. Crucially in order to understand this proposal, abilities must not be confused with mere dispositions.[1]

Let me be clear about what motivates this move. Historically, philosophers have tended to be rather stringent in their demands about concept possession; traditionalists insist, for example, that it requires knowing (if only implicitly) the defining criteria in virtue of which something can be said to belong to a particular extension; to possess the concept of X one must know the necessary and sufficient conditions for being an X. The idea is that dictionarylike knowledge, if not that of the encyclopedic variety, is needed in order to classify and identify kinds correctly. This presumes, of course, that one also has yet more basic, reliable means of telling when something has the right set of properties for kind membership.

Thus to avoid certain standard confusions, it is important to cleanly distinguish

• What a given concept term designates—that is, its worldly extensions
• The nature of individual conceptions relating to those terms (for example, the patterns of judgments one is inclined to make about the topic in question)
• The means or identifying procedures used to determine whether some item belongs in the relevant extension class

Furthermore, there is the question of the skills required for exercising mastery of a conceptual term. These will involve, inter alia, knowing which inferences one is entitled to make when wielding it. In this regard, it is crucial to note that having a basic mastery of a concept need not require an ability to make inferences about its subject matter; it may only imply a capacity to make inferences of other sorts that effectively demonstrate an understanding of a concept. When we say that children have a grasp of the mentalistic concepts, it is really only the latter we are concerned with. It is not that they are able to make many if any inferences about desires and beliefs, but that they can use their understanding of these concepts to make relevant attributions to others, and so on. Certainly, they cannot be said to possess these concepts if we accept the idealized philosophical specifications of what this involves. Typically, developmental psychologists are content to say that child has "a grasp" of a given concept, perhaps a tentative one, if they are able to do certain types of things.

Making this our focus, we can specify what a child's command of any particular concept comes to in terms of the mastery of certain abilities.[2] Relatedly, we can expect that conceptual understanding deepens as a direct function of improved mastery of existing abilities and as new abilities emerge. Furthermore, we can interrogate the basis of any given ability by specifying what underwrites and fosters it. Investigations of this type yield unique "ability profiles" for concept mastery—detailing the conditions required for acquisition, in terms of

• Prerequisite basic abilities/capacities (these might be nonconceptual or conceptual)
• Special supports or cognitive tools that subtend or extend the relevant abilities (for example, material or linguistic constructions)
• Engendering or enabling activities or practices (for instance, parental scaffolding, sociocultural institutions)

Seen in this light, the staged development of the child's linguistically grounded mentalistic understanding is best characterized in terms of children extending and expanding on their embodied practical abilities and skills (not imagined theoretical ones). This is a gradual process. In the next section, capitalizing on the preparatory work of the previous four chapters, I will try to say briefly what it amounts to with respect to how young children get their first grip on the central propositional attitudes, desire and belief.

Linguistically Extended Abilities

Learning how to ascribe propositional attitudes to others is a major step beyond anticipating and becoming attuned to their responses in embodied ways, that are characteristic of how preverbal infants navigate the landscape of social interaction. Children come by this capacity slowly, developing new abilities by mastering certain cognitive tools and exercising these tools in the context of new kinds of practice. Their growing command of language and its internally structured constructions make this possible.

As argued in the previous chapter, young infants attend and respond appropriately to the intentional attitudes of others (e.g., their preferences and goals, which are expressed as intentions-in-action). What changes in the course of their preschool development is that they also become conversant with the use of linguistic signs.[3] This enables them to understand the objects of intentional attitudes in important new, content-involving ways. For example, words—and eventually whole sentences—serve as replacement ways of representing desired items; they allow children to say what it is that someone desires in ways that are unavailable to those restricted exclusively to embodied modes of interpersonal responding.

Calling on their growing command of linguistic forms, children are thus able to make ascriptions about what another wants using symbols to designate the objects in question.[4] As one might expect, children's abilities in this regard develop in tandem with their mastery of particular linguistic constructions. Different constructions are used to ascribe (1) desires for objects, (2) desires that specific actions should be performed, and (3) desires that certain states of affairs should obtain. Thus making attributions such as "Mommy wants ice cream" are of a different form from those that incorporate infinite complements, such as "Mommy wants to go upstairs." Both of these differ from the use of finite complement clauses, such as "Mommy wants that Emerson should go to school." Typically, the last of these—attributions of the full-blown propositional or situational variety—come late in the day and it is not clear how frequently or readily such constructions are used.[5]

The point is that in all of these cases the relevant linguistic constructions serve as new modes of expression and as the basis for more sophisticated, content-mediated forms of attention and joint attention. They are the key points of interest in the simplest kinds of conversational interchanges, which are typically caregiver-led. They provide the basic currency that enables children to say what it is that they want and equally for discussing what parents, siblings, and others want (or even for parents to tell children what it is that they want—see McGeer 2007). As such, these linguistically scaffolded abilities set the stage for social dramas of an entirely different order than those that characterize purely embodied forms of interaction.[6]

By the linguistic route, children come to recognize, in a very particular way, that others may want things that are currently out of sight or temporarily beyond reach. And, as one might expect, this engenders new and more sophisticated kinds of intersubjective expectations—expectations of an inferentially mediated kind. Thus young children in command of these abilities are able to make simple desire-based predictions, albeit of a low-level sort. For example, they are able to reason about what others are likely to do if their desires are fulfilled, frustrated, or merely satisficed (as opposed to properly satisfied).[7]

In light of the discussion of previous chapters, it should be clear that these new methods of representing and understanding the objects of intentional attitudes—that is, eventually coming to understand them as content-involving *propositional* attitudes—are, in an important and clear sense, a natural outgrowth of more rudimentary embodied activity. In other words, to borrow from Hobson (2006), the attitude of "wanting" is already familiar.

Some have claimed that an understanding of desires as propositional attitudes constitutes more than an ability to represent a new kind of mediating focus for intentional attitudes; it is in fact a form of metarepresentational ability because children must represent the other's perspectives on such situations as well (Goldman 2001; Leslie, Friedman, and German 2004; Nichols and Stich 2003). But this looks ill-motivated. Even the most sophisticated case (that of understanding desires-as–propositional attitudes) does not imply having an understanding of divergent cognitive perspectives. Recognizing this is important if we are to honor the notable differences in our understanding of concepts of desire and belief in the traditional way.

Here it is important to note that although the two-year-old capacity to attribute desires is impressive, it falls short of the kind of understanding of other perspectives required to recognize the possibility that another may have a false belief (that is, that some part of the world may not in fact be as another or oneself takes it to be). It is easier to grasp that the other wants something that you do not and even that they want some counterfactual situation to obtain (using a linguistic object to describe the desired non-actual state of affairs) than it is to imagine that the other thinks that a state of affairs obtains when it appears not to or vice versa (at least from the attributer's point of view). Or, put another way, psychological dramas concerning others' desires typically unfold within a single epistemic purview, whereas those involving full-fledged metarepresentational attitudes—that is, beliefs—require one to make leaps of imagination between alternative cognitive perspectives.[8]

Confusion on this score can be alleviated if it is acknowledged that a certain linguistic facility with sophisticated syntax and semantics is necessary, inter alia, for making propositional attitude ascriptions (those that take propostions as the object of *that*-clauses) but is insufficient for making metarepresentational attributions.[9] This is because different types of psychological attitudes can attach to *that*-clauses. Hence, understanding the complex states of minds that are propositional attitudes requires coming to grips with the quite distinctive ways each type of attitude operates. It is no accident that philosophers, for example, appeal to "satisfaction" when it comes to explicating the concept of desire and appeal to the notion of "aiming at truth" when it comes to understanding that of belief. Classically, this is why the desires are said to exhibit a mind-world direction of fit and beliefs exhibit a world-mind direction of fit.

It goes without saying that being able to understand a desire as a full-fledged *propositional* attitude implies a capacity to understand truth-conditional semantic contents. But having this capacity does not entail an understanding of what it is to "aim at truth," which is the sort needed to imagine that one might have contingently true beliefs about the state of the world. By the age of two, children are normally able to produce and respond to simple sentences in short interchanges, but they show no signs of comprehending attributions of knowledge and thought at this point. This changes over time: "Right before the third birthday . . . genuine reference to the mental states of thinking, believing, and knowing appear[s]" (Bartsch and Wellman 1995, 64).[10] Moreover, even once they begin to use these terms appropriately, that use reveals that children start with a grasp of contrasts between ignorance-fact, fiction-reality, and, only later, belief–false belief. The point is that each of these ways of understanding "knowing" states of mind is quite distinct.

For example, knowing of another that they do or do not know that a certain state of affairs obtains does not implicate an understanding of the belief–false belief contrast. When they first start to attribute ignorance and knowledge, children are, in effect, treating others as indicators (reliable or otherwise) about the state of worldly affairs; they are not thought of as claimants or believers. A child may note that "Mommy knows/thinks that Alex is hiding." Yet, even though epistemic verbs feature in the attribution, it does not follow that she therefore possesses a belief-based understanding of the knowledge in question. As discussed in the previous chapter, taken at face value, the evidence from false-belief testing suggests some children below the age of four cannot make sense of the possibility that others might have false thoughts about situations. The point is that this would not prevent them from noting, say, that a state of affairs does not obtain even when the other says it does—as in the case in which Mommy says "Alex is hiding" and, manifestly, he is not. This is likely to provoke such responses as "No, Alex not hiding," "Not hiding," or "There he is," and so on. But these utterances are not equivalent to attempts to correct mother's false belief, based on having first ascribed one to her.

In the imagined case, Mommy's words are not yet interpreted as her having made a claim about the state of the world and this is despite the fact that the child understands full well what they say. It helps if we think of the child as receiving her utterance as a mere factual broadcast—an announcement about how things stand that happens to issue from mother. It is a statement that the child simply endorses or rejects. For those that have only mastered the ignorance/knowledge distinction, although the world may contain falsehoods, there is no false thinking, no false believing as such.

To regard others as the source of factive statements does not require even a weak ability to understand them as adopting attitudes of belief. An understanding of metarepresentation requires grasping the possibility that either oneself or the other might be making errors of judgment. It is only in recognizing this possibility, which involves a capacity to imagine contrasting perspectives, that one can understand what it is to aim at truth. A capacity to imagine possible false beliefs is therefore a condition on understanding beliefs *tout court*.[11]

To think of oneself as having a possibly fallible view of things entails being able to think of one's cognitive take as having, potentially, the same epistemic status as divergent others. It seems that young children do not begin life with this understanding. For, initially when one asks a child, "for the contents of a[nother] person's belief, they consistently, resistantly cite the facts" (Gopnik and Wellman 1992, 152). Until children can make the appropriate distinctions they are not in a position to question the "correctness" of their own or others' epistemic takes in the way adults can.

This makes their state of mind hard to characterize, for it follows that in their younger years they do not understand themselves or others as having "epistemic takes" on the world at all. Thus even in engaging in their first dialogical interchanges, children have yet to step out of what is, in effect, a solipsistic point of view—for each child, the world is *their* world and any knowledge others may have of it is firmly evaluated against how they take things to stand (which, for them, is the same as how things are).[12] At least, this is the most straightforward way to explain why younger children appear to make no distinction between "what they take to be the case" and "what is the case."

Equally, the idea that the concept of belief is acquired late easily accounts for the well-documented gap, of roughly six months, between a child's capacity to make desire attributions and their ability to pass false-belief tests. This shows up very clearly in the developmental profile. Desires come first in our linguistically scaffolded mentalistic understanding of things:

children are capable of attributing these long before they can make competent belief ascriptions.[13] If understanding different kinds of psychological attitudes places uniquely different kinds of demands on children, specifically the ones described above, it is hardly surprising that the concepts of desire and belief are mastered at such a temporal distance.

This prompts the question: What changes in the interactive careers of children such that they are able to get a handle on the concept between the ages of three and four? In a way somewhat reminiscent of the NPH, Nelson has argued that children acquire an understanding of other cognitive perspectives by being exposed to narratives at this critical point in their development.[14] Although I am obviously sympathetic to the idea that certain types of narrative engender folk psychological skills, I do not think that encounters with them are responsible for the child's grasp of the concept of belief per se. This is because although children are typically actively and interactively engaged with early narratives, these remain third-person objects of joint attention for them and their caregivers. Thus it is quite possible that children initially might be engaging with narratives, at least at times, by adopting what Goldie (2004) calls a disengaged "external" perspective. And when they are not—that is, when they are imaginatively and emotionally moved by them—the way this occurs is not of the right sort for introducing the idea that others have different cognitive points of view.

In contrast, being a participant in unscripted conversational exchanges—those of the sort that require one to stake a claim, while attempting to understand and negotiate those of others—provides the appropriate experience. In having conversations of this sort there is no possibility of taking the role of a neutral observer. One has no choice but to deal with the clash of contrasting points of view, coping with the cognitive friction this generates. This requires more than just trading remarks about how things stand in the world—typically one's cognitive perspectives and those of others are up for debate, discussion, and challenge.[15] The most prominent feature of such interchanges is that of participants being unavoidably forced to come to terms with others' peculiar takes. In this way, "Conversation constantly underlines the centrality of point-of-view" (Harris 1996, 218; see also Bohman 2000, 227; Stawarska 2007). Very plausibly, it is by exercising their imaginative abilities in this sort of activity that normally developing children are driven from their early solipsism.

An understanding of belief is fostered by encountering and having to confront and accommodate different cognitive takes during conversations. Ultimately, this kind of practice is the source of metarepresentational understanding. But participating in conversations of the right kind requires special abilities and preparation. We gain insight into these factors by considering the analogue activity involving exclusively intentional attitudes—that is, nonlinguistic joint attention. By performing such acts children will have grown accustomed to using their nonpropositional recreative imagination in a way that is quite similar to the requirements of engaging conversations of the sort that generate cognitive friction—that is, those in which one must cope with clashing points of view. Essentially, both are dynamic affairs involving perspective shifting; both require children to monitor and keep track of different points of view. Importantly, however, the former only requires imagining perspectives in purely embodied as opposed to linguistically mediated ways.

Upon suitable mastery of language, unimpaired children are able to keep track of the cognitive take of others utilizing the same imaginative capacities they used in early life. The only difference is that, when engaged in conversational discourse, they must deal with new objects of interest and trade: propositions. In such cases the perspective taking in question is discursively mediated and content-involving—it is dependent on a prior capacity to understand propositions with truth-conditional content. Conversational interchanges of the appropriate kind demand of children that they play a sophisticated interpersonal game. But although they are playing with new objects, they are still utilizing certain key skills and imaginative machinery used in simpler games.

Assuming the children already understand propositional utterances, know how *that*-clauses work, and have their perspective-shifting capacities intact, they are ready to come to grips with the concept of belief. All they require is enough experience participating in conversations that require them to take stock of the cognitive takes of others. This forces recognition of the fact that one's own take on things is but one among many.

This proposal is one way of making sense of recent findings that reveal conversations to be a critical factor for the onset of metarepresentational understanding. A number of important experiments have confirmed this. For example, it has been discovered that deaf children who lack signing partners in their homes are severely delayed, sometimes even into late adolescence, in their ability to pass false-belief tests.[16] Remarkably, their performances not only fall well below normal thresholds, they are worse than those of individuals with extreme autism (see Peterson and Siegal 2000; Garfield, Peterson, and Perry 2001, 508). No equivalent delays or poor performances are exhibited by deaf children who do have signing partners present in the family home (in effect these children form a naturally occurring control group). The opportunity or lack thereof to engage in conversations (or conversations of the right kind) has been identified as the factor most strongly correlated with this discrepancy.[17] Indeed, since deaf children who are unable to cope with false-belief tasks suffer from no other psychological or neurological deficits, the straightforward explanation of this data in terms of a lack of conversational opportunities is hard to resist.[18]

Nevertheless, in one important sense this evidence is ambiguous. It is unclear whether it is "conversations as such"—which may be about any topic—or "conversations about mental predicates" that matter (Davies and Stone 2003, 316). Of course, it may be that both matter but in different ways. Despite being impaired in their understanding of false belief, the deaf children in these studies also displayed the standard lag in developing this understanding as compared to their grasp of other psychological attitudes, such as desire. Therefore it could be that engaging in "conversations as such" and in "conversations about mental states" make distinct, if roughly concurrent, contributions to the attainment of the concept of belief. Talk about mental states per se may be required for no grander reason than to ensure that children are acquainted with the appropriate labels and terminology. It would take a clever experimental design to filter out these two variables by means of controlled testing since, unless they take up the role of passive observers, even conversations about mental states will typically generate the requisite cognitive friction. In any case, one thing is clear: conversations matter developmentally in some way for getting a grip on the concept of belief.

If I am right in thinking that it is the experience of cognitive friction that matters for getting a handle on the concept of belief, this would complement the NPH perfectly. This would simply mean that children are more or less simultaneously learning what beliefs are while also becoming familiar with the specific role they play in folk psychology. For it is during the period of three to four years of age that they start having the relevant kinds of conversational interplay with caregivers as well as being introduced to people narratives.

Owing to to certain evident similarities, it is worth saying how the above proposal differs from Gordon's account, which makes appeal to a special kind of ascent routine to explain the child's first grasp of the concept of belief. In sketching it, Gordon (1995, 61) writes:

Suppose in simulating another (or herself at a time other than the present)—in describing "the world" as it is within the context of the simulation—she sometimes makes assertions that contradict assertions of her own, that is those she makes from her "home" perspective. In other words, she allows "the facts" to deviate from the actual facts ... all she has to do then is preface these deviant assertions with "I believe ..." or to follow the slightly more sophisticated assent routine, answering the question, "Do I believe that p?" by answering the lower level question, "Is it the case that p?"—and she will be making motivated attributions of false belief. Whether she "passes" a particular false belief test will depend, of course, on how sophisticated she is in making these adjustments.

Without wishing to endorse Gordon's proposal in detail, he is surely right that the capacity for what we might call propositional imagining of other perspectives is essential to the process of coming to grips with the concept of belief.[19] This point of agreement might make it appear as if my account assumes the existence of certain simulative abilities. In a sense this is true; the procedure calls on core imaginative capacities for perspective shifting, which in the conversational case involves imagining another's attitude to propositional objects. But note that this is not a folk psychologically based form of simulation; it does not involve the attribution of *reasons*, only thoughts.

I accept that, in large part, both developmentally and in everyday practice our capacity to make sense of others depends on our being able to co-cognize with them. Co-cognizing is essentially the replication of a target's thoughts in oneself, for the purpose of predicting them. This is done by observing the outcomes of one's own thinking (see Heal 1998a, 491). In this process we "harness our own cognitive apparatus and make it work in parallel with that of the other" (Heal 1998b, 85).[20] Our conclusions about what another is thinking can be justified either by appeal to analogy or by assuming that they have a minimal competence in dealing with aspects of a common world.[21]

This is a vital ability that we call on all of the time in the course of making sense of actions that are done for reasons. Consider how we understand McX's explanation that he reached for the glass of water because he was thirsty (to avoid any accusations that this is a canned example, let us suppose that there was an equally good alternative explanation in the air as to why McX might have done this in the circumstances). If his answer is to dispel my curiosity, I must know what anyone can be expected to know about the relevant properties of water. Yet, since the content of any thought is constrained by the content of other thoughts, knowing such things seems to entail a standing capacity to somehow work through an impossibly large (potentially infinite) number of inferences. For explicitly specifying what "anyone can be expected to know about a particular topic" would require stating all the possible inferential liaisons. In total, this would constitute a description of the whole of our commonsense knowledge on all topics, assuming—of course—that it could be laid out in the form of a series of regulative propositions.

This looks impossible. It would mean that in understanding a person's reasons, apart from making use of the core principles of folk psychology we would need to call on knowledge of an indefinite number of rules detailing both commonsense and specialized knowledge of every possible domain of thought. The mere size of this imagined theory is enough to cast its possibility into doubt.[22] Certainly it would be an utter mystery how anyone could possibly wield it sensitively in real-time, practical applications. For, in any given case, only a small subset of all of the possible inferences that might be drawn would be relevant. To make sense of McX's answer we somehow "just know" which are needed. There is no formula for achieving this.

How would an inherited mechanism ever determine such things? Deciding which thoughts ought to go together, requires understanding the nature of particular judgments that are made in specific circumstances. Hence it is not something that can be specified in advance or once and for all. This business is deeply context sensitive. Judgments of this sort need to be formed on the spot—they are a posteriori. There are simply no algorithms with the right properties that would allow us to anticipate the relevant possibilities. This conclusion is unavoidable if we observe—as we ought—that the nondemonstrative inferences of general cognition are holistic.[23]

Yet, the fact is that such holism is only threatening to those who think that in making sense of the thoughts of others we must be operating with a tractable theory of relevance. In response to this problem, which we can call "Heal's challenge," even theory theorists have wisely confirmed the modesty of their position, clarifying the true scope of their commitments (see Carruthers 1996b; Nichols and Stich 2003, 86, 104). They concede that their proposals concern *only* the core ToM principles, acknowledging that this schema "is all very well as a framework, but it plainly needs to be supplemented in some way if one is to be able to provide fine-grained intentionalistic predictions and explanations" (Carruthers 1996b, 24). This allows them to address the problem by borrowing directly from Heal, endorsing her co-cognition strategy.

Like these hardcore theory theorists, I too want to respond to Heal's challenge in exactly the same way, calling on thought replication to do the hard work. We are able to predict what another is likely to think about any given topic by co-cognizing with them. In doing so, we use our own thoughts and all their typical implications as initial guides to the thinking of others, making interpretative adjustments as necessary (see Hutto 1999b, chap. 5). Since we use our own thought processes to drive this activity, no relevance theory is needed or involved. To achieve an understanding of what another *should* infer about a given topic we need only call on our own first-order commonsense knowledge about the world.[24] For example, provided that I am justified in making certain standard assumptions about Y's initial thoughts, and assuming we are both reasoning in line with accepted norms, the conclusions I reach via reasoning will be a good indicator of what Y thinks (or predictor of what Y will think).

This approach complements the NPH because, as should be evident, pure co-cognition is not sufficient for making sense of the action of others. And this is because our understanding of what it is to act for a reason minimally requires knowing about the interrelations between beliefs and desires (along with their familiar partners). In particular, it requires more than a capacity to enact thought processes that follow the normal course of entailments between thoughts. Put differently, co-cognition does not equate to the use of simulation routines in order to make sense of reasons for action. For that would minimally require the manipulation of propositional beliefs and desires, not just thoughts.[25]

The fact is that the account of this chapter, calling on the apparatus introduced in the past four chapters, shows how co-cognitive abilities arise through the use of more basic imaginative capacities in relation to content-involving attitudes. In this way, propositional forms of co-cognition rest on manipulating the contents of our softwired, linguistically dependent superminds, using a hardwired imaginative mechanism. Basic acts of co-cognition are in this way involved even in the acquisition of our first understanding of belief. Yet, it should be obvious that as they become more proficient at reasoning over time—as children become better supermentalists—they can use this capacity for thought replication in conjunction with their growing folk psychological skills when making sense of intentional actions to good effect, in ever more refined ways.

Having clarified that, I can now summarize the main arguments of the past five chapters. Long before they acquire a practical grasp of mentalistic concepts, children are able to navigate the social matrix using embodied skills, interacting with others in ways that require no understanding of propositional attitudes or reasons for action whatsoever. As their command of language increases, they are able to make use of certain syntactic constructions—in particular embedded complement clauses. This brings new objects of attention and joint attention into view, allowing them to graduate from engaging with others exclusively by responding to intentional attitudes, to possessing a capacity to understand them in terms of propositional attitudes. Initially, this allows children to extend their understanding about what might be desired in content-involving ways. But eventually, after actively participating in conversations and exercising their imaginative abilities appropriately, they come by an understanding of that most important of propositional attitudes, belief.

Therefore, not only does the child's grip on the attitudes of others tighten over time, the very nature of what they have hold of changes. All of these complex, multistaged developments are required to put children in a position to acquire mature folk psychological skills by having narrative encounters of the right sort. This brings us full circle. The proposed account of how and when children come by their first understanding of belief supplies the final piece of the puzzle. We now have everything we need in order to account for the child's prerequisite abilities that allow them to appreciate and learn from their initial encounters with folk psychological narratives.

Throwing Down the Gauntlet

In a bid to better secure the NPH's standing, over the course of the next two chapters I argue that its main competitors are unable to provide an equally compelling account of how the metarepresentational concept of belief is acquired in a way that respects the empirical evidence just cited. If the charge can be made to stick, such accounts are in serious trouble since any decent account of the origins and acquisition of folk psychological abilities must accommodate these findings, in one way or another (Carpendale and Lewis 2004, 82, 84). That conversations play a critical role in developing a folk psychological understanding is beyond reasonable doubt, yet it is open for researchers to take different views about just *how* they make a difference. For example, conversations might be "triggers" that activate and tune inherited mindreading devices or they might be "evidence" used in the construction of a "theory of mind." I claim that neither of these accounts will do. If that assessment is correct, then—recalling the four criteria set out in chapter 2—they fall at the first hurdle, failing a fundamental criterion of adequacy. This would give us strong, if not conclusive, reason to prefer the NPH.

8 No Native Mentalizers

Nobody seemed to know where they came from, but there they were in the forest. ... When Pooh asked Christopher Robin, "How did they come here?" Christopher Robin said, "In the Usual Way, if you know what I mean Pooh," and Pooh, who didn't, said "Oh!" Then he nodded his head twice and said, "In the Usual Way. Ah!"
—A. A. Milne, *Winnie-the-Pooh*

Inherited Mindreading Mechanisms

The idea that our successful everyday navigation of the social world depends on third-person mindreading capacities is extremely popular. It is generally supposed that the latter are constantly but quietly at work, normally unnoticed and behind the scenes, as it were, and that they are responsible for our successful daily dealings with others. As discussed in the first chapter, to date the big issue has not been whether mindreading of this kind happens, only how it is carried off. Do we make use of a built-in theory or simulative procedures that manipulate our own cognitive mechanisms directly?

So far, I have tried to show these imagined feats of mindreading to be unnecessary when it comes to understanding our primary intersubjective engagements. But perhaps my account is not the correct one. Surely, it is equally possible that we might be using tacit mindreading abilities in such cases. To put an end to such speculation, in this chapter I will up the ante, arguing that the idea of built-in ToM mechanisms lacks a credible basis. This is because the proponents of such theories—be they of the standard theory theory (TT) or simulation theory (ST) persuasion—are unable to give an empirically adequate account of the acquisition of the concept of belief. And since it is agreed by all that high-level folk psychological forms of mindreading cannot be conducted without making use of that concept, if true this is a very serious charge.

Initially in what follows, I focus mainly on a prominent version of the theory theory, although my argument applies with equal force against those who defend certain variants of simulation theory, as will become clear in due course.[1] Defenders of what I call inherited theory theory (ITT) hold that our everyday capacity for mentalistic prediction and explanation is best explained by the fact that we—or better, at some level "our minds"—consult contentful principles, principles that detail the basic rules of folk psychology. These describe the lawful interactions between core propositional attitudes and other mental states and how these connect with the world through perception and action. In explicating the "action principle" Botterill (1996, 115) gives a parade example of the form and content of such rules: "If belief-desire psychology has a central principle, it must link belief, desire and behaviour. It could be formulated like this: An agent will act in such a way as to satisfy, or at least to increase the likelihood of satisfaction of, his/her current strongest desire in the light of his/her beliefs."

Accordingly, ITT regards the principles in question as taking the form of "innately cognized propositional contents" (Fodor 1983, 5). Evidently, as a set, the laws in question have "the implicational structure of systems of semantically connected propositions" (Fodor 1983, 7; Segal 1996, 147). This is what puts the "theory" in one's "theory of mind." For the most part the theory is used tacitly. In most acts of mindreading the rules are not consciously rehearsed; indeed they may not even be consciously accessible (or entirely so). For, on this account, in using folk psychology we are typically adopting subpersonal, unconscious states of believing toward the relevant theoretical propositions.[2]

In essence, the state of mind we adopt toward FP principles is allegedly the very same that we adopt toward basic principles of logic. Thus Fodor (1983, 85) speaks of "one's subdoxastic acquiescence in the rule of *modus ponens*," when clarifying his commitment to the existence of propositionally based "knowledge of" and "beliefs about" validity and confirmation. For him, the principles of FP, like those of logic, are explicitly but subconsciously represented.[3]

Defenders of ITT take it that these ToM principles are housed in very special kinds of psychological mechanisms: Theory of Mind Modules (ToMMs). These contain the relevant knowledge base. So, not only do we operate with tacit ToMs, we have built-in ToMMs. Using Fodor's own moniker, ToMMs fall into the class of "neo-Cartesian" devices, and categorizing them as such highlights their distinguishing characteristic—that they are contentful. This is important, for if any neo-Cartesian mechanisms exist they certainly are in a class of their own, being quite unlike all other psychological mechanisms.[4]

And this is not all. For Fodor, the defining feature of modules is not just that they contain propositional contents, but that they are informationally encapsulated—that is, they are only receptive to certain kinds of low-level inputs, typically those of a purely perceptual variety.[5] This allows them to function quite happily in isolation from higher-order cognitive processes—a fact that, apparently, best explains their other special attributes. These include their mandatory high-speed deliveries, cognitive impenetrability, shallow outputs, fixed neural architecture, susceptibility to particular types of malfunction, and characteristic ontogenetic pace and sequencing (see Fodor 1983, part III).

Informational encapsulation is useful in that it putatively fends off debilitating "computational explosions" in basic acts of perception that would otherwise threaten if systems had to "decide" what was relevant in any given case. Indeed, the standard story is that perception is computationally tractable precisely because it does wait around for the verdicts of central cognition. Perceptual modules take in low-level inputs, manipulate these in specific ways, and supply intermediate-level representational outputs. Only then do these feed into belief fixation. Thus modules make no use of background beliefs in conducting their business; quite the contrary, their operation can be described using relatively fixed algorithms.

It should be clear that if there are any such things as ToMMs then they cannot be modules of this kind. For in order for ToMMs to do their specialized interpretative work—the production of accurate mentalistic predictions and explanations—they would need ready access not just to the outputs of other modules, but also to domain-general cognitive processes in some way or other. As discussed in the previous chapter, part of what is involved in making sense of others in terms of their reasons is being able to decide what it is that another is likely to think about any given topic on any particular occasion (and, further, how they are likely to act based on such thoughts). Plausibly, this is achieved by performing acts of co-cognition. Certainly, there seems to be no way to devise a set of regulations that would confer such abilities. If so, ToMMs cannot be isolated modules of the strict Fodorian sort.

This may not matter. There have been robust debates about how to characterize modules in any case. For example, Carruthers has recently argued that ToMMs may be modular (or as he says, quasi-modular) in a non-Fodorian way. In explicating his proposal he draws a distinction between *informational* and *processing* encapsulation. It goes as follows:

A module is a processing system that might be innate or innately channelled in its development, that is targeted on some specific adaptive problem or task (its *domain*), and that is encapsulated *in its processing* from most of the information contained elsewhere in the mind/brain (thus enabling its operations to be computationally tractable). (Carruthers 2004, 260; see also 2003, 77; 1998, 96)

So understood, ToMMs would not be restricted with respect to the kinds of inputs they can receive and manipulate; certainly they would not be defined by having such restrictions. Rather they would be characterized by what they do with the information they receive—that is, how it is processed. Each module would be distinctive in this respect. Thus modules would be distinguished in much the way that practical reasoning is distinguished from its theoretical cousin; it is not the contents they manipulate that set them apart, but what they do with them.[6] Carruthers's modules are encapsulated but only in the way they process contents, not in terms of the kinds of contents that they process.

This characterization of modules is a step away from the mere "library model," according to which any given module is characterized by the theory it contains—that is, the "body of beliefs" that comprises its knowledge base. Yet although Carruthers (2003, 70) places greater emphasis on the processing, he does not deny that modules operate with contentful principles, as is evident from the following remark: "I shall assume that modules contain distinctive processes, at least, even if they also contain domain-specific bodies of information."

Since Fodor did not patent his "modules," it is hard to determine who has property rights to the notion. But this does not matter. Adjudicating this internal dispute will not affect my argument. The important thing is that all card-carrying proponents of ITT accept that ToMMs are neo-Cartesian—that is, they are thought to "contain" theoretical knowledge. This is not negotiable, because failure to acknowledge the existence of a set of core mentalistic principles is tantamount to taking the *theory* out of theory *theory*.

This is the crux, for if ToMMs contain contentful principles then these must be composed of the relevant mentalistic concepts. Fodor (2001a) is admirably clear about this. He acknowledges that "there can't be innate [propositional attitudes] unless there are innate concepts" (p. 110).[7] When thinking about ToMMs, it is pretty clear which "innate concepts" are needed. Leslie claims that such devices contain at least "three basic concepts: BELIEF, PRETENCE, and DESIRE" (Scholl and Leslie 1999, 137; see also 147 especially). One might doubt the need for the concept of pretence, but everyone agrees that to have a working ToMM minimally requires having the concepts of belief and desire.

This is equally true for those who defend what I will call inherited simulation theory (IST). For they do not imagine that mindreading operates in a concept-free way. This is because one cannot make mentalistic attributions without using these core concepts. The kind of simulation of concern here must be understood as a three-stage activity. In the primary or preparatory phase, appropriate targets must be identified (that is, intentional actions or what at least looks to be such). During the second, or what might be called the simulative phase, appropriate inputs—"pretend" thoughts, beliefs, or desires (or the same entertained in a hypothetical manner)—are "fed into" specific subpersonal mechanisms (for example, the practical reasoning mechanism operating in an off-line mode). These states are then internally manipulated so as to yield predictions or explanations.

Mentalistic concepts are not needed for the first two stages of the process. But they are when it comes to attributing mental states to targets in the final phase. This is because making such attributions requires identifying *which* mental states it is that one is ascribing—these must be classified in a complex way both by appeal to their general attitudinal type (belief, desire, hope) and their specific content (that "there are still tickets left for the performance," and so on) (see Goldman 2001, 216). We need concepts to judge or say of Justin that he φed because he believed that p and wanted it to be the case that q.

Beyond this, the unspoken consensus is that the concepts have determinate extensions: the concept of belief is about beliefs—it denotes the mental state of believing (or beliefhood) and nothing else. Interestingly, TT and meaning holism have a long and intimate history—and some think they still belong together. But proponents of ITT break faith with this idea and subscribe to conceptual atomism, at least with respect to mental concepts.[8] The same goes for the prominent defender of IST. Thus atomism about mentalistic concepts is endorsed by Fodor, Leslie, and Goldman alike.

Atomists hold that to have a concept is simply to have "something in one's head" (to use the familiar rubric)—something that refers to, stands for, or otherwise denotes items in the relevant extension class. Crudely, having a symbol in one's "belief box" that stands for Xs is what allows one to represent Xs qua Xs (or to think thoughts about Xs) in a completely determinate way.[9] The content of such concepts, on this view, is entirely determined by what it is that the symbols in question "stand for"—in this case it is not individuals but the class of things that they are about. For many modern thinkers such content is allegedly fixed by token mental symbols standing in the right kinds of informational relations. The structural features of concepts, such as capacity to support inferences of various kinds in virtue, say, of their peculiar syntax, matter not to their content.[10] Or, put another way, possessing content is decidedly not constituted by a concept's role or place in a larger network. Concepts have their meaning first and find their uses later.

A clear consequence of this view is that merely having a concept with an appropriate content requires no background intellectual effort. Or, better, having a concept (as opposed to fully mastering one) does not depend on having the ability to use it in making references or inferences of any sort at all. Indeed, atomists like to argue that the having of content is a logical precondition for making references or inferences in the first place. It should be clear from the discussion in the previous chapter that I think this is a bad way to think about the mentalistic concepts of young children, but for the sake of argument, let us suspend disbelief and pretend that all of this is quite legitimate.

Atomism is attractive for understanding mentalistic concepts because, as we have seen, they appear to be obtained piecemeal, over time. Children do not obtain them as a complete set. Also, atomism enables us to see how such concepts could be the determinate hard points that give theories definition and identity in turbulent times of revolutionary change. As semantic atoms, previously acquired concepts could be the anchors that hold firm throughout theory upheaval. Thus a new concept might be added to an existing theory, augmenting its power, without this in any way affecting the meaning of the preexisting concepts. Acceptance of atomism therefore makes it easy to see how children might have an early "desire psychology" that only operates with the concept of "desire" and not with that of "belief."

Thus ToM devices, whether of the TT or ST variety, might vary in sophistication in the same way that there are different variants of chess. For example, the latter can be played by different rules if it is agreed that specific pieces, say Rooks, are systematically removed from play. By the same token, one could play a version of FP, say, without the concept of belief in play. For all these reasons, atomism is surely the strong favorite for anyone faced with the task of coherently explaining how ToM abilities develop in stages. I have more to say about this and its importance in the next chapter.

Still, defenders of such a view are confronted with the thorny question: Just how is it that children, or more precisely their subpersonal mechanisms, acquire the relevant conceptual atoms? This is an important question for those who think ToM devices have two main jobs: (1) to support mindreading, and (2) to explain the origins of mental-state concepts (Leslie, Freidman, and German 2004, 258, with modifications). Providing a plausible account of this is not straightforward. Ultimately it requires us to consider facts about human prehistory. In the next section, I digress shortly in order to say why.

Ontogenetic Development?

Children become progressively more sophisticated in their understanding of others as they get older. This fact is often taken as evidence that their concepts are developing during ontogeny; as we have seen, a crucial transition is thought to occur between the ages of three and five when they gain a full mastery of the "metarepresentational" concept of belief. Thus when nativists claim that younger children in some sense already "have" the concept of belief they must treat this evidence as having only a prima facie status. It is therefore incumbent on them to explain it in a different way; either that or they must explain it away. Both strategies are found in the literature.

One tactic is to argue that the full set of mentalistic concepts is in place very early on. If so, even very young children have the requisite conceptual equipment needed for passing the false-belief tests but this fact is masked by their performance. Specifically, they have the concept of belief but they are unable to bring it to bear appropriately until they are older. Fodor, for example, advances this sort of line, favoring the idea that "the child's theory of mind undergoes no alteration; what changes is only his *ability to exploit what he knows*" (Fodor 1995, 110).

One way to understand this is to imagine that children have the full set of ToM principles available to them even though they only use a fraction of these when it comes to making sense of intentional actions. Consequently, they might only use heuristic H1 but not H2 (set out below), though they have both available:

H1 Predict that an agent will act in a way that will satisfy his desires.

H2 Predict that an agent will act in a way that will satisfy his desires, if his beliefs were true. (Fodor 1995, 112)

It does not logically follow from the fact that children only operate with very simple ToMs that this is all that they have built into their heads.[11] Others have followed Fodor's lead on this, taking it up in different ways. For example, Scholl and Leslie also argue that the appearance of the conceptual upgrade that enables children to master false-belief tasks is just that—an appearance.[12] In fact, no such change takes place. In their view, the improved performance of older children on such tasks is to be explained entirely in terms of their better developed auxiliary capacity to select and process relevant information, as needed for the effective deployment of their ToMs. In time, children move from a crude default mode of ascription—in which they assign beliefs to others based solely on what they (the children) take to be the case—to the use of a more sophisticated heuristic; that is, that of making sensitively tailored belief content ascriptions.

Crucially, again, younger children already have a metarepresentational understanding of the concept of belief—that is, they know that others can have divergent cognitive points of view—it is just that they are poor at *selecting* contents when it comes to ascribing such beliefs to others. Due to poor executive control they "default attribute," only assigning beliefs to others based on the way the facts look to them. This tendency is curbed at the point at which they are in a position to master false-belief tasks. In a nutshell, it is the child's "selection processor" (or as Leslie et al. call it, their SP) that develops over time, not their ToM concepts or principles— these remain stable throughout.[13] The crux is that we should not confuse the development of supplementary support devices with the development or introduction of core mentalistic concepts.[14]

Yet another possibility has been aired by ToMM theorists who favor nativism. It has also been argued that although young children start life using different precursor mentalistic principles and concepts from those of adults, these develop in genetically fixed ways over time. Full-fledged metarepresentational concepts only appear in the mature phase. Segal, for example, claims that ToMMs unfold diachronically in this way, through a series of staged upgrades. On this model, it is not just an ability to apply preexisting concepts and principles that changes; the core concepts and principles of the ToMMs change as well.

Nevertheless, ToMM development is kept on a very tight leash; it is driven by a genetic blueprint of sorts—thus the way ToMMs mature is constrained in exactly the same way as the growth of hair or teeth.[15] Proponents of this version of the ToMM hypothesis have stressed that there is no incoherence in the idea that modules or mechanisms develop; the interesting question is *"how* they develop" (Scholl and Leslie 1999, 136). They propose that when it comes to theorizing about this, we should think "much less about child 'theories' and much more about mechanisms" (Leslie, Friedman, and German 2004, 532). ToMMs are distinguished by the fact that they only develop in rigidly prespecified ways—it being a case of ontogeny strongly recapitulating phylogeny. Although this account assumes they undergo conceptual change, this is not evidence-driven, as would be the case if concepts were the product of an open-ended scientific investigation. It is just that the way that ToMM concepts roll out can give that appearance.[16]

Ultimately, it seems, nativists have two main choices when making sense of ontogenetic development. The core mentalistic concepts either (1) develop in preset noncognitivist ways, or (2) they do not develop at all (but this fact is masked by performance limitations of one sort or another). According to the first hypothesis the mature ToM is only in place "potentially," rolling out over time in a staged, predetermined way if the conditions are right. According to the second, the mature ToM already exists in its complete form, even though children are unable to make full use of it. If we restrict our attention to considerations of ontogeny, both types of hypotheses are empirically adequate.

Therefore, to get leverage on this question, we must put these proposals to the test by looking at how they fare when it comes to explaining the ultimate origins of the concept of belief. That is what I intend to do in the final section. For it should be evident that if the accounts of the ITT or IST are to work, the concept of belief must have been in place in the minds of our prehistoric forerunners at a suitable point in phylogeny.[17] This must be assumed in light of the simple fact that one cannot bequeath what one does not have. Thus, anyone seeking to explain the development of folk psychological abilities in human children by appeal to one or another of these nativist stories has no choice but to hold that our ancient ancestors possessed the metarepresentational concept of belief.[18]

In what remains of this chapter, I argue that although it is ultimately possible to tell an atomist story about how mindreading mechanisms might acquire the concept of belief—at least, in theory—it is simply not credible that this could have happened in our prehistory. There are empirical grounds for thinking this. I discuss these in the final section, but first let me say why introspectionism looks to be the best option for those seeking to defend a nativist theory about how our putative mindreading apparatus acquires the concept of belief.

The Sustaining Mechanism Objection

The best-developed atomist story about concept acquisition regards it as a noncognitive, mechanical process—a kind of "locking on" to certain properties (such as "being a belief" or *beliefhood*). This is achieved by experiential acquaintance with typical items of the relevant extension class (i.e., typical beliefs) (see Fodor 1998, chap. 6). I have serious doubts about this proposal in general, but I will shelve them in what follows (for an excellent critique of this idea see Viger 2001). In making my argument I will assume that the basic idea of acquiring concepts by locking on is unproblematic. But, please note, this offer is good for a limited time only (over the space of the next few pages)! My aim is to illustrate that even if no complaints are raised about the general nature of such accounts, they face a special problem when it comes to explaining how the concept of belief might be acquired.

To understand this account properly it is necessary to be clear about protoconcepts and how they are supposed get transformed into concepts proper by means of brute-causal, triggering processes. Protoconcepts are concepts in waiting. They are potential vehicles of content, yet while they have this potential they are inherently meaningless. For this reason, unlike true concepts, they cannot be directly modeled on ordinary linguistic signs, words—written or spoken. Getting clear about their nature is not, therefore, straightforward.

Margolis (1998, 351) has proposed that we should think of "a concept as a file whose label specifies which concept it is and whose entries count as knowledge structures that, in one way or another, are associated with the concept." Protoconcepts cannot have labels of this kind since they are not about anything (yet), but if we make use of Margolis's analogy we can think of them as having labels that are almost but not quite blank. The name of their future concept is written on their tag (perhaps in invisible ink) for they are imagined to be specially poised or predisposed to denote only certain things or kinds.[19] Each of these potential concepts is preset, awaiting first contact to be established with at least sample items of their prospective reference classes. To realize this predisposition, like sleeping beauties, they must be properly awakened. When protoconceptual tokens lock onto their extensions—that is, when the tags get firmly attached to the items they denote and protoconcepts become bona fide concepts—they acquire contents to carry.

Protoconcepts are poised to become full-fledged symbols and they do so when they lock onto the right sorts of things—that is, when they are triggered by good examples of the type of things they are innately specified to denote. This innate specification constitutes a kind of preestablished harmony between protoconcepts and certain classes of things.[20] Fodor theorizes that protoconcepts are amodal "symbols-in-waiting" that are predestined to become concepts of certain sorts when they are activated by their proprietary triggers in the right way (Fodor 2001a).[21] Others favor connectionist-based visions of the nature of such potential vehicles, as does Prinz in his account of proxytypes (see Prinz 2002). These differences need not detain us. The fact is that all of those committed to this sort of view hope to provide a noncircular account of the way protoconcepts (whatever form these potential vehicles take) become real concepts.

The account of how this happens is ultimately "adamantly noncognitivist" (Antony 2001, 211). Accordingly, we begin life with certain protoconceptual "potential" vehicles of content. After having the right sorts of perceptual encounters these become vehicles of representational content by lawfully "locking onto" the things in their proprietary reference class. Indeed, "acquiring a concept is getting nomologically locked to the property that the concept expresses" (Fodor 1998, 125; original emphasis).[22] Only after this anchoring are there meaningful conceptual symbols in our heads—symbols that stand for, say, *all* and *only* Xs. Hence, once protoconceptual tokens acquire their semantic properties their subsequent use is forever dogged by the possibility of misrepresentation.

It should be evident that since protoconcepts must be activated by the right kinds of properties before they become concepts proper, this kind of account does not commit one to the view—as is sometimes implied—that concepts proper are simply built into our heads.[23] Protoconcepts start life as "unactivated innate concepts" only taking on contents when appropriately triggered. Hence

on all standard ethological accounts of triggering, part of what is innate in a triggered concept is a *specification of its proprietary trigger*. Since the trigger of an innate concept is both proprietary and innately specified, such concepts can be unvacuously *triggered by reference to what would trigger them*. . . . [Thus] the content of protoconcepts is no particular problem for a semantic externalist, so long as he assumes that it supervenes on (possibly unactualised) dispositions. (Fodor 2001a, 138; emphasis added)

The trouble is that when it comes to explaining the origins of the concept of belief such locking-on mechanisms cannot be of the ordinary perceptual variety. Beliefs are a parade example of the kinds of things that lack perceptual signatures. They have no characteristic looks: there is nothing perceptually salient about them; it seems that there is nothing for sensory detectors to get a lock on. There is a clear tension in acknowledging that beliefs are "invisible, intangible, and abstract" while at the same time claiming that ToMMs enable children to "attend to such states in the first place" (Leslie, Friedman, and German 2004, 531).

As discussed in chapter 6, it seems that there are mechanisms that enable us to sensitively attend to intentional or purposeful actions where goal-directed actions "*are* perceived directly in the bodily activity of humans" (Wilkerson 1999, 61). But the same cannot be said of beliefs. These work behind the scenes (in conjunction with desires) in order to produce sophisticated intentional actions of a different sort. We have no direct perceptual experience of the beliefs of others. By this I mean that we do not even "see" the attitude of believing. Beliefs as propositional attitudes are expressed in utterances, not in bodily ways in the way intentional attitudes are. At best, we might perceive these behavioral analogues of beliefs, these nonindividuative attitudes or factual attitudes as expressed in another's outward behavior. Again, this is not the same as *seeing* a belief, understood as a metarepresentational state of mind.[24] Recognizing that another is intentionally directed at some aspect of the world—even where this is construed as their adopting a kind of psychological attitude—falls far short of spotting a belief.

Even so it might be thought that if beliefs systematically cause certain perceivable phenomena, intentional actions, then perhaps in locking on to good examples of these, one might indirectly lock on to beliefs. One problem with this idea is that beliefs are only reponsible for motivating intentional action when they are partnered in the right ways with other mental states. Since they neither work in isolation nor out in the open it is impossible to lock on to beliefs and beliefs alone by purely perceptual means. Worse still, the relations in question are not that reliable in any case. Being perceptually sensitive to intention-in-actions, and even to have the idea that such actions may have an unobservable cause, does not give a foolproof means of locking on to beliefs per se—for what outwardly appears to be an intentional action might be caused by any number of nondoxastic things, such as ingrained habit, strong desires, and so on. Often what look like actions done for a reason turn out not to be—deciding which are bona fide intentional actions can be a tricky interpretative business, one that requires a prior facility with the concepts of belief and desire. This is precisely why the reductive attempts of behaviorists to explicate individual mental-state concepts in purely observable terms failed so dismally.

The right verdict seems to be that there is really no hope of locking on to beliefs by purely perceptual means. We should avoid accounts that seek to explain the acquisition of concepts of unobservable kinds by appeal to their characteristic perceptual properties. Thus it does not seem possible to explain how we acquire the concept of belief in anything like the way that some hold it to be possible to explain the acquisition of basic color concepts. It seems there are no belief sightings of the sort needed to reliably activate the relevant protoconcepts.

The good news is that we know that crude empiricism is wrong anyway; not all our concepts are straightforwardly perceptually based. Although most of us cannot tell viceroys from monarchs or elms from beeches by looking, our concepts of these things are quite distinct. Or, to take a less beastly example, our concepts of CDs and DVDs are not equivalent, even though in some cases we cannot distinguish one from the other by perceptual means (especially so nowadays, when we are confronted with an unmarked disc). What then is the ultimate basis for these conceptual distinctions?

We rely on other kinds of reliable mechanisms to make the distinctions for us. We know that there are specialists or experts who can identify the flora or fauna for us. We trust that they have some reliable means at their disposal for doing so. Or, focusing on the second case, we stick the offending disc into a laptop and wait for the results, images or sound. The experts and the laptop are both nonperceptual mechanisms that allow us to make the appropriate distinctions. They are prosthetic devices that augment our native resources so that we can acquire new concepts and keep track of them. Crucially, these sorts of mechanisms might perform the same sort of service when converting protoconcepts into true concepts.

The possibility of such augmentation is perfectly consistent with atomism. Nonperceptual mechanisms can mediate the setup and maintenance of the appropriate mind-world relations, as long as it is clear that the mechanisms in question do not play a constitutive role in determining the conceptual contents they help to establish. Only the appropriate lawful links holding between a token and what it denotes do that; it just so happens that sometimes establishing and maintaining the appropriate linkages depend on the existence of certain sustaining mechanisms. Or, put another way, the atomist claims that all that matters for there to be conceptual content is that there is a link between symbols and their propriety reference classes; how such links happen to have been established is immaterial.

Having clarified this, it could be argued that mentalistic concepts are activated and introduced by nonperceptual mechanisms. Other than those of the perceptual variety, two other kinds have been identified: deference-based and theory-based mechanisms (see Margolis 1998).

The idea that deference-based sustaining mechanisms might do the trick looks promising at first glance. It might be thought that mentalistic concepts are introduced and sustained by appeal to knowledgeable others who have special expertise. But as a story about the ultimate origins of the belief concepts this idea suffers for at least two reasons. First, if deference to experts is required in order to reliably identify beliefs, it is difficult to see how folk psychological concepts could be readily deployed in everyday, practical circumstances. Experts are not always on hand to consult and folk psychology would be of pretty limited value if our capacity to correctly identify the relevant mental states was on a par with our unaided capacity to distinguish elms from birches. Second, and more to the point, this only pushes the explanatory problem one step back. An account would still be needed about how the experts got their concept of belief.

While this will not work, proponents of ITT might be naturally inclined to think that the mechanisms introducing mentalistic concepts are theory-based in any case. Margolis discusses the nature of theory-based sustaining mechanisms, and it is worth quoting him at length:

Suppose, for example, that a person has had considerable training in physics and chemistry and has assembled a complex set of beliefs about atomic structure, essentially internalizing both the principles of contemporary physical science and the known procedures for manipulating particles. Then, because of her hard-earned intellectual resources, she would be in a position to infer the presence of a proton when the available evidence together with what she knows about protons compels the conclusion that a proton is present. In other words, her knowledge puts her in a state of mind where protons cause her to token the concept PROTON, the disposition that is the heart of the [Information Based Semantics] treatment of concepts. (Margolis 1998, 354; for a similar account see also Fodor 1998, 157; 2003, 80)

If we swap the references to "proton and PROTON" for "belief and BELIEF" in the above passage it is easy to see how this sort of account might apply to the case in hand. But a moment's reflection reveals that it will not work. Our concern is not what sustains the appropriate links, but how they came to be established in the first place. We can agree that the theory might only act as an introductory mechanism without constituting the meaning of the concepts in question. But even in order to play its limited match-making role the theory in question must already have appropriate content. So, once again we are pushed back a step.

Now the question is how did the theory-based sustaining mechanism get its conceptual contents? As an explanation, appealing to theory-based mechanisms in this case is viciously circular: the only theory that could introduce the concept of belief reliably would be a theory that already contained that very concept. Chickens and their eggs: and in this case there is no competence/performance distinction to appeal to since we are trying to establish the ultimate prehistoric origins of the belief concept.

Perhaps there is a way around this problem—it may be that we have been looking in the wrong direction. It may be that the concept of belief is not acquired by a process of exoperceptual locking on but by using introspective mechanisms that directly target the relevant mental states. After all, the objects of interest—beliefs—are imagined to be located in the minds of thinkers. Or more precisely, mentalistic concepts might be, in part, acquired by means of "inner detection" (Goldman 2000b, 2001).[25] By attending to these attitudes, identifying them by their distinctive phenomenological characteristics, it is at least theoretically possible to lock on to them and thus activate the relevant protoconcepts. All this requires is that each of the various propositional attitudes have their own unique qualitative properties or phenomenological feels. This proposal rests on the idea that there is something-that-it-is-like to experience a belief that is quite different from what-it-is-like to experience a desire, and so forth (Goldman 1993).

This looks like the best bet for proponents of ITT or IST. Yet, even if we allow that the attitudes have distinct qualitative features by which they can be individuated, the idea that we might acquire concepts by looking inward is afflicted with serious troubles. There are deep philosophical difficulties with the very idea that any concepts could be acquired just by means of attending to the contents of our minds (assuming that we have privileged or transparent access to them). Wittgenstein's assault on the concept of a private language, which focused on the acquisition of sensation concepts, constitutes an insuperable objection to such proposals.

The exact nature and force of his argument is often misunderstood. He aimed to provide a kind of exposé—designed to reveal that the imagined private linguist would be unable to establish any rules for the use of even the most basic sensational concepts by simply mentally attending to their experiential properties (allowing, for the sake of argument, that such acts of inner attention are possible). The point is that inner acts of attention and ostension could not possibly establish a standard of the sort required to fix a rule for use. This is why Wittgenstein rejected the possibility that meaning could be established or explained by mere ostensive definition, quite generally. Many interpreters fail to see the true focus of this critique, assuming that Wittgenstein's worry was really only about the subsequent capacity to apply concepts and remembering how to do this. His objection cuts deeper. It reveals that there is no possibility of establishing a rule for the use of concepts through purely introspective (or private ostensive) means. And if one cannot set up a conceptual rule in this way it follows that there is no possibility of applying (or misapplying) it on other occasions—not even in purely hypothetical uses.

At the very least, the onus is surely on proponents of introspective accounts of concept acquisition to address these difficulties. Despite advertisements to the contrary, there has yet to be an adequate rejoinder to Wittgenstein's worries that explains how merely attending to introspectable phenomenal qualities could—even in principle—provide a sufficient basis for establishing a rule for the use of concepts of the kind that would allow for "predictability, with accessibility for truth or falsehood" (Chalmers 2003, 240; cf. Hutto 2006a). I see none on the horizon.

Only if these worries can be overcome could an atomist story that makes use of introspective resources work even "in principle," as they say. But let us assume that it is at least logically possible that the concept of belief could be acquired through some process of locking on. Still, these accounts fail as an adequate explanation of the basis for the ultimate origins of the concept of belief, allegedly first acquired in phylogeny. In the final section, I say why.

The Absent Conversation

Merely having the concept of belief inertly, by having activated the relevant protoconcept, would have been of little use to our ancestors in their interpersonal dealings. For it is not enough just to have concepts; one must be able to deploy them appropriately. Thus if having the concept of belief is imagined to have made a selective difference it follows that it must have been not only on the active-duty roster, but it must actually have been put to good use at some point.

Given the evidence that conversations play a critical role in the acquisition of metarepresentational capacities and the understanding of belief, as discussed in the previous chapter, a natural move for nativists would be to hold that conversational stimuli are what trigger the mature stage of mentalizing to develop, either by actually forging the concept of belief (à la Segal) or by activating other devices that enable its proper use (for example, perhaps by kicking the SP into action à la Leslie). This move looks necessary in any case if proponents of ITT or IST are going to be able to make sense of the existing data.

What's more, it is logically possible to defend this claim while maintaining that our mindreading abilities are innately given. Innateness is, on the best of days, a desperately slippery notion. Indeed, it is so much so that some have asked that it be retired on the grounds that its polysemy makes it unfit for theoretical duty (Griffiths 2002, 70–27). For example, in saying that a trait or device is innate one might be claiming that it has any of a number of properties, including its being

- Present at birth
- Genetically programmed
- Developmentally fixed
- Universal within a species
- Unlearned
- Explanatorily primitive to a given science

This list is not exhaustive, but it suffices to demonstrate the point at issue. The situation is further exacerbated by the fact that each item on the list above is ill-understood. Nearly all biologically based traits/devices develop over time. So to claim that they are "present at birth" is either false (on a literal reading) or ambiguous (if it means that they are present but only potentially so). Still, it might be thought that claims about such potentiality can be easily explicated in terms of genetic blueprints and pre-programming. But this move only prompts further questions. Does genetic preprogramming imply that the trait in question is developmentally fixed? Is it monomorphic (taking only one form); or species typical (does it appear in all members of a species); or is some mix of the above implied?

When defenders of ITT and IST claim that our mature capacity for folk psychological understanding is a gift bequeathed to us by our ancient ancestors, I take it that they are really only minimally committed to saying that it is

- Canalized (that is, impervious to most environmental influences, other than certain specified external triggers; this is why mindreading abilities develop according to a predictable timetable)

- Species typical (that is, barring disorders, when activated in the right way by the right triggers, mindreading abilities emerge in all members of *Homo sapiens sapiens*)
- Pancultural (it is found in all human cultures and groups)
- Monomorphic (it takes just one form—its core elements are not open to local variation)
- Unlearned (the relevant developmental processes are not cognitively driven)

One can accept all of this while holding that the capacity to employ the concept of belief is triggered and tuned by select environmental triggers. Even if the path of mindreading development is fixed in advance, it may require exogenous prompts to act as developmental spurs.[26] If and when these are lacking, mentalizing capacities will be arrested, either partially or completely. The absence of specific environmental input at crucial moments therefore could either delay or completely sabotage a device's proper formation. This would explain the data concerning the effects that a deprivation of conversational stimuli has on certain deaf children.

In this light, to claim that mindreading devices are "innate" need only commit one to the claim that "there exists within the population some mechanism or process that maintains the developmental resources which *very reliably* produce the trait in question" (Maclaurin 2002, 126, emphasis added).[27] So understood, a device can be innate even if it is developmentally dependent on being triggered by specific kinds of external stimuli.

Some might object that this conception of innateness is too weak, for if we accept this criterion, any traits and tendencies that emerge reliably in normal environments will be classed as being innate. Since for humans, their normal environments include stable sociocultural institutions, the result may be that even "highly stereotypical, inherited cultural phenomena (such as religious beliefs) could turn out to be innate" (Maclaurin 2002, 126). Yet we need not get embroiled in a philosophical debate about how to decide the right extension for the term *innate*—all that matters is, those who defend nativist accounts of mindreading would not be breaking any of their own rules if they argued that conversations act as normal triggers for enabling, if not the introduction of the concept of belief then the capacity to apply it. This would simply be a special case of "growth in a normal environment" (Carruthers 1998; cf. Gómez 1998, 92).

Yet, on closer inspection, this proposal will not work. For it assumes that conversations of the appropriate sort were a normal feature of our ancestral environment at the time ancient mindreading mechanisms would have been formed—and the simple fact is this just was not so. Although conversations are today a normal feature of the everyday environments in nearly all human societies, they would have been absent from the Paleolithic world at the point at which that imagined mindreading mechanisms would have had to have been forged. On current best estimates, the last call for the completion of anatomical change in the common ancestors to our species would have been about 100,000 to 120,000 years ago, before the migration "out of Africa."[28] This sets a firm deadline prior to which sophisticated conversational practice would have already had to have been established to feature as a normal environmental trigger that could influence mindreading devices in the appropriate way. But it is not credible that such a complex linguistic practice would have been in play at the right point.

Certainly, we must accept that language-related anatomical changes were completed prior to the dispersal of our common ancestors around the globe. So even if it is possible that there was some coevolution of mindreading devices and some basic linguistic capacities, we cannot assume that languages and related practices had developed enough to enable hominids to participate in sophisticated forms of conversation at the right point in prehistory. There would have been a very long period after language-ready humans first appeared on the scene in which languages themselves, the public cultural products for discursive trade, would have been being founded and their rules hammered out (see Li and Hombert 2002, 178). It seems safe to assume that even after a fully symbolic form of casual language had emerged—that is, one with determinate lexical and syntax elements that were good enough to support basic acts of propositional communication—conversational discourse of the kind that approximates what we witness in modern human societies would have still been a long way off.

Thus even if we assume that linguistic practices of some sort were in place prior to 100,000 years ago they would have been in their infancy at best. Certainly it is implausible (to say the least) that they could have sponsored "conversations as such" or "conversations about mental states." I will say more about this, arguing in more detail against some conjectures to the contrary in chapter 11.

All in all, there is good reason to think that true believers—and claim-staking conversationalists—only arrived on the prehistoric scene at a point after the final touches would have had to have been put on any imagined mindreading devices by the forces of biological evolution. If so, this is devastatingly bad news for defenders of ITT and IST. But perhaps the right story to tell is that only devices for more basic forms of mindreading are inherited—that is, maybe the full-fledged metarepresentational aspects are not inherited but constructed. In the next chapter, I critically examine the most developed version of this idea—the scientific theory theory (STT)—only to conclude that it too fails to live up to the challenge of explaining the origins of the concept of belief.

9   No Child's Science

Scientific Theory Theory

At its core, scientific theory theory (or STT) holds that folk psychology is the result of explicit scientific theorizing on the part of preschoolers—that is, that our mature ToM is in fact the hard-won product of sustained observation, statistical analysis, experimental trial and error, and learning from others (Gopnik 2004, 2003; Gopnik and Meltzoff 1997; Gopnik and Wellman 1992). In particular, the concept of belief is thought to be constructed by each child, individually, during ontogeny—reliably it "appears to be constructed between 3 and 4" (Gopink 1993, 332). In promoting this idea, STT therefore avoids the sorts of problems discussed in the previous chapter that attend nativist proposals. In a crucial respect the proponents of STT are more modest in their views about what our ancient ancestors bequeathed to us.

But their modesty about our cognitive endowments has its limits. They also claim that "infants are born with initial innate theories, and . . . begin revising those theories even in infancy itself" (Gopnik 2003, 241; Gopnik and Meltzoff 1998, 451). The important difference is that these starter theories are not imagined to have the core folk psychological concepts built into them, nor are they preset to acquire them automatically when appropriately stimulated. ToM concepts, and particularly that of belief, are forged as children develop their first, inherited mentalistic theory. Children do not start life with full-fledged ToMMs equipped with all the standard concepts nor are they preprogrammed to acquire them; instead, normally developing children create them for themselves. They are only able to achieve this by making good use of rational theory-construction mechanisms that they have inherited as well. Thus,

the basic idea is that children develop their everyday knowledge of the world by using the *same cognitive devices* that adults use in science. In particular, children develop abstract coherent systems of entities and rules, particularly causal entities and rules. That is, they develop theories. (Gopnik 2003, 240; emphasis added)

In short, supporters of STT hold that our ancient cognitive endowment, relevant to the development of our theory of mind abilities, is two-pronged. It consists of (1) a basic (nonmetarepresentional) theory of mind and (2) mechanisms for scientific theory formation.

Like theory theorists generally, advocates of STT acknowledge that children's theories have the characteristic static features of mature scientific theories—for example, internal coherence, causal implication, and ontological import. Yet, they place much greater emphasis on the claim that children, like adult scientists, engage in the dynamic activity of theorizing where this is understood as the process of collecting, evaluating, and responding to evidence in a rational, truth-seeking manner. Indeed, the core claim of STT is "that *the processes* of cognitive development in children are similar to, indeed perhaps even identical with, *the processes* of cognitive development in scientists" (Gopnik and Meltzoff 1997, 3; emphasis added).

Accordingly, we are told that "the most important and distinctive thing about theories is the fact that the very patterns of representation that occur can *alter* the nature of the representational system itself" (Gopnik and Meltzoff 1997, 44; emphasis added). The emphasis matters, for it is the activity of theory development that is meant to explain how children succeed in fashioning their own genuinely metarepresentational ToMs by the age of four (ceteris paribus) and beyond, since they continue to add to it even beyond this point—undergoing further, less radical, shifts as children become young adults (Gopnik 2004, 23).

Since this process putatively is one of crafting new concepts within an existing framework of laws in a way that involves painstaking assessment of evidence, it is seemingly possible to explain the stages of development in human folk psychological abilities that occur during early childhood. Unlike nativists, supporters of STT take the appearance of conceptual development in ontogeny at face value; they claim that genuine conceptual change occurs as children fashion their theories of mind—that is, that this conceptual change is driven by their activities of theory construction. Our distinctive human understanding of minds is thus *theoretical* in the strongest possible sense, according to STT—both in its very nature and its mode of acquisition.[1]

Significantly, as we will see, the credibility of this constructivist proposal rests on assuming that each child (1) works from a species-universal base theory, (2) encounters the same kind of evidence at the same points in the developmental schedule (and assesses it in the same way as fellow theorists), and (3) operates with the same cognitive toolkit used by adult scientists.

The Disanalogy Objections

The viability of STT depends on making the three assumptions listed above, for it is only by doing so that its defenders are able to reply to a host of objections regularly leveled against their theory. Most of the complaints have taken the form of what we might call "disanalogy objections." The name suits because detractors hold that there is, in fact, no parallel between the intellectual practices of scientists and young children. To many it seems obviously preposterous to claim that infants and young children are in fact capable of engaging in scientific theorizing of essentially the same nature as the adult variety.

A major concern is that actual scientific practice is largely based on working within the framework of a shared tradition, with long periods of training being required to develop the relevant skills and background knowledge to understand existing theories, let alone to begin theorizing for oneself. Initiates into scientific research do not begin their careers by forming and testing theories right away; they begin by becoming familiar with the content of existing theories, mastering experimental techniques, and even learning how to reason formally. This involves being supported and trained by those who are already proficient with such knowledge and techniques. Adult science, in both its early and mature phases, is therefore a social enterprise through and through.[2] This being so, how could a lone agent (in this case, an infant) even begin the task of constructing theories on its own? This would require it to clearly structure what it encounters in conceptual terms, distinguishing what is part of its theory from mere confirming or disconfirming evidence. And it would have to be motivated and able to reason about all this at a very high level.

With respect to the timing of folk psychological developments, in particular, it has been argued that if we took the STT claims seriously children would not only have to be lone scientists, they would have to be amazingly good ones. If the STT is true, they hammer out a viable and fairly sophisticated ToM in hardly any time at all. The creation of such a stable product by the age of four is, surely, anomalously precocious when compared to the length of time it takes professional scientists to work up a theory of equal power and elegance (Goldman 1992a, 106–107). Even if we suppose that infants begin fashioning their theories in the womb, ab ovo—as Gopnik (amazingly) argues—their progress still looks extremely fast by these benchmarks.

Both of these worries point to a more serious underlying puzzle with the STT proposal: How is it possible for all children to converge, so reliably, on the very same ToM despite the fact that they are working alone from the start, without common training or mutual collaboration? It is remarkable, to say the least, that despite their isolation from one another they manage to achieve such an overwhelming consensus about how minds work and their basic components. Adult scientific researchers rarely, if ever, reach a similar level of agreement, even when they are in regular correspondence and share experimental data sets. Agreement about a core theory is most likely to occur, if at all, when scientists work in close-knit research teams and share common traditions, methods, and practices that have been in some way institutionalized. Infants and young children have none of this. One might expect that if they were indeed "little scientists," then, given the conditions under which they operate, we should surely expect their theoretical products to vary to a much greater extent than is the case.

Calling on the assumptions mentioned above, STT theorists have attempted to defend themselves against objections of this kind. For example, they acknowledge that adult science has important social and institutional supports but argue nonetheless that in all cases the process of scientific theorizing is driven by, indeed boils down to, the cognitive activity of individual minds. This, it is argued, is the true basis of science (Gopnik 2003, 248). Ordinary scientific thinking takes place wholly within the heads of particular thinkers and the mechanisms that support it are inherited and thus universal.[3] This is what allegedly secures the rationality of the scientific process for both adults and children.

If scientific theorizing is conducted by means of the operation of subpersonal mechanisms in this way and we assume the existence of relevant starter theories, there is a ready reply to the precocity objection. It is apparently defused by the fact that there are no a priori constraints on how fast children might develop their first theories (Gopnik and Wellman 1992, 167–168). The bottom line is that we have no relevant point of comparison with the speed at which adult scientists develop their theories, for while the processes are identical (if STT is correct), the conditions are not the same. A better test of precocity in ToM development is not therefore how quickly adult scientists fashion theories but how quickly other theories, such as a mature folk physics or a mature folk biology, emerge (presuming, of course, that such theories exist). Here one expects that the speed of constructing a ToM will look quite normal.

Against this background, appeal to assumptions 1 to 3 is needed in order to quell the serious worry about convergence. For

> the [scientific] theory theory proposes that there are powerful cognitive processes that revise existing theories in response to evidence. If cognitive agents began with the same initial theory, tried to solve the same problems, and were presented with similar patterns of evidence over the same period of time, they should *precisely converge* on the same theories at about the same time. These assumptions are very likely to be true for children developing ordinary knowledge. (Gopnik 2003, 248, emphasis added; see also Gopnik and Meltzoff 1997, 52–53)

Still, this reply looks inadequate. Scientific thinking, during its revolutionary phases when new concepts are fashioned, is turbulent—at such times precise convergence is unlikely and heterogeneity is more the norm. This will be so, even when the scientists in question agree about the previous core theories, have been confronted with the same evidence at roughly the same time, and have been making use of the same basic reasoning apparatus.[4]

Examination of the form of existing scientific debates reveals this—for example, this is the state of play with respect to the debates about the character of nonverbal interpersonal intelligence discussed in earlier chapters (does it involve a weak theory of mind, a theory of behavior, unprincipled mindreading abilities, or embodied practices?). Or, even more self-referentially, how should we best explain the acquisition of folk psychological abilities? The various hypotheses, ITT, IST, STT, and the NPH, have all been developed under the conditions described above but there is no precise convergence. Even researchers beginning with the same basic assumptions, using the same basic methodologies, and confronting the same evidence can reach quite different conclusions. Scientific theorizing is not nearly as constrained as the defenders of STT like to insist.

This will be especially so in moments of revolutionary theory change. And this observation is pertinent, since if we take the child-as-scientist proposal seriously, the forging of new mentalistic concepts is a dramatic and creative business; it is not the outcome of "normal science." If we suppose that children engage in it, then our expectation ought to be that there will be widespread divergence in their theorizing, *not* that they hit upon precisely the same theories at roughly the same time. This point will be of importance again when it comes to assessing the STT proposal about how we acquire the concept of belief in the final section of this chapter.

It should be clear however, from earlier chapters, why we might be skeptical about the suppositions that support the STT. The theory depends in part on our willingness to believe that human children regularly engage in private research, as made possible by their native theory-building cognitive apparatus inherited from our hominid ancestors. But it cannot be assumed without argument that hominids were capable of scientific reasoning and theorizing, especially in light of the assessment of chapter 4, which suggests they are not likely to have been capable of bona fide inferential reasoning using propositions. Coupled with the fact that science only made its public debut some 500 years ago, this observation casts the STT into serious doubt (Stich and Nichols 1998, 425). Like its nativist rivals, the STT requires us to believe that our nonverbal ancient ancestors were capable of sophisticated forms of reasoning conducted by means of manipulating contentful mental representations. If, as I have argued, even the most sophisticated nonverbal responding is not content-involving, then both the stronger nativist accounts and the STT are nonstarters, owing to their shared commitment to representationalism.

Here it is important to note that the specific claims STT makes about our cognitive endowment—that is, that it consists of a clutch of "starter theories" and powerful "theory-construction" mechanisms—are allegedly justified, not by appeal to a just-so story about prehuman adventures in a mythic Pleistocene, but on the basis of the best explanation of what is needed—quite generally—in order to explain the cognitive abilities of existing nonhuman animals. As discussed in chapter 6, theory theory is one extreme way of accommodating the growing body of evidence that has been gathered about the sophisticated expectations of nonverbal cognizers (Gopnik and Meltzoff 1998, 451). But, once again, if the assessments of chapters 3 to 6 are correct, it bodes ill for the idea that nonverbals rely on built-in *theories* that coordinate their primary interactions with the world and others.

In this light it looks as if supporters of STT are particularly ill-advised to attempt to secure their claims about the existence of such theories by reasoning abductively about what is required for making sense of nonverbal cognition in general. The more plausible strategy is the very one that Gopnik rejects—that is, focusing specifically on the cognitive capacities of our hominid forerunners, defending the view that these, at least, may have been sophisticated enough to support scientific theorizing. But, as just mentioned, even that strategy looks doomed to failure. There is no compelling reason to interpret even the most advanced of the known nonverbal cognitive activities—the fashioning of the Levallois flake—as involving content-involving inferences. Indeed, as argued in chapter 4, there are good reasons to think otherwise. If hominids were not manipulating propositional representations as practical reasonsers, they surely were not theoretical scientists.

It sorely misrepresents what human infants, in fact, bring to the table to suppose that they start life with a crew of innate theories inherited from our evolutionary forerunners. But even if we suppose this, there is another serious problem for this particular nativist proposal—one that concerns the nature of the concepts of the mentalistic theory with which infants allegedly begin life. For apparently, to have a first theory of other minds seems to require infants to have an understanding of exactly the kind of self/other contrast that they would only be able to gain *after* they had fashioned the concept of belief. For Gopnik (2004, 22) tells us that "infants seem to be *born* believing that people are special and that there are links between their own internal feelings and the internal feelings of others."

It is easy to see why Gopnik says this. Understanding a difference between self and other is a necessary prerequisite for engaging in any kind of theorizing about other minds. One must be capable of understanding "the other" as "other"—more specifically, as a potential locus for attribution of certain kinds of mental states. Before testing the worth of such attributions and developing such constructs, infantile theorizers must have a prior understanding that there are "others" with mental lives of their own (at least potentially). At a bare minimum, this presupposes that infants are capable of recognizing others as appropriate targets for mentalistic ascription of some sort.

The developmental evidence gives us exactly no reason to suppose that infants start life with knowledge of this kind. So, at the very least, if they are to make their opening gambit credible, STT theorists need to specify exactly what kind of self/other contrast is available to newborns. Only in this way can they elucidate what is meant by infants having beliefs about the "links between their own internal feelings and the internal feelings of others" in the passage quoted above. Whatever form that understanding is supposed to take, it had better not rest on an infantile understanding of different cognitive points of view, since that would presuppose that infants start life in possession of the concept of belief.

For the sake of argument, let us pretend that these worries can be dealt with and that there is some answer to the question as to how the imagined starter theories get their content.[5] Ultimately, the primary focus of my critique of STT concerns how it fares in explaining the imagined theoretical construction of the concept of belief, and it calls heavily on the worries raised about convergence mentioned above. Yet before turning to this, it will prove useful to say a bit more about another serious problem that afflicts the STT account of childhood development—a problem that stems from its commitment to a thoroughgoing holism about conceptual content.

A Technical Worry about Holism

According to STT, the concepts that make up the child's theory of mind get their individual meanings or contents by having appropriate links or relations to other concepts. The idea that mentalistic concepts are holistic in this way has a long history, having replaced the previously dominant empiricist theories about the content of such concepts that featured, in different ways, in introspectionist and behaviorist accounts. Radical behaviorists, for example, sought to understand our everyday psychological concepts solely in terms of pairings of visible stimuli and responses in a bid to ensure scientific credibility, in line with the positivist philosophy of science of the day. Other empiricists tended toward more introspectionist proposals. This is a twice-told tale, and I have no wish to bore the reader by repeating it. The idea that mental concepts are theoretical arose in opposition to their treatment by empiricist approaches. In reaction to such views, mental entities were held to be causally efficacious but unobservable. They interacted with one another in complex ways behind the scenes, leading to systematic outputs when set into motion by characteristic inputs. The functionalist motto was and remains: Out of sight, into mind.[6]

Once propositional attitudes are construed as unobservable mental entities, it is natural to think in terms of "abstract" theoretical constructs. In general, knowledge of the existence of theoretical entities is hypothetical; it is indirectly based on evidence because theories posit underlying causes. Indeed, when they are well fashioned this is what gives good theories their depth and potency: unlike a kind of collected wisdom based on threading together many inductive generalizations, theories allow one to place strong bets, quickly and selectively, using minimal evidence. According to tradition, a theory is a good one if it reliably generates predictions and explanations, even in novel circumstances. Theories can do this precisely because they go beyond what is merely observed to have happened in the past (even in the best cases where such observations have been carefully marshaled over time). In this light, it has been claimed that acquiring systematic ways of dealing with others and specific worldly offerings in this

way was "the most important evolutionary benefit of developing theorizing abilities" (Gopnik and Meltzoff 1997, 37). Theories run deep: their
power to anticipate, explain, and control stems from their tapping into the
world of the unseen and the abstract.

These are the primary philosophical motivations for thinking that we
operate with some kind of theory of mind and that our familiar mentalistic vocabulary (that is, our talk of thoughts, feelings, and expectations) is
best understood as a kind of theoretically embedded vocabulary. Crucially,
rejection of the empiricist view of meaning led to the idea that the true
mark of theoretical concepts is that they have their meaning holistically.
Paul Churchland makes this connection clear by renouncing the idea that
meaning might be supplied by certain types of experience; indeed he has
famously advanced the bold claim that all of our judgmental encounters
with the world (and each other) are mediated by theories of one sort or
another.[7]

Advocates of STT apparently buy into content holism of this kind. For
them, its most attractive feature is that it seemingly affords a basis for
thinking that our concepts and categories are not unalterably fixed. Conceptual schemes apparently develop and change over time. Our categories
concerning "what there is" are plastic, pliable, and mutable. Indeed, it is
precisely because our conceptions of the world shift and change that we
can make the sort of rare conceptual advances that constitute the pro-
gressive march of science and the growth of knowledge. This is clearly very
much in line with the STT's constructivist proposal about how theories of
mind develop.

Although it looks prima facie coherent to make sense of the relevant
conceptual change in holistic terms, it is important not to confuse a
desideratum with an explanans. There are deep and difficult problems for
holists when it comes to making sense of how concepts develop. The big
issue is how to make sense of transtheoretic continuity, for only if this can
be achieved in a noncircular and nonvacuous way can it be legitimately
claimed that a single theory or concept develops over time. If this appears
unproblematic to some, it is likely only because when thinking about the
issues uncritically our intuitions typically break faith with the demands of
strict holism.

For, on careful reflection, it seems impossible to get a grip on the idea
of dynamically developing theories and concepts without at the same time
generating serious problems about the idea that conceptual change is even
possible. At bottom, it is simply not clear how we ought to understand the
relations that are supposed to hold between the different versions of a

single theory (and its constitutive concepts) at the different stages of development. This is because the relevant content-conferring relations shift along with the whole theory as it changes.

Really, for holists, it is unclear how concepts could develop at all. In essence, if the having of specific theoretical roles and local liaisons is what defines concepts and gives them their content, it is difficult if not impossible to support the claim that concepts change over time. If holism is true, there cannot really be such a thing as a single evolving theory since, as stressed above, the concepts that are imagined to constitute it shift their meaning as they alter their constitutive relations. Any such alteration in this dimension will yield an entirely distinct theory with entirely distinct concepts. There is no way for a theory to survive changes to any of its constituent contents. Unless we give up strict holism, we can only make sense of mere succession of theories and concepts as opposed to their genuine development.

If it is then agreed that there really are only distinct successor theories with distinct concepts, it is unclear in what ways these are developmentally related—that is, holists are not entitled to talk of one and the same concept developing in the course of the evolution of a single theory as early to later versions emerge. Still it might be thought that the natural way out of this problem is to drop the use of the definite article. Thus, as discussed in chapter 6 in response to Astington's paradox, the child and the adult might be thought to have quite different concepts of, say, intention, concepts with different contours precisely because they play quite distinct roles in quite different theories—the early and the late versions.[8] If so, early and late theories could have different but importantly related concepts. Perhaps, so the story goes, this is because the contents of the early and later versions of the concepts overlap partially; even if the content of the early and late versions are fixed by different surrounding theories such that they cannot be strictly speaking identical, they might be similar nonetheless.

But even this will not do. For, again, nothing stays the same during the theoretic transitions: *Any* change alters all the relevant relations, in which case at best what we have is entirely different theories. How can something "play part of the same role" if what is "the same" about the respective roles cannot be specified in a theory-independent way in the first place? In a word, to accept content holism commits one to the idea that the early and mature mentalistic theories are incommensurable. If theories are distinct in this way, if they merely succeed one another, then we must look to external factors if we are to explain how they are related.[9]

If we want to make sense of transtheoretic continuity it looks as if we must go beyond the confines of a strict content holism. We must abandon the assumption that the contents of mentalistic concepts are interdependent with the global theories of which they are a part. In other words, we must give up the idea that the content of a given theory is a direct function of its constitutive concepts and vice versa. The content of concepts and whole theories had better not come as logically inseparable packages.[10]

This should not bother us too much. After all, what developmentalists really want is to determine which historical factors are responsible for the emergence of new understandings. When it comes to making sense of the course of mentalistic development, my suggestion, as worked out via biosemiotics, is to say that both the infants and the adults target the same psychological phenomenon—intentions—but that they do so in different ways. Thus, for example, we can say that in targeting the same kind of phenomena—for example, goal-directed actions—both children and adults share a common focus. This anchors their developing psychological abilities so they can be said to develop along a single path.

This answer works whether or not the child and adult understand the phenomena in inferentially based ways or even, as I more radically have suggested, if their responses are embodied and nonconceptual at base. Thus the proposal works equally well if mentalistic development advances from nonconceptual responding to more inference-based understandings, of the sort that we might regard as properly conceptual (even if nontheoretical).

The No-Guarantee Objection

So far, I have compiled a number of reasons for wanting to avoid the STT. In this section, I focus on a particular problem it faces when it comes to explaining the acquisition of folk psychology—that is, its inability to accommodate the evidence that conversations are a critical factor in the acquisition of the concept of belief. According to the STT such conversational encounters must be thought of as a source of decisive evidence— evidence that throws up anomalies for young children's early, nonmetarepresentational ToM and drives them to amend the next version in the time-honored way. Children are compelled, as it were, to shift from a normal to a more revolutionary phase of scientific theorizing in order to accommodate the new data constituted or supplied by conversations. Defenders of STT can therefore hold that conversations play an important role in theory construction by acting as *evidential* spurs, instead of as, say, environmental triggers as nativists would have it.[11] This is consistent with the claim that the utterances of others, on this view, are just "another source of information about the structure of the world" (Gopnik and Meltzoff 1997, 7).

Although this seems a viable possibility at first pass, the devil is in the details. A serious problem becomes evident if we attend more closely and ask just how the metarepresentational theory is meant to emerge in response to conversational evidence. And when assessing this it is important to bear in mind that conversations must provide evidence of such a compelling nature that it reliably provokes all normal children to upgrade their early theories of mind by adding the concept of belief to them without fail.

To get a grip on the proposal we must ask: *How* do young children initially understand the linguistic utterances of others at the theoretical stage prior to developing the concept of belief? Clearly, they cannot already be thinking of others as having divergent cognitive perspectives since that would entail that they were already in possession of the concept of belief and metarepresentational capacities. If so, conversations could not be or provide the evidence that prompts the construction of that concept, on pain of circularity.

Perhaps younger children are able to understand what is said to them without understanding that such utterances issue from a particular epistemic point of view, as discussed in chapter 7. It is surely logically possible to understand the sense of a proposition—that is, the conditions under which it would be true or false—without understanding that the source from which that proposition issues, say a person, has a cognitive point of view. This looks to be more than a mere theoretical possibility; given what we know about the abilities of those with autism, it appears to be empirically established fact. Some autistic individuals are quite capable of understanding what others say—of understanding the content of their utterances in the way one might understand a factual broadcast in, say, a newspaper report—without understanding the concept of belief.[12]

If so, STT defenders might hold that it is by engaging with others in sophisticated conversations that children become puzzled by the fact that others frequently say things that are at odds with the facts (as the children know them). Having observed this often enough, children are led to make the imaginative and revolutionary leap of constructing the concept of belief to relieve the tension. That is, they seek to explain the recalcitrant data by upgrading their existing nonmetarepresentational theory.

Yet, it is not at all clear why being frequently confronted with the fact that other speakers are unreliable about the facts (from the child's point of view) would be considered anomalous. This would only be surprising if children had some prior expectation that others are or should be reliable. Without this, even a barrage of false statements (or what look like such) on the part of others would not provoke the need for a theoretical adjustment. This might be interpreted as good evidence that other speakers are poor indicators of worldly affairs. The ample data could be handled in either way. For the young solipsist the latter reading might be the natural, if rather sad, way of accommodating the evidence. In any case, child scientists would surely not be compelled by this evidence to conclude that speakers have cognitive points of view on the world that differ from their own.

Worse still, even if we allowed that at least in some cases some children might creatively construct the concept of belief on the basis of such encounters, there is no reason to think that this would be the norm. Even if we are prepared to think of young children as practiced theoreticians, we must surely draw the line at supposing that they are geniuses, one and all. In this light, it is difficult to see how conversations could be or supply evidence that systematically results in the forging of the concept of belief in preschoolers between the ages of three and four. The relations between theory and evidence are too many and varied—too loose—to make the kind of just-so story required by STT plausible. Indeed, STT would only look more so if a variety of different theories of mind emerged at around this point in the developmental schedule of the normal population of children. In any case, understood as evidential spurs, conversations provide no *guarantee* of the requisite conceptual advance.

This looks fairly damning. But perhaps the STT could be modified so as to avoid these difficulties. It has been long argued that most of its problems stem from its antiquated view of science and theory formation—and in particular its claim that scientific theorizing is essentially individualistic (Stich and Nichols 1998; Carruthers 2003). This makes it an uphill battle for STT supporters to account for the precise convergence we find in the folk psychological abilities of certain populations of normally developing children.

Against this it might be thought that the STT could be softened such that children's conversational encounters with others are understood as playing the same kinds of institutional roles that they serve for adult scientists. Gopnik has recently begun to stress the importance of social interactions, noting the special capacity of humans to learn from others.[13] Certainly, all the evidence suggests that in learning how to understand others in folk psychological terms, children are not working alone! But this is not to say they are working in research teams. It is rather that in learning from others, children are acquiring an established framework in some way; they are not collaborating with adults or their peers in building a new scientific theory in response to evidence and experimentation.

The training children receive by listening to conversations and stories could therefore be construed on this model as being somewhat like that which an undergraduate receives when learning the basics of their scientific field of study. This is a far cry from what established researchers do when they attempt to advance original theories and hypotheses at the cutting edge of science. If we focus on the first stage of scientific practice rather than on the dynamic formation and reformation of theories, perhaps the STT could overcome my no-guarantee variant of the convergence objection.

We might follow Bartsch and Wellman (1995, 207) in supposing that

> naive theories and theory formation processes are not individual, asocial enterprises, contingent purely on the efforts of the individual theorist. . . . A better analogy to the young child might be the fledgling science student. Students learning the accepted framework of a scientific discipline engage in conceptual discoveries and "rediscoveries" but are guided and encouraged by others who already hold the theory.

But the price to pay for making this move is to acknowledge that the developmental process of becoming a folk psychological practitioner does not involve active theorizing at all. Stories and conversations about mental states are not triggers for tuning built-in mechanisms, nor are they evidential fuel for theorizing: they are, just as the NPH would have it, exemplars. Moreover, imparting a tradition to new initiates is surely not a practice unique to science—so there is no residual reason to lean on scientific analogies in order to understand it. It should be obvious that if this turns out to be the best explanation of how folk psychological understanding is acquired, theorizing activity plays no part in the process. Equally, *what* is being imparted need not be understood as a theoretical framework, as discussed in chapter 2. If we make the relevant modifications to make STT more plausible, it turns out that there really is no role for theorizing in this variant of theory theory any longer.

In light of all this it is worth remembering that the major attraction of the STT, especially for developmental psychologists, is that it looks well suited to explain how mentalistic concepts can be acquired in a punctuated way. We come by the pieces needed for folk psychological understanding in stages. But even so we need not understand the process in terms of dynamic theorizing as opposed to the expansion of certain practical abilities when appropriately supported by distinctive sociocultural practices.

A Comparative Assessment

If we cannot explain the regular appearance of the concept of belief in the normal course of development by appeal to the coming online of native mindreading mechanisms or a child's theory-construction abilities, it looks as if the orthodox proposals are ultimately bankrupt when it comes to explaining the basis of our folk psychological abilities. Indeed, it follows that if they are not in a position even to explain the origins or acquisition of the concept of belief, they have no prospect of explaining the understanding children exhibit of the structural interrelations between beliefs and desires. If this appraisal is correct, the NPH is not only a viable new challenger, it appears to be the superior proposal about the origins and acquisition of our folk psychological abilities.

To fully secure this place in the running, it is important to review and challenge certain standard motives for wanting to posit native mindreading devices instead of making appeal to sociocultural factors when thinking about the origins of folk psychology. That is the task of the next chapter.

The Narrative Competency Objection

For all that has been said, it is likely that some readers may still be inclined to believe in the existence of inherited mindreading devices (IMDs), positing these in order to fulfill certain perceived explanatory needs. And it might be thought, for example, that this idea could be combined with a softer variant of the NPH, according to which encounters with folk psychological narratives are needed, but only to put the finishing touches on our capacity to understand intentional action in terms of reasons, not as a *basis* for it.

Yet, before considering whether such a combination is even possible we should determine whether developing this idea is even desirable. In deciding this, it will prove useful to ask that famous question, apparently beloved by actors: "What's my motivation?" With this in mind, my aim in this chapter is to expose and defuse the strongest motivations for thinking that there is a need to postulate some kind of IMD. For, as I see it, it is the tendency to think this that poses the real threat to the full and proper acceptance of the unadulterated variant of the NPH, as presented in chapter 2.

For example, an immediate worry might be about the underlying abilities that children must possess in order to participate in narrative practices that involve stories about people who act for reasons in the first place (see Gallagher 2007b). For, so the thought goes, that ability surely presupposes precisely the kind of understanding that, according to the NPH, exposure to folk psychological narratives is meant to foster. After all, it is not as if the relevant narrative competency is of the general variety: it requires a specific understanding of stories with a distinctive type of mentalistic subject matter. Clearly, the easiest way to explain how children are able to engage with stories would be to suppose that they had preexisting theory of mind (ToM) abilities.

This may be the quickest explanation, but is it the best one? Certainly, if it was the only possible explanation of the narrative competency in question then the NPH would be viciously circular, at least in its strong form: ToM abilities would be required in order for children to appreciate the narratives of the very sort that the NPH holds are responsible for engendering their initial folk psychological understanding. Naturally, I deny this.

In the previous chapters I have been at pains to show that basic folk psychological narrative competence rests on having a raft of abilities—which include at the top end the possession of a sophisticated capacity for cocognition and a practical grasp of the propositional attitudes. Yet, even in sum, these abilities do not add up to having a ToM. Young children come to the table with a great many emotive and imaginative capacities that, even in unison, fall just short of a genuine folk psychological understanding. A range of embodied skills and linguistic skills need to be mastered if they are to become conversant with everyday stories about reasons for action to be sure—but if my appraisal of their nature is correct, it obviates the need to postulate IMDs of any kind whatsoever.

All told, a child's first competence with folk psychological narratives rests on their having a sophisticated command of language, a range of specialized imaginative and interactive abilities, and a prior grasp of the core propositional attitudes. This is what children bring to the relevant storytelling practices during their developmentally rich preschool years. Nevertheless, having this raft of abilities does not equate to having ToM abilities per se. Hence, there is no danger that the NPH is viciously circular.

Technically, therefore, the narrative competency objection has already been dealt with. Still, since theorizing about IMDs is the orthodoxy, I anticipate further resistance to the NPH and its sociocultural proposal about the basis of folk psychology. So, let me try to quell it here and now. To that end, in the next three sections, I put pressure on the three motivating considerations that encourage belief in the existence of IMDs. Polemically, these are often presented as established facts with which any theorist must contend. They are

1. Children's early learning environments lack stimuli of the appropriate kind and quantity to explain how the rules of folk psychology are acquired.
2. Folk psychological abilities are universal through the human species, being exhibited by all unimpaired members of the human race.
3. Mindblindness, brought on by a faulty IMD, is the best explanation of the metarepresentational impairments of autistic individuals.

I intend to cast doubt on each, one by one. The fact is that, despite their combined persuasive force, on close scrutiny, this trio is in fact a rather sorry squad. On examination, they constitute nothing more than (1) an unwarranted prejudice, (2) an empirical blunder, and (3) a weak explanation. I will start with the unwarranted prejudice.

The Poverty of the Stimulus Argument

A prominent reason for believing in IMDs of some sort rests on the assumption that the acquisition of folk psychology "poses the *same degree* of a learnability problem as does the rapid acquisition of linguistic skills, which appears to be similarly rapid, universal and without sufficient stimulus from the environment" (Mithen 2000a, 490; emphasis added). In effect some have tried to advance a Poverty of the Stimulus Argument (PoSA) concerning the acquisition of folk psychology that parallels Chomsky's version, which was developed in support of his claims about the existence of innate linguistic knowledge (Carruthers 2003, 71; cf. Botterill and Carruthers 1999, 52–53).[1]

Accordingly, it has been claimed that our normal developmental environments lack the right kind of ambient information, opportunities, instruction, and training (or enough thereof) to support the claim that folk psychological abilities are not inherited in some way. Indeed, as Sterelny (2003, 214) observes, "The idea that learning a theory of mind would be enormously difficult is close to received wisdom." The corollary is that ToM capacities must be built in.

A precise version of this PoSA has not been presented in any detail, but presumably its basic conceit is that children could not possibly fashion the rich folk psychological product simply by applying their general reasoning abilities in response to sensory encounters. Traditionally, and in general, PoSAs of the sort used to promote nativism about the mind work best when leveled at crude empiricist proposals.[2] Thus they are especially effective against those theories that, for example, regard infants as making their initial way in the world with only minimal predispositions—that is, those that assume children use powerful domain-general cognitive resources in a lonely way so as to construct coherently structured representations of the world. The most extreme version of this idea takes the form of an empiricism that casts the child's mind as an empty container, one that remains so until furnished by sensory encounters. Customary habits of thought are learned through processes of memory, association, and imagination. This is a salient reminder that PoSAs get their prima facie credibility from their opponents' assumptions about the nature of the environmental stimuli that children encounter and also from suppositions about the nature of their minds. PoSAs can be quite compelling if both of these are imagined to be significantly limited.

As argued in chapters 6 and 7, working with such impoverished resources is not the plight of infants and young children. They neither encounter a world of unstructured sensory stimuli on which they struggle to impose order individually, nor do they take up the challenge of developing that understanding by relying on nothing other than domain-general reasoning mechanisms (or open-ended theory-construction devices). Rather, they are predisposed to attend selectively and respond to certain kinds of phenomena in ways that have special actional import for them. Even in their earliest stages of development children are much more sophisticated than traditional empiricists, behaviorists, or Piagetians suppose, despite the fact that they lack concepts and theories.

The correct strategy for dealing with PoSAs is to challenge assumptions that would otherwise lead us to imagine that the minds of early learners and their learning environments are attenuated. Rowlands (1999, chap. 8), for example, has attempted this in the linguistic domain, making a strong case for reconsidering the conditions under which language is initially learned.[3] First and foremost, he observes that the cognitive resources of children are naturally constrained in ways that would make phased learning by means of certain exogenous props possible. Specifically, he claims that humans have come to rely heavily on complex external structures as props for memory stores, as a consequence of the involution of the episodic memories of our early ancestors. If he is right about the effect of this cognitive retreat of our mnemonic capacity it is plausible that children become familiar with the relevant complex structures in piecemeal fashion—that is, memorizing short segments and digestible partial sequences of them a bit at a time. The idea is that when broken down in this way even complex grammatical structures, of the sort found in the primary linguistic corpus, might be dealt with in stages, making the whole business less daunting.

Furthermore, Rowlands has argued that if we look at the learning environment within which children acquire their grammars, it is clear that it is organized such that the language-acquisition process is structured and staged in significant ways. These include activities that make use of standardized routines and games—as found, for example, in infant-directed speech. The relevant activities involve the repeated demonstration of objects and events in ways that serve to shape and regulate the normal expectations of children. In effect, such practices serve as enabling supports; they allow children to explore the linguistic landscape while operating within the "field of promoted action"—that is, their explorations are supported and structured in important respects by others. Clearly, this kind of external scaffolding would greatly reduce the initial cognitive demands on novice language learners.

In effecting a pincer maneuver, by properly characterizing the internal and external constraints that structure a child's learning, the assumptions on which the PoSAs depend are undermined. This strategy is further supported by appeal to the amazing results achieved by Elman's net. Often, these are regarded as a kind of connectionist existence proof that language learning is possible without having to posit the existence of any kind of innate Universal Grammar (UG). The connectionist network in question was able to "learn" both lexical categories (for example, nouns and verbs) and grammatical structures (for instance, agreement and dependence of embedded clauses) after having been subjected to a carefully planned and phased training, during which it was introduced to aspects of the hierarchically ordered sequences in a segmented way. Summarizing the evidence, Prinz remarks that "Elman shows that a dumb pattern detector can pick up on structural relations" (Prinz 2002, 206). With the right kind of environmental scaffolding, it seems that even humanlike grammatical sensitivities can develop using little more than domain-general pattern-completing cognition. If so, it is at least possible that specialized language-acquisition devices (LADs) are not needed.

It is not necessary for us to decide the outcome of that debate, but here is the rub: even if the account sketched above turns out to be insufficient in the final analysis of what is required to tell the whole story about human sensitivities to complex syntactic structures, it should force us to question the assumptions about the limited cognitive resources of young learners, internal and external, that make PoSAs so intuitively plausible. This should suffice for our purposes, for when compared to the task of acquiring complex grammars, picking up folk psychology skills by means of participating in the right kind of storytelling practices would be, well, child's play. To be sure, I have argued that folk psychology is a complex skill, the full mastery of which only comes over time. I have also argued that this only happens if children have the right inherited capacities intact and if they exercise them in the right ways with the support of veterans.

Here it must be remembered that the narratives that serve as exemplars are presented in a rich interactive setting, with engaged participants on both sides. It is helpful to remind ourselves of this, lest we are swayed into thinking that children are disembodied tabulae rasae listening to serial broadcasts from the mouths of their parents, perhaps in the way the citizens of Orwell's dystopia took in announcements from the Ministry of Truth. Nothing could be further from the truth. If I am right, acquiring an explicit understanding of folk psychology through stories is nothing like being taught a set of explicit principles, rules, or regulative propositions. We will only be tempted by this idea if we wrongly imagine folk psychology to be a set of propositions—indeed, only then would it be right to agree with Goldman (1992a, 107) that few children "have mothers who utter [folk psychological] platitudes."

Engaging with folk psychological narratives is not a passive affair: it presupposes a wide range of emotive and interactive abilities. To appreciate what is going on in such stories children must be capable, at least to some degree, of imaginative identification. They are likely to be hooked by the events described to them and moved emotively just as they would in their more basic interpersonal engagements. Thus I agree that "what does seem important for understanding narrative is the kind of emotional resonance that one finds already in infancy, in primary intersubjectivity" (Gallagher 2006, 227). Indeed, as one might expect "if the emotional character of the other person is not in character with the narrative framework—with the story that I could tell about her and her circumstances—it is difficult to understand that person" (Gallagher 2006, 227). This being so, we can assume that "conversations about written and oral stories are natural extensions of children's earlier experiences with the sharing of event structures" (Guajardo and Watson 2002, 307). It is probably no accident that the earliest quasi-narrative encounters of young children are with picture books; the more advanced of these books depict character actions and interactions. Slowly, children graduate to properly discursive stories, those that describe and contextualize the various psychological attitudes of protagonists who find themselves embedded in increasingly complex situations and dramas.

Sophisticated demands are also placed on children in the course of discussing and learning from such stories. It is normal for children to be directed by caregivers to attend to the thoughts, desires, and feelings of story characters. These are often explained to children by placing them in a larger context. And good storytellers will go beyond the strict text—animating their narrations by using voices, enacting character actions and reactions, and supplying relevant asides in order to emphasize and remind listeners of the background motivations and rationales of the dramatis personae. This usually takes the form of a mix of dramatic reenactment, contextualization, giving further examples, and so on. All of this prompts further requests from listeners and creates opportunities for important interventions from storytellers.

It is assumed that throughout these interactions children will be calling on their previously acquired practical grasp of the mentalistic term—that is, belief, desire, hope, fear, and so on. But it is important to note that in this context such terms are not simply *mentioned* by storytellers. In the process, children are shown not only how the propositional and psychological attitudes operate in relation to one another; they are also prompted at crucial points to offer their own explanations using these terms. Thus they may be asked to apply them—and their capacity to do so will be checked and corrected, as need be. For example, in reading stories it is normal for adults to press for answers to questions such as: "Why do you think X did that?" This is a vital developmental opportunity.

Although I have been emphasizing the imaginative, emotional capacities that characterize early engagements with folk psychological narratives, especially in light of the discussion above, I want to stress just how easy it would be for children to pick up the structural template of folk psychology from such encounters. This is important because the propositional attitudes are thought to be inserted into this framework in much the way mathematical arguments are inserted into various equations. This structure lies at the heart of all coherent narrations concerning these attitudes. Similarity-based connectionist accounts of cognitive processing—those that trade in stereotypes, prototypes, and exemplars—could easily explain how it is possible to derive this sort of schema from the relevant presentations. Picking up repeating structures from well-constructed exemplars would be a straightforward job for our pattern-completing, form-finding brains. If so, the underlying mechanisms governing this process can be rendered completely unmysterious. Thus a major advantage of the NPH is that it does not need to characterize the relevant learning process as one of "scaling up" or "bootstrapping." For this reason it cannot be rightly accused of hand waving at this juncture (Gopnik 2003, 243). This is because the training input is identical to learned output: the forms and norms to be acquired are clearly detectable in the relevant exemplars—that is, the folk psychological narratives themselves.[4]

Most importantly, on this view, children are not faced with the lonely task of developing their folk psychological understanding in a vacuum. The narratives to which they are exposed that help them with this task and the context in which this happens cannot be seriously understood on the model of confrontations with unstructured sensory stimuli. And the trainees do not come to the task empty-headed or empty-handed. All the NPH requires for its credibility is the assumption that the child's world is adequately populated with responsive caregivers who relate folk psychological narratives and that children are given enough opportunities to participate with these narratives in storytelling practices of the right kind. This seems to be the case, in most cultures. For most children, the world is simply awash with stories and conversational activity through which countless examples of people acting for reasons are discussed. On the assumption that the relevant narrative practices litter the ground in most human societies, children and their learning environments are anything but impoverished (at least when it comes to the business of acquiring folk psychology).

The Universal Convergence Assumption

It is often said that all children, everywhere—or at least those with a normal developmental profile—reliably develop the capacity to predict and explain actions, like clockwork. That is, they are all thought to develop the same basic approach to making sense of intentional actions using the core folk psychological framework. This capacity, it seems, is universal to our species and thus best explained by a built-in IMD (see Botterill and Carruthers 1999; Mithen 2000a). This line of argument clearly rests on making what I will call the Universal Convergence Assumption.

According to the NPH our capacity to use and understand propositional attitude psychology is not an inherited capacity of all humans, which is gifted to them as a matter of course, merely by their membership in the species. It is acquired if and only if the right sociocultural practices exist and are exploited. For example, if a given culture entirely lacked the relevant narrative practice—that is, the relating of folk psychological stories—the NPH would predict that its populace would lack the relevant folk psychological abilities (even if they had all the other interpersonal capacities on which those abilities are grounded).

It should be clear that despite claiming that folk psychological abilities are not a biological inheritance, the NPH need not be in tension with the Universal Convergence Assumption, for the telling of folk psychological narratives might be a *cultural* universal, like agriculture. Explaining action in terms of reasons may be a pan-cultural phenomenon, found throughout the entire human population, even if there were no inherited mechanisms that explain why this is so. It could turn out that, as a matter of fact, every human culture has developed its own local traditions in a way that reliably supports this special kind of narrative practice. The cultural artifacts that make this possible need not be in written form—they might be embodied in folk tales or even nondiscursive forms of prenarrative practice, such as dramatic reenactment (a possibility that will be discussed further in chapter 11). For example, the Baka, who hail from a nonliterate pygmy society of the Cameroon, reenact stories in which folk psychological activity apparently looms large.[5]

A representation of the spirit Jengi (a Baka male disguised in raffia robes) visits the Baka village. The men seek to mislead the women by treating this representation as the actual spirit and "protect" the women from the Jengi, who supposedly eats women. . . . [This] illustrates how the men seek to use misleading appearances and false-beliefs in their relations with the women. (Avis and Harris 1991, 465)

Although more would need to be done to ensure that this is the right characterization of the practice, it nonetheless serves as a good illustration of how mentalistic notions might become culturally embedded in prenarrative and narrative activity.[6]

Although the possible truth of the NPH is consistent with the Universal Convergence Assumption, it is also consistent with the possibility that the special kind of storytelling practice in question has a unique history and thus is not found everywhere—or at least not in equal measure.[7] There might be a number of reasons why this might occur. Perhaps a society, real or imagined, lacked the linguistic-based practices of reasoning by means of propositional attitudes that would constitute the requisite subject matter for such stories. Or perhaps the telling of such stories might be frowned on for some reason. Or perhaps stories of other kinds predominate such that the folk psychological ones are deemphasized. It remains an open empirical question whether every human group engages in folk psychology and if so, to what extent.

And even if folk psychology is a universal and ubiquitous human practice, it is still possible that cultures diverge widely in the way they tend to understand action because they vary in their storytelling practices. If such cultural differences do exist, the NPH predicts that frequency and competency in the use of folk psychology may vary widely. If so, such skills are best charted along a spectrum and evaluated by degree—culture by culture—rather than being thought of as an all-or-nothing matter.

Ultimately, determining exactly which narrative practices exist and how they impinge on the everyday interpretative skills and tendencies of various peoples is a fascinating and largely underexplored area of empirical research. Conducting this research would require sensitivity not only to the particular content and types of narratives used and emphasized by given cultures, but also the character of the surrounding storytelling and conversational practices. Any of these features might be critical to children getting the training needed for making sense of actions in terms of reasons.

Anticipating heterogeneity in this regard—as opposed to assuming universal convergence—looks to be the right approach. It is far from given that all cultures make sense of intentional actions in terms of reasons. Evidence gleaned from the handful of cross-cultural studies conducted on folk psychological tendencies suggests that even an understanding and use of the concept of belief does not come automatically to all. Tests conducted with children from several non-Western cultures reveal that they do not perform on standard false-belief tasks as readily or with the same proficiency as Westerners do (Vinden 1996, 1999, 2002; Lillard 1997, 1998; Garfield, Peterson, and Perry 2001).

In particular, Vinden's cross-cultural studies, which employ four variants of location-change and false-belief tests, reveal significant variations in the understanding of belief between the children of certain cultures: "The response patterns vary from culture to culture, with the Western children the only ones who were at ceiling on all questions" (Vinden 1999, 32; see table 10.1). In fact, in coping with the false-belief task—where children were asked what a protagonist would "think"—those from the Mofu of Cameroon were only marginally above chance and those from the Tolai and Tainae populations of Papua New Guinea were at chance. These results are even more remarkable given that the children involved were up to eight years old (this was due to problems encountered in finding suitable participants of the desired younger ages).[8] To explain this we might look to the opportunities that children from these cultures have for engaging in the appropriate kinds of conversations—those of the sort that are apparently needed for developing an understanding of belief.[9]

The NPH predicts that if cultures diverge in significant ways in the profile of their narrative practices, we can expect to find different local tendencies and proficiencies in the use of folk psychology. In some non-Western

Table 10.1
Percentage of Correct Responses for Western, Mofu, and Tolai 6-year-olds and Tainae 4- to 8-year-olds

	Western ($n = 13$)	Mofu ($n = 34$)	Tolai ($n = 16$)	Tainae ($n = 12$)
Look	84.6	64.7	43.8	91.7
Think	92.3	55.9	50.0	50.0
Prior	84.6	70.6	43.8	66.7
Subsequent	100	85.3	93.8	58.3

cultures greater emphasis has been shown to be placed on the situational, trait-based, and even supernatural factors.[10] For example, unlike North Americans, the Chinese are less prone to explain a person's behavior by citing their individual beliefs and desires or even by citing personal character traits. Instead, they tend to emphasize social-situational factors (Morris and Peng 1994). Thus the Chinese are apparently more likely to cite things such as the fact that the person was "a victim of the Students' Educational Policy" or that they had "recently been fired" rather than mentioning facts about their character, their personality, or their psychological set when explaining behavior. The NPH predicts that we may well find a similar pattern with respect to the content of the narratives that are preferred or emphasized in Chinese cultures. Thus one possible explanation of the data may be that the Chinese may not favor the use of narratives of the specified folk psychological sort during childrearing. Or, to the extent that they do make use of them, these stories may not have the same prominence that they do in Western cultures.

Certainly, the evidence shows that we must be especially careful when making assumptions about cultures whose intellectual and political histories diverge significantly from those of the West in ways that might impinge on the relevant narrative practices. Relating and emphasizing folk psychological narratives to children—those in which the main characters act for reasons of their own—may be a primarily Western institution, one that has nonaccidental links to the ethicopolitical vision of individualism (see also Kusch 2007).[11] Of course, the evidence does not suggest that the Chinese are incapable of making sense of actions in terms of reasons or that they never do so. The point of citing this case is merely to underline the fact that when one looks carefully at the interpretative practices of other cultures, one finds more diversity in the explanatory tendencies and methods used in understanding human behavior than one might initially expect.

As long as we do not equivocate in our use of terms, the previous point does not imply that folk psychology takes different forms in other cultures (or that they have different folk psychologies). Claims about intercultural heterogeneity with respect to folk psychological practice must not be confused with claims that folk psychology is culturally relative in the sense of being polymorphic—that is, that it varies from culture to culture. The claim is not that folk psychology is not found in different *forms* elsewhere, but rather that it may not be used everywhere (or used to the same extent or with the same skill everywhere). It is a point of logic that the practice of making sense of intentional action in terms of reasons (stricto sensu) simply could not be different in different parts of the world. This is, of course, wholly consistent with the possibility that the practice itself is not universal but only relative to specific cultures.[12]

It is also important to be clear about the polemic force of the preceding observations. This evidence has not been cited in order to discredit the very idea of IMDs (I have used other arguments for that purpose).[13] What it does show is that the claim that all human cultures possess a built-in understanding of belief/desire psychology cannot be used as a motivation for thinking that IMDs must exist. For, on the face of it, it seems that not *all* humans in *all* cultures wind up with the very same folk psychological skills—at least, not as a matter of course.

We are not entitled to conclude that folk psychological practice is universal to all human populations simply because there are strong patterns of intracultural convergence, as revealed by running tests on subjects that hail from the industrial West.[14] The similarities in the folk psychological abilities and tendencies of European and American subjects are likely best explained by the fact that their early childhoods will have been crowded with folk psychological narratives. These narratives will have been encountered in fairy tales, children's books, comic books, television, films, and everyday conversations (Richner and Nicolopoulou 2001, 408; Nelson 2003, 22). And it is not just the form, content, and focus of these stories that is similar (in some cases, such as those involving canonical texts, exactly the same). In most Western societies, even the character of the storytelling practices, parenting styles, and schooling patterns is alike. Where such tight intracultural convergences exist with respect to narrative practices, we can expect to find similar levels of explanatory proficiencies and tendencies.

In sum, looking at the data from the few cross-cultural studies that have been conducted, we should be discouraged from making the Universal Convergence Assumption. And if we do not make that assumption, then another standard motivation for wanting to believe in built-in mindreading devices vanishes.

The "Mindblindness" Explanation of Autism

Children with autism have well-documented, and in some cases, profound difficulties with social interaction. In the debates concerning the basis of ToM abilities, the most discussed symptom of the disorder is the inability to pass false-belief tests, even when strong levels of general intelligence are demonstrated. It has been known for some time that "even with a mental age of 7 years, these children mostly fail in tasks which are normally passed around ages 3 and 4" (Leslie and Frith 1988, 315).

In contrast, children with Williams' syndrome display the opposite pattern of abilities and disabilities. For despite suffering from moderate mental retardation and severe difficulties with spatial cognition, individuals with Williams' syndrome exhibit extreme, sometimes overexuberant, hypersociability and affective responding. Thus, quite unlike children with autism, they regularly seek to engage others emotionally and have a tendency to attend closely to the facial expressions of others.

The existence of this double dissociation has helped to promote the idea that damaged or malfunctioning domain-specific mechanisms, some kind of innate mindreading device, may be responsible for the poor performances of children with autism in their dealings with others and, specifically, when it comes to passing false-belief tests. According to the received view, when functioning properly, mindreading mechanisms enable unimpaired children, or at least those of the appropriate age, to perform such tasks successfully. Against this background, debates have ensued for many years over which type of IMD—those of the theory-based or simulative variety—might be best suited to explain the observed patterns of mentalistic understanding exhibited by the normal and autistic populations.

Positing failed IMDs is the root idea of the "mindblindness" hypothesis. The catchy label might suggest that the heart of autism lies in an inability to "see other minds." But this is not remotely plausible. There are a great many symptoms associated with the disorder, both social and nonsocial. Typically, these are categorized under three broad headings: social interaction, communication, and creative imagination (see Baron-Cohen 2000). In more detail, individuals with autism are typified by a range of more specific difficulties, relating to

- Eye-gaze monitoring
- Joint attention
- Imitating facial expressions, gestures, and movement
- Rigidity and repetitiveness of behavior
- Reciprocal relating and empathy
- Distinguishing appearance from reality
- Pretend play/role-play
- Executive function/forward planning tasks
- Understanding cognitive emotions
- Understanding false-beliefs/beliefs about beliefs
- Pronominal usage
- Conversational pragmatics
- Use of prosody, metaphor, and irony

· Understanding and constructing mentalistic narratives
· Gestalt understanding/recognition of significance or relevance

This list is indicative, not comprehensive, but it suffices to show that if individuals with autism are mindblind, they are not *only* mindblind. An appraisal to the contrary would seriously mischaracterize the scope of the disorder. Indeed, it is unlikely that its many symptoms have a single cause. Although some attempts have been made to provide global explanations of the full spectrum of autistic difficulties, in recent times there has been a growing tendency to regard it as a multidimensional syndrome with a wide range of characteristic symptoms rather than as a unitary syndrome with a single common cause.[15]

Yet even if we restrict our concerns to the more obviously mentalistic items on the list, it turns out that those with autism are not entirely mindblind. They are oblivious to some but not all aspects of the psychological life of others. Autistic individuals seemingly understand some psychological concepts perfectly well. For example, Goldman (1992a, 112) cites a case in which

an able autistic young man who despite suffering from autism is very helpful with household chores and errands. One day, as his mother was mixing a fruit cake, she said to him "I haven't got any cloves. Would you please go out and get me some." The son came back a while later with a carrier bag full of girlish clothes, including underwear, from a High Street boutique. Clearly, the boy had misperceived the word "cloves" as "clothes." But what normal young man would assume his mother asked him to casually buy her clothes, just like that?

It is natural to suppose that the boy's mistake in this case derives from an inability to read the situation—a failure to grasp what it is normal for someone to ask for in these circumstances. This explains why he does not question what ought to seem a strange request from his mother. Perhaps, as some have proposed, this indicates a problem with being able to appropriately contextualize relevant information. This may be the case, but the example certainly reveals that the boy has a sound understanding of what it is for someone to "want" something. His actions show that he grasps this notion perfectly well, even if his understanding of what is likely to be wanted in such circumstances is decidedly peculiar. What matters is that he has an adequate understanding of the concept "desire."[16]

The mindblindness hypothesis is only credible therefore if it isolates its explanatory concerns to giving an account of why individuals with autism encounter problems in acquiring and using the metarepresentational concept of belief. Construed in this more precise way, it has been claimed that "mindblindness" is the "core and possibly universal abnormality of autistic individuals" (Baron-Cohen 2000, 3). Yet, even this claim is untenable given that not every autistic individual fails false-belief tests. Only some do; between 15 and 60 percent pass (Happé 1995).[17]

Less ambitiously, the mindblindness hypothesis can be interpreted as a proposal about how best to explain the performances of just that subset of autistic individuals who, in fact, fail false-belief tests. Their failures, it might be argued, should be attributed to the lack of a properly functioning IMD—that is, they lack "the relevant normally developing mechanism . . . for creating and handling *meta-representations*" (Leslie and Frith 1988, 315; original emphasis). Let us call this the Restricted Mindblindness Hypothesis (RMH).

It should be obvious from the discussion that opened this chapter that even the RMH directly threatens the NPH. For if the best explanation of autistic individuals' performance on false-belief tasks is malfunctioning IMDs (for example, ToMMs), this naturally implies that the true basis of metarepresentational understanding exhibited by the normal populace depends on their IMD functioning normally. The same line of argument can be replayed with respect to folk psychological understanding more generally.

Indeed, at first glance, the RMH looks like the best way to explain the unique pattern of narrative skills exhibited by autistic individuals. As compared with the normal population, they show serious problems when it comes to producing and digesting people narratives—that is, mentalistic ones—even though they can cope, in a basic way, with narratives that merely concern the antics of inanimate objects and agents who act in accord with simple behavioral scripts (see Baron-Cohen 1995, 72; Frith 1989, 163–165). Or, to be more precise, autistic individuals have proven themselves capable of coherently ordering and correctly sequencing cartoon frames relating to such topics, suggesting a very minimal narrative competence at least.[18]

If the relevant narrative competencies of the normal populace are best explained in terms of their use of IMDs, clearly our capacity to appreciate folk psychological narratives presupposes the existence of ToM abilities—in which case, my preferred variant of the NPH is in serious trouble. It is therefore crucial to the NPH's viability that another, non-IMD account is found to explain the metarepresentational incapacities of certain autistic individuals.

Supplying an alternative is not difficult once it is recalled that the false-belief-related impairments of autistic individuals boil down to inabilities to imagine divergent cognitive perspectives. Neutrally understood, this characterizes our explanans. For, as discussed in chapter 7, to have a practical understanding of belief is nothing other than being able to distinguish oneself as a believer in a contrast space of other believers. Like younger children, some autistic individuals seem incapable of this—the very idea of there being cognitive perspectives on factual situations, their own being just one among others, is what eludes them.[19]

Despite the popularity of the RMH, the available evidence only securely establishes that folk psychological understanding is highly domain specific. And this fact in no way lends conclusive support to the claim that an inability to successfully execute mentalistic tasks is best explained by damaged or imperfect IMDs. The big question is whether the RMH is the only or the best way to explain this particular inability. As a general rule, we should be suspicious when an explanans so conveniently meets the needs of its explanandum (that is, failures in metarepresentational tasks are best explained by malfunctions in metarepresentational mechanisms). Still, with appropriate modifications, it seems that failures of certain autistic individuals on false-belief tasks are best explained by the malfunction of some kind of inherited mechanism—only the mechanism in question is not best understood as a kind of IMD.

At root, the inability of some autistic individuals to imagine that others have different cognitive takes may stem from an impaired capacity for "perspective shifting." If so, their difficulties in this regard may take the form of a basic imaginative deficit—one that may also explain why they find it hard, if not impossible in some cases, to cope, even with nonlinguistic joint attention—that is, those forms of interpersonal responding that only involve the mutual recognition of intentional attitudes. And the fact is that autistic individuals have profound difficulties in this regard.[20] Often, these are quite fundamental; they fail even to meet the eyes of others or to attract another's attention.[21] These tendencies are "missing in the development of even quite able autistic children" (Kennett 2002, 347; Andrews 2002). What's more, problems with joint attention are strong indicators of later failure on false-belief tasks (Baron-Cohen and Sweetenham 1996; Gerrans 1998).

In line with my proposal about how children normally come to understand the concept of belief, as set out in chapter 7, I hold that an imaginative inability to shift perspective underlies the metarepresentational inability to imagine cognitive perspectives (that is, content-involving, linguistically represented, propositional attitudes). This same imaginative inability presents in failures in joint-attention tasks as an inability to imagine alternative visual perspectives on objects or situations. Since the former depends developmentally on the latter, again as argued in chapter 7, there is no need to postulate the existence of a dedicated metarepresentational mechanism at all. Although different sorts of attitudes are involved in the two activities—propositional as opposed to intentional—the same mechanism or mechanisms that enable the imaginative-capacity to perspective-shift is implicated in both joint attention and metarepresentation.

It follows that anyone with the relevant imaginative defect would be prevented from fruitfully engaging in conversations of a kind that require giving mutual attention to statements and keeping track of one's own propositional attitudes and those of others. It seems that participating in conversational dynamics of this kind is precisely what is beyond the ken of those with autism (Sigman, Yirmiya, and Capps 1995, 170–171; Barker and Givón 2005). I have suggested that a basic understanding of belief is fostered by exercising one's imagination in the relevant ways by engaging in such regular activity. If so, the failure of some autistic individuals on false-belief tasks can be put down to their congenital inability to partake in such exchanges, thus being robbed of a critical developmental opportunity. This in turn would be sufficient to explain why they are unable to appreciate and construct folk psychological narratives in particular and not narratives of other kinds.

It must also be noted that my alternative explanation is entirely consistent with the existence of "double dissociations." Indeed, because the imaginative capacity for perspective shifting is plausibly an ancient biological endowment, my proposal is not even at odds with the idea that this symptom of autism is ultimately neurologically based (see also Gallese 2006).

It has been claimed that the mechanisms that enable pretense may be the true source of our metarepresentational abilities—and that even the simplest acts of pretense involve "an early manifestation of the ability to understand mental states [and hence represent] the specific innate basis of our commonsense theory of mind" (Leslie 1987, 412). But in the stated form this conjecture has not held up well under scrutiny. The fact is that early forms of pretend play have no direct connection to an ability to imagine the mental states or propositional attitudes; instead they mostly involve imagining that certain objects are of a different kind than they in fact are. While it is hard to deny that this kind of imaginative capacity is related to metaphorical thinking, it surely does not entail an ability to think of others as having possibly divergent cognitive takes on situations—

that is, it hardly constitutes or need be based on a metarepresentational ability. The mere fact that children without autism engage in pretend play as early as age two is enough to suggest that these imaginative feats are at best a platform for a metarepresentational activity that develops later on, rather than the other way around.

Recent evaluations of experiments using picture-choice tasks support this conclusion—for children systematically pass these tests early on when the relevant requests are framed using the language of pretending, but not that of thinking (Astington and Jenkins 1999, 1318). And it has been demonstrated, in a way that is even more directly pertinent, that in a number of trials, "3-year olds understand pretence in terms of observable action, whereas 4-year olds are capable of attributing relevant states about a pretend sequence to an absent actor" (Berguno and Bowler 2004, 541). Making direct reference to Leslie's earlier work, the authors of this more recent study argue that a failure to make this kind of distinction has resulted in the data from previous experiments on pretense being interpreted ambiguously. It therefore seems safe to conclude that a basic capacity for pretense is not identical to a capacity for metarepresentation (nor does it developmentally presuppose the latter).

What is empirically well established is that children with autism demonstrate great difficulty in simultaneously entertaining or imagining more than one perspective on events and/or situations.[22] This shows up not just in their basic interpersonal interactions but also in more advanced forms of pretend play. For this reason, although autistic individuals are sometimes characterized as having an impoverished perspective on others, it is in fact closer to the truth to say that they are unable to recognize that others (or indeed that they themselves) have perspectives on situations at all.

All of this is consistent with the claim that a basic ability to engage in imaginative acts of perspective shifting is necessary (but not sufficient) as a platform for bona fide metarepresentational understanding. That kind of understanding develops when other conditions are also in place, such as a command of complex linguistic forms and the experience of engaging in conversations. That is how children normally come to recognize what it is to have a contrasting cognitive take on things.

Looked at in this light perhaps at least some of the core symptoms of autism might be related. It may be that problems in carrying off imaginative perspective shifts have a kind of domino effect; they may be the root cause of a range of further problems and exponentially bad effects. For example, if a basic imaginative deficit affects metarepresentational abilities it is likely to interfere with metacognition more generally. This might manifest itself when it comes to entertaining counterfactual possibilities and making complex future plans—the sorts of activities associated with executive control (see Currie 1996, 253). A fundamental imaginative inability may also be the source of the ultraliteral interpretive tendencies of autistic individuals and their related difficulties in understanding metaphor and analogy, all of which involve a kind of aspect switching. Plausibly, it could also shed light on why they have particular problems in the use and understanding of pronouns and in negotiating conversational pragmatics quite generally (see Frith 1989, chaps. 8, 11).[23]

Failures on these fronts would lead to other problems too since, by and large, "we establish and maintain relationships to others in dialogue and conversation" (Bohman 2000, 224). If, as suggested in chapter 2, folk psychological narratives constitute one important route into the norm-ridden social world that most of us occupy, then an inability to cope with them may partly explain why those with autism behave in socially awkward ways, showing only a very limited capacity to understand such things as jokes and exhibit a kind of obliviousness to the ethical dimension of most situations (see McGeer 2001, 113). And if people narratives help to establish our cultural "second natures," this may go some distance to explaining why autistic individuals have such trouble seeing what is "important, meaningful or relevant" (Frith 1989, 109; see also 5–6, 12, 108, 120, 134). Imaginative flexibility may be a nonnegotiable requirement for developing not only alternative sets of values, but also our own very first set. Finally, our sense as a person existing across time may depend on our ability to situate and understand ourselves as figuring in larger narratives. If so, a fundamental inability to understand and produce even short folk psychological narratives may even have the potential to explain why autistic individuals have only limited self-understanding (see Hobson 1993, 236–237).

This loose set of speculations has some prima facie plausibility. But a defense of the NPH does not depend on their holding good. All that is required is that there is a viable alternative to the "faulty IMD" explanation of why some autistic individuals fail false-belief tests. There is at least one. These might be adequately explained by a more fundamental imaginative disorder that interferes with or disrupts perspective shifting.

If I am right, the proponents of the RMH have things exactly backward; it is not that autistic individuals lack the concept of belief because they lack a working IMD! Rather, more fundamental imaginative deficits prevent them from coming to grips with the concept of belief; this in turn prevents them from properly mastering folk psychology. After all, having a practical understanding of *belief* is necessary for understanding *reasons*— and folk psychology requires having an understanding of reasons (minimally, the possible interrelations that can hold between beliefs and desires). That is something children only achieve by participating in a distinctive kind of narrative practice.

A Final Challenge

In all, there is no need to postulate a dedicated IMD to explain the abilities on which folk psychological competence rests. Although something more than a practical grasp of the forms and norms of folk psychology is required in order to make sense of others in everyday life, this does not take the form of inherited mindreading capacities. At best, our folk psychological understanding of action must be supplemented by a range of embodied, imaginative abilities, including abilities for nonpropositional perspective shifting and co-cognition.

The job of the NPH is only to explain how, when suitably supported, children become skilled folk psychologists. It also reminds us that making sense of action in terms of reasons is essentially a narrative practice. But it still only provides part of the story of how we make sense of others in everyday practical situations. A wide range of strategies and alternative methods are deployed for that purpose. Making sense of others by folk psychological means is only the tip of a much larger iceberg.

Yet there is one residual concern that must be aired and dealt with to ensure that the NPH is not regarded as false or at least radically incomplete. It can be cast in the form of a question. If folk psychology has its basis in a late-arriving sociocultural practice, how is it that our immediate ancestors, the hominids, succeeded in their sophisticated interpersonal interactions without it?

11 First Communions

How did humans bridge the tremendous gap between symbolic thought and the nonsymbolic forms of intelligence that still dominate the rest of the animal kingdom?

—Donald 1991, 4

The Missing Cognitive Link

The existence of chimpanzee ToM abilities was once a very hot topic of debate. As early as 1978 Premack and Woodruff asked, in a paper by the same name, "Does the chimpanzee have a theory of mind?" Of all the primates, it was initially thought that chimps alone engage in acts of genuine tactical deception.[1] It was thought that if this could be established then it would have settled the matter; to deceive with intent apparently involves representing the beliefs, desires, and intentions of others—implying that chimpanzees have the capacity for metarepresentational intentional attribution. For true intentional deception calls on a *sophisticated* mentalistic understanding not only of states of mind such as desires but, crucially, also beliefs (Hauser 1997).

Early assessments, based on anecdotes of the behaviors of individual animals, encouraged a positive answer to the Premack and Woodruff question. There were reported cases of what seemed to be genuine intentional deception (and even counterdeception) on the part of at least some chimpanzees. One such sophisticated interplay took the form of tactical exchanges in the context of food-harboring contests between two chimps, Belle—a female—and Rock—the dominant male. These contests, which were arranged as part of a series of experiments conducted by Menzel, had the virtue of revealing aspects of behavior in what would be relatively ecologically normal settings for these apes (Bryne and Whiten 1991).

The setup was such that Belle was privileged by being shown the whereabouts of hidden food by the researchers. However, she soon discovered any attempt on her part to openly alert others to its presence, resulted in Rock's taking it. This led her to adopt a series of deceptive tactics whenever Rock was nearby. Initially, she would sit on the food—until Rock caught on and began regularly pushing her aside to check beneath her. After this she consistently stopped short of the actual location of the food whenever Rock was in the vicinity. By way of reply, Rock started searching the area around her ever more widely, until he successfully obtained the food. The moves in this dance became increasingly more elaborate, step by step, much to Belle's frustration no doubt.

Chimpanzees learn quickly from trial-and-error experience. There can be no question that these apes closely monitor one another (and even monitor another's monitoring of them). They are also capable of remembering the past behaviors and attitudes of individuals and the circumstances in which they are likely to be evoked. This would be sufficient to explain how they develop fresh plans of action that are swiftly adjusted and adapted, as need be, on the hoof in light of new developments. But this suggests that their antics can be adequately explained without positing any understanding of other minds at all. For example, Belle and Rock might just be very talented behaviorists. Those who have pushed for the mindreading interpretation have long been aware of this killjoy alternative and its undermining force (see Byrne and Whiten 1997, 9).[2]

Against the deflationary interpretation, one of Rock's advanced stratagems was cited as compelling evidence that chimpanzees, as a species, must have mature ToM abilities. In one interaction, Belle employed a new tactic of waiting until Rock was seemingly distracted before moving toward the food. Rock eventually countered this by pretending to look away, and even sometimes by heading off in another direction, apparently to give the impression that his attention was occupied elsewhere. For all intents and purposes, it seemed as if this was done purposefully in order to lull Belle into a false sense of security, for after going a certain distance, Rock would suddenly turn—without warning—to catch her, using her as a guide to the food's location. Admittedly, this sort of behavior is not the norm in the chimpanzee repertoire but if one animal could achieve it, it must be within the species' cognitive reach. Most importantly, it seems impossible to make sense of Rock's pretense—his tactic of feigning disinterest—without attributing to him a capacity for mentalistic attribution. The suggestion was therefore made that this particular chimpanzee must in fact have had a capacity for intentional attribution of a third-order of magnitude: "Rock *believes* that Belle will *think* that he no longer *wants* to discover what she *knows* about hidden food" (Bryne and Whiten 1991, 131).

Many methodological reasons have been given for resisting the conclusion that Rock is a sophisticated metarepresentationalist. Observations that rely heavily on anecdote always have a high risk of overinterpretation. To properly assess how an individual animal actually achieves its feats, it is vital to know every aspect of its entire learning history so as to rule out any alternative explanations (and that is not typically possible). It is especially important to handle even the most careful observations of this kind with extreme care, given our strong tendency to interpret others in our own mentalistic image. And even if it could be established that Rock was a mentalizer of some sort, it is never a good policy to extrapolate from a single case to draw conclusions about the cognitive capacities of an entire species. In light of these risks, it seems that serious progress on the question of whether chimpanzees are mindreaders demands conducting rigorous experiments—experiments that incorporate appropriate controls and permit replication (Premack 1988; Bryne and Whiten 1997).

One landmark experiment has taken the heat out of the debate over great-ape ToM abilities considerably. It used a simplified version of the "location-change" false-belief test adapted for use with nonverbals and conducted with chimpanzees and orangutans (Call and Tomasello 1999). Although the apes displayed a solid grasp of the task logistics in pretest controls, their performance under actual test conditions was dismal; with a success rate of only 10.7 percent in trials they were performing well below chance. Strong correlations between performances of four- and five-year-old human children on the standard verbal and this nonverbal version of the test imply that the latter is an adequate indicator of false-belief understanding.

On the basis of these results there is now a well-established consensus that chimpanzees are not metarepresentationalists—that is, that they are incapable of understanding the concept of belief (Papineau 2003; Povinelli and Vonk 2003; Tomasello, Call, and Hare 2003a; Sterelny 2003).[3] The live issue of today is therefore no longer whether chimpanzees have metarepresentational ToM abilities but to what extent they have any degree of genuine mindreading ability at all. Primatologists have shifted the debate to a new level. The main question now occupying the field is: How do apes manage their sophisticated intersubjective interactions *without* full-blown mentalizing? What form does their social cognition actually take? There are at least four ways we might possibly understand it. Chimpanzees might be using (1) a primitive theory of mind, (2) a theory of behavior

(ToB), (3) an early mindreading system, or (4) unprincipled embodied expectations.

These results, and those discussed in chapter 6, can be regarded as evidence for the claim that chimpanzees might be operating with a primitive type of ToM—one that allows for the attribution of low-level goals and the recognition of agency, providing a rudimentary conceptual understanding of knowledge/ignorance and seeing/not seeing (Whiten 1997, 161; Premack 1988, 175, 179). Yet it is the second option that is now in ascendancy among primatologists; it is now widely thought that chimpanzees might be coping in their dealings with one another by reasoning about behaviors and not minds. It may be that they are in fact nothing more than extremely proficient behaviorists.[4] This claim is, for example, the central plank in the reinterpretation hypothesis (or RIH). According to the RIH, the pattern of profound dissimilarities as well as points of overlap in chimpanzee and human social psychology is best explained by a two-level account (Povinelli and Vonk 2003, 158). Uniquely human ToM abilities are thought to build on and reinterpret ToB products, bringing new explanatory depth and predictive possibilities to the earlier nonmentalistic mode of theorizing. A distinctive feature of this proposal is the claim that the more ancestral ToB "remained undisturbed by the evolution of theory of mind" (Povinelli 2003, 59). ToMs therefore only provide a new system for "coding" the very same behaviors that the ToB initially classifies. In this way the ToM abilities of humans are simply "woven" in around the old capacities; they are straightforwardly additive.[5]

In support of this proposal, Povinelli and Vonk have argued that in every case, the behavior of the chimpanzees could be explained by a reliance on purely behavioral predictions. Their claim is that we can be sure of this since some behavioral abstraction or other must serve as the logical basis for even low-level mentalistic ascriptions. Thus they have speculated that chimpanzees may be using rules such as "Don't go after the food if the dominant has oriented toward it", but without adding the mentalistic twist: *because he has seen it, and therefore knows where it is* (Povinelli and Vonk 2003, 159). The food-competition experiments, discussed in chapter 6, were explicitly designed to rule out this possibility. In certain trials the subordinates could not have been influenced by any online cues from the dominant, for in them the following conditions held jointly: (1) the subordinate was given an early head start before entering the room, and (2) the dominant's door was completely lowered. In those cases, at least, subordinates will have had to act based only on what they remembered since there were no "live" behavioral cues for them to read. Thus the subordinates will have had to recall what the dominant had seen in the past (as opposed to what he was currently orienting toward) (Call 2001). But this misrepresents the nature of the ToB proposal—it treats it as entirely cue-based and contrasts it with more robust cognitivist proposals. However, those who defend the ToB theory are clear that chimpanzee social cognition is thought to be grounded in representations and is not a mere sensitivity to cues.

Accordingly, chimps are first-class cognizers. These apes are not just reading behaviors, they are making use of behavior-based conceptual abstractions, calling on their understanding of rules of behavior. Abstract behaviors are classified and categorized into higher-order types and the links between these are understood inferentially. For example, in classifying a given behavior as "threat display," chimps are able to reason about and predict what is likely to follow, such as charging or hitting. Hence ToB theorists maintain that "chimpanzees undoubtedly form concepts related to the statistical regularities in behaviour" (Povinelli and Vonk 2003, 157). Rules and representations are required for ToB predictions in just the same way they are needed for those of the ToM variety; it is their contents that differ. Chimpanzee reasonings about behavior are therefore based in the use of principles that constitute an organized, coherent body of knowledge; presumably these are explicitly represented at some level.[6]

This being so, there is no reason to think that chimps using a ToB would need greater access to online cues in order to make predictions than they would if they were using a primitive ToM. Moreover, it is possible that what they remember is not what the dominant had seen/not seen but what he previously oriented toward/did not orient toward. This would be enough to fuel a behavioral rule appropriate to the situation.[7]

We need to be clear about the degrees of sophistication as well as about the relevant limitations exhibited in chimpanzee intersubjective engagements when assessing proposals about their basis. The mere fact that the two dominant cognitivist proposals for understanding chimpanzee social cognition take the form of a primitive theory of mind or a theory of behavior should give us pause for thought. If chimpanzees' capacities can be explained in this way, it might be wondered why chimpanzees need any theory at all in order to prosecute their social dealings. For example, it is within the realm of possibility that they might simply be making inductions based on past experience, noting perhaps that Xs (or some particular X) tend to Y in circumstances Z (Gauker 2003; Andrews 2003).[8] As a basic rule of thumb, the weaker a given theory is imagined to be, the easier it will be to imagine that one could get by without it using nontheoretical methods.

As argued in chapter 6, the ability profile of chimpanzees suggests that their intersubjective capacities are at best parochial; they neither make predictions of the sort that are applicable in a wide range of contexts nor do they apply them to a wide range of targets. This being so it is unclear why this would drive us to suppose that they must be operating with abstract rules or concepts of any kind. We should be suspicious of the idea that chimpanzees are theorists at all. This conclusion is especially compelling when conjoined with the more serious worry about representationalist theories, again as discussed in chapter 6. For the fact is that "how chimpanzees might have acquired such rules is not specified, nor is there any speculation about how they might understand them" (Tomasello, Call, and Hare 2003b, 239). This certainly is a pressing concern. Those who favor what I have called the "principled approach" must face up to the problem of explaining how the relevant concepts and rules—those that form the basis of their respective theories—get their contents.

Here the work of earlier chapters begins to pay off. I propose that informational sensitivity to the other's intentional attitudes drives specific behavioral routines that can be elaborated on by individual learning. These constitute the embodied expectations and anticipations that chimpanzees have about others. Such responding is therefore not based on the use of concepts, principles, or theories. It does not even involve the representation of behaviors or mental states but only a direct responsiveness to them (when conditions are normal).

In responding to another's seeing or knowing, chimpanzees are not representing these in propositional attitude terms. Instead they have embodied expectations about intentional attitudes of significant others. Thus even when their "purposeful" engagements are tailored to deal with specific individuals on specific occasions, these are not based in beliefs per se. They are not grounded in propositional knowledge of any kind, even though they constitute sometimes quite sophisticated attempts to control, direct, or respond to the behavior of others. This more minimalist proposal provides an obvious way of reassessing what lies at the heart of those acts of tactical deception in which at least some chimpanzees, such as Rock, engage.

Whether one accepts this or not, the unequivocal conclusion is that "apes do not have a 'theory of mind' in the sense of understanding the false beliefs of others.... [Thus such abilities] must have arisen in the human lineage only after human beings split from chimpanzees some 6–8 million years ago" (Call and Tomasello 1999, 393; see figure 11.1). Most researchers involved in experimenting with chimpanzees now agree on this much (Tomasello, Call, and Hare 2003a, 2003b; Povinelli 2003; Povinelli and Vonk 2004; Call and Tomasello 2005). This is important, for whatever we ultimately decide about the nature of the basis of the inter-subjective engagements of apes, it is well established that "only a small amount of social cognition involves reasoning about mental states" (Povinelli 2003, 59).

If mature mindreading capacities must have emerged at a point in our prehistory sometime *after* the human line broke from that of the great apes, they must have shown up within the million years or so just prior to the beginning of recorded human history—that is, at some point during the Pleistocene. The received wisdom is that hominids must have had a gradual development of metarepresentational IMD, since ascribing beliefs to one another must have constituted at least one of their most used party tricks. It is typically thought that such mechanisms underpin a range of

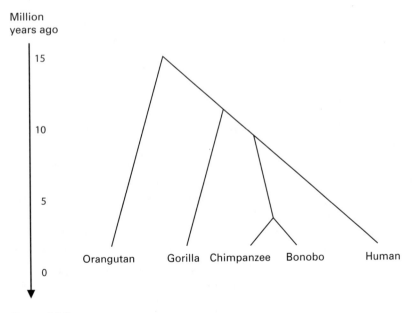

Figure 11.1
The Evolutionary Trees of the Greater Apes (reprinted from P. Gärdenfors, *How Homo Became Sapiens: On the Evolution of Thinking*, 7, Oxford University Press. Copyright © 2003. Used with permission from P. Gärdenfors).

unique hominid talents, including those for (1) advanced toolmaking, (2) social cohesion, and (3) language formation/learning (Baron-Cohen 1999; Mithen 2000a). The idea is that the dedicated mindreading mechanisms that allowed for all of this were formed and fashioned by biological evolution, thus inherited directly by us, having been built into our species.

Close scrutiny of the available evidence gives no reason for believing this to be true—indeed it suggests a superior, alternative explanation. I call it the mimetic ability hypothesis (or MAH). In essence, it claims that growing recreative imaginative abilities funded impressive mimetic skills and that these best account for the sophisticated social engagements of the hominids—even those implicated in their capacity to form and learn symbolic language. For example, a capacity for reciprocal mimesis is well suited for explaining what grounds the shared norms and basic intersubjective agreement needed to sponsor basic rule-following activity. In contrast, ToM-based accounts are not appropriately equipped to explain this. When the two proposals are compared side by side, the explanatory virtues of the MAH become evident and the suggestion that modern humans inherited metarepresentational mindreading devices from our nearest ancestors looks like a weak and somewhat incredible hypothesis. At the very least, the mere availability of the MAH reveals that we have no overriding reason to suppose that hominids must have had a sophisticated capacity for folk psychological understanding.

How might we decide between these two possibilities? Cognitive archaeology—the attempt to understand ancestral minds by drawing on insights of psychology applied to remnants of prehistory—is a highly speculative business. Not only is the archaeological record gappy, with only fragmentary material evidence having been preserved and much of it yet to be discovered, there are no live subjects to test. This means we do not even know, with any certainty, which kind of activities our ancestors engaged in and what abilities they may have had. And, as just shown by the debates over the cognitive capacities of nonhuman primates, even when we have live subjects to examine there is scope for competing interpretations about how precisely to characterize and explain the basis of social-psychological abilities. By comparison, the task of deciding between rival conjectures about prehistoric cognition is trickier still.

Matters are helped somewhat by the general consensus about the level, if not the nature, of the cognitive capacities of chimpanzees. Placed alongside what we know about the abilities of modern humans—both infants and adults—this yields at least a very rough sense of the cognitive distance that hominids must have covered. That is, in thinking about the common ancestor we shared with chimpanzees, we know roughly where our forerunners must have started and where they ended up, even if details of the precise route taken remain obscure. Despite its sketchiness, the archaeological record gives us a general picture, though to be sure a changeable and contestable one, of the large features of the terrain they covered and the likely timing of their specific movements. However imperfect, this is the evidence against which we must test the plausibility of proposals about our ancestors' likely cognitive powers and what may have driven them.

It is beyond doubt that there was a cognitive change—or series of changes—of considerable magnitude that took place over the period spanning from the emergence of a common ape-human ancestor approximately six million years ago to the appearance of *Homo sapiens* (see figure 11.2). If we assume a neo-Darwinian perspective, it is likely that such changes will have happened gradually, presumably under a variety of selection pressures. Since the perceived cognitive gulf between apes and humans is so great, despite the fact that we share at least 95 percent of the same genetic makeup, the Pleistocene is regarded by evolutionary

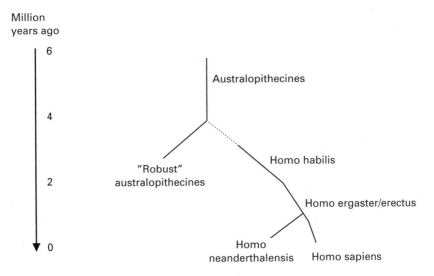

Figure 11.2
A Simplified Evolutionary Tree of the Hominids (reprinted from P. Gärdenfors, *How Homo Became Sapiens: On the Evolution of Thinking*, 7, Oxford University Press. Copyright © 2003. Used with permission from P. Gärdenfors).

psychologists as the environment of evolutionary adaptiveness (for more on these issues see Dupré 2001, chap. 2; Sinha 2004); it is the home of the missing cognitive link or links that paved the way for the eventual development of distinctively human cultures and our unique linguistic abilities.

Recognizing these limitations, in the remainder of this chapter I review the existing evidence and challenge the assumptions that lend prima facie support to the familiar and widely held view that the gradual development of sophisticated mindreading devices must have constituted at least *one* important hominid upgrade.

Imitation and Social Learning

Going back to the very first hominids, there is no reason to think that their lifestyles offered challenges of a significantly different kind from that faced by the apes—certainly, no drastic change occurred in this respect until long after the passing of *Australopithecus afarensis* and after the arrival of *Homo habilis*. With the latter's appearance we see the first major spurt in brain size (which increased roughly 1.5 times in cranial capacity compared to that of the australopithecines). Indeed, the fossil record tells a story of just two such instances of encephalization in human prehistory. The first, and most remarkable, roughly coincides with the emergence of simple Oldowan tool manufacture—a craft supervised by these first members of the *Homo* line (see figure 11.2). Although the tools made during this period would have been extremely basic in many respects, by today's standards, their fashioning would have constituted an impressive achievement—a genuine innovation—when compared with what had come before (or rather what had not).

The stone-knapping techniques involved in the production of such tools would have required a good sensitivity to fractural dynamics and strong eye-hand coordination, capacities that far outstrip those required for making simple repetitive actions (Mithen 1996, 2000b; Wynn 2000). And an off-line imaginative ability to reenact and practice complex routines would have been needed not only for the technical proficiency of fashioning the final products but also for the collection and preparation of materials. Acts of imagination—perceptual reenactments—look likely to have funded these aspects of the early toolmaker's craft.

Clearly, not even weak ToM abilities would have been needed for the individual acts of making of such tools, but they might have played a crucial part in enabling the social learning on which the tool industries themselves were founded. For more than an individual's potential to fashion such tools would have been needed to keep the practice alive; such crafts had to be maintained over time.[9] Could it be that ToM abilities might have played a critical pedagogical role in ensuring this? In assessing this idea, let us simply accept the consensus view that "the Paleolithic record suggests very strong social learning of such skills" (Mithen 2000b, 496).[10] Very well, but what is the exact connection with ToM abilities? Mithen suggests that

it seems most probable that these technical skills and traditions were intentionally taught from generation to generation, or acquired by passive watching and active imitation. A modern-like theory of mind appears *essential* to either task. Instructed learning requires that both the teacher and the novice take account of what is in each other's mind. (Mithen 2000a, 496, emphasis added; Mithen 2002; see also Baron-Cohen 1999, 263)

Despite this rather bold statement, the idea that passive watching and active imitation implies ToM abilities (of any sort) is surely false. Demonstrating this is of particular importance because there is a strong independent reason to suppose that hominids must have had impressive imitative abilities. Humans are natural mimics and our basic abilities in this regard seem to be inherited, though they may be elaborated and extended by epigenesis (see Sinha 2004). Human neonates, as is well known, engage in facial imitation even at the tender age of thirty-two hours old (indeed it has been claimed that they are capable of this when they are less than an hour old) (Meltzoff and Moore 1977, 1994; Gopnik and Meltzoff 1997, 131).

Young chimpanzees have shown similar abilities (see Myowa-Yamakoshi et al. 2004). Yet the claim is not that humans alone are natural-born mimics, it is that we are also mimics of the first rank. Recent work on imitation carefully distinguishes a number of different forms, including stimulus enhancement, goal emulation, response priming, and imitation proper (Billard and Arbib 2002, 344; Rizzolatti, Graighero, and Fadiga 2002, 52; Hurley 2005). The first three abilities on this list only require capacities for detecting and responding to intentional attitudes—for example, involving only copying the simple behaviors of others in order to achieve a particular goal. True or complex imitation, by way of contrast, stands out in that it requires the capacity to copy both the novel ends and means of another's complex action.

When compared with humans, apes are much less good at complex forms of imitation (see Donald 2005, 285–286; Jones 2005). The fact is that it remains a matter of some dispute whether they are capable of true imitation at all. Monkeys are able to copy simple actions, such as a movement sequence tied to a particular goal but they cannot reproduce complex ones involving hierarchically structured repertoires. They can copy bodily movements but without adoption of specific goal structures with multiple substeps. Chimpanzees too may only be capable of limited forms of imitation involving uncomplicated movements—their performances only becoming reliable after considerable training. Exactly what level of ability chimpanzees really have in this regard remains a somewhat open question (Zlatev, Persson, and Gärdenfors 2005; Whiten, Horner, and Marshal-Pescini 2005). But what is not in doubt is that their abilities stand in stark contrast to those of young human infants who are able to masterfully copy complex and novel movements and actions—even those segmented into discrete ordered parts—with no training and little effort. Putting these thoughts together, it seems hard to deny that distinctively human imitative abilities are inherited from the hominids.

I take this as established common ground. But, *pace* Mithen, there is simply no reason to think that imitative abilities in any way entail ToM abilities. To see this, it helps to have a clear picture of just what imitation involves. Bermúdez (1998, 125) neatly characterizes the problem that infants must solve in order to imitate faces:

Facial imitation involves matching a seen gesture with an unseen gesture, since in normal circumstances one is aware of one's own face only haptically and proprioceptively. If successful facial imitation is to take place, a visual awareness of someone else's face must be apprehended so it can be reproduced on one's own face.

If we model what is going on in the infant on the way a suitably well informed adult might attempt to solve this sort of problem, using a set of explicit propositional instructions, then their ability to converge on precisely the right gesture to be imitated will be regarded as "the product of inference-like processes and . . . not merely reflexive" (Gopnik and Meltzoff 1997, 130). And it would seem to follow that "very young infants represent a variety of aspects of human action; they can make inferences on the basis of these representations; they think of themselves and others as fundamentally sharing the same psychological states" (Gopnik and Meltzoff 1997, 133). If so, we must presuppose that infants are aware of at least some sort of substantive self/other contrast from birth—and this might imply some sort of ToM capacity (Gopnik 2004, 22). But this line of thought raises a number of difficult questions. What is the character of this neonatal understanding of the self/other contrast? What is the precise content of the representations that these infants are allegedly using, and what is their origin? And, crucially, what account can be given of the subpersonal mechanisms that make use of these representations in order to effect the appropriate manipulation of infants' faces and bodies?

In offering a straight choice between inferentialist accounts and merely reflexive ones, theory theorists, such as Gopnik and Meltzoff, have missed a trick.[11] Research into mirror neuron systems (MNSs) holds out the promise of a better way of understanding the mechanics of simian and human neonatal abilities to imitate buccal and facial expressions and other gestures (Gallese 2003; Rizzolatti 2005).

Even though research in this area is still at the early stage it is widely agreed that "a mechanism with the characteristic of the mirror system appears to have the potentiality to give a neurophysiological, mechanistic explanation of imitation" (see Rizzolatti, Craighero, and Fadiga 2002, 55). This is an instance in which we have some reason to believe that the promissory note for future explanations might actually get cashed.

The fact that MNSs of apes are not as sophisticated as the human variety could explain their limited capacity for complex forms of imitation; the differences are empirically well established, having been demonstrated by various brain-imaging studies (Knoblich and Jordan 2002, 115; Rizzolatti and Luppino 2001; Arbib 2005). Also, more importantly, in the human case the potential fit with the basic type of inherited mimetic abilities to be explained is ideal. It is easy enough to imagine that our early hominid ancestors might have started their mimetic careers with abilities akin to those of "young children [who] spontaneously imitate adults in a *mirror-like* fashion" (Wohlschläger and Bekkering 2002; emphasis added). Just as children only begin to make the appropriate adjustments for cross-lateral differences when imitating others as they get older, so too the mimetic capacities of hominids may have become similarly enriched over evolutionary time.[12] Looking to embodied accounts for an explanation of imitative abilities is surely a better bet than positing modules with the relevant declarative knowledge to do such work.

Sterelny (2003, 64) identifies and deftly defuses the assumption that can make it look as if a ToM might be needed for these basic kinds of imitative tasks:

The link between imitation and theory of mind depends on the supposition that imitation involves a translation between points of view: the mimic represents something like the model's motor pattern as seen by an onlooker, and turns it into a representation of a motor pattern as seen by the agent himself. But that is not the only possibility. . . . If the mimic represents the model's behaviour functionally—pick up the rock in the grasping hand; hold the nut facing away; place it on smooth hard surface—there is no need to transform between points of view.

There are good reasons to opt for the simpler functional interpretation of this process, appealing to resonance pattern research in order to understand its mechanics. Although I have said that the mirror systems of humans are much more sophisticated than those of other primates, taking stock of the lessons of chapter 6, we must not suppose that the basic acts of imitation they sponsor have any of the standard features of mentalistically based simulations per se. Certainly, they do not implicate the kinds of simulation procedures that involve the manipulation and attribution of propositional attitudes (see Goldman 2005, 82; Gallagher 2007a). Here it pays to remember that Gallese and Goldman (1998, 498), who were the first to claim that the discovery of mirror neurons might lend respectable empirical backing to ST, only ever took the evidence to show that there were primitive precursors that might be related to explicit, mentalistic forms of simulation. As such, it is clear that the kind of responsiveness associated with these precursor abilities cannot be identified with or understood in terms of ToM capacities of either the TT or ST variety. The bottom line is that there is simply no need or warrant to postulate any inferential or theoretical activity on the part of the embodied systems that supports basic forms of imitation. And it is mimetic abilities of this sort that suffice to explain how technical skills are acquired and developed by attending either to one's own or another's action routines (whether selectively or otherwise) so that these can be recalled and reenacted. In this context, it is important to remember a lesson from chapter 4, which Donald (1999, 145) has taken pains to underscore: "The process that generates these action-patterns relies on a principle of perceptual resemblance; accordingly I have labeled the skill 'mimesis' or 'mimetic skill'."

Worse still, the truth is that Mithen's claim that our ancestors would have needed ToM abilities for the social transmission of technical skills does not hold up even if we imagine that basic acts of imitation do involve representing the representational contents of the others' minds. Thus, even if we suppose that the minds of ancient toolmakers were filled with sets of instructions about how to fashion their artifacts, representing these would have been of little use to the trainee. A clutch of rules—here imagined as a series of conditional statements—is the wrong sort of medium for technical training and instruction of the kind needed to learn basic tool manufacture. Quite the opposite: it is often the case when learning a practical craft that mastering a set of explicit rules is a positive hindrance. This fact will be salient to anyone who has tried to build a do-it-yourself product using only a pictureless set of instructions, with no blueprint for guidance. Call this the "Ikea constraint."

Technical training is not about passing on procedural knowledge *that*, but of engendering a kind of know-*how*. Novices typically get the knack by direct hands-on practice. And where this is not possible, they must attend to what the other does and attempt to reenact the appropriate steps using their visuomotoric imagination in a cross-modal way (consider how one might learn the relevant skill of fashioning the Levallois flake using a diagram such as figure 11.3).

This sort of need is felt even today, as when surgeons are given the chance to "*see* one done" before actually performing operations. It is therefore hardly surprising that verbal instruction, even when it is readily available as an accompaniment, appears to play a minor role in craft apprenticeship, even among modern humans (Donald 1991, 213; Wynn 1991). Mimesis of the kind discussed is perfectly suited to enable the nongenetic copying required for the passing down of technical skills through the generations by imitative means. Social training of this kind takes the form of showing not saying (of imagining not thinking, for that matter).

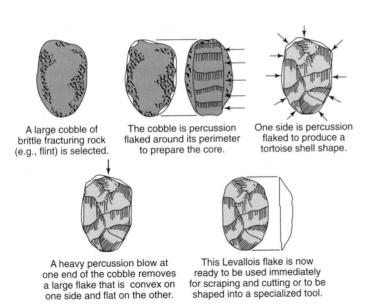

A large cobble of brittle fracturing rock (e.g., flint) is selected.

The cobble is percussion flaked around its perimeter to prepare the core.

One side is percussion flaked to produce a tortoise shell shape.

A heavy percussion blow at one end of the cobble removes a large flake that is convex on one side and flat on the other.

This Levallois flake is now ready to be used immediately for scraping and cutting or to be shaped into a specialized tool.

Figure 11.3

Technique for Fashioning the Levallois Flake (reproduced from http://anthro .palomar.edu/homo2/archaic_culture.htm or http://anthro.palomar.edu/homo2/ default.htm. Used with permission from Dennis O'Neil).

This is consistent with the fact that the mimetic skills in question develop over time; this happened in ontogeny and is likely to be recapitulated in phylogeny too, in an epigenetic manner: imitative learners might become more selective and discriminating in the sorts of routines that they choose to mimic (see Harris and Want 2005; Sinha 2004).

The Mimetic Ability Hypothesis

If ToMMs are neither implicated in the maintenance of tool industries nor the basis of imitative capacities, perhaps they were needed to fund sophisticated social skills of the hominids. This seems most unlikely. *H. habilis* looks to have been living in groups only marginally larger in size than that of australopithecines, and both would have kept within relatively tight geographic boundaries (Mithen 1996). There is no compelling reason to think that the social circumstances of the very early hominids would have changed enough to require more powerful tools for engaging in or monitoring social dynamics of a qualitatively different sort than those afforded to apes. Very much in line with current thinking about the abilities of our simian relatives in this regard, Mithen—who has done more than most in thinking about the likely stages of ToM development—surmises that the Oldowan toolmakers would have had "an equivalent theory of mind ability to that found within chimpanzees today. As an alternative they would have been extremely clever behaviorists" (Mithen 2000a, 500).

Things changed decisively with the coming of *Homo ergaster/erectus* in the Lower Paleolithic period.[13] Their arrival was accompanied by a remarkable new way of life, which some regard as constituting the first Hominid Revolution. Unlike its predecessors, the extent of *H. ergaster/erectus* movements—coming out of Africa and spreading across Europe and Asia—were unprecedented. During this period the quality of tools improved quite dramatically, so much so that "archaeologists require months of training and practice to become good at creating Acheulian tools" (Donald 1991, 179). This could be explained by an increase in mimetic ability, which would have also conferred advantages with respect to other technical crafts such as shelter construction.

But such skills would have also permitted new and more complex forms of social coordination. Many animals, but particularly those who form cohesive social units, faithfully produce and respond to characteristic expressive behaviors of others, normally conspecifics (Allen and Saidel 1998). They can signal shifts in emotional temperament or mood and otherwise indicate their readiness to engage in characteristic kinds of action. For example the bearing of teeth, the arching of backs, and the lowering of heads can be early warnings that the other is preparing to fight, or mate, or retreat, and so on. Being able to faithfully produce and respond to such recognizable behaviors makes basic social coordination possible.

The mimetic ability with which hominids appear to have been gifted would have been qualitatively unlike these other animal signal systems, not just in its special mirroring character but in being securely under voluntary control.[14] Although it is likely that our ancestors would have used the full range of facial, vocal, and postural gestures, at least to some limited extent, it is likely that manual gestures would have dominated (Donald 1991; Arbib 2005). It is likely that the tree-based living of their simian forefathers would have prepared the early hominids with the prodigious dexterous freedom and control—a freedom that the shift to bipedalism would have allowed them to capitalize on (Corballis 2003; Lieberman 2000, 151–153). Also, being self-cueing and self-regulating, the hominid ability to imitate would have constituted a major step beyond the more stereotypically circumscribed patterns of interaction that characterize the intersubjective engagements of other social creatures, those that depend mainly on inherited routines alone to structure the basic form of their engagements. A flexibility conferred by mimetic skills in conjunction with recreative imaginative abilities for practice and rehearsal would have vastly increased the developmental possibilities for social expression and engagement, as discussed in chapter 6 (see also Sinha 2004).

This openness would have introduced new challenges; coordinating intersubjective interactions in stable and effective ways would require taming or regulating these newfound capacities for freedom of expression, at least within local communities. It is very plausible that this was achieved by the development of a kind of mimetic culture. Donald has convincingly argued that the establishment of such culture would have funded the emergence of games, rites, and well-defined norms of a kind unlike anything found in simian "societies." A kind of mutual miming—which Donald (1991, chap. 6) calls "reciprocal mimesis"—is the plausible basis of nonlinguistic conventions.[15] Such interactions could have acted as powerful social glue.

In fact, it may be that reciprocal mimesis can be called on to do some heavy philosophical lifting: offering a potential solution to the rulefollowing paradox (see Hutto 2003/2006, chap. 4). Although I will not explore this idea further at this juncture, I leave it for the reader to imagine the possibilities for taking it forward by considering two pregnant passages from Wittgenstein:

If one of a pair of chimpanzees once scratched the figure |– –| in the earth and there-upon the other series |– –| |– –| etc., the first would not have given a rule nor would the other be following it, whatever else went on at the same time in the minds of the two of them.

If however there were observed, e.g., the phenomenon of a kind of instruction, of *shewing how* and of *imitation*, of lucky and misfiring attempts, of reward and pun-ishment and the like; if at length the one who had been so trained put figures which he had never seen before one after another in sequence as in the first example, then we should probably say that the one chimpanzee was writing rules down, and the other following them (RFM VI §42; Wittgenstein 1978, 345, emphasis added).

This was our paradox: no course of action could be determined by a rule, because every course of action can be made out to accord with a rule. . . . What this shows is that *there is a way of grasping a rule which is not an interpretation but which is exhib-ited* in what we call "obeying the rule" and "going against it" in actual cases. (PI 201; Wittgenstein 1953; reprinted 1989, 81e, emphasis added)

At the very least, the development of mimetic abilities that sponsored the emergence of a unique hominid culture is a credible explanation of changed living patterns and augmented technical and social abilities of *H. ergaster/erectus*, without the need to postulate that these hominids were in command of anything like a modern language. Certainly, a capacity for reciprocal miming and the establishment of a mimetic culture could have played a central part in an impressive list of important activities and prac-tices, such as childrearing, coordinated hunting and gathering, food sharing, and defining community recognized social ranks and statuses. Mimetic abilities look well suited to explain norm governed social inter-actions of the sort needed for the remarkable and wide-ranging achieve-ments of *H. ergaster/erectus*. Yet all of this would have been available "in the absence of language" (Donald 1991, 174). For, as Donald makes quite clear, "Language is not necessary for the development of complex social roles and rules, but mimesis is essential" (p. 175).

A steady increase along this cognitive trajectory might explain why, although the second period of significant encephalization was still a long way off, hominid brain sizes were increasing slightly all the while. And this needs explaining since having larger brains came at a heavy price. They are costly to run and feeding them on small stomachs requires a high-quality diet—one that is not easy to acquire. Big brains will have made other demands too, especially for bipeds. Not only do they require more energy, they make birthing difficult (Lovejoy 1980).[16] This has other con-sequences. Having bigger-brained offspring is problematic for those who walk on two legs, for it meant that babies had to be pushed through rather narrow birth canals. The solution to this problem, to have immature off-spring, saddled hominids with all the burdens of dealing with prolonged periods of "childhood." This is not seen in other primates but is most pro-nounced in humans. *H. ergaster/erectus* would have required dedicated prac-tices of pedagogy and childcare. Thus, even though it is not possible to draw direct conclusions about specific modes of cognition based on brain size, we can conclude that there must have been some major trade-off (or trade-offs) for all of these changes.

It seems plausible that expansion of domain-general (not general-purpose) mimetic abilities, which may have reached a first plateau with *H. habilis*, may have been at least partly responsible for the first major growth in neural volume. The further enhancement of these abilities could have been the source, not only of the more advanced technical skills exhibited by *H. ergaster/erectus* but also the basis for their dramatically different kinds of social engagements. Both technical and social advantages conferred by imaginative-imitative abilities would have had a ratcheting-up effect, inde-pendently spurring on and reinforcing their selection. This might explain why, despite the seemingly great achievements of hominids during the reign of *H. ergaster/erectus*, there is an extended period of steady but unre-markable brain growth—which lasted until the arrival of the early humans. This is surely consistent with the hypothesis that with *H. ergaster/erectus* mimetic capacities had reached an apex, coming into full swing for the first time. To give this proposal a name, let us call it the Mimetic Ability Hypothesis (or MAH).

Mimetic Sharing without Theory of Mind

Once the MAH is articulated it puts strong claims that our ancient ances-tors would have *needed* ToMMs in order to get by in their daily routines under great pressure. In this regard, it is worth noting that the claim that mindreading devices would have been necessary for hominids gets much of its credibility from equivocation about the level of abilities we are seeking to understand. Thus it has been argued that ToM abilities would have been needed in order to share a plan or a goal, as required to develop and implement sophisticated hunting tactics or erecting various structures (Baron-Cohen 1999, 264). Yet this thought must be weighed against the fact that even wild chimpanzees and other group animals are quite capable of coordinating their hunting efforts, despite a manifest lack of mature ToM abilities (Boesch and Boesch-Achermann 2000; Brinck and Gärdenfors 2003). At the very least, such facts encourage taking extreme caution when drawing inferences about the degree of mentalizing capacity that might have been needed by our ancestors.

Some have exercised it. For example, Mithen speculates that—at most—only a desire-based psychology would have been needed in order to account for the kinds of behaviors that would have been witnessed from the time of *H. ergaster/erectus* to the rise of archaic humans. The trouble for those who postulate IMDs is that it is easy enough to understand a purely desire-based psychology in terms of an appropriate capacity for unprincipled embodied engagements—the having of a kind of intentional attitude psychology—as discussed in chapter 6.

In this light, Dunbar's claim that more would have been needed at this intermediate phase of hominid evolution becomes particularly important. He has offered special reasons for thinking that nothing short of full metarepresentational ToM abilities would have been required. For, he argues, it is only by having such abilities that those hominids could have managed to have lived in the large groups to which they were accustomed. Dunbar (1992, 1993) has independently established that there is a direct correlation between neocortical volume in primates and the maximal size of their workable social groups. Extrapolating from this data, and estimating the brain size of *H. ergaster/erectus*, he suggests that these hominids may have been operating with social groups with as many as 150 members. There are good reasons to believe this might have been so. Groups of this size would have afforded greater protection; improved capacities to defend and access resources and new opportunities for predation—but at a price. For, on reaching a critical ceiling they would have become hard to manage. The maintenance of social cohesion certainly would not have been possible using the same methods as their predecessors.

A crucial factor in keeping a handle on this more complex social matrix would have been to keep tabs on personal relationships—one's own, as established with specific individuals, as well as monitoring the third-party alliances and interactions of others. A quantitative increase in domain-general capacities for reidentifying particulars and stronger working memory, not unlike that of apes, would be sufficient to explain this achievement. But keeping track of a social space and one's place in it is one thing, securing and maintaining one's relationships within it is quite another. Monkeys and apes manage the latter through one-to-one physical grooming, but this requires direct contact and interaction with a restricted number of others. While effective, this method is a thief of time and—in any case—once groups get too large and physically disperse such intensive interactions would have been impossible.

Using cranial comparisons with apes and indexing these to their social habits as a baseline, Dunbar calculates that the budget of time required for physical grooming would have reached pressure point in groups of the size that *H. ergaster/erectus* would have been operating in (see also Mithen 1996, 111). If so, these hominids would have been forced to find fresh methods to substitute for personal grooming. Dunbar's (2003, 2004) proposal is that they switched to linguistic as opposed to tactile means for achieving this— our early ancestors would have had to learn to gossip.

If we assume that these linguistic exchanges involved the conveyance of and conversations about propositional attitudes then mature ToM abilities are entailed. In arguing that we should accept this, Dunbar assumes the truth of an intention-based semantics and a particular version of the communicative view of language. Crudely, on this view, the primary role of language is to clothe the preexisting private thoughts of conversationalists—it provides the conventional forms that serve as the public medium for the sharing of these. Comprehension and production are understood in translational terms, involving the appropriate coding of outputs from and the decoding of inputs to the language of thought of each participant. This has been aptly named the "inner process model" (Rowlands 2003, 76–77). It casts natural language signs in the role of mere facilitators, lacking any intrinsic representative power of their own.

If one accepts this picture of the function of language, then metarepresentational devices would have been necessary preadaptations for such public exchanges. They would be crucially implicated in the translational processes since a hearer's grasp of a speaker's meaning would depend on deciphering the speaker's communicative intention—understood as their sincere assertion—that is, they would be giving expression to what they believe (Grice 1989). If public communication is, at root, an attempt by hearers to grasp what individual speakers have in mind—that is, the content of what they intend to assert by their utterances—then anyone engaged in such activity must be presumed to have intact metarepresentational ToM abilities (and the relevant mechanisms to support these). In this way, folk psychological abilities would have played a vital role "in ensuring temporal cohesion of large dispersed groups" (Dunbar 2000, 250). Dunbar is explicit about the relevant implications:

Theory of mind is probably *essential* for language, not so much because it is involved in the production of speech *per se* but because it provides a mechanism that both enables speakers to ensure that their message has got through and allows hearers to figure out what the speaker's message actually is (subtext and all). (Dunbar 2003, 224; emphasis added)

Although in some quarters the communicative view of language still has the status of being the received view, it deserves to be treated with skepticism (Gauker 2003). In its strong form it rests on the assumption that pre-verbal individuals would have been capable of propositional thought prior to developing a public medium appropriate for the expression of such thoughts. Yet, if my argument against the very idea of content holds good this idea is thrown into serious doubt and the communicative conception of language along with it, as discussed in chapter 5.[17]

These considerations alone suffice to make Dunbar's conclusions precarious, to say the least. But his proposal is implausible in any case, if we accept widely held views about the arrival dates of a symbolic language with the sort of complexity that would have been needed for the reliable formation, encoding and public expression of content-involving propositional attitudes. Since they lacked vocal tracts of an equivalent kind to that of modern humans, "The anatomy necessary to produce the full range of human speech was absent in *H. [ergaster/]erectus* and certain, if not all, Neanderthals" (Lieberman 2000, 136). It might be thought that this was only a barrier to the expression of content-involving propositional attitudes. But, as I argued in chapter 5, if there could be no such attitudes prior to the establishment of public languages with stable meanings then there would have been no thought contents for these early hominid speakers to express in any case.

In all, if we assume, in line with standard thinking, that the kinds of linguistic practices needed to support discursive conversational exchange were still a long way off it is much more likely that grooming-at-distance was achieved by the making of "pleasant but meaningless noises" (Bickerton 2003, 79). This may have involved the exchanging of familiar idiosyncratic calls and would have required a reasonable vocal control—of the sort we find in the "duetting" used by chimpanzees, gorillas and baboons; this is used by these animals to keep in touch with each other when they are out of one another's sight. Signature calls used in this way may have served as a vocal analogue of the repeated actions normally involved in manual grooming. These performances would be, in key respects, like infant-directed speech. This is a more plausible hypothesis than Dunbar's if we suppose, as seems likely, that, at this stage, hominids would only have had the capacity to engage in protoconversational exchanges that had "none of the properties of conversation" (Corballis 2003, 203).

Building directly on Dunbar's work, Dautenhahn has proposed that the capacity to produce and comprehend narratives, taking the form of conversational gossip, may have evolved in order to resolve the dilemma of living in larger social groups mentioned earlier: "The evolutionary origin of communicating in stories coevolved with the increasing social dynamics among our human ancestors, in particular the necessity to communicate about third-party relationships" (Dautenhahn 2002, 103–104; 2001, 252). Stated in this way, Dautenhahn's proposal seems to inherit all of the problems that haunt Dunbar's account. But, in fact, these evaporate if we distinguish between two importantly different kinds of narrative, those of a purely dramatic reenactive sort and those which are linguistically based.[18]

A mimetic culture could have plausibly sponsored the former, calling on established canonical forms, roles, and figures in doing so. These would have been the obvious precursors to oral myth and story, but they cannot be identified with them. There is a more modest rendering of Dautenhahn's scenario, according to which the dramatic reenactments of social happenings would have taken the form of stories *that were literally played out*. These would have had a recognizable prenarrative format and structure of the sort that would make these embodied stories ripe for verbal rendering (Dautenhahn 2001). Thus, as Donald (1999, 146) suggests, "If hominids could comprehend and remember a complex event, such as the killing of an animal or the manufacture of a tool, they should have been capable of re-enacting such events, individually or in groups, once mimetic capacity was established."

Regular reenactments of events of special significance may have eventually become deeply ingrained in the social fabric, thus supporting the establishment of common customs and habits. Established dramatic re-enactments and nonlinguistic conventions would have been a powerful substitute means of ensuring social cohesion, supplanting or at least supplementing the physical grooming of individuals. Mimetic interactions of this kind would have helped to solidify within-group identities, obviating the need for more direct and physically taxing forms of one-one social maintenance.[19] Either way, if only nonlinguistic grooming methods were used then there is no need to suppose that the early hominids would have needed (mature) ToMs.

Similar considerations defeat the claim that "pretending *necessarily* requires a theory of mind" (Baron-Cohen 1999, 265; emphasis added). For if the MAH is even *possibly* true then a capacity for quite sophisticated forms of pretense—those powerful enough to have fueled a robust "public theater"—surely did not rest on having a ToM. Here it helps to recall the recent evidence that has been effectively marshaled against Leslie's claim that this sort of pretense involves metarepresentation, as discussed in the previous chapter.

Moreover, there is a clear connection between the kinds of imaginative reenactments that a mimetic culture would have sponsored and the basis for the kind of narrative competency young children first exhibit (see Hutto 2006h). Social dramas are, of course, the very stuff of many narratives—such engagements set the broad parameters for deciding which events are interesting; these provide the subject matter for much narration. Without question, stories *could* have been told about the actions of our ancient ancestors. Certainly, their lives would have been dramatic enough. Nevertheless, lacking the appropriate medium and established practice, they were in no position to tell such stories. We must be clear about the order of appearance: narratives could not have been related orally or conversationally in the early stages of our prehistory on the assumption that "there can be no narrative without narration, a point sometimes overlooked by those who see human life in terms of narratives untold or waiting to be told" (Lamarque 2004, 394).[20] And assuming that *H. ergaster/erectus* lacked a (sufficiently complex) language, the resources for conducting discursive conversation and telling stories would have been missing (Dunn 1991). In place of such discourse, a blossoming capacity for mimesis may have taken up the slack.

First Communions

Even if they lacked language it is widely supposed that the hominids as far back as *H. ergaster/erectus* would have used a kind of protolanguage—one that had some but not all the features of a full-fledged language. Specifically, if we follow Bickerton, such a "language" would have consisted of grammarless utterances, rather like the one and two-word offerings of two-year-olds, being comparable to pidgins. Thus it might be thought that metarepresentational abilities must be implicated in the formation of such a basic protolanguage and its subsequent acquisition. The forging and learning of a public lexicon is based on a capacity for coreference, and on the received view, "Children require some type of theory of mind. They need to have an idea of what the parent is thinking and how his/her mind differs from their own to be so very good at associating the correct utterance with the correct reference" (Mithen 2000a, 497). If so, perhaps metarepresentational mechanisms played an instrumental part in the development of the very first public "languages." The assumption here is that the formation and learning of a public lexicon rests on the most sophisticated kind of preverbal intersubjective engagement—joint attention. And the idea is that joint attention looks hard to account for without invoking ToM abilities of some kind or other.

Baron-Cohen claims that "understanding that words refer presumes the concept of intention or goal" (Baron-Cohen 1999, 267). Yet, if the argument of chapter 6 succeeds there is no reason to assume that, even if this is true, it implies a capacity for metarepresentation. For, even if one were to insist that some "concept of intention" is needed it need not be equivalent to that of the mature folk psychological variety. It is much more plausible that even in the normal case, where basic language learning is supported by children and adults mutually engaging in prelinguistic acts of joint attention, that these only involve a mutual responsiveness to one another's intentional attitudes.

Not only that, but the argument suffers in any case since having joint attentional abilities is not even necessary for learning the basics of a language. Consider that

children with autism show us just how useless a language capacity is without a theory of mind. Strip out a theory of mind from language use and you have an individual who might have *some syntax, the ability to build a vocabulary,* and a *semantic system.* Crucially, what would be missing from their language use and comprehension is 'pragmatics'. . . . Language without a theory of mind is not of course entirely useless. It allows literal communication, acquisition of information from others, requesting, ordering, etc. (Baron-Cohen 1999, 266, emphasis added; second quotation from note on 267)

The very existence of such linguistic abilities in individuals with autism serves as a kind of existence proof; it demonstrates the falsity of the claim that it is necessary to have ToM abilities in order to learn words. As the above quotation makes amply clear, some individuals with autism are surely capable of learning and using language competently to some extent, despite their ToM deficiencies. Presumably they are able to achieve this because, even though they cannot jointly attend with others, they are supported by veteran language users who can. Without the normal forms of feedback and checking, their teachers therefore must make even stronger assumptions than usual about what it is that the autistic child is attending to when the relevant associations are being forged. It is their job to ensure, to the best of their abilities, that the initiate is making the appropriate connections between items of reference and local labels (see

Hutto 1999b, 133–134; 2000, 31–35). I presume that the same is true for those great apes who manage to learn a few symbols, despite lacking a human-level capacity for joint attention.

Indeed this line of argument is made more implausible still when it is observed that full-fledged ToM abilities are not only unnecessary, but that to use them during basic word-learning situations would be downright unhelpful. Doing so would make it difficult even to establish basic referential triangles in the first place. Ironically, this fact is most evident in the cases of primitive lexicon forging and learning. It has been noted that

> young children's deficits in understanding intentional diversity may actually *benefit* word learning. As many theorists have noted, the task of interpreting novel words presents a complex inductive problem because, logically speaking, any given word could mean any of an infinite set of possible things. (Sabbagh and Baldwin 2005, 172)[21]

It is clear that without a basic agreement about how to respond to things, symbol grounding and word learning would not get off the ground. But it could be argued that something akin to the tendency for "default attribution," in which children use the simple heuristic of attributing beliefs to others based on what they take to be the case, is at play here (Leslie, Friedman, and German 2004). This would obviate the need to decide between the countless possible ways of construing the other's communicative intentions. Perhaps, so the thought goes, hominids had full-fledged ToM abilities after all, but these were only used at their lowest setting during acts of lexicon formation. But, for obvious reasons, this is a very poor strategy for arguing that hominids would have needed sophisticated ToM abilities. If anything, it shows that even if they had them they surely did not *need* them. After all, the question is not whether imagining that hominids might have had sophisticated ToMs is in some sense logically possible, we are trying to assess if there is any reason to think they actually had them.

Rather than supposing that nonlinguistic joint attention rests on prior facility with referential symbols, it is much more plausible that it—scaffolded by imitative abilities and the conventions of a mimetic culture—enabled the fashioning of very first symbols. This would have permitted a kind of objective thinking—an awareness of sharing a world with others—of a kind that, when further supplemented with imaginative and mimetic abilities, could have been a bridge from perceptually based forms of intersubjective interaction to amodal symbolic thinking (see Arbib 2003, 2005; Sinha 2004; Hutto 2006g). Being able to learn to use genuinely referring symbols is dependent on our capacity to have a shared awareness of things, not the other way around.

There are various proposals about the stages of this process on the market. It is plausible that most rudimentary forms of mime exploited shared "mimetic schemas"—those that tap deeply into what lies at the base of our readily familiar embodied activities, the kind of activities that can be enacted and reenacted (Zlatev 2005). These would have served as the initial points of connection with others, drawing on the common ways of acting in the world such as running, hitting, kicking, and so on. Mimetic schemas are more fundamental than their abstract cousins "image schemas." Still, even the latter can be thought of as deriving from what is common to basic, embodied ways of responding in relation to certain normally encountered situations and activities. These yield certain familiar contrasts, such as "UP-DOWN, IN-OUT, FRONT-BACK, LIGHT-DARK, WARM-COLD, MALE-FEMALE" (Lakoff and Johnson 1980, 58). Dichotomies of this kind have a sort of universal resonance because they feature in everyday ways of acting, reacting, and interacting with the world and others. Moreover, it is plausible that material artifacts—tools, buildings, furniture, and so on—which can be the focus of joint attention, act as intersubjective anchors, since the activities they afford are nonarbitrarily constrained in important ways and habits of use can be made canonical through convention (see Sinha 2005, 1542–1543). Although more needs to be said about their nature, it is plausible that commonalities fostered by embodied engagements in a common world would have provided the means of getting ancient mimetic acts of the basic sort off the ground.

Indeed, our tendency to make use of mime has stayed with us even after the establishment of symbolic language. For example, we typically adorn purely linguistic speech acts with gestures—even when these are of no use to the hearer either for adding expression or for helping to establish significance, such as when one gestures while speaking on the telephone (Corballis 2003). This deeply ingrained way of connecting with others through mime looks to have stayed with us as something more than an inert cognitive vestige. Thus it has been convincingly argued that to a large and interesting extent, we only feel we have satisfactorily understood or grasped something once we retreat to embodied schemas of some kind or other, which shows that they are plausibly the prelinguistic ground of the metaphors by which we live.

However we ultimately choose to make sense of basic mimetic activities, it is from this sort of starting point that it is possible to sketch the gradual stages of likely linguistic development in hominids. For once the practice of jointly attending was well established it is plausible that a basic capacity for mime would have developed into a more rudimentary form of communication, one involving a kind of reference to common focal points (where these might be happenings, actions or objects) even in their absence. In such cases, communicators would need to bring the relevant objects before the other's mind by some means: the referents would have to be in some way invoked. It is plausible that early mimes might have achieved this by drawing on bonds of visuomotor associations of a sort that would have been familiar to all participants. In doing so they would have had to tap into associations holding between certain worldly things (objects of potential coattention) and certain salient aspects of mimetic acts which resemble these or would successfully remind the other of them. For example, this might be done by using highly stylized gestures, such as wriggling one's arm in slithering fashion to mimic the movements of a snake.[22]

Mimetic acts of this kind are not signals since they involve prior communicative intent. They are not attempts to effect more straightforward coordinations such as initiating imitation (that is, getting the other to use their arms in a similar way) or to directly cue a certain kind of action routine on the part of the other (that is, by inspiring characteristic responses that the presence of snakes normally calls forth). To use one's arm so as to invoke thoughts of snakes is not an imperative act, but an attempt at intentional communication, albeit of a crude and unstable one. That this is possible is evident by the fact that games such as charades are so much as possible, but, of course, that sort of game has important structural supports that the imagined mimetic acts just described would have lacked (or would have lacked in the first instance).

It should be clear that even a rudimentary capacity to use and appreciate mime would have brought unheralded degrees of freedom and new possibilities for communication. In key respects, its advent would have made the character of our ancestors' first communicative efforts, quite literally, "dramatically" different from the sorts of signals used for coordination by other animals, even those of our closest living cousins.[23] Mimetic communication requires that others make the appropriate connections: they must recognize the *significance* of the communicative act. And, lacking established conventions, early mimetic acts would have depended on strong associations and resemblances, and these could hardly be relied on. It is not easy to communicate by means of pantomime, even when using additional supports. To be sure, it is a hit-and-miss affair—definitely more miss than hit, that is, unless the activity is structured and supplemented in important ways. For example, such acts can be made more reliable through the use of conventionalized gestures as these help to more immediately disambiguate their meaning.

Communicating by pantomime using only nonlinguistic resemblance based modes of quasi-reference is a weak and highly ambiguous mode of communicating. Failures at successful indication would have been a spur to fall in line with publicly established norms. This is a matter of negotiating and adjusting one's methods of communication to suit a public standard, as prompted by requests for clarification. Participants forge a common understanding by recasting the communicative offerings in line with conventional requirements. This would have been a crucial step on the road from contextual, indicational communications to true predicative symbolic use.

In sum, although mimetic communions are certainly *intentional* acts in some sense, they do not rest on a prior ability to convey or interpret propositional attitudes, rather by enabling the formation and use of stable symbols they make this possible. There is simply no compulsion to think that a nonverbal mime's intended communications are based in intentions to convey beliefs about the state of the world or that they require a capacity on the part of speakers and hearers to understand and decode such intentions. Capacities for protodeclarative pointing, joint attending, mimesis, and the practice of ostensive naming would surely have been necessary preconditions for formation of the symbols that would have made propositionally based thought possible. It seems that in order to understand our prelinguistic engagements we have every reason to appeal to intentional attitudes and shared awareness of them, as supported, extended and elaborated by mimetic abilities and the norms they ground. If so, we can get by without making the standard assumption that intentional communication is always grounded in propositional trade involving sophisticated mindreading. As a result we can knock away arguments to the effect that hominids would have had to have had a metarepresentational ToM in order to engage in and repair their intentional communications, in the course of speaking with, persuading and deceiving others.

The unresolved question is: If not during the era of *H. ergaster/erectus*, just how much later did full-fledged folk psychological abilities arrive on the scene? If the NPH is right, they were late-developing and socioculturally based developments, not biological ones. I say something about this in the final chapter.

The Intensional Representation Requirement

When thinking about the prehistoric origins of folk psychology, it is important to realize that our hominid ancestors (with the possible exception of the early humans) were without the resources of a grammatically complex language. For this reason I hold that they would have been unable to act for reasons of their own and equally without the ability to interpret their compatriots as having done so. They lacked facility with sophisticated public languages with a compositional semantics that would have been needed for having and representing such complex states of mind.

In a nutshell, the hominids would have lacked the essential *cognitive* resources needed for conducting folk psychology. Recall that making sense of intentional action involves more than just having a handle on the mentalistic concepts of the attitudes; it requires being able to specify and understand how these interrelate. And this means that any would-be folk psychologist needs to be able to "represent representations"—in particular, representations that have propositional content and structured logical forms—that is, representations in which the relevant propositional contents are composed of meaningful parts. This must be the case since it is only by means of the linkage of the subpropositional components that the attitudes in question are bound together in appropriate ways. To predict, explain, or understand intentional actions requires being able to characterize these complex states of mind (at least potentially). And this means having the capacity to represent the structured MoPs, those under which the relevant believed or desired propositions are grasped or the way they are apprehended.

Characterizing another's state of mind in propositional attitude terms, which is a capacity all folk psychologists must have, requires a fine-grained understanding that goes beyond a capacity to make crude broad-content ascriptions. Making such ascriptions is of some general use, but only in those straightforward cases in which explaining the other's behavior does not require knowing how things appear to them or are construed from their point of view. This works in cases where the target of the other's thought is, as it were, transparent to the observer—that is, those in which they can be read off their behavior directly. Crucially, there are two quite different ways that one might achieve this: either by not using folk psychology at all—as discussed in chapter 6—or by using folk psychology at its lowest setting, by making any adequate intensional ascription without presupposing that it necessarily specifies the way in which the target apprehends the situation in question.

In contrast, understanding and attributing reasons in interesting cases—those in which reason explanations and predictions are called upon to do hard labor—demand specifying just how thinkers think about situations (as in the case of me and my wife cited at the end of chapter 1). In some cases absolute precision is required in specifying what someone thinks, if we are to understand his or her reasons for acting. If you have trouble bringing such cases to mind, think of the stock-in-trade of situation comedies or Greek tragedies. Failing that, there are always the examples in the philosophical literature (see Quine 1956; Kripke 1979). Often in these instances we must be "hypersensitive" to the MoPs under which a thinker apprehends a situation if we are to make sense of their reasons.

It is easy to see what this comes to if we follow Segal in thinking of the relata of propositional attitudes as total forms. According to his definition, "A total form is an abstract, linguistic object. It is a syntactic structure that has a variety of properties associated with it. It contains words, which are themselves spelt and pronounced in specific ways. The words have meanings, and the whole structure has a meaning (derived systematically from the words' meanings and syntactic structure)" (Segal 1998, 149). If we individuate and attribute propositional attitudes using this sort of apparatus then specifying what someone thinks, believes or desires can be achieved in an extremely fine-grained manner. For example, to borrow from Segal, in light of transatlantic differences in the conventions concerning spelling, (1) and (2) express different beliefs: Zelda is psychologically related to different "total forms" in each case (obviously, the same goes for any conventional differences concerning pronunciation).

1. Zelda believes that black and white are colours.
2. Zelda believes that black and white are colors.

As I said, it is easy enough to imagine cases in which ascribing (1) to Zelda but not (2) would be pertinent to understanding why she acted. Yet, clearly, there is a spectrum of possibilities here. For most mundane purposes, I concede that making intensional attributions, let alone hypersensitive ones, is not only unnecessary, it would be a downright hindrance. Use of such a demanding criterion would make it impossible to pass easy comment on the propositional attitudes of foreign-language speakers, for example, in the causal way we often do. To borrow from Segal one last time, if we are thinking in terms of total forms then it is—strictly speaking—false to say of Caesar that he thought that "Rome wasn't built in a day." Not being an English speaker it is not possible that he could have thought *this*—at best, he could have held a belief about this state of affairs using a total form that is the Latin equivalent of this English sentence. It would be pedantry to insist on this degree of specification in most everyday cases. Typically, we really do not need (or care) to understand the exact mindset of the others in this kind of detail. But those are also the sorts of cases in which we really do not need to understand *their* reasons. When we need to bring our folk psychological understanding to bear it is important to know *how* the other thinks about things and how their propositional attitudes are linked together in, perhaps, quite quirky chains of reasoning. A creature only capable of understanding intentional attitudes (or propositional attitudes in purely extensional terms) would be incapable of making such linkages explicit.

Again, this is not to suggest that doing so is necessary or pertinent in every case of folk psychological understanding or ascription. Truncated explanations will often do well enough. My point is rather that any creature capable of understanding what it is to act for a reason must be capable of representing such complex states of mind (even if in many cases they do not need to do so). That is, they must have the cognitive capacity to detail the relevant interrelations and logical connections that hold between the propositional attitudes—at least potentially, as need be. Call this the Intensional Representation Requirement (IRR).

The IRR must be satisfied by any bona fide folk psychologist, whether we imagine that their business is conducted by explicitly representing (and reasoning theoretically about) reasons or merely by internally modeling them (say, by directly manipulating their own propositional attitudes in complex ways to mirror those of others). The issue here is not one of accuracy. How reliably or otherwise a mentalistic attribution characterizes the target's state of mind is not to the point. In drawing attention to the IRR my aim is simply to acknowledge a necessary condition that must be met by any mind capable of understanding (and attributing) reasons. My hope is that this is an uncontroversial reminder.

Having the capacity to manipulate linguaform representations of some kind or other is not simply the easiest way of satisfying the IRR, if we deny the existence of an LoT it looks as if it is the only way of doing so. For if we rule out the LoT hypothesis as a live option, it is clear that there are limits to the cognitive capacities of languageless creatures in this regard: it is simply not possible for creatures restricted to imagistic modes of thought and mimetic modes of communion to represent another's belief contents. We can conclude from this that if understanding reasons requires a capacity to manipulate linguaform representations, then any adequate account of the cognitive capacities of folk psychologists entails a commitment to characterizing their minds in line with the sentential paradigm.

So it looks as if our very ancient ancestors would have been incapable of acting for reasons because they lacked the requisite linguistic forms to support truly supermental thinking. By the same token, they would have lacked the cognitive resources needed for understanding intentional actions performed for reasons. We can be fairly sure of this. Although there is still a great deal of speculation about the exact character of early hominid "languages"—perhaps they used a gestural protosign, or a vocal protospeech or both at different stages—it is widely agreed that whatever their precise form they would have "consisted of single-symbol utterances, lacking combinatoriality" (Jackendoff 2002, 23; see also Bickerton 1990; Arbib 2005). Using such limited modes of communication, the semantic import of their protolinguistic acts would have been inescapably context-sensitive. And even if we suppose that such utterances might, in theory, have been used to convey messages about complex states of affairs (that is, by suitably encoding these), the utterances themselves would have lacked the right sort of structure needed to support logical reasoning, even for practical purposes.[1] For that one needs to operate with a symbol system that decomposes into discrete elements, each taking the form of stable units of meaning that can appear in more than one expression.

A creature that is at best only capable of holophrastic "utterances" would not be able to form intentions or to act for reasons of its own. A language with a combinatorial syntax and semantics is needed for even the most basic kind of supermental thinking. So again, it seems that our early ancestors were not even capable of genuine practical reasoning, let alone folk psychological interpretation. They simply could not have been in the folk psychology business as they were bereft of the essential tools and equipment needed for prosecuting it.[2] In saying this, I am assuming two things: (1) that sententialism is nonnegotiable both for having and, crucially, for representing reasons (that is, that neither could be achieved by a mind that used only nonlinguaform representations), and (2) that the hominids lacked a LoT.

Pretty obviously, if this verdict is right, it is hardly possible that such creatures could have bequeathed such abilities to modern humans by supplying us with the appropriate cognitive mechanisms, as a kind of biological endowment. This is devastatingly bad news for those inclined to believe in the existence of nativist mindreading mechanisms of any sophistication.

The Late Arrival of Discursive Practices

Let me run the argument a different way. If sophisticated hominid ToM abilities existed at all then they must have coevolved with language. This joint venture, Mithen (2000b, 500) conjectures, may have been related "to the encephalization after 600,000 years ago leading to modern size brains by 150,000 years ago." This late-in-the-day proposal, according to which mature ToM abilities make their first appearance with archaic humans, is at least prima facie credible. Nevertheless, it cannot be concluded without further ado that "the increased sociality, complex technology and cooperative hunting undertaken by the early humans *imply* a significantly enhanced theory of mind over that found within earlier members of *Homo* or the australopithecines" (Mithen 2002, 29; emphasis added).

The real issue is whether it is more plausible to suppose that sophisticated ToM abilities appeared (1) along with the emergence of language or (2) only after its establishment. Here, as observed in chapter 8, we must carefully distinguish between the origins of language and the evolution of linguistic preadaptations. And when we are reminded of this distinction it drives us to prefer option (2), the one that runs counter to Mithen's proposal. For despite its intuitive plausibility, it is difficult to see what factors would have driven the emergence of a metarepresentational mechanism alongside the linguistic developments that would have taken place prior to our ancestors' migration out of Africa. This is especially so if it is accepted that having and expressing reasons requires having content-involving propositional attitudes and that this would have only been possible, minimally, *after* the establishment of a language with stable symbolic meanings and appropriate predicate-argument structures.

Only then would early humans have been able to form and express propositional attitudes. Given Mother Nature's scruples, if a less-than-mature ToM (or no ToM at all) was in fact good enough to coordinate the relevant social interactions prior to this, then we must ask: What selective pressures would have pushed for the development of more sophisticated devices? To borrow a quip from Gómez, just as "a corkscrew would not succeed in a world devoid of wine bottles," so too would metarepresentational IMDs have been a luxurious extravagance in a world of creatures incapable of expressing their reasons, either in word or deed (allowing, for the sake of argument, that they could have acted for reasons of their own!) (Gómez 1998, 90). Call this the external-pressure objection.

This objection holds even if we accept that the folk psychological framework has at least a crude instrumental value in making third-person predictions—for example, allowing one to anticipate the behavior of what are, strictly speaking, nonbelievers (that is, animals, rivers, etc.), as per Dennett's intentional stance proposal. That ability could have been of some use to our ancestors. But the question is not whether, in some open-ended sense, it might have been useful in principle—it is rather, how could languageless creatures acquire the relevant framework without recourse to the practices that made the right sort of use of complex languages, languages with recombinatorial properties of the sort needed for representing reasons?

To see the contours of the problem, it helps to imagine what it would be like to be a complete outsider to an established linguistic practice faced with the task of making sense of it; this is the situation of a Davidsonian radical interpreter, here played by Frankenstein's monster:

By degrees I made a discovery of still greater moment. I found that these people possessed a method of communicating their experiences to one another by articulate sounds. I perceived that the words they spoke sometimes produced pleasure or pain, smiles or sadness, in the minds and countenances of the hearers. This was indeed a godlike science, and I ardently desired to become acquainted with it. But I was baffled in every attempt I made for this purpose. Their pronunciation was quick, and the words they uttered, not having any apparent connection with visible objects, I was unable to discover any clue by which I could unravel the mystery of their reference. By great application, however, and after having remained during the space of several revolutions of the moon in my hovel, I discovered the names that were given to some of the most familiar objects of discourse; I learned and applied the words, "fire," "milk," "bread," and "wood". . . . I cannot describe the delight I felt when I learned the ideas appropriated to each of these sounds and was able to pronounce them. (Shelley 2003/1817, 94–95)

Like the monster, to make sense of such sophisticated behavior requires a method both for tracking the enormously fine-grained structures of thought and a means of seeing how it is tied down to extralinguistic items. In theory, it should be possible to develop basic axioms about certain metalinguistic references and, in turn, these could be used to get to grips with more complex constructions. Or, at least, this is in principle possible—if one makes certain charitable assumptions. Frankenstein's creature provides a fairly accurate account of the first steps of the process of deciphering sophisticated thought evident in the linguistic expressions of others (for more detail see Hutto 1999b, chap. 5).

But imagine his predicament if those he wished to interpret, made *no* internally structured utterances at all—that is, if they used only holophrastic expressions with no repeating elements. In this situation, how would the outsider ever decipher the reasons for which such "speakers" acted? In this light—even if one were prepared to allow that propositional attitudes might exist prior to a properly grammaticalized language—I take it to be more than a mild understatement to say that "language facilitated communication, especially of those beliefs and desires that may be difficult to transmit through gesture alone" (Mithen 2002, 32).

The fundamental worry with this statement is that it presupposes that our ancestors had propositional beliefs and desires with intensional contents to be transmitted prior to developing the external linguistic structures that were needed to form these—that is, what kind of beliefs and desires would have needed to be expressed in gestures alone at this point in prehistory? Before the emergence of stable symbolic thought it might be wondered at what kind of contents would these states of mind have been directed? Mime might allow one to convey a nonpropositional desire for some item or other, but as anyone who has played charades will know, it is difficult to convey the content of a specific proposition by such means (as would be needed to convey a propositionally focused desire for some situation to obtain or corresponding belief that one thinks that it does). It is a good take-home exercise to try to mime the contents of one's beliefs without using linguistic clues. That is hard enough, but it would surely have been beyond the capacity of an imaginary hominid Hamlet to express his reasons using mime, even if he were gifted with the skills of a Chaplin or a Marceau.

On the assumption that early humans were limited to a nonsyntactic protolanguage, they would have been unable to form reasons of their own (stricto sensu) or to give adequate public expression to them. But should we suppose early humans were so restricted in their means of communication? After all, unlike their predecessor hominids,

early modern humans . . . had the anatomical prerequisites for fully modern human speech . . . we can be certain that the human FLS [functional language system] existed 100,000 years ago, at the time of the migration of humans from Africa and their subsequent dispersal throughout most of the world over the next 50,000 years. (Lieberman 2000, 148)

If we accept the MAH, it is reasonable to conclude that members of *H. ergaster/erectus* may have been capable of forging meaningful, but non-compositional, symbols even though they would have been physically incapable of fully modern speech productions. Precisely how grammatical abilities arose in our prehistory is undecided. Some speculate that a general sensitivity to structural hierarchies may have issued from the same cognitive spring that permitted our ancestors to produce ordered and iterated action sequences, as required for the creation and use of, say, composite tools. This assumes that sophisticated manual manipulations are reasonable analogues of complex linguistic activities, such as the embedding of clauses within clauses. Hence the basic thesis is that sensitivity to syntax might be explained by a more general sensitivity to recursive patterns in other tasks domains (Greenfield 1991; Byrne 2002b).

This idea has not been widely accepted by linguists. It is claimed that although the iterated activity just described bears *some* resemblance to syntactical activity, the fit is not good enough. It has been seriously questioned, for example, whether this proposal could explain what is most central to syntactic sensitivity—that is, why complex languages have a characteristic noun phrase/sentence distinction (Carstairs-McCarthy 1999, 184–187, 63).

This has prompted an interesting alternative hypothesis: that human sensitivity to basic sentence structure derives from our sensitivity to core syllabic structure. It has been conjectured that the latter is what provided a basis for syntax-as-it-was for our ancient ancestors.[3] Call this the core syllabic-syntax hypothesis (CSSH). There is a strong body of linguistic evidence that supports it (Carstairs-McCarthy 1999, 151).[4] Natural languages are distinguished, in part, by their basic set of phonemes, consonants, and vowels. Although meaningless, these combine in ordered ways to form recognizable speech patterns. Speech of any kind presupposes a capacity to produce and recognize these. Picking up on this, the primary claim of the CSSH is that the basis of core syntactic sensitivity may ultimately derive from the same source as this syllabic sensitivity. If so, basic grammatical ability is not best explained by the grasping of principles about linguistic universals; it is more likely that the syntactic filters that underlie it were forged by the same changes that were responsible for our capacity to articulate and perceive phonological aspects of speech.

In any case, whichever story we decide to tell about this, it was the combining of a generative capacity with lexical abilities that would have been the eventual basis for the emergence of a symbolic protospeech—a proto-speech of a kind that would have required forging of conventional links between vocal gestures and their referents, converting the former into conventionalized symbols; these would have been the ultimate basis on which the first language makers developed stable symbol *systems*.[5] This first practice of lexicon formation may have already been established in earlier hominids; that is, they may have already developed it mimetically—perhaps using a kind of protosign, based primarily on *manual* gestures (Arbib 2005).[6] If so, it is easy to imagine how, using new voice talents, they might have put those capacities to similar use.[7]

Given the vast number of possible vocal gestures, treating each vocal gesture as a distinct call sign would have been unproductive since it would have required associating special routines of action (and this would have quickly outstripped their cognitive capacities). Unless systematized, there would have been simply too many calls, and too many related protocols to cope with, identify, and remember each of them. And this is not the way things went in any case. Human language stands out not simply because of its recursive properties. Humpbacks and songbirds generate recurring and embedded patterns of well-formed strings in their vocalizations; the difference is that these lack a *symbolic* dimension. Only in humans did the capacity to produce and cope with internally complex recursive structures unite with meaning-making abilities so as to permit the fashioning of the endless productive, fully combinatorial symbol systems, such as those found in modern natural languages. If syntactic and meaning-conferring capacities developed along separate lines—lines that crossed uniquely in human prehistory—this would explain, rather neatly, why human languages are peculiar in having a duality of linguistic patterning with both autonomous meaningless (for example, phonological) and meaningful (for example, semantic) dimensions. This proposal is consistent with the continuist view that sees human language as having ultimately evolved from primate call systems, but it is equally at home with the claim that the emergence of a mimetic capacity originally fostered a gesture-based mode of communication in hominids.

The path of the development of linguistic competence in hominids and early humans may well have been elliptical—having gone through a period in which manual gestures dominated and only later shifted back to speech-centered modes of communication and expression. Positing this circuitous route of the evolution of language-related abilities is at least one credible selectionist explanation of how humans came to have brains and bodies that are so apt to receive and use language. This was not achieved by the forging of a single linguistic module—it was, instead, a multistage, gradual evolutionary development, one that exploited the normal features of archaic human environments, as sustained and extended by material cultures. The ability to acquire and use language therefore rests on several biologically driven anatomical foundations, all of which look likely to have been uniquely constructed in the homo line.

The point is that the creation and use of symbolic languages would have only been possible after our ancestors had undergone several distinct and specific preadaptations—those that separately fueled the development of their morphological, lexical, and syntactic capacities. Yet, once again, the evolution of linguistic capacities must not be confused with the origin of languages. Although we must accept that language-related anatomical changes were completed prior to the dispersal of our common ancestors around the globe, it does not follow that grammatically complex symbolic languages (with combinatorial semantics) would have been fully in place at that point (Li and Hombert 2002, 178). Early humans were surely making use of their linguistic abilities to some extent, but it cannot be freely assumed that the relevant linguistic practices themselves would have been in play at this stage. Languages—as opposed to the capacity to form and use them—are complex cultural products; it is likely that it would have taken some time to establish a lexicon that could support a truly symbolic symbol system with a combinatorial semantics.

And, more to the point, even if grammatically complex languages did come early and played a role in the support of basic communicative acts, there is good reason to suspect that there may have been quite a long gap between the point at which language-ready humans first appeared on the scene and the time at which anything that we might recognize as complex discursive practices, such as conversation and narration, will have arrived. It would have taken a long time before practices such as these became embedded in our ancestors' social fabric.

If such discursive practices arrived late this could explain why there was such a long delay between linguistic activity of the early humans (whatever form it took) and the "Great Leap Forward," which occurred sometime between 30,000 and 60,000 years ago. For, at that moment in prehistory, our ancestors achieved technical and cooperative feats that had no previous parallel, such as crossing the seas to colonize Australia and fashioning large quantities of complex tools of a quality that far outstripped anything that had gone before. They also began working with new materials, such as bone and ivory, using these for adornments and decorations. It is commonly held that the cave paintings and elaborate stone sculptures that appeared at this time, along with practices of burying the dead with grave goods, marked the beginnings of the symbolic practices of art and religion. The trouble is that if we assume discursive practices were already in full flow thousands of years before this, it leaves us with a mystery about what was responsible for the sudden uplift of human culture in the Middle/Upper Paleolithic period.

Carruthers has offered to explain this by putting a very late date on the development of a capacity for imaginative pretense. He suggests that its late emergence, restricted to *H. sapiens sapiens*, solves this very puzzle. The onset of this imaginative capacity, along with the amassing of cross-domain knowledge as made possible by exploiting the medium of public language, resulted in an avalanche of creative thinking, the generation of cultural artifacts, and novel modus vivendi for our ancient ancestors (Carruthers 1998, 115). Carruthers finds support for his hypothesis in the putative fact that if earlier hominids, such as *H. ergaster/erectus*, had exercised their imaginations, we would have seen a much greater impact of this in the patterns of their life. Yet Carruthers may be looking for the wrong sort of evidence in this regard, for instead of appearing in the form of symbolic art, the recreative imagination may have left its mark visibly on toolmaking industries and more invisibly on a mimetic culture, as argued in the previous chapter.

Moreover, while it seems right to suppose that the ability to use complex language was a necessary foundation for all these developments, it must also be remembered "that syntactized language enables but does not compel. . . . What human language confers is not a technological strait-jacket but freedom" (Bickerton 2003, 92). In this light, a more convincing explanation of the major cultural changes is that they marked the beginnings of certain sophisticated discursive practices. In evaluating this suggestion it is worth bearing in mind that the so-called cultural explosion was "not so much a single big bang as a whole series of cultural sparks that occurred at different times in different parts of the world between 60,000 and 30,000 years ago" (Mithen 1996, 152). My suggestion is, of course, sheer speculation. Sheer, but not wild. For we do know that structurally complex symbolic languages are themselves culturally grounded and that the emergence of even basic languages of this kind would have had to wait for the development of certain sociocultural *practices*, such as naming, classifying, and reporting. It is therefore reasonable to suppose that the more complex uses of languages, such as relating myths and stories, would have taken even longer to emerge.

The proposal is at least prima facie plausible. Importantly, it obviates the need to suppose that metarepresentational ToM abilities would have played any role at all in the onset of this Paleolithic creative culture. There is, for example, no reason to suppose that "cave painters were also mind readers" (Mithen 2000a, 495). Certainly, the technical capacities required for the production of such art does not support this conclusion. For, as even Baron Cohen (1999, 269) observes, those suffering from autism are often highly adept at drawing, despite their ToM deficits. In this light, it might be thought that discoveries such as the half-human, half-lion statuette from Hohlenstein-Stadel, which dates from 30,000–33,000 B.P., offer better evidence of ancient ToM abilities. Allegedly, this is because such artifacts are fictions in which imaginary elements are combined. Thus it has been argued that "Upper Palaeolithic art includes within it certain images that may provide compelling evidence for the existence of a theory of mind" (Mithen 2000b, 495; Baron-Cohen 1999, 269).

While these products are surely evidence that our ancestors had fertile recreative imaginations and symbolic tendencies, it is not at all clear why this implicates them in the possession of ToM capacities. To make that connection one must also suppose, for example, that these items were used in religious rituals, in which the gods and spirits they represent were perhaps thought to be endowed with supernatural agency—intentional agency. Yet, even if we assume this was the case (despite the complete lack of evidence), there are surely no grounds for supposing that our ancestors imagined that these supernatural agents acted for reasons of their own per se—as opposed, say, to acting out emotion or other intentional attitudes.

It must be remembered that folk psychology (stricto sensu) is only needed to enable us to make sense of subjects that act for reasons of their own—and only those capable of using complex language would have been in a position to do this. Moreover, only those with such a capacity would have been able to express and explicate their reasons for acting. Assuming this, it is more plausible to suppose that if ToM abilities developed at all, they would have done so at some point *after* discursive practices, such as conversation and narration, were well established. For at that point there would have been interesting new patterns of behaviors to deal with—complex linguistic ones—and there would have been an attendant pressure to make sense of them. The need to interpret these kinds of linguistic utterances of others in order to understand their reasons for acting is the right kind of pressure to have been a causal factor in the evolution of full-fledged folk psychological abilities—on the assumption that these were the product of biological evolution (Godfrey-Smith 2002, 64).

Yet there is an obvious problem for nativists if we assume this. For the relevant discursive practices (and thus the need to make folk psychological interpretations) look likely to have become established quite late in our prehistory—too late to have coevolved with or have been shaped along with any imagined built-in metarepresentational mechanisms. These developments will have postdated, by far, the anatomical preadaptations that made language possible. This matters since even the staunchest proponents of the idea that ToM abilities are products of biological evolution place *very* late dates on the emergence of their mature form:

It is only around 50,000 years ago that fully modern theory of mind abilities evolve. (Mithen 2000a, 496)

A theory of mind had in all likelihood evolved by 40,000 years ago, but . . . before this time there is as yet no clear evidence for it. (Baron-Cohen 1999, 273)

The trouble is that if the relevant mindreading mechanisms are supposed to have been built into our species, these dates are just too late. Recognizing this, it has been suggested that "a more powerful argument is that 'theory of mind' *must* have been present in *H. sapiens* 100–150,000 years ago or at least before the dispersion from Africa. Otherwise, one would have to assume parallel evolution of theory of mind" (Baron-Cohen 1999, p. 274; emphasis added).

This is indeed a powerful argument. But it is also one with a clear potential to backfire. For, it invites us to reject the idea that metarepresentational mechanisms could have been the products of biological evolution. This conclusion is especially compelling given the independent reasons just sketched for supposing that folk psychological abilities came late in the day. For, as is implied by Baron-Cohen's remark, the only way to accommodate a biological-evolution story in light of this fact would be to posit the parallel evolution of hardwired mechanisms in diverse human groups over a very short timescale. To say the least, against this, it is much more likely that folk psychology had (and has) a sociocultural basis rather than a biological one.

Sophisticated conversational discourse and narrative practices (not some built-in mindreading mechanism), it seems, fostered the development of our understanding of beliefs and grounded folk psychological practice. Our capacity to understand intentional action in terms of reasons will have only arrived on the scene long *after* the last possible date for universal anatomical change in early humans. Selection pressures may have still operated beyond this point, favoring practical reasoners and folk psychologists over others when there was such competition, but they will not have forged dedicated biological mechanisms to support those abilities throughout the whole of our species.

The NPH can be understood as a special case of the thesis that material culture and its enduring artifacts—in this instance stories of a particular kind—are responsible for "extending" our cognitive and interactive possibilities in important and transformative ways.[8] If we want to understand the basis of our folk psychological abilities, we must look to social practices involving narratives of a quite distinctive variety. It is folk psychological narratives and not inherited biological theory of mind mechanisms or built-in capacities for the construction of such theories on which our interpretative skills for making sense of intentional action rest.

This provokes the question: How and when did folk psychology get started? To address this properly, it is important to revisit the conclusion of the first chapter—that is, that folk psychology has its *primary* application in second-person contexts and its use in supporting third-person speculations is derivative (and not very reliable). Adopting the spectatorial stance when engaging in folk psychology is simply not a very reliable basis for accurately predicting or explaining intentional actions *in those sophisticated cases where there is a need to do so*. And in less sophisticated cases in which there is not—where the imagined mindreading mechanisms are set to their supposedly lowest or default setting—there are simpler and more convincing explanations of how basic intersubjective coordination is effected—explanations in which the ascription of beliefs and desires does not feature at all.

This matters not only because it helps us to understand the role folk psychology is best suited to play in our contemporary dealings but also because it poses a direct challenge to received thinking about its ultimate origins. Apart from the considerations of this and the previous chapter, this gives us a quite independent and sufficient reason for doubting that our ancient predecessors would have needed sophisticated folk psychological abilities in order to conduct their social dealings. On its own it upsets the supposition that the development of third-person mindreading abilities would have been an effective adaptive solution to a problem that arose for them during the Pleistocene epoch: "The rapid comprehension and prediction of another organism's behavior" (Baron-Cohen 1995, 12; cf. Mithen 2000b).

If the arguments of preceding chapters hold good, we would do well to rethink the role folk psychology plays, not just in our lives, but also in those of our forerunners. We should not simply assume that its basic function was to fuel third-party speculations about the reasons for which others *may* have acted. Note that the fact that folk psychology is not mainly about prediction and explanation in no way detracts from its importance in our lives and practices—indeed, recognizing that it serves other, much more vital ends should enhance its status. For Emerson to say why he has acted and for Alex to understand him, serves as a kind of social glue; this sort of activity drives some of our most sophisticated forms of interpersonal relations and bondings (Andrews 2007). It is centrally bound up with our ability to monitor and regulate each other—to hold one another accountable (McGeer 2007).

To state why one acted on a given occasion—to give one's reasons—is not just to give a backward-looking explanation or explication, it is also to lay down tracks. Such an avowal establishes a special sort of future-oriented commitment—although it also sets up expectations in others about what one *ought* to do in relevantly similar circumstances. It does this, in part, by sending a message about what kind of person you are; saying why you have acted on a particular occasion can speak volumes about one's character. And giving one's reasons is revelatory in other ways too. In certain contexts, the mere choice to speak up and say why one acted is equally revealing. Certainly, this is true of the way one does so—both by *what* is said and *how* it is said. Storytellings of this kind—even short narratives—are thus best understood as expressive actions that can and typically do have enormous social and ethical import (see Goldie 2004, chap. 5).

Communal, as opposed to personal, narratives have a similar role and it is likely that they are the more venerable: "Narratives emerged as social forms, which include *explanatory* myths, among other genres that support the coherence and cohesiveness of the community" (Nelson 2003, 22; emphasis mine). Even today such narratives serve this sort of function in existing cultures. Canonical texts, myths, fables, yarns, legends, parables, and traditional tales all play their parts in this. These cultural artifacts constitute a powerful normative force both in first weaving and maintaining the social fabric.

The Myth of Jones (Remix)

What then should we say about the ultimate origins of our folk psychological abilities? Here I take a leaf out of Sellars's book, in making clear the limit of my ambitions while also adapting the central feature of his basic proposal. Sellars concocted a famous myth—which he explicitly identifies as a piece of anthropological science fiction—in order to show the conditions under which our Rylean ancestors—who would have been wedded to a kind of methodological behaviorism—might have graduated to a more nonobservationally based understanding of "inner episodes of thought." This is accomplished, Sellars imagines, by a genius, whom he calls Jones, who came among them. The great Jonesean insight was to model the inner thoughts of his compatriots on their overt speech acts and by doing so he developed a new means of explaining their intelligent acts, even when these were unaccompanied by any outward verbal behavior (Sellars 1956/1997, 102–107).

In the very same way, we can imagine that reasons—minimally, logically interlaced belief/desire pairings—might have been originally modelled on overt narrations. These would have been temporally extended, public speech acts that detailed, at bare minimum, the episodes of practical reasoning constituting one's rationale for acting. They would have provided accounts, for example, of plans constructed and acted on on the basis of manipulating contentful beliefs and desires in appropriate ways. We can suppose then that just like the overt speech acts that served as Jones's original inspiration, these more complex narratives would have been supplied by the authors of these activities, in the first instance. Of course, this assumes that these narrators had command of a logically complex discursive forms, since they would have had to be at home with the practice of making plans based on bouts of practical reasoning involving propositional attitudes, expressing themselves in this way, and so on.

What matters is that in such storytellings one's reasons for acting would have been put on exhibit for all to see. Presumably, such narratives would have been public spectacles, taking the form of complex third-person representations for the benefit of a shared audience—issued in second-person contexts. In short, we can imagine that such public narrations would have provided the model for what it is to act for a "reason" in just the same way that less complex utterances served Jones in developing his understanding of inner episodes of thought.

The importance of this version of Sellarsian myth is that it serves to remind us of the primacy of second-person, public practices in establishing our understanding of ourselves and others as persons who act for reasons. Given this ambition it may seem odd that I have borrowed from Sellars. After all, he is frequently presented as an arch theory theorist, indeed possibly even the progenitor of the kind. Surely, his myth is better suited to support the idea that, at its root, folk psychology is a model used for third-person explanation. Indeed, it is common to hear that "early formulations of the notion of folk psychology stressed the idea that folk psychology is an explanatory theory. This is much to the fore, for example, in Sellars' influential mythical account of how folk psychology might have emerged"

(Bermúdez 2003a, 47). However, one really should not read too much into Sellars's talk of a Jones having created a "theory," especially given the source of his model. Certainly, the way the story plays out, Jones uses his model in order to effect third-person speculations. And this is surely a possible use of folk psychology, though it is—to be sure—not a very reliable one. Yet, this gives us no reason to suppose that supporting such third-person speculation is or was the primary use of the folk psychological framework.

Still, it might be objected that Sellars emphasis is on the way Jones constructs his model of nonobservational "inner episodes of thought" in order to bring out a parallel with the way in which theoretical posits are, in general, constructed. This is nearer the mark. But consider too that he only ever claimed that his "story helps us to understand that concepts pertaining to such inner episodes are primarily and essentially *intersubjective*, as intersubjective as the concept of a positron, and that the reporting role of these concepts—the fact that each of us has a privileged access to his thoughts—constitutes a dimension of the use of these concepts which is built on and presupposes this intersubjective status" (Sellars 1956/1997, 107). I too have been at pains to stress this intersubjective, indeed sociocultural, basis of our understanding of reasons, but this hardly commits me—or anyone who follows suit—to the idea that that understanding is theory based, theorylike, or formed as a product of explicit theorizing.

To see this it may help if one observes that in my new version of the Sellarsian myth, my Jones, like the orginal one, is not really a creative mastermind; he is more an attentive listener. He pays close attention to the stories of his fellows who act for reasons. For it is by hearing these often enough (or, more plausibly, by actively participating in conversations about these) that he becomes acquainted with a basic understanding of what it is to act for a reason. This deals with another worry that is often raised about Sellars's myth, understood as an acquistional account:

As Sellars tells the story, Jones actually set out a theory and taught it to his compatriots. But nothing like that seems to go on in our current practice. We don't explicitly teach our children a theory that enables them to apply mental terms to other people. Indeed, unlike Jones and his friends, we are not even able to state the theory, let alone teach it. (Stich and Ravenscroft 1996, 120–121)

Certainly, Jones neither taught nor do we teach folk psychology as an explicit set of propositions or theoretical posits. But if the NPH is right we do teach it all the same, but through stories. Through the same kind of medium Jones could have been supplied with the relevant framework and thus developed his skill for making sense of actions performed for reasons. My proposal is that the story is essentially the same with us.

Postscript

For all that I have said, some may still think it a weakness of the NPH that it postulates no dedicated inherited inner mechanisms in order to explain our competence with people narratives, for this bucks the popular trend. The tendency of right-thinking folk nowadays is to think of the mind as "massively modular," such that any important job that needs (or better, needed) doing is likely to have its own dedicated module. As a result, in some areas of cognitive science one witnesses a kind of knee-jerk postulation of mechanisms for every (and any) cognitive task that wants explaining. Hence, modules include among their number:

A face recognition module, a spatial relation module, a rigid objects mechanics module, a tool-use module, a fear module, a social-exchange module, an emotion-perception module, a kin-oriented motivation module, an effort allocation and recalibration module, a child care module, a social inference module, a friendship module, a semantic-inference module, a grammar acquisition module, a communication-pragmatics module, a theory of mind module, and so on. (Mithen 1996, 45; Tooby and Cosmides 1992)

For those tempted by this way of thinking, despite all I have argued, it is natural to suppose that a competence with folk psychological narratives must be served by its own dedicated mechanism, one that, presumably, depends on the operation of sophisticated innate mindreading devices. The fact that I deny this might be considered as a weakness of the NPH *if* the rival offerings had anything positive to offer. I have argued that on close inspection, they do not.

I want to close this book with a final, Parthian shot (and a less considered argument). Despite the free flow of talk of modules and mechanisms as the "best explanations" for this or that cognitive capacity, the fact is that in the end we are typically offered little more than promises and excuses when details are called for. Thus, when push comes to shove, it is not uncommon to hear remarks such as the following:

We still don't know, in detail, how these theory-formation mechanisms work, either in science or cognitive development. (Gopnik 2003, 245)

We don't have a detailed account of the cognitive mechanisms that underlie this process. There *must* be *some* mechanism (or, more likely, a cluster of mechanisms). (Nichols and Stich 2003, 35; first emphasis added)

Thus in having no story to tell about the inner mechanisms that underwrite folk psychological narrative competence it seems I am in good company. The difference is my account does not *try* to supply any such story and it promises none. If the details of the sketches concerning inter-subjective engagements provided in this book can be fleshed out it in full, we could potentially tell the whole story (and at least we would know how to go about this). Certainly, the basic proposal of the NPH can be evaluated for its viability and credibility in its entirety, just as it stands. Nothing I have claimed rests on the future hope of discovering some yet-to-be-understood mechanism in order to complete the account. I take it to be a virtue of the NPH that it is completely easy on the scientific eye, requiring no special pleading of any sort. This verdict applies equally to its partners, the MAH and the account I have given of unprincipled embodied engagements. Together they are best placed to explain the basis of our capacity to generate and understand folk psychological narratives.

Notes

Preface

1. Some prefer to talk of "commonsense psychology" as opposed to "folk psychology." This is because the latter label was pejoratively fashioned by the enemies of this practice in order to highlight its weak scientific credentials. Calling it "folk" psychology was meant to signal that its tenets are outmoded, limited, and backward—that is, to highlight the fact that it is indeed "folksy." However, I do not think our everyday practice of making sense of actions in terms of reasons can be usefully thought of as theoretical, nor can virtues and vices be compared in any straightforward manner with what is promised by a scientific psychology. Thus, in talking of folk psychology I happily ally myself with the vulgar without shame or embarrassment (see Hutto 1999a).

Chapter 1

1. One might say that I am concerned with reasons *under the aspect* in which they motivate actions. Falling in line with tradition, I take this to be distinct from the question of whether the reason in question might be designated a "good" one. For more on this distinction and a challenge to the tradition see Dancy 2000.

2. Strictly speaking, practical reasoning does not result in action but always only in an intention to act (see Broome 2002). Malle (1999) offers five criteria for having the mature "folk concept of intentionality." Crucially, among these criteria he defends the traditional view that "a belief or desire functions as a reason only if the agent considered it in at least a rudimentary reasoning process and formed an intention in light of it" (p. 26). I agree.

3. Anscombe's classic work, *Intention*, published in 1957, is often cited as the modern locus classicus on this topic, but the idea has a much more venerable history. It appears in rudimentary form even in Aristotle, who tells us that "intellect itself moves nothing. . . . Hence choice is either desiderative thought or intellectual desire" (EN, 1139a 35–36, 1139b 4–5).

4. Note that I have identified folk psychology as a certain kind of practice. This is important because often the labels "folk psychology" and "theory of mind" are used to denote a set of rules or propositions—those that putatively underlie or explain our capacity to engage the everyday practice of giving and understanding reasons. To accept this characterization would be to get ahead of ourselves, to muddle the explanandum with a possible explanans.

5. I accept that "belief-desire reasoning forms the core of commonsense psychology" (Baker 1999, 3).

6. Terminology—or rather its associated effects—matters. Loose talk sinks ships, so they say, but it can also keep them afloat. As long as our talk is unregulated it is impossible to assess claims properly.

7. To understand *why* it is generally supposed that the primary job of folk psychology is to effect third-person prediction and explanation, we must look at some rather big movements in the recent history of the philosophy of mind and cognitive science. For what one finds is that the standard vision of the function of folk psychology is structurally supported at several points. Essentially, a number of factors conspired to make theory theory the reigning view, leaving simulation to play the role of its natural, if relatively conservative, rival. For it was the rise of the idea that folk psychology is best understood as a kind of low-level theory that gave credence to the now popular idea that its core business is predictive-explanatory in character. For a detailed account of the received view and its ideological history, see the introduction to Ratcliffe and Hutto 2007.

8. Gallagher (2001, 96) is right to stress that "a more basic question is whether our ordinary attempts to understand other people are best characterized as explanations and predictions." For one thing, it is not plausible that we could take a detached interest in the movements of all those we encounter, for to do so would surely sap our intellectual resources. It is much more likely that we only tend to track those actions of others that have some potentially direct impact on us, since doing so is vital if we are to successfully coordinate our actions (see Morton 2003, chap. 1).

9. I have defended an account of nonconceptual content and connectionist processing that would suit this style of approach (see Hutto 1999b, chaps. 3, 4). Henderson and Horgan (2000) also develop an explanation along similar lines.

10. According to the *Oxford English Dictionary*, *common sense* is defined as "normal understanding, good practical sense in everyday affairs, general feeling of mankind or community." This is apposite and it resonates well with the term's etymology. As Taylor (1955, 83–84) relates, "Aristotle's language about 'common sensibles' is, of course, the source of our expression 'common sense,' which, however, has an entirely different meaning. The shifting of sense has apparently been effected through Cicero's employment of the phrase *sensus communis* to mean tactful sympathy, the feeling of fellowship with our kind on which the Stoic philosophers laid so much stress."

11. There are, of course, other non–folk psychological normalizing explanations, but if an action is performed for a reason, then to understand it one must have facility with the folk psychological framework.

12. It is hardly surprising that philosophers of mind schooled in a neopositivist view of science often mix talk of prediction and explanation interchangeably. For example, in making a case for the pervasiveness and indispensability of commonsense psychology, Fodor (1987, 3) switches without warning from talk of "predictive adequacy" to talk of "explanation."

13. In this respect, the notion of an "ideal rational agent" could be replaced by something like "any typical person," as Perner suggested (Perner 1996, 92; see also Hempel 1966, 472, and Arkway 2000, 118–120).

14. Given his general views on the irreducibility and anomalousness of reason explanations, I find it both surprising and somewhat misleading for Davidson (1984, 158) to say that folk psychology is a "familiar mode of explanation of human behaviour and must be considered an organised department of common sense which may as well be called a theory."

15. Following Dretske's lead, he regards their structure as essentially contrastive in nature, in that they answer what-if-things-had-been-different questions. In contrast, theoretical explanations are designed to answer a whole range of what-if-things-had-been-different questions at once.

16. Importantly, we can conclude nothing interesting about the nature of our subpersonal mechanisms from the mere fact that veteran commonsense psychologists (or, more likely, philosophers) can unearth the skeleton of the folk psychological framework. Certainly, this in no way justifies the assumption that what is being articulated is a set of preexisting theoretical principles that exists in the minds of all those capable of engaging in folk psychology. We should not reason, as Socrates did in the Meno, to the conclusion that simply because we can articulate folk psychological principles (to some extent) it follows that such principles exist in our minds innately. Access to a preexisting subpersonal theory is not needed in order to explain our ability to explicate the core folk psychological schema.

17. Heal's (1998a, 1998b) co-cognition variant of the simulation theory only seeks to illuminate how we come to understand and predict the thoughts of others in cases of this kind. Specifically, it can only be used in those in which the object is to determine (1) which thoughts will likely ensue from the other's confrontation with their environmental circumstances, (2) which future thoughts will likely ensue from the other's current thoughts, and (3) which bodily movements will likely ensue from the other's current thoughts.

18. As the name indicates, supporters of this sort of view claim that when predicting and explaining other minds we engage in "a kind of *practical* simulation" (Gordon 1986, 161; emphasis added). Two major proponents of this view, Gordon

and Goldman, frequently speak of applying simulation to obtain both predictions and explanations of intentional action. For example, Goldman (1989, 169–170) openly claims that "the simulation procedure can also be used for explanatory, or 'retrodictive,' assignment of mental states." Gordon too has emphasized that his version of simulation is meant to explain how reason explanations are achieved where these "perform an explanatory function beyond merely portraying the action as reasonable from the agent's point of view. They surely do answer 'Why?' questions, and they may have the form 'A X'd because p,' where 'p' states a reason for A's X'ing" (Gordon 2000, 63; see also Gordon 1986, 158, 163–164; 1992, 12).

19. Views diverge widely about what exactly acts of simulation involve. The major players have heterogeneously characterized the process as a form of imaginative transformation (Gordon 1995); thought replication or co-cognition (Heal 1998a, 1998b); introspective modeling (Gopnik and Wellman 1992); and off-line practical reasoning (Goldman 1989). Nichols and Stich (2003, 133–134) provide a comprehensive and detailed survey of the many varied things that simulation might be. Because the list is so long they fear that only equivocation follows from the use of such a broad term, and they have reiterated an earlier call for it to be "retired." While it is true that different theories of simulation need to be more cleanly distinguished, it would surely be a mistake to throw away the central insight that has inspired these theories: the supposition that when predicting actions (and for some, in explaining them too), folk psychologists draw on nothing but their own cognitive (and, for some, emotional) resources in order to get a handle on other minds. This is precisely what makes simulation theories interesting and promising, however exactly the process is to be understood. I will argue, in later chapters, that the simulation heuristic's only nonspeculative contribution to folk psychological understanding derives from its role in Healish "co-cognition." This is discussed in chapter 7. An embodied form of simulation may also fund basic interpersonal responding but, crucially, the mental states that drive such "simulations" are not propositional attitudes and the activity in question is not best understood as a kind of mind-reading. I discuss this in chapter 6. Of course, to make these claims fully credible it is incumbent on me to say precisely how such "simulations" are carried off and how these abilities are first acquired.

20. A major attraction of this proposal is its ontological economy. One and the same mechanism is postulated in order to explain (1) how we deliberate and generate intentions to act, (2) how we consider possible actions in counterfactual situations, and (3) how we manage to predict and explain the actions of others.

21. "Theory of mind" terminology allegedly made its first appearance in psychology with Premack and Woodward's famous 1978 paper and found its way into philosophy independently in 1980, as introduced by Adam Morton in his *Frames of Mind*, under the alias "theory theory." This was to highlight the fact that the idea that folk psychology is a theory is itself a theory, and not obviously a true one.

22. For example, Goldman (1992b, 22) tells us that nothing "excludes the mixed hypothesis that people use both a simulation heuristic and some form of nomological information. Some kind of mixed theory, I suspect, is unavoidable." In a similar spirit, Heal (1996, 75, 50) instructs us that "philosophers and psychologists should not oppose simulation to theory, but should rather ask what is the appropriate realm of each and how they interact."

23. Early on folk psychology was sometimes characterized as if it *included* such rough nomological information. So understood it would not only incorporate principles about the propositional attitudes but also a series of anthropocentric facts about how humans generally react, tend to feel, or usually think in particular situations (Churchland 1981; see also Loar 1981, 133).

24. In a different context, but also focusing on the limitations of third-person explanations, Juarrero has also noted this: "We will never be able to specify any dynamical system's initial conditions to the requisite (infinite) degree, *a fortiori* we will never be able to capture all the details and circumstances of anyone's life and background. Given this limitation, we must always keep in mind that reconstructing specific instances of behaviour will always be, at best, an interpretation not a deduction—a *much more fallible type of explanation* than we had previously hoped was available. . . . When we are dealing with complex adaptive systems, surprises are unavoidable. . . . Knowing someone is ambitious will not tell you what specific path her behaviour will take" (Juarrero 1999, 225; emphasis mine).

25. It is worth saying something about the defining features of narratives per se. A very minimal definition will suffice. Lamarque tells us that for something to be a narrative "at least two events must be depicted in a narrative and there must be some more or less loose, albeit non-logical relation between the events. Crucially, there is a temporal dimension in narrative" (Lamarque 2004, 394; see also Lamarque and Olsen 1994, 225). This neutral characterization easily lends itself to the idea that there are different types of narratives and that these can be classified by such common features as their constituents and subject matter. Folk psychological narratives are distinguished by being about or centrally featuring agents who act for reasons.

Chapter 2

1. Bartsch and Wellman (1995, 149–150) cite many examples of children talking about and attributing desires and thoughts to others quite early on.

2. Wimmer and Perner developed the original version of this task, but it has been further modified by others (see Wimmer and Perner 1983; Baron-Cohen, Leslie, and Frith 1985). It now travels under the alias of the Location Change task in order to distinguish it from newer versions such as the Deceptive Box task (see Perner, Leekham, and Wimmer 1987).

3. Bloom and German (2000, B30) have convincingly argued that "the false belief task should be considered in its proper context. It is an ingenious, but very difficult task that taps one aspect of people's understanding of the minds of others. Nothing more, nothing less."

4. Children only begin to make explanatory attributions *over time*, during the course of their early school years (Pillow and Lovett 1998). The reason for the delay between getting a handle on the concept of belief and deploying it in this way may be in part that "whereas pre-school-aged children tend to connect events in a linear fashion, 5-year-olds begin to use complex syntax to impose a causal-temporal hierarchy that contrasts important events with background information" (Capps et al. 2000, 201).

5. As Bartsch and Wellman (1995, 215) note, "Interest in people begins in infancy and strengthens in early childhood. This interest manifests itself in children's conversations . . . [Their] talk is dominated by a focus on parents, siblings, friends, babies, adults, television and book characters, and of course, themselves. It is worth noting that this talk arises in family interactions. Children grow up in a family world filled with discourse about each other."

6. That said, many short discussions will not reveal the *full* framework of FP in the way that those of the longer, more involved sort can. Our workaday folk psychological narratives are often of the truncated kind, in line with the rules of conversational implicature.

7. Even so, it has been argued that we should not place too much weight on the need to presuppose rationality in our explanations of action (see Fodor 1981, 109; Dennett 1985, 16–22; Dennett 1987, chap. 4; Stich 1990, chaps. 2–3). For example, it is a great advantage of Gordon's (1992, 15) approach that it "predicts—correctly— that we will sometimes attribute irrationality to others, something that would not be readily predicted by . . . the [strict] 'rational norms' approach."

8. Distanced feelings pervade the lives of those with this disorder. Another patient describes his situation in similarly alienated terms: "I really didn't know there were other people until I was seven years old. I then suddenly realized that there were other people. But not like you do" (Hobson 1992, 247).

9. It is common to describe FP as being akin to theories in the physical sciences— that is, as being a "set of propositions" (Sedon 2005, 5; see also Bickle 1998).

10. The NPH is consistent with recent empirical findings. Several studies have established that there are important links between narrative abilities and our capacity to understand others (Astington 1990; Dunn et al. 1991; Feldman et al. 1990; Lewis 1994; Lewis et al. 1994; Furrow et al. 1992; Peterson and McCabe 1994). Exposure to stories is a critical determiner of FP abilities, and it has been shown that this relation is stronger than mere correlation. Apparently narrative training at least causally influences the basic theory of mind skills for the better (Guajardo and Watson 2002).

Controlled studies have shown that narrative training is responsible for improving performances on false-belief tasks. Thus, it has been concluded that narrative is an effective tool for "at least modest improvements in children's theory of mind development" (Guajardo and Watson 2002, 320). Similarly, it has been observed that "frequent conversations about the mind can accelerate growth of a ToM" (Garfield et al. 2001, 513).

Chapter 3

1. Cats and mice are the animals of choice in giving parade examples of nonverbal believing and desiring: "Taking the object of propositional attitudes as sentences does not require the subject to speak the language of the object sentence, or any. A mouse's fear of a cat is counted as his fearing true a certain English sentence" (Quine 1960, 213). Most famously, Fodor (1987, x) regails us with tales of Greycat who "has, and acts out of, beliefs and desires."

2. Belief/desire psychology used in this way has been described as a type of calculus for predicting behavior of many, many complex systems. As such, it has only instrumental value—its predicates need be treated like "calculation-bound" entities generally. We need take their existence no more or less seriously than that of centers of gravity, as Dennett has long argued. Accordingly, he invites us to think of the "posits" of intentional psychology as species of *abstracta* and not as serious theoretical posits (that is, *illata*). An example of abstracta would be Dennett's (1991, 28) lost sock center, defined as "the center of the smallest sphere that can be inscribed around all the socks I have ever lost in my life."

3. Notably, even Dennett (1987, 23) draws a line at ascribing propositional attitudes to such things as lecterns, arguing that in order to treat something as boring as an inanimate object as an intentional system would require tailoring its "beliefs and desires in a quite unprincipled way."

4. The Fregean approach has well-known problems and there are many different ways of unpacking the metaphor of "Modes of Presentation." We should not take it too literally to be sure.

5. The claim that thoughts (propositional contents) must have an independent objective existence is traditionally motivated by noting that when one says "It is snowing" in English and "Il neige" in French, one says the same thing. Making an ontological head count, based on this simple observation, it looks as if we have three things here: two well-formed, complex linguistic tokens—each hailing from different natural languages—and one meaningful propositional content that is expressed by both. This is what Millikan (2004, 92) calls "the philosophers' notion of a proposition."

6. Accordingly, Fodor's (1987, 12) theory of thinking "attributes contents and causal powers to the very same mental things that it takes to be semantically

evaluable. . . . A chain of thought is presumably a causal chain in which one semantically evaluable mental state gives rise to another."

7. Accordingly, it is possible for "subjects to be in a state with a content p, [even if]
they do not possess the concepts which are canonical for p" (Crane 2001, 152). This
is because "the content of the experience is what you would put in words if you
had the words in question" (see Crane 2001, 144). Or in a slightly different formulation: "If you put your thoughts into words, then *what* you put into words is the
content" (Crane 2006; emphasis added).

8. Crane illustrates the difference neatly as follows: "To believe that a certain pig is
flying you have to have the concept of a pig, but that to see that this pig is flying
you don't need to" (Crane 2001, 152–153). Perceptual experience is usually singled
out as being paradigmatically nonconceptual because its content "is more detailed,
more specific, containing more information than the contents of beliefs and other
propositional attitudes" (Crane 2001, 151).

9. For example, Dretske writes of natural indicators that: "More is needed to be a
representation. E.g. the only way . . . [information-carrying] natural signs can misrepresent is if . . . they fail to indicate something they are supposed to indicate"
(Dretske 1988, 67).

10. A creature might have developed an informational sensitivity to the presence
of Xs by means of detecting Ys. We can imagine that in certain context, say an isolated island, Ys might be unequivocal signs of Xs *and only* Xs: that is, in a restricted
domain the correlation might be perfect (at least for a while). Alternatively, a creature's environment might be noisier—Ys might covary with other things too. This
might not matter so long as Xs could be picked out and tracked by means of picking
out and tracking Ys *often enough* in order to serve the organism's purposes (here
"often enough" can be read as having been good enough in order to have beaten
out the local competition).

11. For example, we can see that Dretske is committed to some such account,
because he holds that much "informational content" is lost in reformatting—when
it is converted from analogue form to digital form. The counterpoint to this idea is
that some property-specific information "contained" in signals is also preserved.
Thus we are told: "Typically, the sensory systems overload the information-handling
capacity of our cognitive mechanisms so that *not all that is given to us in perception*
can be digested" (Dretske 1981, p. 148). Consequently, "Until information is lost
. . . an information-processing system . . . has failed to classify or categorise, failed to
generalise, failed to recognise the input as being an instance (token) of a more
general type" (Dretske 1981, 141; cf. Jacob 1997, 71).

12. The modern inspiration is—of course—Kantian: "The data which sensitivity
gives us is brought under intellectual control by the understanding" (Bennett 1981,
16).

13. For example, Fodor recently took up the sword in defense of the idea in London at The Royal Institute of Philosophy's Annual Lecture for 2006, entitled "The Revenge of the Given: Mental Representation without Conceptualization."

14. I have borrowed from Goldie, who borrows from Griffiths' (1997) notion of an affect program. I prefer Goldie's formulation because he concentrates more on steps 1 and 5 (Goldie 2000, 94, 105).

15. Millikan, as usual, has the right idea: "There are lots of ways of doing things right rather than wrong without making claims or holding theories. . . . Erroneous identification is not a failure at the level of know-that but failure on the level of know-how. It is failure in an activity. Standing back from the failed activity it is often possible to explain its failure by pointing to some proposition that, had it only been true, would have prevented the failure. Had that wrinkle in the rug not been there, I would not have tripped. It doesn't follow that my attempt to walk involved a judgement that no wrinkles were in the rug" (Millikan 2000, 172).

16. The informational links to things of importance need not be straightforward. Millikan supplies the unsavory but effective example of goose droppings that signify the presence of geese passing through, which in turn signifies the onset of winter. Importantly, because covariance relations are transitive the droppings might serve to signify the onset of winter *directly* for a suitably calibrated organism.

17. Akins gets this just right: "Information that is carried by, but not encoded in, a signal is information that is available only in theory. To say that the information is present is to say only that there exists a computable function which, if used, would yield the correct result. . . . It is present, as it were, from the point of view of the universe. But no creature has ever acted upon information that is available only in principle" (Akins 2003, 381).

18. Millikan makes it absolutely clear that there are many other, more interesting, kinds of representations. Thus "the public language representations of humans and surely also human beliefs, desires and intentions, may differ quite radically from more primitive inner and outer representations having the same satisfaction conditions, representations that are either used by humans below the level of explicit belief, desire, and intention or used by other species" (Millikan 2004, 93).

19. Millikan once remarked that if you "put (an analogue of) the bee dance inside the body so that it mediates between two parts of the same organism and you have . . . an inner representation" (Millikan 1993, 164). I think this is a mistake.

20. Relatedly, if one were to move honeybees that originally hail from above the Tropic of Cancer to a location below the Tropic of Capricorn, their use as guides would be thrown off, or this would be so unless or until their dances and their respondents were suitably recalibrated. This is because the correlations they depend upon in guiding action assume that the sun is always in the south (not the north).

21. Consider Elder's rendering of the content of marine bacteria representations. He writes, "The bacteria have not a single thought about oxygen, and could not recognize it if it were right in front of them. So it is misleading to suggest that the content of a given tug is 'oxygen-free water thither'; it would be better to say, 'safe travel that-away'" (Elder 1998, 360). It would be better to say nothing at all. If I am right, we have no need to make such attempts, other than to satisfy our own interpretative tendencies (Hutto 1999b, 84–86; Godfrey-Smith 2002).

22. I once tried to make sense of "nonconceptual content" by appeal to what I called a "modest biosemantics" (Hutto 1999b, chap. 3). Although the substance of my position has not changed, I now realize that both labels are misleading since the view I promote is that basic kinds of end-directed responding are not to be understood as involving reference or truth.

23. I agree with Akins (2003, 386): "Of course, it is true that, as a whole, an animal's behaviour must be directed toward certain salient objects or properties of its environment. Objects (and their properties) are important to the survival of all creatures. But from this fact alone, one cannot infer that the system of sensory encoding, used to produce that behavior, uses a veridical encoding. That is, it does not follow from the fact that the owl's behaviour is directed toward the mouse or that the brain states bear systematic relations to stimuli, that there are any states of the owl's sensory system that are about or serve to detect the property of being a mouse."

24. This is not to be confused with the quite implausible claim that, in general, by having beliefs we manufacture truth-makers.

25. Russellian propositions—the objects of thought—just are "certain complex" worldly objects. Russell, like Moore, believed that these thought-objects were literally composed of terms (or concepts) standing in certain relations to one another, as specified by the particular way individual propositions are constructed. But, for Russell, reality is exhausted by terms—the very constituents of propositions. Hence, the latter cannot be understood as standing in a truth-bearing relation to something else that they are about. Propositions cannot be about something beyond themselves, since *they are* the facts that made up the very bedrock of reality. On this understanding of how reality is populated, there simply is no room for relations of truth, understood in terms of correspondence or of referential relations understood in terms of denotation. Rather, propositions—the objects of thought—are somehow identical with their subject matters. Thinkers of Russellian thoughts are directly acquainted with the complex objects that comprise the world—facts; these are identified with the set of true propositions.

26. When making quotidian, off-the-cuff belief or desire ascriptions for the purposes of predicting (as opposed to genuinely explaining) the behavior of complex systems, it does not matter which of the great range of possible belief/desire pairings is ascribed; that is, it is not necessary to specify the belief or desire contents nonver-

bals harbor. Indeed, it does not seem possible to do this (for examples, see Hutto 1999b, 90–91).

27. This proposal is in clear opposition to Carruthers's claim that a rudimentary practical reasoning system has extremely venerable ancestry. If true, even very simple animals manipulate belieflike representations—representations that cooperate with goal-based motivations in order to generate action. Desert ants and honeybees are the flagship examples (Carruthers 2004).

28. There appears to be a growing consensus about this. As Papineau remarks, "non-human animals are sophisticated in many different ways, but . . . there is no compelling reason to think them capable of means-end reasoning in particular" (Papineau 2003, 99). Or, in Akins's words, "Much of a simple organism's behavioural repertoire can be accounted for without the use of anything other than narcissistic systems without anything that looks like an internal representation of objects and properties" (Akins 2003, 388).

29. Despite the fact that modules manipulate representations of the right form and content to participate in inferential operations they are imagined to be shut off from the operations of central cognition: in a word, they are "encapsulated." A virtue of the biosemiotic account is that it relieves the need to explain how or why the domain-specific "representations" of the various modules are "corralled" from the rest of cognition in this way.

Chapter 4

1. According to Bermúdez the LoT hypothesis "is seriously limited when it comes to the epistemological dimension of nonlinguistic thought and is of little practical use in grounding psychological explanation at the nonlinguistic level" (Bermúdez 2003b, 20; see also 28, 31). This is because it provides no way of specifying *which* contents are being used by nonverbals.

2. The friends of success semantics acknowledge that "it is in fact neither vacuous nor easy to characterise beliefs by the actions which, along with the desires, they generate. In particular, it is not easy to say in general how changes in beliefs affect behaviour" (Mellor 1991, 31).

3. To suppose otherwise is to be under the sway of a passive picture of perception and cognition, according to which the recognition of sameness boils down to nothing more than regularly exhibiting the same response to specific types of stimuli (Millikan 2000, chaps. 8, 9). But that picture seriously underestimates what is required for bona fide reidentification. Recognizing some particular as the *same again* requires being able to do so even when it is identified by quite different identification procedures.

4. Thus he also confesses to simplifying the experimental evidence somewhat. Although the empirical literature provides statistical analyses of the performance of

whole groups of rats in different kinds of maze, Bermúdez presents the data as if a single rat had been subject to such trials, using the same type of maze. He also assumes that this imaginary rat doesn't switch strategies, suddenly enlisting diverse ways of "thinking about" food in different trials, even though he also notes that studies show that the salience of landmarks does in fact matter to the way rats "code locations" (Bermúdez 2003b, 101, 103). He takes it that such modifications are not important since his hope is only to show, in general, "how a theorist might go about resolving the inevitable indeterminacies generated by applying success semantics to a target behavior" (p. 103).

5. For Millikan, even linguistically based methods of re-identification should not be understood in terms of MoPs. She writes "Opaque descriptions characterise aspects of conceptions, that is, aspects of ways of identifying substances. They do not describe ways of thinking of substances. 'Via a definite description' and 'via a proper name' are not ways of thinking of things. Nor, of course, is 'by recognizing her face' or 'by recognizing her voice' a way of thinking of a person" (Millikan 2000, 176). Quite generally, for her "Fregean senses and their kin . . . have to pretty much be trashed" (Millikan 2000, 13). But in light of the argument presented, one could argue that language users are capable of having MoPs even these cannot feature in non-verbal responding. This would be consistent with the claim that "some sorts of confusion are best explained in terms of modes of presentation and the false identity judgements they make possible" (Lawlor 2005, 32).

6. The SIH is the hypothesis that the high levels of general intelligence displayed by simians is in some way a by-product of their social intelligence. First canvassed by Jolly (1966) and Humphrey (1976) in slightly different forms, the basic claim has been explored most thoroughly in a series of papers and anthologies focusing, inter alia, on the way primates develop and deploy strategies about: whom to cooperate with (and when), whom to defer to (and when), and whom to deceive (and when). To successfully implement these not only requires keeping track of the sociable tendencies of other individuals (as well as their rank and status) but also of one's one previously formed alliances and enemies.

7. Papineau illustrates the limitation in the following way: "Imagine a simple animal who has information along the lines of *shaking those trees will yield apples* implicit in one behavioural disposition, and information like *throwing apple-sized objects will repel bears* implicit in another, it will have no way of putting these together so as to figure out that it would be a good idea to shake a tree when a bear is prowling around and no suitably throwable objects are yet to hand. Of course, this information may itself come to be embodied implicitly in some disposition, if natural selection or learning instills a specific disposition to shake trees and throw the resulting fruit when bears are nearby. But the general point will still apply. While the organism will have various bits of general information implicit in its various behavioural dispositions, it will have no system for combining them and using them

to infer the worth of behaviour that is not already directed by its cognitive architecture" (Papineau 2003, 97). The distinction between generalizations that are in sensu composito and in sensu diviso is useful when it comes to characterizing their modes of thought (see Clapin 2002, 50).

8. Consider, for example, the proposal that dispositions themselves might the vehicles of nonlinguistic thought. Papineau (2003, 96) writes, "An animal who is disposed to drink from ponds must differ in some substantial causal way from an animal who hasn't learned to do this. So why not let this real difference, whatever it is, serve as the vehicle of the content 'pond drinking yields water?'" In explicating this, he goes on to talk of a "disposition as a perfectly explicit representer" (p. 97). But, on the face of it, this suggestion looks hopeless: a creature's dispositions will at best serve to *exhibit* its reasoning capacities; they cannot be the *basis* for conducting said reasoning.

9. Motor imagery has special features. When thinking about it, it is important to bear in mind that "motor imagery is imagined perception of action, it is not imagining you are perceiving action. . . . What you are imagining is, exactly, moving your body, just as what you are imagining when you visually imagine a cat is a cat" (Currie and Ravenscroft 2003, 87–88).

10. There is a respectable body of empirical findings that point to (1) strong continuities in subject performances on tasks involving imagery and visual experience, (2) strong discontinuities in performances on those tasks involving imagery and verbal responding, and (3) interference and enhancement effects on tasks of the sort that one would expect if there was a link between perception and imagination (Currie and Ravenscroft 2003; Hutto 2000, chap. 1).

11. Consider the labors of Putnam's ant: "An ant is crawling on a patch of sand. As it crawls, it traces a line in the sand. By pure chance the line that it traces curves and recrosses itself in such a way that it ends up looking like a recognizable caricature of Winston Churchill. Has the ant traced a picture of Winston Churchill, a picture that *depicts* Churchill? Most people would say, on a little reflection, that it has not. The ant, after all, has never seen Churchill, or even a picture of Churchill, and it had no intention of depicting Churchill. It simply traced a line (and even that was unintentional), and a line that we can 'see as' a picture of Churchill" (Putnam 1981, 1).

12. My focus here is on Prinz's account of cognitive processing and not his concept empiricism and detection-based semantics more generally. In advocating his new-order empiricism he avails himself of connectionist resources (Prinz 2002, 143–144). I only intend to make appeal to his work on the combinatorial properties of similarity-based accounts without buying into his theory of categorization, which is based ultimately on his providing an adequate account of determinate, referential content.

13. Also, "When prototypes combine compositionally, they do so in a context-sensitive way. If combination is context-sensitive, the ability to combine concepts in one context may not carry with it the ability to combine them in another" (Prinz 2002, 295, 299).

14. Those influenced by the Fregean tradition hold that images, feelings (the "ideas" of the empiricists) and other subjective denizens of the mind are unfit subject matter for logicians. Frege rejected such psychologism in his attempt to cast logic as an objective science, concerning only the laws of thought (Hutto 2003/2006, chap. 1). Today's cognitive scientists tend to reject imagistic mediums of thought and resemblance theories of reference. The corollary is that the best models of mind are computational. In effect, the move has been to depsychologize psychology. Rollins captures the basic logic in the following passage: "The image can have a multitude of meanings; thus, by itself it is cognitively impotent. The language of thought therefore cannot be iconic" (Rollins 1986, 57; cf. Fodor 1975, 177–184; Carruthers 1996a, 31–33). Many are happy to catalogue, in great detail, why "the imagist theory of thought is hopelessly inadequate as an account of all forms of thinking—or, indeed, as an account of any of our propositional thoughts" (Carruthers and Boucher 1998, 7).

15. This is fully in the spirit of Carruthers's suggestion about how Köhler's apes might have solved their problems by means of visual imagination. He writes: "It may be that what the chimp has to be able to do, to arrive at a sudden solution to such a problem, is imagine the boxes piled one on top of the other, and to visualise, and then act on, the result. Although this is intelligent and sophisticated, there is no reason to believe that the chimp must also be capable of thinking about its own sequence of images" (Carruthers 1996a, 221).

Chapter 5

1. I favor a Davidsonian line on most of these issues, but especially so when it comes to understanding what is involved in thinking and uttering everyday contextual truths (see Hutto 1999b, chap. 5; 2000, chap. 7).

2. There are also nontrivial and nonaccidental parallels between the verbs of propositional attitudes and the verbs of saying. For a full discussion of the general virtues of sententialism, in both its semantic and psychological varieties, see Richard 1990. For details of its Mentalese version see Fodor 1975, 31–32, 1978; Mahoney 1989, 3–19.

3. The basic claim, unchanged for decades, is that "psychological processes are typically computational and computation presupposes a medium for representing the structures over which the computational operations are defined" (Fodor 1975, 51; Mahoney 1989, 18).

4. Thus, "LoT wants to construe propositional-attitude tokens as relations to symbol tokens. According to standard formulations, to believe that P is to bear a certain

relation to a symbol that means that P . . . Now all symbol tokens have intentional contents and their tokens are physical in all known cases. And—*qua* physical—symbol tokens are the right sorts of things to exhibit causal roles" (Fodor 1987, 135–137).

5. Fodor has recently argued that there has been decisive philosophical progress on this issue, claiming that "the same considerations that guarantee that no epistemic conditions are constitutive of the content of words or concepts strongly suggest that thoughts must have content in the first instance" (Fodor 2001b, 6).

6. Mentalese might be ontologically distinct from and explanatorily prior to language, without being temporally prior to it. It is not clear just how far back Mentalese is thought to go, but Fodor has argued we certainly have linguaform mental representations but that organisms in the lower branches of the phylogenetic bush, such as paramecia, do not (see Fodor 1986; cf. Churchland 1986, 388). Therefore it is even possible that only our own species enjoys Mentalese representations. It would be consistent with the argument of the last chapter that the LoT only arrived very late in the day—being restricted to modern humans (*Homo sapiens sapiens*). This would also be in line with recent arguments that propositional representation and inferential reasoning only look to be features of "human cognitive capacities" (Von Eckardt 2003). However, this would mean that an entirely new form of mental representation emerged with the speciation event that gave rise to modern humans, arriving just prior to the advent of full-fledged language use. While this hypothesis is consistent with Fodor's best argument for believing in a LoT—his concept/language learning ur-argument—in many respects this sudden emergence of Mentalese would be harder, not easier to explain. It is not, for example, obvious which selection pressures would have driven it, presumably *alongside* the other preadaptations necessary for natural language competency.

7. Many are suspicious of this argument because it apparently leads to a regress. But the postulation of the LoT is precisely meant to avoid a regress since it is language that one does not need to learn. If one could account for its semantics by some other route the problem would indeed be solved. But the fact is that there is no credible story about how Mentalese content is acquired.

8. There are reasons for doubting that the LoT hypothesis could ever be put to the test. For example, some have claimed that the failure to find any sentences in the brain shows it to be false (Churchland 1991, 65). Yet, from the very start, Fodor has always maintained that his hypothesis must not be confused with a crude thesis about how the proposed mental architecture is implemented at the neural level. All that it requires for its truth is that the higher-order symbolic operations are somehow implemented at the neural level. Mentalese symbols are natural computational kinds that do not make themselves known to neurological investigations. This is consistent with their being spatiotemporal particulars with genuine causal powers in the same way that the entities of interest to other special sciences might be. In line with token materialism, it is argued that although every symbolic kind

is also a physical kind, there need be no robust or systematic correlations between the symbolic and the neural. This is certainly an internally consistent position, but as far as empirical hypotheses go, it makes the claim that symbols of the lingua mentis are natural kinds awkward if not impossible to falsify. At least, no evidence for or against it can be amassed by carrying out physiological or neuroscientific investigations into the actual working of brains.

9. Fodor has argued that *only* Mentalese sentences are in a position to explain compositionality (see Fodor 2001b). This is a feature that natural language sentences allegedly inherit from the underlying Mentalese thoughts (as Fodor would have it this is true of their semantic properties quite generally). Compositionality requires the existence of stable semantic building blocks that can play recurring roles across contexts. And Fodor's claim is that natural language, being "strikingly elliptical and inexplicit" about the thoughts it expresses, could not possibly be compositional in anything like strict detail (Fodor 2001b, 11). Its indeterminacy renders natural language incapable of supplying the basic constituents needed to underwrite a recombinant and constructive semantics. I have addressed this argument in detail elsewhere, and rejected it (see Hutto 2007c). If Fodor's argument can be successfully defused, we can endorse the proposal that "words serve as anchors that allow us to speak and defer to people in our linguistic community. As long as we have this much, we can generate a representation for an unfamiliar category using purely compositional means. That is all the compositionality we need" (Prinz and Clark 2004, 61).

10. Frankish and I differ in our characterization of the basic mind. He understands it in propositional attitude terms, despite the fact that no acts of explicit conscious reasoning occur at this level. In contrast, I hold that it is only in the ratiodiscursive, linguistic domain that we can *legitimately* talk of propositional attitudes.

11. One can endorse the TNL account without taking sides in the debate about the "location" of the relevant cognitive processing. There is disagreement within the extended mind camp about whether or not supermental cognition involves an internal reconfiguration of procedures to which our biological brains are accustomed or merely the manipulation of external vehicles (Clark 1998; Dennett 1998; Mithen 2000b).

12. Papineau provides the raw sketch of a similar kind of account in which means-end reasoning and communication coevolved on the back of complex language. He too speculates that an "initial stage of means-end reasoning made use of visual imagination" (Papineau 2003, 127).

13. There remains a tremendous gulf between ape and human capacities for learning symbols. Encultured apes struggle to learn even a small number of basic symbols and the process is very, very slow (Li and Hombert 2002, 190).

14. Unlike cases of purely indexically or iconically based responding, this really is a situation in which a simple public sign is being used to stand for something, denotationally and referentially. Here we might *begin* to talk of content legitimately.

15. Even more speculatively, if reasoning by means of natural language structures did constitute such a vast improvement to the cognitive possibilities of early humans, this might potentially explain why modern humans are almost unique in the animal kingdom as having so completely out-competed all other species within its taxonomic family (Li and Hombert 2002, 176).

16. Carruthers issued this complaint against Bickerton's version of the claim that propositional thought and language coevolved together. Another of his concerns is that such a hypothesis undercuts the possibility that human intelligence could have coevolved with brain size *prior* to the arrival of complex language. And he holds that this is the best explanation of the encephalization evidence. But this worry is easily dealt with if we suppose that the selective pressures that drove the slow development of a language-ready brain operated on multiple fronts. There are many factors other than linguistically based reasoning that are likely responsible for brain growth and reorganization during the period just prior to the birth of language. I will discuss this in chapter 11.

Chapter 6

1. I say "if" so as not to prejudge the possibility that children may "have" the belief concept earlier, even though they show no outward signs of being able to use it. This might be so if they lack the capacity or motivation to apply it, perhaps because they favour simpler heuristics instead. This view, which has been defended by Leslie, German and others, will be discussed again in the next chapter (see Leslie 1994).

2. In some quarters, the tendency to assume that concepts of some sort are needed when it comes to characterizing such responses is almost automatic. For example, in her introduction to a recent anthology on joint attention Eilan recognizes the seriousness of this problem but fails to note that she forecloses on important ways of approaching it by labeling it the "Concept question" (Eilan 2005).

3. For details of the use of these methods on nonhuman primates see Hauser 1998; Munakata et al. 2001.

4. That such differences exist is a well-known fact to practicing magicians who must vary their routines significantly when dealing with these two classes of audience (cf. Gopnik and Meltzoff 1997).

5. At a minimum, it presupposes that there exists "a complex set of relations between concepts, usually with a causal basis" (Murphy and Medin 2000, 246).

6. Stich and Nichols express the same worry when they say, "we find it a bit hard to take this proposal seriously.... What reason do we have to suppose that the

infant takes the entities posited by his theory (whatever exactly these are) to be "closely, lawfully, related with one another," or that the infant is interpreting anything in a causal way, or that his knowledge supports counterfactuals, or that what he knows has an explanatory force?" (Stich and Nichols 1998, 432).

7. Prinz bring this out in describing how the infant mind is imagined to be like "a little university, divided into departments. Each of these departments has its own subject matter, and its own general principles for making sense of that subject matter. Innate principles are often presumed to require innate concepts" (Prinz 2002, 212).

8. To think otherwise belies a misguided attachment (if only tacit) to what Millkan calls the "passive" conception of perception and cognition. As usual, she hits the nail on the head: "Substances need not be grasped by understanding the principles that structure them and hold them together, but merely by knowing *how* to exploit them for information-gathering purposes. Just as one does not have to be able to describe or even to recognize the conditions required for exercise of one's other abilities, for example, just as a child can swim without understanding Archimedes' principle and ride a bicycle without understanding the laws of dynamics, neither does one need to understand the ontological principles on which one's successful projections of substance invariances depend. Analysis of the world structures that permit the possibility of human knowing is not the same thing as analysis of the inner psychological structure of the knowing" (Millikan 2000, 74).

9. Rehearsing the moves between empiricists and rationalists in the ancient debate over the existence and nature of innate ideas, Louise Anthony gives a clear example of how a formalist might understand some innate principles. Appealing to the concept of "identity," she writes, "There is, at any rate, nothing to show that there must be a concept of identity in *the sense of a mental symbol that expresses identity*—there might simply be the mind's tendency to segregate and desegregate experiences in a way that permits abstraction. . . . What Hume may have shown—and no surprise—is that *our innate 'knowledge' of the principle of induction may be entirely 'knowledge-how' rather than 'knowledge-that'*" (Antony 2001, 202; emphasis added).

10. Although dismissed by the founders of the cognitive revolution, the idea that *knowledge how* as opposed to *knowledge that* might underlie many cognitive acts is once again back in vogue. A new enactivist movement has been begun; one which rejects the idea that skilful activity depends upon the manipulation of underlying tacit representations of a pre-given world (Varela, Thompson, and Rosch 1991, 148; Hutto 2005a, 2006b).

11. The claims is that, "the distant ancestors of modern humans had nothing much like the contemporary capacity to read minds. . . . What they did have, however, were all the components of the mind . . . beliefs, desires, an inference mechanism, a practical reasoning mechanism, a planner . . . though they had no inkling that

they had minds like this nor did they have any idea that conspecifics or other organisms did" (Nichols and Stich 2003, 61–62).

12. Somewhat confusingly, Nichols and Stich also claim that the concept of a goal is, in itself, a kind of theory. They write: "One glorious day (well it probably took longer than a day) a new idea emerged—but it was more than an idea, really. It was a theory. The central theoretical notion in the theory was the concept of a goal" (Nichols and Stich 2003, 62). What might at first seem like theoretical looseness in their talk of "having a concept" is in fact just the application of a general (and I think sensible) policy of not wanting to get embroiled in philosophical debates about the possession conditions for concepts: "So at what point do their concepts and ours count as really being the concept of *goal, desire, belief*, etc.? On our view, there is no principled way of answering this question and it is not a question we propose to take seriously" (Nichols and Stich 2003, 68).

13. Nichols and Stich are utterly explicit that the EMS must make "use of the attributer's beliefs about the world" (Nichols and Stich 2003, 84). They are less clear, however, about what "having a belief" comes to at the subpersonal level. Given their choice of examples one might expect them to endorse the LoT hypothesis. They cite, as instances of having propositional attitudes, having the representation "Socrates was an Athenian" stored in one's belief box and having the representation "It will be sunny tomorrow" stored in one's "desire box." Yet, when it comes to discussing the nature of such representations they adopt a neutral line, observing that "many advocates of the representational account of cognition will also assume that the representation tokens subserving propositional attitudes are linguistic or quasi-linguistic in form. This additional assumption is no part of our theory" (Nichols and Stich 2003, 15). The fact is that such openness will not do; that is, unless an alternative theory of representation is provided that shows how such contentful ascriptions are warranted without assuming a sententialist theory.

14. Papineau sees matters clearly. He writes that "standard accounts of understanding of mind only make sense if we suppose that 'mind-readers' are already capable of means-end thinking. This applies to both the 'simulation-theory,' which holds that understanding of mind rests largely on the ability to simulate the decision-making of others, and theory-theory, which holds that understanding of mind derives from an articulated theory of mind . . . an ability to perform such reasoning 'off-line' presupposes a prior ability to do it on-line" (Papineau 2003, 120–121).

15. Thus, as Goldman and Sripada argue, "we do not regard the creation of pretend states, or the deployment of cognitive equipment to process such states, as essential to the generic idea of simulation. The general idea of simulation is that the simulating process should be similar, in relevant respects, to the simulated process. Applied to mindreading, a minimally necessary condition is that the state ascribed to the target is ascribed as a result of the attributor's instantiating, undergoing, or experiencing, that very state. In the case of successful simulation, the experienced

state matches that of the target. This minimal condition for simulation is satisfied [in Gallese's model]" (Goldman and Sripada 2005, 208).

16. Conversely, Gallese has also seen a potential link between his account of embodied attunement and my NPH. Referring to my paper on the limits of spectatorial folk psychology he writes, "A possibility is that embodied simulation mechanisms might be crucial in the course of a long learning process required to become fully competent in how to use propositional attitudes, like during the repetitive exposure of children to the narration of stories" (Gallese 2006, 7).

17. The mere fact that recognition-and-response ties *can* be undone testifies that Wittgenstein was right to insist that characteristic emotional expressions are best treated as *symptoms* of their associated emotions and not as *criteria* for them. This is what makes it possible for stage actors to ply their trade, even those in the wild.

18. This way of thinking is pervasive, as is evidenced by the fact that Nichols and Stich regard the term *mindreading* to have a kind of theoretical neutrality (Nichols and Stich 2003, 2). Behind this thought lies the supposition that our primary interpersonal transactions are third-personal and that the only serious options for understanding these will be some variant of TT and ST, or their combination.

19. This proposal about embodied responding is flexible enough to capture both shared and contrastive reactions in its net—that is, by factoring in variables of character, history and context, we can appeal to different general patterns of response in order to explain, at least in part, why sometimes our way of attuning to others requires us to mirror their psychological state and at others times not. Sometimes your anger might fuel my anger, at other times it might induce fear in me.

20. In claiming this I am going against a certain familiar trend in current thinking. Apparently, "It is almost universal among philosophers to think that all social interactions are governed by psychological explanations taking this general form—that we are *only* able to navigate the social world because we constantly deploy belief-desire explanations to make sense of what is going on around us" (Bermúdez 2003b, 46, emphasis added; Davies and Stone 2003, 305–306). This standard assumption supports some rather bold claims that have been made about the importance of propositional attitude psychology. For example, we have been told that "we have no other way of describing behaviors and their causes" (Fodor 1987, 8); that "everyday affairs are well nigh unthinkable without the apparatus of the attitudes" (Baker 1995, 4); that intentional psychology is "the best way to make sense of the action of others" (Baron-Cohen 1995, 21). The received view appears to be that "our *basic* grip on the social world depends on our being able to see our fellows as motivated by beliefs and desires" (Currie and Sterelny 2000, 145; emphasis added).

21. In the above I have said nothing about the experiential character of such reactions—that is, of the sensations and feelings that are part and parcel of the activities and states of readiness to act that characterize such encounters. I discuss this

topic elsewhere; see Hutto 2006a, 2006b, 2006c. In my view, these phenomenal aspects are neither additionally generated mental properties nor intentional contents; rather I propose they must be understood in actional ways.

22. It is possible that the basic scripts and core mechanisms for intersubjective responding derive and build on prior adaptations. For example, it is plausible that "some sorts of facial expression—for example barring of the teeth in anger—which were serviceable for some purpose in our remote ancestors, may in humans have taken on the secondary function of signalling an emotion to other members of the same species" (Goldie 2000, 97). However, it is equally possible that some of these recognition and response systems are primary adaptations, having evolved to serve entirely social ends. In emphasizing the importance of sexual selection, Carruthers (2003, 74) usefully reminds us that "many of the behaviors and behavioral tendencies that we think of as distinctively human—story-telling, jokes, music, dancing, sporting, competition, and so on—are products of sexual selection, functioning as sexual displays of one sort or another. . . . [Similarly] emotional dispositions such as kindness, generosity, and sympathy, for example, may be direct products of sexual selection."

23. These original findings were replicated in other variants. Not only did the subordinates take more food under these conditions than in tests using transparent barriers, they clearly preferred to enter the room when the location of the food was switched without the dominant seeing that this had happened.

24. Interestingly, chimpanzees do better in such tasks when body movements and vocalizations are used in conjunction with gaze.

25. Through the use of longitudinal studies Povinelli and his team ruled out the possibility that the chimpanzees had *developed* an understanding of seeing over time. In a follow-up series of tests a year after the initial set were conducted it was discovered that the apes had not retained what they had learned. Faced again with the same conditions they were performing below chance until after they had undergone four scores of trials. The results were replicated by re-testing as they verged on adulthood.

26. More controversially, it may be that such intelligence is also displayed in the wild during certain types of cooperative activities, such as collaborative hunting. Interestingly, even these involve an element of competition, occurring both within and across groups. Caution should be exercised when it comes to explaining the form of psychological intelligence that underlies such interactions since lions and wolves also engage in it, at least to some extent (Boesch and Boesch-Achermann 2000). It matters that these collaborations are a far cry from the sophisticated human versions. Others have noted this too. Thus—very much in line with the arguments of this book—Brinck and Gärdenfors (2003) claim that future-directed cooperation of the kind that is based on the symbolic representation of means and ends is only achieved by linguistically competent humans.

27. As Call and Tomasello (2005, 59) note, it is important to distinguish between "perceptual access (whether others can or cannot see something), perspective taking (how others perceive something from their vantage point), or attention (what aspect of something others are focusing on . . .). Currently, there is evidence that chimpanzees reach the first level of understanding the visual access of others." This is a much clearer statement of an earlier verdict according to which it was ambiguously claimed that "Chimpanzees actually know something about *the content* of what others see" (Tomasello, Call, and Hare 2003a, 155; emphasis added).

28. By my lights, behaviors can be properly classed as cognitive even if there is no underlying manipulation of mental representations which makes them so. Carving the conceptual space up in the traditional way encourages researchers to draw a clear-cut dividing line between those behaviors that are representationally driven and those which are merely mechanically driven (for example, reflexive, associative). Concomitantly, this is usually taken to be the fault line that separates those responses which exhibit intentionality and those which do not. It should be obvious that the biosemiotic approach I promote redraws these boundaries.

29. Joint attention of this kind has never been shown to be mastered by apes, not even adult apes. Indeed, the gulf between their abilities and ours in this domain is so wide that it suggests that to the extent that they can attend jointly at all it is "an evolutionarily different version" (Gómez 2005, 80; see also Leekam 2005, 225).

30. It seems likely therefore that the first nonsyntactic protolanguage would have been manually based. If so, it would follow that language evolution took a circuitous route—that is, speech-dominated language would not have emerged *directly* from primate call systems. Some claim that the latter is the more straightforward explanation (Dunbar 2003). That is certainly so, but there is simply no a priori reason to suppose that straightforward explanations are always the best ones.

Chapter 7

1. My reasons for thinking that abilities are not dispositions are essentially those of Millikan (see Hutto 1999b, chap. 3). She is bolder than I am on this topic; she identifies concepts with *abilities* (Millikan 2000).

2. The line taken here is that:"Children's social knowledge is based on action. . . . Understanding others is at first practical" (Carpendale and Lewis 2004, 85).

3. As Eilan notes, "First words emerge during the thirteenth month, on average, and from then on until the end of the second year, attentional behaviors become progressively more sophisticated—for example, we find progressively sensitive checks of where the adult is looking, before, during and after pointing initiated by the infant, or showing of objects to adults, the bouts of attending together to an object become longer and able to sustain the beginning of extended play with, and conversations about the object(s) attended to" (Eilan 2005, 5).

4. On the view I am propounding, "theory of mind depends on language" (Astington and Jenkins 1999, 1319). Although I reach this verdict through philosophical reflection, Astington and Jenkins come to it on the basis of a detailed longitudinal study. It should therefore be of no surprise that "by far the most significant variable in predicting success on ToM tasks is the production and comprehension of sentences containing propositional complement clauses. . . . It is precisely familiarity with discourse in which propositions figure as objects ('Sally says/thinks that [proposition]') that enables children to propose mental states in which propositions figure as objects" (Garfield, Peterson, and Perry 2001, 520). It would seem that mastery of complementation is needed for the kind of metarepresentational attributions that rely on embedding propositional clauses (de Villiers and de Villiers 1999). While the empirical discoveries of Astington and Jenkins are surely consistent with this hypothesis—in that they found that syntactical abilities in particular were most strongly correlated with ToM abilities—they acknowledge the softer possibility that the mastery of syntax in question might not take the form of mastery of complementation per se.

5. Up until the age of two years, English-speaking children typically use only simple two-word constructions (Pinker 1994). Some children can make use of fully tensed *that*-clauses to represent the complex objects of desires at an early age; apparently this is true of German children (Perner et al. 2003).

6. It has been argued that only once suitably reformatted, it is possible that propositional desires can play their part in practical reasoning—either by taking the form of imperatives or by modalizing the indicative form (Mahoney 1989, 20–21; Carruthers 2004).

7. For example, Wellman and Wooley discovered that 2½ year olds predicted different responses from story characters when, in seeking a desired object, they were confronted with three different types of outcome: finds-nothing, finds-wanted, finds-substitute (Wellman and Wooley 1990; Wellman and Phillips 2001, 130).

8. As Harris proposes, even when it comes to understanding advanced desires it is sufficient to regard others as "goal-directed agents." In contrast, to understand others as believers requires being able to see them as "epistemic subjects" in their own right (Harris 1996).

9. In this context it is of interest that, although German children master that-clauses much earlier than their Anglophone counterparts, they do not manifest an earlier understanding of false belief (Perner et al. 2003).

10. Interestingly, against the idea that children make default attributions of belief to others (that is, using a heuristic that exploits what they know to be the case), Bartsch and Wellman (1995, 64) observe that "we find no evidence of an early stage in which children erroneously think of thoughts as connections instead of representational mental states."

11. Or, as Davidson (1985, 487; 1999) would say, having the *concept* of the concept of belief is required for having the concept of belief.

12. Given these connotations, solipsism is a good label for this. As Nelson (2003, 29) observes, "Piaget calls this egocentrism but it is an egocentrism that simply lacks perspective because there is no possible alternative view but one's own. There are no insights into another's life because there is no vehicle except shared actions through which experience can be shared."

13. Evidence gleaned from the conversations of young children reveals that they "do not use such terms as intend to, on purpose, or mean to until about 3, 4, or 5 years, but as early as 1½ years they talk about persons' goals and desires, primarily with the term want" (Wellman and Phillips 2001, 130).

14. Nelson's claim is that stories are the medium for "understanding of different perspectives on the world of experience, perspectives that are revealed especially in narrative discourse and that are not discernable in actions alone" (Nelson 2003, 29).

15. In this respect it is "the child's growing experience, not as an agent, but as a conversationalist [that] plays a critical role" (Harris 1996, 209–210).

16. It has been discovered that "profoundly deaf children who grow up in hearing families often lag several years behind hearing children in their development of an understanding of false belief, even when care is taken to include only children of normal intelligence and social responsiveness in the deaf sample . . . it was not until age 13 to 16 that deaf children's success rates were seen to approximate those of normally developing 4-year-old's" (Peterson and Siegal 2000, 127; see especially their summary on 138).

17. We are told that "The results of the studies . . . combine to suggest that the ease with which deaf children develop a theory of mind may be related to the nature and extent of their exposure to conversation in the home while growing up as preschoolers" (Peterson and Seigal 2000, 131).

18. That proposal about the role of conversations is one way of accommodating the wealth of data, including longitudinal studies, that shows the strong influence that family environments and socioeconomic circumstances have on developmental patterns and ToM performances of individual children. The relevant factors include: number and age of siblings; frequency and content of discussions; security, quality, timing and styles of parent-child interactions (Appleton and Reddy 1996; Brown, Donelan-McCall, and Dunn 1996; Dunn, Brown, and Beardsall 1991; Perner, Ruffman, and Leekam 1994; Lewis et al. 1996; Watson et al. 1999; for a general summary of see Carpendale and Lewis 2004).

19. We can rule out the possibility that this could be achieved by a lone thinker merely imagining alternative cognitive perspectives on their own. The evidence about the importance of actual conversations with others tells against this, as does

the fact that self-ascriptions of belief are harder and occur later than other ascriptions in the developmental timetable (see Bogdan 2005).

20. For Heal this is not an a posteriori hypothesis about subpersonal mechanisms, but an a priori truth about a substantial part of our personal-level method of psychological understanding. Thus, unlike Goldman, her position is not dependent on a commitment to the Basic Architectural Assumption (BAA) or the existence of hardwired, inherited practical reasoning mechanisms. It is entirely compatible with the "Thinking in Natural Language" hypothesis.

21. Heal (2000, 12) does not construe the process as involving pretend "beliefs"; rather it is one that manipulates seriously held beliefs entertained in hypothetical contexts. Thus she writes, "Given the assumption of such very minimal rationality, we can show why reliance on co-cognition is a sensible way to proceed in trying to grasp where another's reflections may lead. The other thinks that p_1-p_n and is wondering whether q. I would like to know what she will conclude. So I ask myself "Would the obtaining of p_1-p_n necessitate or make likely the obtaining of q?" To answer this question I must myself think about the states of affairs in question, as the other is also doing, that is, I must co-cognise with the other. If I come to the answer that a state of affairs in which p_1-p_n would necessitate or make likely that q, then I shall expect the other to arrive at the belief that q" (Heal 1998a, 487).

22. The problem is well known to defenders of classical cognitivist approaches to artificial intelligence. It is widely accepted that if one requires explicit theoretical knowledge of the full range of possibilities that might obtain in a given domain in order to take appropriate action then—to sum up the worry with a slogan—agents would need to know practically *everything* in order to be able to do almost *anything*. As Varela, Thompson, and Rosch (2000, 148) observe, "After two decades of humblingly slow progress, it dawned on many workers in cognitive science that even the simplest cognitive action requires a seemingly infinite amount of knowledge, which we take for granted." More pithily, as Clark (1997, 6) remarks, "A little reflection suggests that there would be no obvious end to the 'common-sense' knowledge we would have to write down to capture all that an adult human knows."

23. Fodor, who has done the most to highlight this difficulty, has gloomily pronounced that if a great deal of cognition really were holistic in this way then cognitive science has seen the harbinger of doom (Fodor 1983, part IV; 2000, chap. 2). He speaks of the "ruinous holism" that follows from assuming "the units of thought are much bigger than in fact they could possibly be" (Fodor 2000a, 33). In failing to face up to this challenge he accuses cognitive scientists of being in "deep denial" (p. 39). In an even gloomier assessment he writes "cognitive science hasn't even started; we are literally no farther advanced than in the darkest days of behaviourism" (p. 129).

24. As a consequence, co-cognition is afflicted with the "Dr. Watson constraint" (Botterill and Carruthers 1999, 90). That is to say, when using this method on its

own we are only ever able to *downgrade* our understanding of what others are likely to think; we can never upgrade it. Due to his limited deductive capacities and knowledge, Dr. Watson (not to mention Lestrade) always comes up short when trying to work out what Holmes will think about any particular topic. In co-cognizing we too will always be constrained by the limits of our own intellectual capacities in a similar way.

25. Noting this, Heal is very clear about the limits of her simulative proposal. She observes that her co-cognitive account is about predicting the outcomes of certain thought processes and is therefore not in the business of accounting for how we go about "interpreting and explaining behaviour" (Heal 1998b, 86). If co-cognition used principles it would need only one:"When an agent A acquires the belief that p and a rational thinker ought to infer q from the conjunction of p with other beliefs that A has, A comes to believe that q" (Botterill 1996, 116).

Chapter 8

1. When I talk of Simulation Theory in making this argument I am only thinking of the version that claims that everyday mindreading is conducted by means of the manipulation of propositional attitudes, minimally beliefs and desires (see Goldman 2005).

2. This is much weaker than claiming that tacit mindreading involves "having some sort of awareness of the principles involved" (Botterill 1996, 114). *Awareness* is a tricky term at the best of times. It has treacherous connotations and in this context it can be avoided.

3. Not everyone is as clear as Fodor is in spelling out their commitments on this front. For example, Leslie et al. tell us that "the principle that people act to satisfy their desires in light of their beliefs is *represented implicitly* in the ToMM-[selection processor]'s mode of operation" (Leslie, Friedman, and German 2004, 531; emphasis added). I take it that this is not a slip but an acknowledgement that FP principles may be implicit in the sense of "not being consciously accessible to their users." Yet it is quite consistent to claim this while holding that the tacit principles must be *explicitly represented* at the subpersonal level. The danger is that we must not confuse these two senses of implicit. The implicit/explicit distinction of interest to Fodor is the centerpiece of his famous debate with Dennett about what goes on in chess-playing computers. The former takes up the realist sword, insisting that "according to [the representational theory of mind], programs—corresponding to the 'laws of thought'—may be explicitly represented; but 'data structures'—corresponding to the contents of thoughts—have to be. Thus, in Dennett's chess case, the rule 'get it out early' may or may not be expressed by a 'mental' (/program language) symbol. That depends on just how the machine works; specifically, on whether consulting the rule is a step in the machine's operations. I take it that in the machine that Dennett has in mind, it isn't: *entertaining the thought 'Better get the*

queen out early' never constitutes an episode in the mental life of that machine" (Fodor 1987, 25, first emphasis added; see also Dennett 1985, 64). Fodor (1987, 25) is, for these reasons, obdurate in claiming that "if the occurrence of a thought is an episode in a mental process, then [a representational theory of mind] is committed to the explicit representation of its content."

4. Fodor famously chides Chomsky for failing to pin his colors to the mast on this score. In promoting talk of specialized "mental organs," Chomsky is explicitly trying to revive certain Platonic ideas, reclothing them in modern dress. He claims that "certain aspects of our knowledge and understanding are innate, part of our biological endowment, genetically determined, on a par with the elements of our common nature that cause us to grow arms and legs rather than wings" (Chomsky 1988, 4). But Fodor objects to loose talk of "mental organs" since, in his eyes, it fails to capture what is most distinctive about cognitivist proposals—that is, that the postulated mechanisms must be characterized by their representational contents. Thus to be a cognitivist is to be committed to the existence of "domain specific propositional attitudes not [just] . . . domain specific 'devices'" (Fodor 2001a, 107). Attributing propositional knowledge to subpersonal mechanisms, he reminds us, is *"the* characteristic feature of contemporary cognitivist theorizing" (p. 109; emphasis added).

5. Although Fodor never supplies a hard and fast definition of modules, he states that "the informational encapsulation of the input systems is, or so I shall argue, the essence of modularity" (cf. Fodor 1983, 37, 71; see also Currie and Sterelny 2000, 148, for a fuller discussion). Accordingly, modular systems are characterized by the fact that they only respond to "a restricted range of inputs, and can only be influenced in a limited way (if at all) by background knowledge" (Carruthers 2003, 76).

6. Characterized in this way, practical reasoning mechanisms *might* be modular, despite the fact that they manipulate propositional attitudes with contents about *any* topic. Some welcome placing this formal capacity "on the side of the modules." Papineau, for example, regards means-end reasoning not as a coordinating metadevice, but as one blade among others in the "Swiss Army knife" of the mind. For him, it is "an add-on that arrived late in evolution" (Papineau 2003, 85–86; see also 125). Others however worry that Carruthers" move deflates the notion of a module too greatly, making it so weak that modules will be found in abundance (Nichols and Stich 2003, 121–122).

7. Fodor is openly steadfast in his commitment to the existence of innate concepts. For instance, he criticizes Cowie's attack on nativism for having avoided this very issue. Indeed, he wonders with amazement how a book that seeks to reconstruct the debate between nativists and empiricists "could miss the point that it was an argument about whether there are innate ideas" (Fodor 2001a, 103; see also 110).

8. If mentalistic concepts are atomistic then presumably ToM principles get their content from the particular arrangement of these constituent semantic atoms—that

is, this happens when they are brought together in the right way to form properly structured propositions.

9. Fodor has been the most dedicated contemporary defender of conceptual atomism and he is quite open about his allegiances. Qua Cartesian, he insists that "having a concept is having something in one's head that serves to represent the objects of one's thoughts. . . . What Cartesians deny is just that our putting our concepts to the uses that we do is constitutive of the concepts or our having them" (Fodor 2003, 21). He holds that "there is nothing at all to meaning except denotation" (Fodor 1990, 162; 1994, 6).

10. It is possible to opt for a mixed or two-factor theory of content, removing this restriction. Prinz (2002) has recently offered a theory of concepts of this kind. But this move has been frowned on by those who want to ensure the clear-cut determinacy and identity of concepts since the mixed view creates problems about the precise individuation of *contents* (see Fodor 1987). Nor is it entirely what such an approach offers of value in return.

11. As Fodor writes, "Adults can afford to insist on better warranted predictions— ones that take into account more of what the predictor knows about the predictee's cognitive circumstances. But the price of warrant is computational complexity and since, as a matter of fact [the heuristic of simply predicting that the other will act to satisfy their desires] is reliable most of the time, the advantages of growing up, though no doubt real, might be easy to overestimate" (Fodor 1995, 118).

12. According to Scholl and Leslie, "The 3-year-old does indeed have a metarepresentational notion of BELIEF which is simply obscured by performance limitations" (Scholl and Leslie 1999, 147). Nichols and Stich have also defended this line, claiming that this understanding is more clearly evidenced in explanatory (as opposed to predictive) tasks. They write: "The ability to generate discrepant belief explanations . . . is in place quite early in development. In one study, children were shown a drawing of a girl and told, "Here's Jane. Jane is looking for her kitten. The kitten is hiding under a chair, but Jane is looking for her kitten under the piano. Why do you think Jane is doing that?" (Bartsch and Wellman 1989, 949). From the age of three, children will correctly note that Jane is behaving this way because she thinks that the kitten is under the piano. This is noteworthy since children succeed on this task earlier than they succeed at the standard false belief task" (Nichols and Stich 2003, 91; see also 112–114). Of course, it may be that a concept of belief is available to three-year-olds without it being the case that it is built into a ToMM.

13. Allegedly, through a process of triggering and tuning the SP begins to make better use of its "learned database of circumstances relevant to selecting between candidate beliefs" (Leslie, Freidman, and German 2004, 532).

14. In support of this idea, great weight is placed on the fact that younger children who fail the false belief tests are able to imagine "what is not the case" in pretend

scenarios, regularly treating such things as bananas as telephones and so on. I discuss this data in a way that tells against the metarepresentational proposal in chapter 10.

15. The plans for ToMM development are "built into our genes. . . . The modularity theory thus reduces conceptual development in childhood to a kind of process that is reasonably well understood in general terms, and applies across a very wide range of phenomena" (Segal 1996, 155).

16. The difference between this variant of ITT and scientific theory theory (STT) is perhaps best illustrated by a thought experiment dreamt up by Gopnik and Melt-zoff. They conjectured that if the child's ToM was in fact dynamically open and responsive to evidence, like any good scientific theory, we should expect children to adjust their theories as appropriate to the novel variations in their local evidence base. Thus, if we were to place a child in an alien universe in which they encoun-tered other minds that were radically different from those of our own world, they could still hammer out a workable ToM—one sensitive to the local scene. On the other hand, if the modularists are right, then we should expect that these children will simply acquire their familiar ToM, come what may (Gopnik and Meltzoff 1997, 50). Actually, this is probably not so since the alien world would presumably lack the appropriate triggers to spur on ToMM development. Nevertheless, the example illustrates what is different about the two accounts.

17. In characteristic tongue-in-cheek fashion, Fodor (1987, 132) once quipped that he would have gifted humankind with a working ToMM that was both innate and true, were he God. Of course, this will not do. Theistic answers do not wash with naturalists. They really have no choice but to look to natural history.

18. We must assume this if the explanatory buck is not to be passed from phylogeny back to ontogeny. Segal looks to be in danger of doing just this when he writes: "It is not implausible to suppose that the early theories of mind—the two-year-old's, three-year-old's and so on—are *a hangover from phylogenetically prior stages*. . . . The false representations of, say, the three-year-old are a product of a *relatively primitive system that was present in the species some while ago*. The system was, indeed, good enough for survival" (Segal 1996, 156; emphasis added).

19. It is thus imagined that protoconceptual "word shapes" of the vehicles of the mental lexicon *already* have a special relationship to that which they denote. Protoconcepts are in this way unlike the shapes of the words in natural lan-guage, which bear only an arbitrary relation to their semantic content. The English word *dog* could just as easily have been used to denominate cats. Nothing about its visual or auditory *shape* predecides anything about its meaning or wider func-tional roles that is, it could easily have been a verb and not a noun (in English, the word *dog* has both uses). Such things are fixed once it is decided what a word stands for.

20. Positing this kind of "special relation" is vital, lest protoconcepts be identified as nothing more than the internal mechanisms that reliably happen to underwrite the acquisition of particular concepts. On such a weak reading there would be nothing proprietary about them at all; certainly nothing to warrant thinking of them as unactivated concepts. Indeed, without appeal to the idea of innate specification they would simply be mechanisms implicated in the attainment of concepts—and as Cowie (1999, 84) notes, "Everyone . . . can agree we have innate protoconcepts in this weak sense." It follows that to adequately explain how protoconcepts become true concepts (that is, how they come to have contents) requires explaining what makes the Proprietary Triggers proprietary (or, putting things the other way around, it requires explaining the basis of the Pre-Established Harmony).

21. Fodor has tried to defend the claim that such predestiny is not in tension with naturalism. In the course of browbeating Cowie, he remarks: "We have, in short, good reason to take for granted that there's a substantive notion of innateness because biology needs one" (Fodor 2001a, 102). But, in fact, this is not something we can simply take for granted. There are many reasons to think that "the innateness concept is irretrievably confused and the term 'innate' is one that all serious scientific researchers should eschew" (Griffiths 2002, 70). It is somewhat ironic that while philosophers of biology have begun to retreat from the notion of innateness, philosophers of mind typically look to the biological sciences to secure its credibility. Apparently, they live in the hope that even without a respectable account of innateness of their own, the concept can be used in explanatory good faith by borrowing from others. This is never a good strategy.

22. Thus Fodor (1998, 156) writes: "We typically get a concept from instances that exemplify its stereotype." As this account assumes the truth of informational theories of content, Fodor calls it Supplemented Informational Atomism (SIA).

23. Fodor's reputation as a radical concept nativist is in this respect somewhat overstated. Prinz notes this as well. In his recent attempt to revive concept empiricism he argued that Fodor's "mad-dog nativism may be interpreted as a radical empiricist thesis. . . . Fodor's views reveal a surprising kinship with Locke's. Mad dogs and Englishmen have much in common" (Prinz 2002, 235).

24. Even some ToMM theorists acknowledge this: "After all, it is not as if a parent can simply point and say, "See that? That's a belief'" (Scholl and Leslie 1999, 133).

25. Inner detection is only *part* of Goldman's story. On his dual representation account, mental state concepts have both inner and outer components. Thus, for example, "Children learn to match inner features detectable in their own goal or desire experiences with behavioral cues utilized in identifying goals or desires" (Goldman 2001, 21). Ultimately, he hopes to ground this supramodal matching by appeal to Janus-facing mirror neurons.

26. The development of some traits and devices will be even more highly canalized than this. They show up, come-what-may, often according to a strict timetable, whatever the environmental influences. The growth of hair and fingernails are endogenously controlled in this way. Even so, no trait is *entirely* impervious to environmental influences. Obtaining appropriate nutrition is, for instance, a quite general constraint on the possible appearance of any trait.

27. Although Maclaurin talks of the "reliable appearance" and "regular production" of traits, which can suggest that a merely statistical analysis will suffice, it is clear from his examples—specifically, concerning ducks and imprinting—that he regards trait emergence as indexed to the historically normal environments of the creatures in question.

28. Paleontologists tell us that "in Africa one can follow a gradual evolutionary development in the fossil record from *H. ergaster* through archaic *H. sapiens* to *H. sapiens sapiens*" (Mithen 2000b, 492). And also that "after 100,000 years ago *H. sapiens sapiens* dispersed rapidly across the Old World displacing early human populations" (Mithen 2000b, 493).

Chapter 9

1. Unsurprisingly, this bold hypothesis is regarded as "an unabashedly extreme version of the theory theory. It's Theory Theory to the Max!" (Stich and Nichols 1998, 422).

2. The fact is that "scientists do not and never have worked alone but constantly engage in discussion, co-operation and mutual criticism with peers. If there is one thing which we have learned over the last thirty years of historically oriented studies of science, it is that the positivist-empiricist image of the lone investigator, gathering all data and constructing and testing hypotheses by him- or herself, is a highly misleading abstraction" (Carruthers 2003, 77). It is precisely because of this that "science is, in fact, a bad model for the cognitive processes of ordinary thinkers" (Carruthers 2003, 76).

3. Indeed, the activity of theorizing is itself "implicit," on this view: "The developmental evidence suggests that children *construct* a coherent, abstract account of the mind which enables them to explain and predict psychological phenomena. Although the theory is *implicit* rather than explicit, this kind of cognitive structure appears to share many features with a scientific theory. Children's theories of the mind postulate unobserved entities (beliefs and desires) and laws connecting them, such as the practical syllogism. Their theories allow prediction, and they change (eventually) as a result of falsifying evidence" (Gopnik 1993, 333; emphasis added).

4. As Kitcher (1993, 71) observes, "Co-workers in a scientific discipline often recognize one another as having distinctive cognitive styles. Faced with the same problem, different scientists will pose it and reason about it in different ways. . . .

Variation in inferential success may vary from jumpers to stick-in-the-muds, depending on the kinds of problem situations in which those propensities are called into play. If so, there will be no sense to the ideal of a single method, a unique description of the 'properly functioning scientific mind.'"

5. Actually, it is especially problematic for proponents of STT to supply a credible naturalistic account of the ultimate origin of the content of the supposed native theories. This is because they tend to subscribe to meaning holism. But it is not clear how one might begin to develop a holist account of inherited content. For, according to holists, if there is to be any content at all it implies the existence of a whole *set* of concepts, each with its own well-defined theoretical roles. The trouble is that it is hard to see how a coherent first *theory* could have sprung into being fully formed. In contrast, it is easy enough to imagine that evolution might have individually fashioned a series of specialized mechanisms with specified biological functions—mechanisms that eventually came to cooperate in important and systematic ways. The fact is that I know of no well-developed holistic proposal about how first contents are naturalistically acquired.

6. Being unobservable is not, strictly speaking, a necessary condition for theoretical status. It is possible to make theoretical entities visible, as has been achieved with DNA, electrons, and so on. Rather, what is important is that our understanding of theoretical terms is simply based on "restatements of the data" (Gopnik and Meltzoff 1997, 35; see also Wellman 1991, 20).

7. Churchland reasoned as follows: "If the meaning of our common observation terms is determined not by sensations, but by the network of common beliefs, assumptions, and principles in which they figure, then, barring some (surely insupportable) story about the incorrigibility of such beliefs, assumptions, and principles, our common observation terms are semantically embedded within a framework of sentences that has all the essential properties of a theory" (Churchland 1979, 37; cf. Goldman 2001, 212–213).

8. This strategy has been used by those still persuaded by the merits of theory theory. In specifying the "early" concept of intention they simply see it as having different conceptual connections. Thus Wellman and Phillips "argue that young children understand persons as intentional, as sensibly having desires for things and for actions while understanding little if anything about beliefs (see also Bartsch and Wellman 1995). Even this early intentional understanding, however, if genuine, must encompass some necessary connections between desires and other states and experiences. In particular, desires and intentions seem inextricably related to emotional and to perceptual experiences. If Jill wants to do X, and then fails, she'll be displeased, unhappy, even angry" (Wellman and Phillips 2001, 126–127).

9. It is equally unexplanatory, for these purposes, to observe simply that in the early stages of their careers children somehow "have" the relevant concepts *potentially*. For if holists are right in thinking that the surrounding concepts play a constitutive

role in determining the content of any particular concept, then no concept can be thought of as "having" its content based on merely *potential* relations to other concepts (however likely these are to obtain in the future). This is simply to describe the situation that wants explaining; it is precisely not to explain it.

10. The obvious move would be to opt for some kind of conceptual atomism. But this tactic suffers from other problems, as discussed in the previous chapter.

11. Gopnik (2004, 28) notes that unlike nonhuman animals there is good evidence that human children "learn from others" and that this fact may play a vital role in enabling them to "learn far more about the world than other animals." But she neither says how such learning proceeds nor how this claim sits with her claim that theory construction is essentially a process of individual minds. Is learning from others a central part of theory building (and if so how) or is just allied to it (that is, as an enabling condition). In a very loose sense the NPH can be seen as a "learning from others" account, but it is one that stands in stark contrast to the constructivism of the "child as scientist" proposal.

12. Andrews (2002) claims that the existence of linguistically competent autistic individuals offers "a clear counterexample to Davidson's view: a person who speaks but who does not understand belief, and does not interpret the vocalizations of others by attributing mental states or rationality." According to Davidson, to be a believer at all requires that one has the concept of the concept of belief because this is needed if one is to understand the distinction between truth and falsity—that is, it is needed to understand a speaker's proposition as "saying something" in the sense of making a claim. This is the primary reason he maintains that to be a believer of propositions requires "the gift of tongues" (p. 473). It is, however, possible to accept that Davidson was right about this without accepting that having the concept of belief is necessary for understanding what a proposition (as opposed to a speaker) means.

13. She writes that "scientists and babies alike learn from the interventions of others. Scientists read journals, go to talks, hold lab meetings, and visit other labs" (Gopnik 2004, 27). But she expands on the point in a way that suggests that this kind of activity plays only a supporting role, for it allows the sharing of data: "We scientists make the assumption that the interventions of others are like our own interventions, and that we can learn similar things from both sources" (p. 27).

Chapter 10

1. Fodor was perhaps the first to use this kind of argument in the domain of folk psychology. Some time ago he claimed that there "are, thus far, precisely no suggestions about how a child might acquire the apparatus for intentional explanation 'from experience' (Unless by introspection?!)" (Fodor 1987, 133). In line with a general policy of his, he regarded the lack of credible alternative hypotheses as a kind of empirical evidence.

2. Indeed, as Antony observes, "The poverty-of-the-stimulus strategy seeks to establish that there is either not enough sensory data, or not of the right kind, available to a particular organism to have attained a certain cognitive state *via* some particular mechanism. The strategy *cannot be employed except against specific non-nativist theories of acquisition*" (Antony 2001, 200; emphasis mine).

3. Rowlands's (1999, 201) primary objective was to loosen the grip of the internalist picture by resisting the extremely "attenuated" view of the child learning environment that inspires it. He builds on the idea that "considerably more structure is latent in the environment than one might have guessed" (Elman et al. 1998).

4. It should also be noted that although the folk psychological framework is derived from stories, this does not in any way detract from the power and depth it affords in making sense of others in particular cases. It still allows one to go beyond the evidence when explaining and predicting what actors are likely to do or why they did what they did in novel cases. That said, as I argued in chapter 1, there are serious limits to the reliability of such third-person speculative uses.

5. Baka children (of a mean age of five years) demonstrated a reliable capacity to pass a "look" variant of the false-belief task—one that also required them to make certain inferences about the likely feelings of others (Avis and Harris 1991). Yet it may be that these children were relying on more basic strategies for interpersonal enagement, rather than on an understanding of belief as a propostional attitude, to get by in these tests.

6. In an exchange about this case, Vinden rightly asks: "How do the Baka really interpret the event? It seems to me that we can't use these events as 'proof' of a mentalistic view of reasons and explanations of events unless we have a clear indication from the people themselves that they see things that way. My feeling is that you would likely not get talk about misleading appearances or false beliefs or anything like that from the Baka! I would expect them to talk about the disguised figure as if he were really Jengi. But then the absence of talk about something doesn't necessarily mean the concept is absent. Then there is the question as to whether or not anyone is really fooled in this situation, except very young children" (Vinden, personal communication, August 2006).

7. It is not obvious that even the concept of belief is universal. In examining its history Needham (1972, 50) traced its origins to two convergent lines in Western culture, "one manifesting itself in a series of related lexical forms in the Indo-European family of languages, and the other in a religious history that combines Jewish, Greek, and Christian concepts."

8. Similar results from cross-cultural comparisons concerning "person conceptions" of a more general sort have "directly challenged the assumption of a single, universally applicable conception of the person and, perhaps, even more fundamentally, the view that treats the development of this conception as a straightforwardly

individual and socioculturally dexcontextualized process" (Richner and Nicolopoulou 2001, 402).

9. Interestingly, certain Papua New Guinean populations "rarely comment on reasons for action, even their own" (Lillard 1997, 13; Fajans 1985). This has been put down to their epistemological scruples—their belief that they cannot know what others are thinking. As a result, "They do not fill in children's statements, presuming their intended meanings, as Americans routinely do" (Lillard 1997, 13).

10. Hence, it appears that favored modes of action explanation, like children's "models of personhood," take "shape in an active interplay with culturally available models of personhood, which are not uniform either between or within societies" (Richner and Nicolopoulou 2001, 401).

11. Acting for one's own reasons is held up as an ideal of rationality in the West (Richner and Nicolopoulou 2001, 399). This may go some distance to explain why it has such sway on certain philosophical imaginations despite a lack of supporting evidence.

12. It is important to be clear about this, since in some cases when cross-cultural studies are discussed the term *folk psychology* is clearly being used with much wider scope; there it seems to denote "whatever methods are used in understanding others." Thus, for example, Lillard (1997) includes in the range of different folk psychologies explanations of human behavior that involve interventions by supernatural beings and astrological forces.

13. To be sure, on its own, this evidence does not provide a secure basis for mounting an effective argument against the existence of IMDs. Drawing a comparison with culturally diverse folk theories of vision, Scholl and Leslie insist that "even specific beliefs about the concept of belief are not necessarily relevant: the concept of belief could be universally grounded in a module even though most cultures do not recognize the 'modular account' in their own folk psychology" (Scholl and Leslie 1999, 137). Nevertheless, the very fact of such cross-cultural divergence takes on new importance in light of the independent arguments I have mounted against the existence of IMDs in previous chapters.

14. Lillard (1997, 268) stresses this, remarking that "in examining our everyday, folk understanding of mind and behavior, we draw mainly on a database of information culled from European-American experience . . . [yet] extrapolations based on this one cultural group might not hold up well in other cultures."

15. Even defining autism is no simple matter (see Boucher 1996, 225–226).

16. Stich and Nichols (1995, 104) objected to Goldman's reading on the grounds that "neither the term 'want' nor any other mentalistic language occurs in the anecdote, and there is no indication that the young man 'has a perfectly good grasp of the mentalistic notion of wanting.'" But in such cases actions speak louder than

words. Surely, if we are only interested in practical (not theoretical) knowledge then the relevant understanding is implicit in how the boy responds to the request.

17. It has been frequently observed that "although most autistic children fail tests which assess their mentalizing ability, there is a substantial minority of such children who regularly succeed" (Coltheart and Langdon 1998, 143). In light of their work with high-functioning autistics and those with Asperger's syndrome, Ozonoff and colleagues (1991, 1181) have concluded that "the lack of theory of mind deficit may not be primary to all of the autistic continuum, but may be a correlated deficit, present in more severely affected autistic individuals."

18. Autistic individuals are able to construct narratives relating to these topics but only in a very minimal sense. Their true level of ability in this regard has not as yet been well studied: "There have been surprisingly few detailed investigations of narrative abilities in individuals with autism.... Children with autism tended to produce impoverished narratives, more frequently made grammatical errors, included bizarre or otherwise inappropriate information, neglected to mention central themes, and misinterpreted story events.... In addition to these global narrative deficits, individuals with autism have also been shown to exhibit specific difficulty narrating stories that revolve around character's mental states" (Capps, Losh, and Thurber 2000, 194). Autistic narrators tend to simply label affective and cognitive states when these are mentioned at all and in general they veer toward describing or chronicling as opposed to narrating per se. Beyond this, they have manifest difficulties even when it comes to simply retelling stories (Dautenhahn 2001, 256). This is in direct contrast to the competencies displayed by children with Williams' syndrome. They are excellent narrators who make frequent and effective use of dramatic devices—such as sound effects, character voice, and so on. These are used in order to stress emotional content and to enrich and elaborate their narratives in line with listener's needs and interests (Losh et al. 2000).

19. This is likely what explains why autistic individuals have problems in understanding complex emotions. Thus Baron-Cohen (1995, 79) reports that in viewing photographs of people expressing emotions, "Most children with autism were able to match happy and sad, but significantly more children with autism made errors in matching pictures of surprised expressions. They mistook these for noncognitive states such as yawning or being hungry, focusing on the open mouth." It is plausible that the reason for this is that surprise is a belief-based emotion, one that is likely to require recognition of the other's *cognitive* take on things.

20. It is known that "although autistic children may make requests for objects and actions and may understand other people's pointing gestures that convey instructions, they rarely make gestures such as showing, giving or pointing in order to share awareness of an object's existence or properties or comprehend such gestures when they are made by others" (Hobson 1993, 242; see also Baron-Cohen 1995, 66).

21. By the end of their first year infants are normally beginning to engage in social referencing. They respond appropriately, even in experimental conditions, when confronted by such things as visual cliffs, *only* after taking cues from their mothers' emotional orientations. Thus a mother's expressions of happiness or anxiety systematically affect infant reactions. Describing this perhaps too richly, Hobson (1993, 235) remarks that what such interactions involve is something like the recognition that "I am seeing this as a frightening situation, she sees it as OK."

22. Hobson (1993, 243) puts this down to "their difficulty in disembedding from a particular point of view and acquiring the capacity to adopt a variety of 'co-orientations' to given objects or events, for example to pretend a matchbox 'is' a car." This incapacity might also be implicated in their failure on appearance-reality tests in which, "most children with autism made largely 'phenomenalist' errors, saying 'It looks like an egg,' 'It really is an egg,' and similar things" (Baron-Cohen 1995, 82).

23. The link is that "pronouns and deictic terms must be produced and understood with respect to a given point-of-view" (Harris 1996, 218).

Chapter 11

1. Deception is commonplace throughout the animal kingdom. Predators and prey constantly set about misinforming one another about their actual resources and capacities in order to gain special advantages. This takes many forms, ranging from simple camouflage to more complex Batesian and self-mimicry. Batesian mimics typically make use of the colorful call-signs of their less than palatable fellows in order to ward off discriminating predators, whereas self-mimics use their body parts to attract or distract prey. For example, the frogmouth catfish uses its tongue protrusions to serve as lures and the "two-headed" snake of Central Africa manipulates its tail (which resembles a head) and its head (which resembles a tail) in order to baffle its opponents. No one supposes these to be intentional acts of deception. Such "strategies" do not involve any decisions on the part of such creatures themselves, not at any level. Indeed, it is acknowledged that even much more complex and flexible "deceptive" behaviors may merely be the products of general inductive learning of a kind that does not entail that an animal has attributed "intentions to its victims" (Byrne and Whiten 1991, 127). In an early review of collected data on deception in primates, Byrne and Whiten (1991, 129) concluded that of all the species considered, only the common chimpanzee (*pan troglodytes*) was "clearly" capable of true intentional deception. They subsequently extended this claim to include other species of great apes—gorillas and orangutans—but, based on subsequent investigations, they also weakened its force, making it more tentative since the strength of their original convictions had waned over the years (Byrne and Whiten 1997, 10).

2. This possibility has ever dogged the steps of those that defended more mentalistic interpretations in the domain of primate social cognition generally; the "smart behaviorist" option has long been the leading alternative (Bennett 1991; Cheney and Seyfarth 1991; Smith 1996). Indeed, its ready availability has always made switching sides in this debate from richer to leaner interpretations a very straightforward affair.

3. The following assessments are now the norm: "the ape 'ToM,' even on the most charitable reading is considerably impoverished as compared with that with which a four-year-old Homo sapiens is endowed" (Garfield, Peterson, Perry 2001, 500); "Convincing experimental data that a mindreading system is present in nonhumans is somewhat thin on the ground" (Nichols and Stich 2003, 99). Indeed, as Nichols and Stich acknowledge, the strongest prima facie evidence of such capacities still comes from the work of Premack and Woodruff, which was conducted with a single chimpanzee who had undergone extensive training.

4. This is a natural point of retreat for those persuaded that great apes lack metarepresentational ToM abilities. After all, being a capable behaviorist is thought to be a necessary step on the path to becoming a competent folk psychologist. This assumption is plausible on the grounds that in order to make mental state attributions at all—that is, to infer that others harbor specific beliefs and desires—one must first recognize, and presumably be able to categorise, the behaviors that these states putatively underlie, produce and explain. Thus acknowledging that certain types of stimuli reliably generate certain types of responses is the very basis for speculation about the intermediary causes that stand between these inputs and outputs. Being *au fait* with the observable action-related behavioral patterns, which might be construed as having a theory of behavior (or ToB), is regarded by some as a prerequisite for developing a ToM in any case. To be a folk psychologist, by this reasoning, one must go via the weigh station of behaviorism. This is plausible on the assumption that "mindreading is not telepathy" (Whiten 1996).

5. This honors the idea that evolution rarely throws anything away that is in good working order—that is, unless it carries other unacceptable costs. Mother Nature prefers to tinker and build on what has already proven itself in the field.

6. Povinelli writes in a way that lends itself to a robust, neo-Cartesian reading. In speaking of the chimpanzee form of "folk physics" he tells us that "by 'principle' we mean a basic rule or heuristic about the regularities in the world that guide chimpanzees' interactions with objects" (Povinelli 2003, 303). Elsewhere he commits to the claim that "brains translate . . . information into a neural code that reduces and 'represents' the external world" (p. 58).

7. Despite their complaints, Call and Tomasello (2005, 59) have now recently made it clear that they too are persuaded by the idea that, in large part, chimpanzees (and other primates) get by with "a representational understanding of the behaviour of others."

8. Gauker (2003, 244) is surely right to observe that "one of the main ways to predict people's behaviour is just by generalizing from the past, that is by straight induction. . . . The reference class for such generalisations may be the actions of people in general, or just the actions of the particular person in question, or just the actions of the particular person in question in circumstances like the present." Andrews (2003, 203) too stresses this: "We do not always need to attribute beliefs and desires to predict what a person will do next. . . . It often suffices to refer to past events, and use statistical induction to conclude that a person will behave in future the way she did in the past."

9. Donald (1991, 179) puts the point beautifully: "Innovative tool use could have occurred countless thousands of times without resulting in an established tool making industry, unless the individual who 'invented' the tool could remember and reenact or reproduce the operations involved and then communicate them to others."

10. This assumes the truth of the standard, progressivist stories about tool manufacture. For a deflationary alternative, see Davidson 2003. He argues that the products found are not the result of a tradition or cultural industry but the much more mundane fact that stone knapping will produce a limited range of outcomes for anyone who engages in the process. Archeologists are accused of imposing their own intentional forms on the workmanship of these periods rather than our ancestors having done so. If Davidson is right, not only is the crafting of such items *not* rooted in any kind of tool tradition—it is much less skilled than is generally supposed.

11. For these reasons the theory-theory approach compares negatively with the account that Gallagher advances, which makes appeal to body schemas. He claims that "the imitating subject depends on a complex background of embodied processes, a body-schema system involving visual, proprioceptive, and vestibular information. . . . This intermodal *intra*-corporeal communication then, is the basis for an *inter*-corporeal communication" (Gallagher 2005, 76). Although Gallagher suggests that infants may be capable of experiencing a difference between self and other, he argues that "the concept of the self starts out closer to an embodied sense than to a cognitive or psychological understanding" (p. 79).

12. Interestingly, those who suffer from autism have difficulty in replicating the manner and style of another's response (see Hobson 2007).

13. There is current debate about whether the early African *H. ergaster* (meaning workman) or the later Asian *H. erectus* was the direct ancestor of modern humans. Indeed, there is debate over whether or not the former is merely a subspecies of the latter. Either way, they will have established the Achulean stone industry before their offspring will have left Africa to become *H. heidelbergensis*, our last common ancestor shared with the Neanderthals.

14. It seems safe to assume that such abilities were under the voluntary control of the hominids. Whether some other animals have some degree of control over their

vocalizations is still an open question (Allen and Saidel 1998; Hauser and Marler 1993a; 1993b; Marler and Evans 1995; see also Corballis 2003, 202).

15. The development of domain-general mimetic abilities obviates the need to postulate the "emergence of an evolved mechanism for identifying, memorizing and reasoning about social norms, together with a powerful motivation to comply with such norms. And with norms and norm-based motivation added to the human phenotype, the stage would be set for much that is distinctive in human cultures" (Carruthers 2003, 75).

16. For a discussion of the running costs of brains see Aiello and Wheeler 1995.

17. The argument developed here only targets those versions of the communicative view of language that presuppose the existence of meaning-conferring LoT. It may be possible to accept a Gricean analysis of mature language, while rejecting the claim that beliefs would have been a prerequisite for it. In other words, linguistic utterances have representational content, the conventional meanings of which are mutually known, but in both ontogeny and phylogeny, language use does not get its life from belief-based understandings; rather it enables the establishment of such understandings, in time (see Zlatev 2007; cf. Eilan 2005, 13–14).

18. We can thus rename Dautenhahn's Narrative Intelligence Hypothesis, which is a direct descendant of Dunbar's, the Pre-Narrative Intelligence Hypothesis (PIH) to avoid confusion. This recognizes that there are "two aspects of children's narrative activity which are too often treated in mutual isolation: the discursive exposition of narratives in storytelling and their enactments in pretend play" (see Richner and Nicolopoulou 2001, 408).

19. This may explain why, being in the same form as the dramatic reenactments of our ancient ancestors, "Children's first narrative productions occur in action, in episodes of symbolic play by groups of peers, accompanied by—rather than solely through—language. Play is an important developmental source of narrative" (Nelson 2003, 28).

20. Or more succinctly: "A story must be told, it is not found" (Lamarque 2004, 394).

21. For those with full-fledged interpretational abilities the early indicational phase is initially "extremely idiosyncratic: one or only a small number of interlocutors can understand what the child is indicating—i.e., grasp what aspect of the environment it is to which the child is drawing attention" (Rowlands 1999, 196).

22. This is a description of what Zlatev (2007) calls triadic mimesis.

23. Apes, for example, rarely use declarative as opposed to imperative gestures—in fact, only those with extensive human contact do so at all. Hence, it has been speculated that "although apes can master the 'referential triangle' in their interactions with humans for instrumental purposes when they are raised in humanlike cultural

environments, they still do not attain humanlike social motivations for sharing experience with other intentional beings" (Tomasello and Call 1997, 393).

Chapter 12

1. It is surely a *live* possibility that "means-end reasoning only emerged after our ancestors had first developed a relatively sophisticated language" (Papineau 2003, 122).

2. Bermúdez (2003b) makes much the same argument. Assuming the falsity of the LoT hypothesis, he claims that "a belief can only be attributed if the thought that is the content of the belief can be represented by the attributer, which requires it to have a vehicle. . . . The only candidate vehicles are linguistic" (p. 172). Our languageless prehistoric ancestors could not have been folk psychologists because "public language vehicles are required for thoughts to be the object of further thoughts" (p. 191).

3. Carstairs-McCarthy is exercised by the question of why human languages should have evolved along their existing syntactic lines, incorporating the basic grammatical divisions they do, such as the noun phrase-sentence distinction, rather than quite different ones. For, it is easy enough to imagine complex linguistic phrases and word orderings which lack the sort of grammar inherent in modern human syntax. In a series of convincing thought experiments, he shows that human language could still have served its basic communicative functions even if it had evolved such that it had either much *less* complex or much *more* complex syntaxes than the kind it currently enjoys. Thus, "We may be tempted to see it as self-evident that a communication system that does what human language does *must* inevitably distinguish between mentioning things (or referring) and making assertions about them (or making true and false statements). But, even if we grant for argument's sake that this distinction is important, it does not follow that it must be reflected in syntax" (Carstairs-McCarthy 1999, 28). As a result, the distinction between noun phrases and sentences, evident in all human languages, wants explaining, as it need not have developed at all.

4. The CSSH is made more plausible once we realize that core syntax need only have provided enough structural support to make *basic* forms of *spoken* language possible. Complex grammars of the sort familiar to modern human languages will have only appeared very late in human history. These will have been sponsored by cultural innovations rather than anatomical changes, with some developments only following on the heels of written languages, which arrived some 5,000 years ago. Although it is not often observed, there are a great many important grammatical differences between casual, spoken language and established written ones. Recognizing this matters if it is also acknowledged that "much of what generative linguistics consider as canonical grammatical constructions are formalized or conventionalized in written language" (Li and Hombert 2002, 199). Doubtless this

affects intuitions about Primary Linguistic Data (or PLD). Thus the reasons for believing in linguistic universals may stem from a polluted phenomenology since the "linguistic intuitions" on which our understanding of these universals is based are strongly influenced by familiarity with well-established grammars, those of sophisticated writers, not casual speakers. No such principles are likely to have been in place at the dawn of spoken language since refined syntactical niceties would not have mattered to the first linguistic productions.

5. The emergence of protospeech may have coincided with the second major burst of encephalization roughly 250,000 to 500,000 years ago. Brain development, both in size and organization is likely to have been driven by the need to accommodate new linguistic abilities. For example, the second major spurt of increased brain size may have been the result of the need to remember all the various associated meanings relating to the new lexical forms and to access, plan, and manage discourse. Human natural languages have enormous vocabularies and even a simple combinatorial syntax would yield an enormous increase in communicative possibilities.

6. For these reasons, it is plausible that "an intermediate stage in evolving a phoneme-based vocabulary might have been based on the syllable rather than the phoneme as the generative unit. The syllable is basically a unit of articulatory gesture, and . . . the rhythmic organization of language (stress and timing) revolves around the syllable rather than the individual phoneme" (Jackendoff 2002, 143). Donald may be right to be impressed by Darwin's suggestion that the development of rudimentary song in hominids was crucial moment in our evolutionary history (Donald 1991; Mithen 2005).

7. Hominid mimetic abilities would have played an important part in this in more than one way. For imitation is not only implicated in establishing meanings, it is also necessary for reliably reproducing and recognizing complex sounds and structural forms—in establishing a morphophonology (Jackendoff 2002, 242; Donald 1999). The MAH therefore helps to explain the unique prerequisites of the linguistic abilities of human children on at least two fronts.

8. This can be understood as a proposal about embodied cognition, but "the key notion of 'embodiment' [needs] to be extended beyond its focus on the humanly corporeal, the 'brain-in-the-body,' to take account of the way that cognitive and cultural schemas find material realization—are embodied—in the artefacts of material culture. . . . Cognition extends beyond the individual; embodiment goes beyond the skin" (Sinha 2005, 1538).

References

Aguiar A, Baillargeon R. 2002. Developments in young infants' reasoning about occluded objects. *Cognitive Psychology* 45(2): 267–336.

Aiello LC, Wheeler P. 1995. The expensive tissue hypothesis. *Current Anthropology* 36: 184–193.

Akins K. 1993. What is it like to be boring and myopic? In *Dennett and His Critics*, ed. B Dahlbom. Oxford: Basil Blackwell.

Akins K. 1996. Of sensory systems and the "aboutness" of mental states. *Journal of Philosophy* 113: 337–372.

Akins K. 2003. Of sensory systems and the "aboutness" of mental states. In *Philosophy and the Neurosciences: A Reader*, ed. W Bechtel, P Mandik, J Mundale, S Stufflebeam. Oxford: Basil Blackwell.

Allen C, Saidel E. 1998. The evolution of reference. In *The Evolution of Mind*, ed. DD Cummins, C Allen. New York: Oxford University Press.

Andrews K. 2002. Interpreting autism: A critique of Davidson on thought and language. *Philosophical Psychology* 15: 317–332.

Andrews K. 2003. Knowing mental states: The asymmetry of psychological prediction and explanation. In *Consciousness: New Philosophical Perspectives*, ed. Q Smith, A Jokic. Oxford: Oxford University Press.

Andrews K. 2005. Chimpanzee Theory of Mind: Looking in all the wrong places? *Mind and Language* 20: 521–536.

Andrews K. 2007. Critter psychology: On the possibility of nonhuman animal folk psychology. In *Folk Psychology Reassessed*, ed. DD Hutto, M Ratcliffe. Dordrecht: Springer.

Antony LM. 2001. Empty heads. *Mind and Language* 16: 193–214.

Antony LM, Hornstein N. 2003. *Chomsky and His Critics*. Malden MA: Blackwell Publishing.

Apperly IA, Williams E, Williams J. 2004. Three- to four-year-olds' recognition that symbols have a stable meaning: Pictures are understood before written words. *Child Development* 75: 1510–1522.

Appleton M, Reddy V. 1996. Teaching three-year-olds to pass false belief tests: A conversational approach. *Social Development* 5: 275–291.

Arbib M. 2002. The mirror system, imitation, and the evolution of language. In *Imitation in Animals and Artifacts*, ed. K Dautenhahn, C Nehaniv. Cambridge, MA: MIT Press.

Arbib M. 2003. The evolving mirror system. In *Language Evolution*, ed. M Christiansen, S Kirby. Oxford: Oxford University Press.

Arbib M. 2005. From monkey-like action recognition to human language: An evolutionary framework for neurolinguistics. *Behavioral and Brain Sciences* 28: 105–124.

Arbib M, Billard A, Iacoboni M, Oztop E. 2000. Synthetic brain imaging: Grasping, mirror neurons and imitation. *Neural Networks* 13: 975–997.

Aristotle. 1984. *The Complete Works of Aristotle: The Revised Oxford Translation*. Princeton, NJ: Princeton University Press.

Arkway A. 2000. The simulation theory, the theory theory and folk psychological explanation. *Philosophical Studies* 98(2): 115–137.

Astington J. 1990. Narrative and the child's Theory of Mind. In *Narrative Thought and Narrative Language*, ed. BK Britton, D Pellegrini. Hillsdale, NJ: Erlbaum.

Astington J. 1996. What is theoretical about a child's Theory of Mind?: A Vygotskian view of its development. In *Theories of Theories of Mind*, ed. P Carruthers, P Smith. Cambridge: Cambridge University Press.

Astington J. 2001. The paradox of intention: Assessing children's metarepresentational understanding. In *Intentions and Intentionality: Foundations of Social Cognition*, ed. B Malle, LJ Moses, DA Baldwin. Cambridge, MA: MIT Press.

Astington JW, Jenkins JM. 1999. A longitudinal study of the relation between language and Theory of Mind development. *Developmental Psychology* 359(5): 1311–1320.

Avis J, Harris PL. 1991. Belief-desire reasoning among Baka children. *Child Development* 62: 460–467.

Avramides A. 1999. Davidson and the New Sceptical Problem. In *Donald Davidson: Truth, Meaning and Knowledge*, ed. U Zeglen. London: Routledge.

Avramides A. 2001. *Other Minds*. London: Routledge.

Ayer AJ. 1954. *Philosophical Essays*. London: Macmillan.

Baillargeon R. 1987. Object permanence in 3.5- and 4.5-month-old-infants. *Developmental Psychology* 23: 655–664.

Baillargeon R. 1995. Physical reasoning in infancy. In *The Cognitive Neurosciences*, ed. MS Gazzaniga. Cambridge, MA: MIT Press.

Baillargeon R, Spelke E, Wasserman S. 1985. Object Permanence in five-month old infants. *Cognition* 20: 191–208.

Baird JA, Baldwin DA. 2001. Making sense of human behaviour: Action parsing and intentional inference. In *Intentions and Intentionality: Foundations of Social Cognition*, ed. F Malle, LJ Moses, DA Baldwin, 193–206. Cambridge, MA: MIT Press.

Baker LR. 1988. *Saving Belief: A Critique of Physicalism*. Princeton, NJ: Princeton University Press.

Baker LR. 1995. *Explaining Attitudes: A Practical Approach to the Mind*. Cambridge: Cambridge University Press.

Baker LR. 1999. What is this thing called "commonsense psychology"? *Philosophical Explorations* 1: 3–19.

Baker LR. 2000. *Persons and Bodies: A Constitution View*. Cambridge: Cambridge University Press.

Baldwin DA, Baird JA, Saylor M, Clark A. 2001. Infants parse dynamic action. *Child Development* 72: 708–717.

Baldwin J. 1896. A new factor in evolution. *American Naturalist* 30: 441–451.

Barker M, Givón T. 2005. Representation of the interlocutor's mind during conversation. In *Other Minds: How Humans Bridge the Divide between Self and Others*, ed. B Malle, S Hodges. New York: Guilford Press.

Barkow JH, Cosmides L, Tooby J, eds. 1992. *The Adapted Mind: Evolutionary Psychology and the Generation of Culture*. Oxford: Oxford University Press.

Baron-Cohen S. 1991. Precursors to a Theory of Mind. In *Natural Theories of Mind*, ed. A Whiten. Oxford: Blackwell.

Baron-Cohen S. 1995. *Mindblindness: An Essay on Autism and Theory of Mind*. Cambridge, MA: MIT Press.

Baron-Cohen S. 1999. The evolution of Theory of Mind. In *The Descent of Mind: Psychological Perspectives on Hominid Evolution*, ed. MC Corballis, SEG Lea. Oxford: Oxford University Press.

Baron-Cohen S. 2000. Theory of Mind and autism: A fifteen year review. In *Understanding Other Minds: Perspectives from Developmental Cognitive Neuroscience*, ed. S Baron-Cohen, H Tager-Flusberg, D Cohen. Oxford: Oxford University Press.

Baron-Cohen S, Cross P. 1992. Reading the eyes: Evidence for the role of perception in the development of a Theory of Mind. *Mind and Language* 6: 173–186.

Baron-Cohen S, Leslie A, Frith U. 1985. Does the autistic child have a "Theory of Mind"? *Cognition* 21: 37–46.

Baron-Cohen S, Sweetenham J. 1996. The relationship between SAM and ToMM: Two hypotheses. In *Theories of Theories of Mind*, ed. P Carruthers and P Smith. Cambridge: Cambridge University Press.

Barsalou LW. 1999. Perceptual symbol systems. *Behavioral and Brain Sciences* 22: 577–660.

Barsalou LW. 2003. Situated simulation. *Language and Cognitive Processes* 18: 513–562.

Barsalou LW, Niedenthal PM, Barbey AK, Ruppert JA. 2003. Social embodiment. In *The Psychology of Learning and Motivation*, ed. BH Ross. New York: Academic Press.

Barton RA, Dunbar RIM. 1997. Evolution of the social brain. In *Machiavellian Intelligence II: Extensions and Evaluations*, ed. RW Byrne, A Whiten. Cambridge: Cambridge University Press.

Bartsch K, Wellman H. 1989. Young children's attribution of actions to beliefs and desires. *Child Development* 60: 946–964.

Bartsch K, Wellman H. 1995. *Children Talk about the Mind*. New York: Oxford University Press.

Bavelas J, Black A, Lemery C, Mullett J. 1987. Motor mimicry as primitive empathy. In *Empathy and Its Development*, ed. N Eisenberg, J Strayer. Cambridge: Cambridge University Press.

Bennett J. 1981. *Kant's Dialectic*. Cambridge: Cambridge University Press.

Bennett J. 1991. How to read minds in behaviour: A suggestion from a philosopher. In *Natural Theories of Mind*, ed. A Whiten, 97–108. Oxford: Blackwell.

Berguno G, Bowler D. 2004. Understanding pretence and understanding action. *British Journal of Developmental Psychology*. 22: 531–544.

Bermúdez J. 1998. *The Paradox of Self-Consciousness*. Cambridge, MA: MIT Press.

Bermúdez J. 2003a. The domain of folk psychology. In *Minds and Persons*, ed. A O'Hear. Cambridge: Cambridge University Press.

Bermúdez J. 2003b. *Thinking without Words*. New York: Oxford University Press.

Bickerton D. 1990. *Language and Species*. Chicago: Chicago University Press.

Bickerton D. 2003. Symbol and structure. In *Language Evolution*, ed. M Christiansen, S Kirby. Oxford: Oxford University Press.

Bickle J. 1998. *Psychoneural Reduction: The New Wave*. Cambridge, MA: MIT Press.

Billard A, Arbib M. 2002. Mirror neurons and the neural basis for learning by imitation: Computational modelling. In *Mirror Neurons and the Evolution of Brain and Language*, ed. M Stamenov, V Gallese, 345–352. Amsterdam/Philadelphia: John Benjamins.

Bloom P. 1998. Some issues in the evolution of language and thought. In *The Evolution of Mind*, ed. DD Cummins, C Allen. Oxford: Oxford University Press.

Bloom P, German T. 2000. Two reasons to abandon the False Belief Task as a test of Theory of Mind. *Cognition* 77: B25–B31.

Boesch C, Boesch-Achermann H. 2000. *Chimpanzees of the Tai Forest: Behavioural ecology and evolution*. Oxford: Oxford University Press.

Bogdan R. 1997. *Interpreting Minds: The Evolution of a Practice*. Cambridge, MA: MIT Press.

Bogdan R. 2005. Why self-ascriptions are difficult and develop late. In *Other Minds: How Humans Bridge the Divide between Self and Others*, ed. B Malle, S Hodges. New York: Guilford Press.

Bohman J. 2000. The importance of the second person: Interpretation, practical knowledge, and normative attitudes. In *Empathy and Agency*, ed. HH Kogler, KR Stueber. Boulder: Westview Press.

Botterill G. 1996. Folk psychology and theoretical status. In *Theories of Theories of Mind*, ed. P Carruthers, P Smith. Cambridge: Cambridge University Press.

Botterill G, Carruthers P. 1999. *The Philosophy of Psychology*. Cambridge: Cambridge University Press.

Boucher J. 1996. What could possibly explain autism? In *Theories of Theories of Mind*, ed. P Carrtuthers, P Smith. Cambridge: Cambridge University Press.

Bowler D. 1992. "Theory of Mind" in Asperger's syndrome. *Journal of Child Psychology and Psychiatry* 33: 877–893.

Brandom R. 1994. *Making it Explicit*. Cambridge, MA: Harvard University Press.

Brinck I. 2001. Attention and the evolution of intentional communication. *Pragmatics and Cognition* 9: 259–277.

Brinck I. 2004. Joint attention, triangulation and radical interpretation. *Dialectica* 58: 179–205.

Brinck I, Gärdenfors P. 2003. Co-operation and communication in apes and humans. *Mind and Language* 18: 484–501.

Broome J. 2002. Practical reasoning. In *Reason and Nature: Essays in the Theory of Rationality*, ed. J Bermúdez, A Millar. Oxford: Oxford University Press.

Brower TGR. 1982. *Development in Infancy*. San Francisco: Freeman.

Brower TGR, Broughton JM, Moore MK. 1971. Development of the object conception as manifested in changes in the tracking behaviour of infants between 7 and 20 weeks of age. *Journal of Experimental Child Psychology* 11: 182–193.

Brown HI. 1986. Sellars, concepts and conceptual change. *Synthese* 68: 275–307.

Brown JR, Donelan-McCall N, Dunn J. 1996. Talk about mental states? The significance of children's conversations with friends, siblings, and mothers. *Child Development* 67: 836–849.

Bruner J. 1983. *Child's Talk: Learning to Use Language*. New York: Norton.

Bruner J. 1990. *Acts of Meaning*. Cambridge, MA: Harvard University Press.

Butterworth G. 1991. The ontogeny and phylogeny of joint visual attention. In *Natural Theories of Mind*, ed. A Whiten. Oxford: Blackwell.

Byrne R. 1999a. Human cognitive evolution. In *The Descent of Mind: Psychological Perspectives on Hominid Evolution*, ed. MC Corballis, SEG Lea. Oxford: Oxford University Press.

Byrne R. 1999b. Imitation without intentionality. Using string parsing to copy the organization of behaviour. *Animal Cognition* 2: 63–72.

Byrne R. 2002a. Imitation of complex novel actions: What does the evidence from animals mean? *Advances in the Study of Behavior* 31: 77–105.

Byrne R. 2002b. Seeing actions as hierarchically organized structures: Great ape manual skills. In *The Imitative Mind: Development, Evolution and Brain Bases*, ed. AN Meltzoff, W Prinz. Cambridge: Cambridge University Press.

Byrne R. 2004. Detecting, understanding, and explaining animal imitation. In *Perspectives on Imitation: From Neuroscience to Social Science*, ed. S Hurley, N Chater. Cambridge, MA: MIT Press.

Byrne RW, Whiten A. 1991. Computation and mindreading in primate tactical deception. In *Natural Theories of Mind*, ed. A Whiten. Oxford: Blackwell.

Byrne RW, Whiten A. 1997. Machiavellian intelligence. In *Machiavellian Intelligence II: Extensions and Evaluations*, ed. RW Byrne, A Whiten. Cambridge: Cambridge University Press.

Call J. 2001. Chimpanzee social cognition. *Trends in Cognitive Sciences* 5: 388–393.

Call J, Hare B, Tomasello M. 1998. Chimpanzee gaze following in an object choice task. *Animal Cognition* 1: 89–100.

Call J, Tomasello M. 1996. The effect of humans on the cognitive development of apes. In *Reading into Thought*, ed. AE Russon, K Bard, ST Parker. New York: Cambridge University Press.

Call J, Tomasello M. 1999. A nonverbal false belief task: The performance of children and great apes. *Child Development* 70: 381–395.

Call J, Tomasello M. 2005. What chimpanzees know about seeing, revisited: An explanation of the third kind. In *Joint Attention: Communication and Other Minds*, ed. N Eilan, C Horel, T McCormack, J Roessler. Oxford: Oxford University Press.

Capps L, Losh M, Thurber C. 2000. "The frog ate the bug and made his mouth sad": Narrative competence in children with autism. *Journal of Abnormal Child Psychology* 28: 193–204.

Carey S. 1988. Conceptual differences between children and adults. *Mind and Language* 3: 167–181.

Carey S, Spelke E. 1996. Science and core knowledge. *Philosophy of Science* 63: 515–533.

Carlson SM, Wong A, Lemke M, Cosser C. 2005. Gesture as a window on children's beginning understanding of false belief. *Child Development* 76: 73–86.

Carpendale JLM, Lewis C. 2004. Constructing an understanding of the mind: The development of children's social understanding within social interaction. *Behavioral and Brain Sciences*: 79–151.

Carpenter M, Akhtar N, Tomasello M. 1998. Fourteen through eighteen month old infants differentially imitate intentional and accidental actions. *Infant Behaviour and Development* 21: 315–330.

Carruthers P. 1996a. *Language, Thought and Consciousness*. Cambridge: Cambridge University Press.

Carruthers P. 1996b. Simulation and self-knowledge: A defence of theory-theory. In *Theories of Theories of Mind.*, ed. P Carruthers, P Smith. Cambridge: Cambridge University Press.

Carruthers P. 1998. Thinking in language? Evolution and a modularlist possibility. In *Language and Thought: Interdisciplinary Themes*, ed. P Carruthers, J Boucher. Cambridge: Cambridge University Press.

Carruthers P. 2003. Moderately massive modularity. In *Minds and Persons*, ed. A O'Hear. Cambridge: Cambridge University Press.

Carruthers P. 2004. Practical reasoning in a modular mind. *Mind and Language* 19: 259–278.

Carruthers P, Boucher J. 1998. Introduction: Opening up options. In *Language and Thought: Interdisciplinary Themes*, ed. P Carruthers, J Boucher. Cambridge: Cambridge University Press.

Carruthers P, Boucher J, eds. 1998. *Language and Thought: Interdisciplinary Themes*. Cambridge: Cambridge University Press.

Carstairs-McCarthy A. 1999. *The Origins of Complex Language: An Inquiry into the Evolutionary Beginnings of Sentences, Syllables and Truth*. Oxford: Oxford University Press.

Chalmers D. 2003. The content and epistemology of phenomenal belief. In *Consciousness: New Philosophical Perspectives*, ed. Q Smith, A Jokic. Oxford: Oxford University Press.

Cheney DL, Seyfarth RM. 1991. Reading minds or reading behaviour? Tests for a theory of mind in monkeys. In *Natural Theories of Mind*, ed. A Whiten. Blackwell: Oxford.

Cheung H, Hsuan-Chih C, Creed N, Ng L, Ping Wang S, Mo L. 2004. Relative roles of general and complementation language in Theory-of-Mind development: Evidence from Cantonese and English. *Child Development* 75: 1155–1170.

Chomsky N. 1986. *Knowledge of Language: Its Nature, Origin, and Use*. New York: Praeger.

Chomsky N. 1988. *Language and Problems of Knowledge: The Managua Lectures*. Cambridge, MA: MIT Press.

Chomsky N. 1995. *The Miminalist Program*. Cambridge, MA: MIT Press.

Christensen WD, Bickhard MH. 2002. The process dynamics of normative functions. *The Monist* 85: 3–28.

Christiansen M. 2004. On the relation between language and (mimetic) culture. In *Perspectives on Imitation: From Neuroscience to Social Science*, ed. S. Hurley, N Chater. Cambridge, MA: MIT Press.

Churchland PM. 1979. *Scientific Realism and the Plasticity of Mind*. Cambridge: Cambridge University Press.

Churchland PM. 1981. Eliminative materialism and propositional attitudes. *Journal of Philosophy* 78: 67–90.

Churchland PM. 1988. Perceptual plasticity and theoretical neutrality: A reply to Jerry Fodor. *Philosophy of Science* 55: 167–187.

Churchland PM. 1989. *A Neurocomputational Perspective: The Nature of Mind and the Structure of Science*. Cambridge, MA: MIT Press.

Churchland PM. 1991. Folk psychology and the explanation of human behaviour. In *The Future of Folk Psychology*, ed. JD Greenwood. Cambridge: Cambridge University Press.

Churchland PM. 1992. Activation vectors versus propositional attitudes: How the brain represents reality. *Philosophy and Phenomenological Research* 52(2): 419–424.

Churchland PM. 1993a. Evaluating our self conception. *Mind and Language* 8(2): 211–222.

Churchland PM. 1993b. State-space semantics and meaning holism. *Philosophy and Phenomenological Research* 53(3): 667–672.

Churchland PM. 1998. Conceptual similarity across sensory and neural diversity: The Fodor/Lepore challenge answered. *Journal of Philosophy* 95(1): 5–32.

Churchland PM, Churchland PS. 1998. *On the Contrary: Critical Essays, 1987–1997*. Cambridge: MIT Press.

Churchland PS. 1986. *Neurophilosophy: Toward a Unified Science of the Mind-Brain*. Cambridge, MA: MIT Press.

Clapin H. 2002. *Philosophy of Mental Representation*. Oxford: Oxford University Press.

Clark A. 1989. *Microcognition*. Cambridge, MA: MIT Press.

Clark A. 1993. *Associative Engines*. Cambridge, MA: MIT Press.

Clark A. 1997. *Being There*. Cambridge, MA: MIT Press.

Clark A. 1998. Magic words: How language augments human computation. In *Language and Thought: Interdisciplinary Themes*, ed. P Carruthers, J Boucher. Cambridge: Cambridge University Press.

Coltheart M, Langdon R. 1998. Autism, modularity and levels of Explanation in Cognitive Science. *Mind and Language* 13: 138–152.

Corballis MC. 2003. Gestural origins of language. In *Language Evolution*, ed. M Christiansen, S Kirby. Oxford: Oxford University Press.

Costall A. 1995. Socializing affordances. *Theory and Psychology* 5: 467–481.

Cowie F. 1999. *What's Within: Nativism Reconsidered*. Oxford: Oxford University Press.

Crane T. 1992. The nonconceptual content of experience. In *The Contents of Experience*, ed. T Crane. Cambridge: Cambridge University Press.

Crane T. 2001. *Elements of Mind: An Introduction to the Philosophy of Mind*. Oxford: Oxford University Press.

Crane T. 2003. The intentional structure of consciousness. In *Consciousness: New Philosophical Perspectives*, ed. Q Smith, A Jokic. Oxford: Oxford University Press.

Crane T. 2006. Intentionality and emotion. In *Consciousness and Emotion: Special Issue on Radical Enactivism*, ed. R Menary. Philadelphia: John Benjamins.

Currie G. 1995a. Imagination and simulation: Aesthetics meets cognitive science. In *Mental Simulation*, ed. M Davies. Oxford: Blackwell.

Currie G. 1995b. Visual imagery as the simulation of vision. *Mind and Language* 10(1–2): 25–44.

Currie G. 1996. Simulation-theory, theory-theory and the evidence from autism. In *Theories of Theories of Mind*, ed. P Carruthers, P Smith. Cambridge: Cambridge University Press.

Currie G. 2007. The expression of mind in narrative. In *Narrative and Understanding Persons.*, ed. DD Hutto. Royal Institute of Philosophy Supplement. Cambridge: Cambridge University Press.

Currie G, Ravenscroft I. 1997. Mental simulation and motor imagery. *Philosophy of Science* 64(1): 161–180.

Currie G, Ravenscroft I. 2003. *Recreative Minds*. Oxford: Oxford University Press.

Currie G, Sterelny K. 2000. How to think about the modularity of mind-reading. *Philosophical Quarterly* 50: 145–160.

Cussins A. 1990. The connectionist construction of concepts. In *The philosophy of artificial intelligence*, ed. M Boden, 368–440. Oxford: Oxford University Press.

Dautenhahn K. 2001. The narrative intelligence hypothesis: In search of the transactional format of narratives in humans and other social animals. In *Proceedings of the Fourth International Cognitive Technology Conference: CT 2001: Instruments of Mind*, ed. M Beynon, CL Nehaniv, K Dautenhahn. Berlin, Heidelberg: Springer-Verlag.

Dautenhahn K. 2002. The origins of narrative. *International Journal of Cognition and Technology* 1: 97–123.

Davidson D. 1980. *Essays on Actions and Events*. Oxford: Clarendon Press.

Davidson D. 1984. *Inquiries into Truth and Interpretation*. Oxford: Clarendon Press.

Davidson D. 1985. Rational animals. In *Actions and Events: Perspectives on the Philosophy of Donald Davidson.*, ed. E Lepore, B MacLaughlin. Oxford: Basil Blackwell.

Davidson D. 1987. Problems in the explanation of action. In *Metaphysics and Morality:*, ed. P Pettit, R Sylvan, J Norman. Oxford: Blackwell.

Davidson D. 1990. The structure and content of truth. *Journal of Philosophy* 87(6): 279–328.

Davidson D. 1991. Three varieties of knowledge. In *A J Ayer Memorial Essays*, ed. P Griffiths. New York: Cambridge University Press.

Davidson D. 1996. Subjective, intersubjective, objective. In *Current Issues in Idealism*, ed. P Coates, DD Hutto. Bristol: Thoemmes Press.

Davidson D. 1999. The emergence of thought. *Erkenntnis* 51: 511–521.

Davidson I. 2003. The archeological evidence of language origins: States of art. In *Language Evolution*, ed. M Christiansen, S Kirby. Oxford: Oxford University Press.

Davies M. 1994. The mental simulation debate. In *Objectivity, Simulation and the Unity of Consciousness,* ed. C Peacocke. New York: Oxford University Press.

Davies M. 1998. Language, thought and the Language of Thought (Aunty's Own Argument Revisited). In *Language and Thought: Interdisciplinary Themes,* ed. P Carruthers, J Boucher. Cambridge: Cambridge University Press.

Davies M, Stone T. 1995a. *Folk Psychology: The Theory of Mind Debate.* Cambridge: Blackwell.

Davies M, Stone T. 1995b. *Mental Simulation.* Cambridge: Blackwell.

Davies M, Stone T. 2003. Psychological understanding and social skills. In *Individual Differences in Theory of Mind: Implications for Typical and Atypical Development,* ed. B Repacholi, V Slaughter. New York and Hove: Psychology Press.

Davies PS. 2001. *Norms of Nature: Naturalism and the Nature of Functions.* Cambridge, MA: MIT Press.

Deacon T. 1997. *The Symbolic Species: The Coevolution of Language and the Human Brain.* London: Penguin Books.

Deak GO, Ray SD, Brenneman K. 2003. Children's pervasive appearance-reality errors are related to emerging language skills. *Child Development* 74: 944–964.

Dennett DC. 1985. *Brainstorms.* Cambridge, MA: MIT Press.

Dennett DC. 1987. *The Intentional Stance.* Cambridge, MA: MIT Press.

Dennett DC. 1991. Real Patterns. *Journal of Philosophy* 88: 27–51.

Dennett DC. 1998. Reflections on language and mind. In *Language and Thought: Interdisciplinary Themes,* ed. P Carruthers, J Boucher. Cambridge: Cambridge University Press.

Dennett DC. 2000. Making tools for thinking. In *Metarepresentations: A Multidisciplinary Perspective,* ed. D Sperber. Oxford: Oxford University Press.

Dennett DC. 2001. The evolution of culture. *The Monist* 84: 305–324.

de Villiers JG. 2000. Language and Theory of Mind: What are the developmental relationships? In *Understanding Other Minds: Perspectives from Developmental Cognitive Neuroscience,* ed. S Baron-Cohen, H Tager-Flusberg, DJ Cohen. Oxford: Oxford University Press.

de Villiers JG, de Villiers P. 1999. Linguistic determinism and the understanding of false beliefs. In *Children's Reasoning and the Mind,* ed. P Mitchell, K Riggs. New York: Psychology Press.

Donald M. 1991. *Origins of the Modern Mind: Three Stages in the Evolution of Culture and Cognition.* Cambridge, MA: Harvard University Press.

Donald M. 1999. Preconditions for the evolution of protolanguages. In *The Descent of Mind: Psychological Perspectives on Hominid Evolution*, ed. MC Corballis, SEG Lea. Oxford: Oxford University Press.

Donald M. 2005. Imitation and mimesis. In *Perspectives on Imitation: From Neuroscience to Social Science. Volume 2: Imitation, Human Development and Culture*, ed. S Hurley, N Chater. Cambridge, MA: MIT Press.

Doyle AC. 1887–1927/1986. *The Complete Illustrated Sherlock Holmes*. Chatham: Omega Books Ltd.

Dretske F. 1981. *Knowledge and the Flow of Information*. Cambridge, MA: MIT Press.

Dretske F. 1988. *Explaining Behavior: Reasons in a World of Causes*. Cambridge, MA: MIT Press.

Dretske F. 1991. Dretske's replies. In *Dretske and His Critics*, ed. BP McLaughlin. Oxford: Basil Blackwell.

Dreyfus HL. 1993. *What Computers Still Can't Do: A Critique of Artificial Reason*. Cambridge, MA: MIT Press.

Dunbar RIM. 1992. Neocortex size as a constraint on group size in primates. *Journal of Human Evolution* 20: 469–493.

Dunbar RIM. 1993. Coevolution of Neocortical Size, Group Size and Language in Humans. *Behavioural and Brain Sciences* 16: 681–735.

Dunbar RIM. 2000. On the origin of the human mind. In *Evolution and the Modern Mind: Modularity, Language and Meta-Cognition*, ed. P Carruthers, A Chamberlain. Cambridge: Cambridge University Press.

Dunbar RIM. 2003. The origin and subsequent evolution of language. In *Language Evolution*, ed. M Christiansen, S Kirby. Oxford: Oxford University Press.

Dunbar RIM. 2004. *Grooming, Gossip and the Evolution of Language*. London: Faber and Faber.

Dunn J. 1991. Understanding others: Evidence from naturalistic studies of children. In *Natural Theories of Mind*, ed. A Whiten. Oxford: Blackwell.

Dunn J, Brown JR, Beardsall L. 1991. Family talk about emotions and children's later understanding of others' emotions. *Developmental Psychology* 27(3): 448–455.

Dupré J. 2001. *Human Nature and the Limits of Science*. Oxford: Oxford University Press.

Eilan N. 2005. Joint attention, communication and mind. In *Joint Attention: Communication and Other Minds*, ed. N Eilan, C Horel, T McCormack, J Roessler. Oxford: Oxford University Press.

Eisenmajer R, Prior M. 1991. Cognitive linguistics correlates of "Theory of Mind" ability in autistic children. *British Journal of Developmental Psychology* 9: 351–364.

Elder C. 1998. What versus how in naturally selected representations. *Mind* 107: 349–363.

Elman JL, Bates EA, Johnson MH, Karmiloff-Smith A, Parisi D, Plunkett K. 1991. *Rethinking innateness: A connectionist perspective on development.* Cambridge, MA: MIT Press.

Elugardo R, Stainton RJ. 2003. Grasping objects and contents. In *Epistemology of Language,* ed. A Barber. Oxford: Oxford University Press.

Evans G. 1982. *The Varieties of Reference.* Oxford: Oxford University Press.

Evans JSTB, Over D. 1996. *Rationality and Reasoning.* Hove: Psychology Press.

Fajans J. 1985. The person in social context: The social character of Baining "psychology". In *Person, Self and Experience,* ed. GM White, J Kirkpatrick. Berkeley: University of California Press.

Farah MJ. 1985. Psychological evidence for a shared medium for mental images and percepts. *Journal of Experimental Psychology* 114: 91–103.

Feldman CF, Bruner J, Renderer B, Spitzer S, eds. 1990. *Narrative Thought and Narrative Language.* Hillsdale, NJ: Erlbaum.

Fine A. 1996. Science as child's play: Tales from the crib. *Philosophy of Science* 63(4): 534–537.

Fodor JA. 1968. *Psychological Explanation: An Introduction to the Philosophy of Psychology.* New York: Random House.

Fodor JA. 1975. *The Language of Thought.* Cambridge, MA: Havard University Press.

Fodor JA. 1978. Propositional attitudes. *Monist* 61: 501–523.

Fodor JA. 1981. *Representations: Philosophical Essays on the Foundations of Cognitive Science.* Cambridge, MA: MIT Press.

Fodor JA. 1983. *The Modularity of Mind.* Cambridge, MA: MIT Press.

Fodor JA. 1986. Why paramecia don't have mental representations. *Midwest Studies in Philosophy* 10: 3–23.

Fodor JA. 1987. *Psychosemantics.* Cambridge, MA: MIT Press.

Fodor JA. 1990. *A Theory of Content and Other Essays.* Cambridge, MA: MIT Press.

Fodor JA. 1994. *The Elm and the Expert: Mentalese and Its Semantics.* Cambridge, MA: MIT Press.

Fodor JA. 1995. A theory of the child's Theory of Mind. In *Mental Simulation*, ed. M Davies, T Stone. Oxford: Blackwell.

Fodor JA. 1998. *Concepts: Where Cognitive Science Went Wrong.* New York: Clarendon Press.

Fodor JA. 2000a. *The Mind Doesn't Work That Way: The Scope and Limits of Computational Psychology.* Cambridge, MA: MIT Press.

Fodor JA. 2000b. Replies to critics. *Mind and Language* 15(2–3): 350–374.

Fodor JA. 2001a. Doing without what's within. *Mind* 110: 99–148.

Fodor JA. 2001b. Language, thought and compositionality. *Mind and Language* 16(1): 1–5.

Fodor JA. 2003. *Hume Variations.* Oxford: Oxford University Press.

Fodor JA. 2004a. Having concepts: A brief refutation of the twentieth century. *Mind and Language* 19: 29–47.

Fodor JA. 2004b. Reply to commentators. *Mind and Language* 19: 99–112.

Fodor JA, Lepore E. 2002. *The Compositionality Papers.* Oxford: Oxford University Press.

Fodor JA, McLaughlin BP. 1995. Connectionism and the problem of systematicity. In *Connectionism: Debates on Psychological Explanation*, ed. C. Macdonald. Oxford: Blackwell.

Fodor JA, Pylyshyn ZW. 1995. Connectionism and cognitive architecture: A critical analysis. In *Connectionism: Debates on Psychological Explanation*, ed. C Macdonald. Cambridge: Blackwell.

Foley WA. 1997. *Anthropological Linguistics: An Introduction.* Oxford: Basil Blackwell.

Forrest B. 2000. The possibility of meaning in human evolution. *Zygon* 35(4): 861–879.

Forster EM. 1962. *Aspect of the Novel.* London: Pelican Books.

Frankish K. 1998. Natural language and virtual belief. In *Language and Thought: Interdisiplinary Themes*, ed. P Carruthers, J Boucher. Cambridge: Cambridge University Press.

Frankish K. 2004. *Mind and Supermind.* Cambridge: Cambridge University Press.

Frith U. 1989. *Autism: Explaining the Enigma.* Oxford: Blackwell.

Frith U, Happe F. 1994. Autism: Beyond "Theory of Mind." *Cognition* 50: 115–132.

Fuller G. 1995. Simulation and psychological concepts. In *Mental Simulation*, ed. M. Davies. Cambridge: Blackwell.

Furrow D, Moore C, Davidge J, Chiasson L. 1992. Mental terms in mothers' and children's speech: Similarities and relationships. *Journal of Child Language* 19: 617–631.

Gallagher S. 2001. The practice of mind: Theory, simulation or primary interaction? *Journal of Consciousness Studies* 8(5–7): 83–108.

Gallagher S. 2004. Understanding interpersonal problems in autism: Interaction Theory as an alternative to Theory of Mind. *Philosophy, Psychiatry, Psychology* 11: 199–217.

Gallagher S. 2005. *How the Body Shapes the Mind*. Oxford: Oxford University Press.

Gallagher S. 2006. The narrative alternative to Theory of Mind. In *Consciousness and Emotion: Special Issue on Radical Enactivism*, ed. R Menary.

Gallagher S. 2007a. Logical and phenomenological arguments against simulation theory. In *Folk Psychology Re-Assessed*, ed. DD Hutto, M Ratcliffe. Dordrecht: Springer.

Gallagher S. 2007b. Pathologies in narrative structure. In *Narrative and Understanding Persons*, ed. DD Hutto. Royal Institute of Philosophy Supplement. Cambridge: Cambridge University Press.

Gallagher S, Hutto DD. 2007. Understanding others through Primary Interaction and Narrative Practice. In *The Shared Mind: Perspectives on Intersubjectivity*, ed. J Zlatev, T Racine, C Sinha, E Itkonen. Amsterdam/Philadelphia: John Benjamins.

Gallese V. 2001. The "shared manifold" hypothesis: From mirror neurons to empathy. *Journal of Consciousness Studies* 8: 33–50.

Gallese V. 2003. The manifold nature of interpersonal relations: The quest for a common mechanism. *Philosophical Transactions of the Royal Society of London* 358: 517–528.

Gallese V. 2005. "Being like me": Self-other identity, mirror neurons and empathy. In *Perspectives on Imitation: From Neuroscience to Social Science*, ed. S Hurley, N Chater. Cambridge, MA: MIT Press.

Gallese V. 2006. Intentional attunement: A neurophysiological perspective on social cognition and its disruption in autism. *Cognitive Brain Research* 1079: 15–24.

Gallese V, Fadiga L, Fogassi L, Rizzolatti G. 1996. Action recognition in the premotor cortex. *Brain* 119: 593–609.

Gallese V, Goldman A. 1998. Mirror neurons and the simulation theory of mindreading. *Trends in Cognitive Sciences* 2: 493–501.

Gärdenfors P. 2003. *How Homo Became Sapiens: On the Evolution of Thinking*. Oxford: Oxford University Press.

Gardner H. 1983. *Frames of Mind: The Theory of Multiple Intelligences*. New York: Basic Books.

306   References

Gardner H. 1993. *Multiple Intelligences: The Theory in Practice*. New York: Basic Books.

Garfield JL, Peterson CC, Perry T. 2001. Social cognition, language acquisition and the development of the Theory of Mind. *Mind and Language* 16: 494–541.

Gauker C. 2003. *Words without Meaning*. Cambridge, MA: MIT Press.

Gerrans P. 1998. The norms of cognitive development. *Mind and Language* 13: 56–75.

Gigerenzer G. 1997. The modularity of social intelligence. In *Machiavellian Intelligence II: Extensions and Evaluations*, ed. RW Bryne, A Whiten. Cambridge: Cambridge University Press.

Godfrey-Smith P. 2002. On the evolution of representational and interpretative capacities. *The Monist* 85: 50–69.

Godfrey-Smith P. 2003. Folk psychology under stress: Comments on Susan Hurley's "Animal action in the space of reasons." *Mind and Language* 18: 266–272.

Goldie P. 1999. How we think of others' emotions. *Mind and Language* 14(4): 394–423.

Goldie P. 2000. *The Emotions: A Philosophical Exploration*. Oxford: Oxford University Press.

Goldie P. 2003. One's remembered past: Narrative, thinking, emotion and the external perspective. *Philosophical Papers* 32: 301–320.

Goldie P. 2004. *On Personality*. London: Routedge.

Goldie P. 2006. Emotional experience and understanding. In *Consciousness and Emotion: Special Issue on Radical Enactivism*, ed. R Menary. Philadelphia: John Benjamins.

Goldie P. 2007. There are reasons, and reasons. In *Folk Psychology Reassessed*, ed. DD Hutto, M Ratcliffe. Dordrecht: Springer.

Goldman AI. 1989. Interpretation psychologized. *Mind and Language* 4: 161–185.

Goldman AI. 1992a. In defense of the simulation theory. *Mind and Language* 7: 104–119.

Goldman AI. 1992b. Empathy, mind, and morals. *Proceedings and Addresses of the American Philosophical Association* 66: 17–41.

Goldman AI. 1993. The psychology of folk psychology. *Behavioural and Brain Sciences* 16: 15–28.

Goldman AI. 2000a. Folk psychology and mental concepts. *Protosociology* 14: 4–25.

Goldman AI. 2000b. The mentalizing folk. In *Metarepresentations: A Multidisciplinary Perspective*, ed. D Sperber. New York: Oxford University Press.

Goldman AI. 2001. Desire, intention, and the simulation theory. In *Intentions and Intentionality*, ed. B Malle, LJ Moses, DA Baldwin. Cambridge, MA: MIT Press.

Goldman AI. 2005. Imitation, mind reading and simulation. In *Perspectives on Imitation: From Neuroscience to Social Science. Volume 2: Imitation, Human Development and Culture*, ed. S Hurley, N Chater. Cambridge, MA: MIT Press.

Goldman, AI. 2006. Simulating minds: The philosophy, psychology and neuroscience of mindreading. New York: Oxford University Press.

Goldman AI, Sripada C. 2005. Simulationist models of face-based emotion recognition. *Cognition* 94: 193–213.

Gómez JC. 1991. Visual behaviour as a window for reading the mind of others in primates. In *Natural Theories of Mind*, ed. A Whiten. Oxford: Blackwell.

Gómez JC. 1998. Thoughts about the evolution of LADs. In *Language and Thought: Interdisciplinary Themes*, ed. P Carruthers, J Boucher. Cambridge: Cambridge University Press.

Gómez JC. 2005. Joint attention and the notion of subject: Insights from apes, normal children and children with autism. In *Joint Attention: Communication and Other Minds*, ed. N Eilan, C Horel, T McCormack, J Roessler. Oxford: Oxford University Press.

Goody EN. 1997. Social intelligence and language: Another rubicon? In *Machiavellian Intelligence II: Extensions and Evaluations*, ed. RW Bryne, A Whiten. Cambridge: Cambridge University Press.

Gopnik A. 1988. Conceptual and semantic development as theory change. *Mind and Language* 3: 197–216.

Gopnik A. 1990. Developing the idea of intentionality: Children's theories of mind. *Canadian Journal of Philosophy* 20: 89–113.

Gopnik A. 1993. How we know our own minds: The illusion of first-person knowledge of intentionality. In *Readings in the Philosophy of the Cognitive Sciences*, ed. A Goldman. Cambridge, MA: MIT Press. (Originally published in *Brain and Behavioral Sciences* 16 (1993): 1–14).

Gopnik A. 1996a. The scientist as child. *Philosophy of Science* 63: 485–514.

Gopnik A. 1996b. Reply to commentaries. *Philosophy of Science* 63: 552–561.

Gopnik A. 1996c. Theories and modules: Creation myths, developmental realities and Neurath's boat. In *Theories of Theories of Mind*, ed. P Carruthers, P Smith. Cambridge: Cambridge University Press.

Gopnik A. 1998. Explanation as orgasm. *Minds and Machines* 8: 101–118.

Gopnik A. 2003. The theory theory as an alternative to the innateness hypothesis. In *Chomsky and His Critics*, ed. LM Antony, N Hornstein. Oxford: Blackwell.

Gopnik A. 2004. Finding our inner scientist. *Daedalus* 133: 21–28.

Gopnik A, Capps L, Meltzoff A. 2000. Early Theories of Mind: What the theory can tell us about autism. In *Understanding Other Minds: Perspectives from Developmental Cognitive Neuroscience*, ed. S Baron-Cohen, H Tager-Flusberg, D Cohen. Oxford: Oxford University Press.

Gopnik A, Glymour C. 2002. Causal maps and Bayes nets: A cognitive and computational account of theory-formation. In *The Cognitive Basis of Science*, ed. P Carruthers. Cambridge: Cambridge University Press.

Gopnik A, Meltzoff AN. 1997. *Words, Thoughts, and Theories*. Cambridge, MA: MIT Press.

Gopnik A, Meltzoff AN. 1998. Theories vs. modules: To the max and beyond: A reply to Poulin-Dubois and to Stich and Nichols. *Mind and Language* 13: 450–456.

Gopnik A, Wellman HM. 1992. Why the child's Theory of Mind really "is" a theory. *Mind and Language* 7: 145–171.

Gordon RM. 1986. Folk psychology as simulation. *Mind and Language* 1: 158–171.

Gordon RM. 1992. The simulation theory: Objections and misconceptions. *Mind and Language* 7: 11–34.

Gordon RM. 1995. Simulation without introspection or inference from me to you. In *Mental Simulation,* ed. M Davies, T Stone. Oxford: Blackwell.

Gordon RM. 1996. Radical simulationism. In *Theories of Theories of Mind*, ed. P Carruthers, P Smith. Cambridge: Cambridge University Press.

Gordon RM. 2000. Simulation and the explanation of action. In *Empathy and Agency*, ed. HH Kölger, KR Stueber. Boulder: Westview Press.

Gordon RM. 2005. Intentional agents like myself. In *Perspectives on Imitation: From Neuroscience to Social Science. Volume 2: Imitation, Human Development and Culture,* ed. S Hurley, N Chater. Cambridge, MA: MIT Press.

Greenfield P. 1991. Language, tools and brain: The ontogeny and phylogeny of hierarchically organised sequential behaviour. *Behavioral and Brain Sciences* 14: 531–595.

Grice P. 1989. *Studies in the Way of Words*. Cambridge, MA: Harvard University Press.

Griffiths P. 1997. *What Emotions Really Are*. Chicago/London: University of Chicago Press.

Griffiths P. 2002. What is innateness? *The Monist* 85: 70–85.

Grush R. 2003. The architecture of representation. In *Philosophy and the Neurosciences: A Reader*, ed. W Bechtel, P Mandik, J Mundale, S Stufflebeam. Oxford: Blackwell.

Guajardo NR, Watson A. 2002. Narrative discourse and Theory of Mind development. *Journal of Genetic Psychology* 163: 305–325.

Guaker C. 2003. *Words without Meaning*. Cambridge, MA: MIT Press.

Haden C, Haine RA, Fivush R. 1997. Developing narrative structure in parent-child reminiscing across the preschool years. *Developmental Psychology* 33: 207–307.

Happé F. 1995. The role of age and verbal ability in the Theory of Mind task performance of subjects with autism. *Child Development* 66: 843–855.

Hare B, Call J, Tomasello M. 2001. Do chimpanzees know what conspecifics know? *Animal Behaviour* 61: 139–151.

Harley K, Reese E. 1999. Origins of autobiographical memory. *Developmental Psychology* 35: 1338–1348.

Harris P. 1992. From simulation to folk psychology: The case for development. *Mind and Language* 7(1–2): 120–144.

Harris P. 1996. Desires, beliefs and language. In *Theories of Theories of Mind*, ed. P Carruthers, P Smith. Cambridge: Cambridge University Press.

Harris P, Want S. 2005. On learning what not to do: The emergence of selective imitation in tool use by young children. In *Perspectives on Imitation: From Neuroscience to Social Science. Volume 2. Imitation, Human Development, and Culture*, ed. S Hurley, N Chater. Cambridge, MA: MIT Press.

Hauser MD. 1997. Minding the behaviour of deception. In *Machiavellian Intelligence II: Extensions and Evaluations*, ed. RW Byrne, A Whiten. Cambridge: Cambridge University Press.

Hauser MD. 1998. Expectations about object motion and destination: Experiments with a nonhuman primate. *Developmental Science* 1: 31–38.

Hauser MD, Marler P. 1993a. Food associated calls in rhesus macaques (*Macaca mulatta*). I. Socioecological factors. *Behavioral Ecology* 4: 194–205.

Hauser MD, Marler P. 1993b. Food associated calls in rhesus macaques (*Macaca mulatta*). II. Costs and benefits of call production and supression. *Behavioral Ecology* 4: 206–212.

Heal J. 1994. Simulation vs theory theory: What is at issue? In *Objectivity, Simulation and the Unity of Consciousness*, ed. C. Peacocke. New York: Oxford University Press.

Heal J. 1995. How to think about thinking. In *Mental Simulation*, ed. M Davies. Cambridge: Blackwell.

Heal J. 1996a. Simulation and cognitive penetrability. *Mind and Language* 11(1): 44–67.

Heal J. 1996b. Simulation, theory and content. In *Theories of Theories of Mind*, ed. P Carruthers, P Smith. Cambridge: Cambridge University Press.

Heal J. 1998a. Co-cognition and off-line simulation: Two ways of understanding the simulation approach. *Mind and Language* 13(4): 477–498.

Heal J. 1998b. Understanding other minds from the inside. In *Current Issues in Philosophy of Mind*, ed. A O'Hear. New York: Cambridge University Press.

Heal J. 2000. Other minds, rationality and analogy. *Proceedings of the Aristotelian Society, Supplementary Volume*: 1–19.

Heal J. 2005a. Joint attention and understanding the mind. In *Joint Attention: Communication and Other Minds*, ed. N Eilan, C Horel, T McCormack, J Roessler. Oxford: Oxford University Press.

Heal J. 2005b. Review of mindreading: An integrated account of pretence, Self-awareness and understanding other minds. *Mind* 114: 181–184.

Heider F, Simmel M. 1944. An experimental study of apparent behavior. *American Journal of Psychology* 57: 243–259.

Heiser M, Iacoboni M, Maeda F, Marcus J, Mazziotta JC. 2003. The essential role of Broca's area in imitation. *European Journal of Neuroscience* 17: 1123–1128.

Hempel C. 1966. Laws and their role in scientific explanation. In *The Philosophy of Science*, ed. R Boyd, P Gasper, JD Trout. Cambridge, MA: MIT Press.

Henderson D, Horgan T. 2000. Simulation and epistemic competence. In *Empathy and Agency*, ed. HH Kölger, KR Stueber. Boulder: Westview Press.

Hernandez Cruz JL. 1998. Mindreading: Mental state ascription and cognitive architecture. *Mind and Language* 13: 323–340.

Heyes C. 2001. Causes and consequences of imitation. *Trends in Cognitive Sciences* 5: 253–261.

Hobson P. 1991. Against the theory of Theory of Mind. *British Journal of Developmental Psychology* 9: 33–51.

Hobson P. 1992. Social perception in high level autism. In *High Functioning Individuals with Autism*, ed. E Schopler, GB Mesibov. New York: Plenum.

Hobson P. 1993. The emotional origins of social understanding. *Philosophical Psychology* 6: 227–249.

Hobson P. 2000. The grounding of symbols: A social-developmental account. In *Children's Reasoning and the Mind*, ed. P Mitchell, K Riggs. Hove: Psychology Press.

Hobson P. 2005. What puts the jointness in joint attention? In *Joint Attention: Communication and Other Minds*, ed. N Eilan, C Horel, T McCormack, J Roessler, 186–204. Oxford: Oxford University Press.

Hobson P. 2006. From feeling to thinking (through others). In *Consciousness and Emotion: Special Issue on Radical Enactivism*, ed. R Menary.

Hobson P. 2007. We share, therefore we think. In *Folk Psychology Re-Assessed*, ed. DD Hutto, M Ratcliffe. Dordrecht: Springer.

Hobson P, Lee A. 1999. Imitation and identification in autism. *Journal of Child Psychology and Psychiatry* 40: 649–659.

Humphrey N. 1976 (reprinted 1988). The social function of intellect. In *Machiavellian Intelligence: Social Expertise and the Evolution of Intellect in Monkeys, Apes and Humans*, ed. RW Bryne, A Whiten. Oxford: Oxford University Press.

Hurley S. 1998. *Consciousness in Action*. Cambridge, MA: Harvard University Press.

Hurley S. 2003a. Animal actions in the space of reasons. *Mind and Language* 18: 231–256.

Hurley S. 2003b. Making sense of animals: Interpretation vs. architecture. *Mind and Language* 18: 273–280.

Hurley S. 2005. The shared circuits hypothesis: A unified functional architecture for control, imitation, and simulation. In *Perspectives on Imitation: From Neuroscience to Social Science. Volume 1. Mechanisms of Imitation and Imitation in Animals*, ed. S Hurley, N Chater. Cambridge, MA: MIT Press.

Hutto DD. 1997. The story of the self: The narrative basis of self-development. In *Critical Studies: Ethics and the Subject*, ed. K Simms. Amsterdam: Rodopi.

Hutto DD. 1999a. A cause for concern: Reasons, causes and explanations. *Philosophy and Phenomenological Research* 59(2): 381–401.

Hutto DD. 1999b. *The Presence of Mind*. Amsterdam: John Benjamins.

Hutto DD. 2000. *Beyond Physicalism*. Amsterdam: John Benjamins.

Hutto DD. 2002. The world is not enough: Shared emotions and other minds. In *Understanding Emotions*, ed. P Goldie. Aldershot: Ashgate.

Hutto DD. 2003. Folk psychological explanations: Narratives and the case of autism. *Philosophical Papers* 32: 345–361.

Hutto DD. 2003/2006. *Wittgenstein and the End of Philosophy: Neither Theory nor Therapy*. Basingstoke: Palgrave Macmillan.

Hutto DD. 2004. The limits of spectatorial folk psychology. *Mind and Language* 19: 548–573.

Hutto DD. 2005a. Knowing what? Radical versus conservative enactivism. *Phenomenology and the Cognitive Sciences* 4: 389–405.

Hutto DD. 2005b. Starting without theory: Confronting the paradox of conceptual development. In *Other Minds: How Humans Bridge the Divide between Self and Others*, ed. B Malle, S Hodges. New York: Guilford Press.

Hutto DD. 2006a. Turning hard problems on their heads. *Phenomenology and the Cognitive Sciences* 5: 75–88.

Hutto DD. 2006b. Unprincipled engagements: Emotional experience, expression and response. In *Consciousness and Emotion: Special Issue on Radical Enactivism*, ed. R Menary. Philadelphia: John Benjamins.

Hutto DD. 2006c. Impossible problems and careful expositions: Reply to Myin and De Nul. In *Consciousness and Emotion: Special Issue on Radical Enactivism*, ed. R Menary. Philadelphia: John Benjamins.

Hutto DD. 2006d. Both Bradley and biology: Reply to Rudd. In *Consciousness and Emotion: Special Issue on Radical Enactivism*, ed. R Menary. Philadelphia: John Benjamins.

Hutto DD. 2006e. Against passive intellectualism: Reply to Crane. In *Consciousness and Emotion: Special Issue on Radical Enactivism*, ed. R Menary. Philadelphia: John Benjamins.

Hutto DD. 2006f. Embodied expectations and extended possibilities: Reply to Goldie. In *Consciousness and Emotion: Special Issue on Radical Enactivism*, ed. R Menary. Philadelphia: John Benjamins.

Hutto DD. 2006g. Four Herculean labours: Reply to Hobson. In *Consciousness and Emotion: Special Issue on Radical Enactivism*, ed. R Menary. Philadelphia: John Benjamins.

Hutto DD. 2006h. Narrative practice and understanding reasons: Reply to Gallagher. In *Consciousness and Emotion: Special Issue on Radical Enactivism*, ed. R Menary. Philadelphia: John Benjamins.

Hutto DD. 2007a. First communions: Mimetic sharing without Theory of Mind. In *The Shared Mind: Perspectives on Intersubjectivity*, ed. J Zlatev, T Racine, C Sinha, E Itkonen. Philadelphia: John Benjamins.

Hutto DD. 2007b. Folk psychology without theory or simulation. In *Folk Psychology Reassessed*, ed. DD Hutto, M Ratcliffe. Dordrecht: Springer.

Hutto DD. 2007c. Getting clear about perspicuous representations: Wittgenstein, Baker, and Fodor. In *Perspicuous Presentations: Essays on Wittgenstein's Philosophy of Psychology*, ed. D Moyal-Sharrock. Basingstoke: Palgrave Macmillan.

Hutto DD. 2007d. The Narrative Practice Hypothesis. Origins and applications of folk psychology. In *Narrative and Understanding Persons*, ed. DD Hutto. Royal Institute of Philosophy Supplement. Cambridge: Cambridge University Press.

Jackendoff R. 1999. What is a concept, that a person may grasp it? In *Concepts: Core Readings*, ed. E Margolis, S Laurence. Cambridge, MA: MIT Press.

Jackendoff R. 2002. *The Foundations of Language: Brain, Meaning, Grammar and Evolution*. Oxford: Oxford.

Jackson F. 1999. All that can be at issue in the theory-theory simulation debate. *Philosophical Papers* 28(2): 77–96.

Jacob P. 1997. *What Minds Can Do*. Cambridge: Cambridge University Press.

James W. 1909. *The meaning of truth*. London: Longman, Green and Co.

Jeannerod M. 2001. Neural simulation of action: A unifying mechanism for motor cognition. *Neuroimage* 14: S103–S109.

Jolly A. 1966 (reprinted 1988). Lemur social behaviour and primate intelligence. In *Machiavellian Intelligence: Social Expertise and the Evolution of Intellect in Monkeys, Apes and Humans*, ed. RW Byrne, A Whiten. Oxford: Oxford University Press.

Jones S. 2005. Why don't apes ape more? In *Perspectives on Imitation: From Neuroscience to Social Science: Volume 1: Mechanism of Imitation and Imitation in Animals*, ed. S Hurley, N Chater. Cambridge, MA: MIT Press.

Juarrero A. 1999. *Dynamics in Action: Intentional Behaviour as a Complex System*. Cambridge, MA: MIT Press.

Karmiloff-Smith A. 1995. *Beyond Modularity: A Developmental Perspective on Cognitive Science*. Cambridge, MA: MIT Press.

Kennett J. 2002. Autism, empathy and moral agency. *Philosophical Quarterly* 52: 340–357.

Kerby P. 1993. *Narrative and the Self*. Indiana: Indiana University Press.

Kitcher P. 1993. *The Advancement of Science: Science without Legend, Objectivity without Illusions*. Oxford: Oxford University Press.

Knobe J. 2007. Folk Psychology: Science and morals. In *Folk Psychology Reassessed*, ed. DD Hutto, M Ratcliffe. Dordrecht: Springer.

Knoblich G, Jordan JS. 2002. The mirror system and joint action. In *Mirror Neurons and the Evolution of Brain and Language*, ed. M Stamenov, V Gallese. Amsterdam/Philadelphia: John Benjamins.

Kölger HH. 2000. Empathy, dialogical self, and reflexive interpretation: The symbolic source of simulation. In *Empathy and Agency*, ed. HH Kölger, KR Stueber. Boulder: Westview Press.   '

Kölger HH, Stueber KR. 2000a. *Empathy and Agency*. Boulder: Westview Press.

Kölger HH, Stueber KR. 2000b. Introduction: Empathy, simulation, and interpretation in the philosophy of social science. In *Empathy and Agency*, ed. HH Kölger, KR Stueber. Boulder: Westview Press.

Kripke S. 1979. A puzzle about belief. In *Meaning and Use*, ed. A Margalit. Dordrecht: Reidel.

Kusch M. 2007. Folk Psychology and freedom of the will. In *Folk Psychology Re-Assessed*, ed. DD Hutto, M Ratcliffe. Dordrecht: Springer.

Lakoff G, Johnson M. 1980. *Metaphors We Live By*. Chicago: Chicago University Press.

Lamarque P. 2004. On not expecting too much from narrative. *Mind and Language* 19: 393–408.

Lamarque P, Olsen S. 1994. *Truth, Fiction and Literature*. Oxford: Oxford University Press.

Laurence S. 1998. Convention-based semantics and the development of language. In *Language and Thought: Interdisciplinary Themes*, ed. P Carruthers, J Boucher. Cambridge: Cambridge University Press.

Lawlor K. 2005. Confused thought and modes of presentation. *The Philosophical Quarterly* 55: 21–36.

Leekam S. 2005. Why do children with autism have a joint attention impairment? In *Joint Attention: Communication and Other Minds*, ed. N Eilan, C Horel, T McCormack, J Roessler. Oxford: Oxford University Press.

Leslie A, Friedman O, German TP. 2004. Core mechanisms in "Theory of Mind." *Trends in Cognitive Sciences* 8: 528–533.

Leslie AM. 1987. Pretense and representation: The origins of "Theory of Mind." *Psychological Review* 94: 412–426.

Leslie AM. 1994. Pretending and believing: Issues in the theory of ToMM. *Cognition* 50: 211–238.

Leslie AM, Frith U. 1988. Autistic children's understanding of seeing, knowing and believing. *British Journal of Developmental Psychology.* 6: 315–324.

Leslie AM, German TP. 1995. Knowledge and ability in "Theory of Mind: One-eyed overview of a debate. In *Mental Simulation*, ed. M Davies. Oxford: Blackwell.

Lewis C. 1994. Episodes, events and narratives in the child's understanding of mind. In *Children's Early Understanding of the Mind*, ed. C Lewis, P Mitchell. Hillsdale, NJ: Erlbaum.

Lewis C, Freeman NH, Hagestadt C, Douglas H. 1994. Narrative access and production in preschoolers' false belief reasoning. *Cognitive Development* 9: 397–424.

Lewis C, Freeman NH, Kyriakidou C, Maridaki-Kassotaki K, Berridge DM. 1996. Social influences on false belief access: Specific sibling influences or general apprenticeship? *Child Development* 67: 2930–2947.

Lewis D. 1970. How to define theoretical terms. *Journal of Philosophy* 67: 427–446.

Lewis D. 1972. Psychophysical and theoretical identifications. *Australasian Journal of Philosophy* 50: 249–258.

Lewis M, Ramsay D. 2004. Development of self-recognition, personal pronoun use, and pretend play during the 2nd year. *Child Development* 75: 1821–1831.

Li CN, Hombert J. 2002. On the evolutionary origin of language. In *Mirror Neurons and the Evolution of Brain and Language*, ed. M Stamenov, V Gallese. Amsterdam/Philadelphia: John Benjamins.

Lieberman P. 1984. *The Biology and Evolution of Language*. Cambridge, MA: Harvard University Press.

Lieberman P. 1998. *Eve Spoke: Human Language and Human Evolution*. New York: Norton.

Lieberman P. 2000. *Human Language and Our Reptilian Brain: The Subcortical Basis of Speech, Syntax, and Thought*. Cambridge, MA: Harvard University Press.

Lieberman P, Kato ET, Friedman J, Tajchman G, Feldman LS, Jiminez EB. 1992. Speech production, syntax comprehension and cognitive deficits in Parkinson's disease. *Journal of Nervous and Mental Disease* 179: 360–365.

Lillard A. 1997. Other folks' theories of mind and behaviour. *Psychological Science* 8: 268–274.

Lillard A. 1998. Ethnopsychologies: Cultural variations in Theories of Mind. *Psychological Bulletin* 123: 3–32.

Loar B. 1981. *Mind and Meaning*. Cambridge: Cambridge University Press.

Lohmann H, Tomasello M. 2003. The role of language in the development of false belief understanding: A training study. *Child Development* 74: 1130–1144.

Losh M, Bellugi U, Reilly J, Anderson D. 2000. Narrative as a social engagement tool: The excessive use of evaluation in narratives from children with Williams syndrome. *Narrative Inquiry* 10: 265–290.

Lovejoy CO. 1980. Hominid origins: The role of bipedalism. *American Journal of Physical Anthropology* 52: 250.

MacIntyre A. 1984. *After Virtue*. London: Duckworth.

Maclaurin J. 2002. The resurrection of innateness. *The Monist* 85: 105–130.

Mahoney JC. 1989. *The Mundane Matter of the Mental Language*. Cambridge: Cambridge University Press.

Malle B. 1999. How people explain behaviour: A new theoretical framework. *Personality and Social Psychology Review* 3: 23–48.

Maraschal D, French RM. 1999. A connectionist account of perceptual category learning in infants. In *Proceedings of the 21st Annual Conference of the Cognitive Science Conference*. Mahwah, NJ: Lawrence Erlbaum and Associates.

Margolis E. 1998. How to acquire a concept. *Mind and Language* 13: 347–369.

Markman EM. 1989. *Categorization and Naming in Children*. Cambridge, MA: MIT Press.

Marler P, Evans C. 1995. Bird calls: Just emotional displays or something more? *Ibis* 138: 26–33.

McGeer V. 2001. Psycho-practice, psycho-theory and autism. *Journal of Consciousness Studies* 8: 109–132.

McGeer V. 2007. The regulative dimension of Folk Psychology. In *Folk Psychology Re-Assessed*, ed. DD Hutto, M Ratcliffe. Dordrecht: Springer.

McGinn C. 1989. *Mental Content*. Oxford: Basil Blackwell.

McMullin E. 1984. A case for scientific realism. In *Scientific realism*, ed. J Leplin. Berkeley: California University Press.

Mellor DH. 1991. *Matters of metaphysics*. Cambridge: Cambridge University Press.

Meltzoff AN. 1995. Understanding the intentions of others: Re-enactment of intended acts by 18-month-old children. *Developmental Psychology* 24: 470–476.

Meltzoff AN, Moore MK. 1977. Imitation of facial and manual gestures by human neonates. *Science* 198: 75–78.

Meltzoff AN, Moore MK. 1994. Imitation, memory and the representation of persons. *Infant Behaviour and Development* 17: 83–99.

Mendola J. 2003. A dilemma for asymmetric dependence. *Nous* 37: 232–257.

Millikan RG. 1984. *Language, Thought and Other Biological Categories*. Cambridge, MA: MIT Press.

Millikan RQ. 1989. Biosemantics. *Journal of Philosophy* 86: 281–297.

Millikan RG. 1993. *White Queen Psychology and Other Essays for Alice*. Cambridge, MA: MIT Press.

Millikan RG. 1998. A common structure for concepts, individuals, stuffs and real kinds: Mama, more milk and more mouse. *Behavioral and Brain Sciences* 21: 55–160.

Millikan RG. 2000. *On Clear and Confused Ideas*. Cambridge: Cambridge University Press.

Millikan RG. 2001. Purposes and cross-purposes: On the evolution of languages and language. *The Monist* 84: 392–416.

Millikan RG. 2004. *Varieties of Meaning: The 2002 Jean Nicod Lectures*. Cambridge, MA: MIT Press.

Mithen S. 1996. *The Pre-History of the Mind: A Search for the Origins of Art, Religion and Science*. London: Thames and Hudson.

Mithen S. 2000a. Mind, brain and material culture: An archeological perspective. In *Evolution and the Modern Mind: Modularity, Language and Meta-Cognition*, ed. P Carruthers, A Chamberlain. Cambridge: Cambridge University Press.

Mithen S. 2000b. Paleoanthropological perspectives on the Theory of Mind. In *Understanding Other Minds*, ed. S Baron-Cohen, H Talgar-Flusberg, D Cohen. Oxford: Oxford University Press.

Mithen S. 2002. Human evolution and the cognitive basis of science. In *The Cognitive Basis of Science*, ed. P Carruthers, S Stich, M Siegal. Cambridge: Cambridge University Press.

Mithen S. 2005. *The Singing Neanderthals: The Origins of Music, Language, Mind and Body*. London: Weidenfeld and Nicolson.

Morris MW, Peng K. 1994. Culture and cause: American and Chinese attributions for social and physical events. *Journal of Personality and Social Psychology* 67: 949–971.

Morton A. 1980. *Frames of Mind: Constraints on the Common Sense Conception of the Mental*. Oxford: Oxford University Press.

Morton A. 2003. *The Importance of Being Understood*. London: Routledge.

Morton A. 2007. Folk Psychology does not exist. In *Folk Psychology Re-Assessed*, ed. DD Hutto, M Ratcliffe. Dordrecht: Springer.

Moses LJ. 2001. Some thoughts on ascribing complex intentional concepts to young children. In *Intentions and Intentionality*, ed. B Malle, LJ Moses, DA Baldwin. Cambridge, MA: MIT Press.

Munakata Y, Santos LR, Spelke ES, Hauser MD, O'Reilly RC. 2001. Visual representation in the wild: How rhesus monkeys parse objects. *Journal of Cognitive Neuroscience* 13: 44–58.

Murphy GL. 2002. *The Big Book of Concepts*. Cambridge, MA: MIT Press.

Murphy GL, Medin DL. 2000. The role of theories in conceptual coherence. In *Concepts: Core Readings*, ed. E Margolis, S Laurence. Cambridge, MA: MIT Press.

Myin E, De Nul L. 2006. Feelings and objects. In *Consciousness and Emotion: Special Issue on Radical Enactivism*, ed. R Menary.

Myin E, O'Regan JK. 2002. A way to naturalize phenomenology? *Journal of Consciousness Studies* 9: 27–46.

Myowa-Yamakoshi M, Tanaka MT, Matsuzawa T. 2004. Imitation in neonatal chimpanzees (*Pan troglodytes*). *Developmental Science* 7: 437–442.

Needham R. 1972. *Belief, Language and Experience*. Oxford: Blackwell.

Nelson K. 2003. Narrative and the emergence of a conscious of self. In *Narrative and Consciousness*, ed. GD Fireman, TEJ McVay, O Flanagan. Oxford: Oxford University Press.

Newell A, Simon H. 1976/1990. Computer science as empirical enquiry: Symbols and search. In *The Philosophy of Artificial Intelligence*, ed. M Boden. Oxford: Oxford University Press.

Nichols S, Stich S. 1998. Rethinking co-cognition: A reply to Heal. *Mind and Language* 13(4): 499–512.

Nichols S, Stich S. 2003. *Mindreading: An Integrated Account of Pretence, Self-Awareness and Understanding of Other Minds*. Oxford: Oxford University Press.

Nichols S, Stich S, Leslie A, Klein D. 1996. Varieties of off-line simulation. In *Theories of Theories of Mind*, ed. P Carruthers, P Smith. Cambridge: Cambridge University Press.

Osherson DN, Smith ES. 1981. On the adequacy of prototype theory as a theory of concepts. *Cognition* 9: 35–58.

Over D. 2002. Rationalty of evolutionary psychology. In *Reason and Nature: Essays in the Theory of Rationality*, ed. J Bermúdez, A Millar. Oxford: Oxford University Press.

Ozonoff S, Miller JN. 1995. Teaching Theory of Mind: A new approach to social skills training for individuals with autism. *Journal of Autism and Developmental Disorders* 25: 415–433.

Ozonoff S, Pennington B, Rogers S. 1991. Executive function deficits in high functioning autistic children. Relationship to Theory of Mind. *Journal of Child Psychology and Psychiatry* 32: 1081–1105.

Oztop E, Arbib M. 2002. Schema design and implementation of the grasp-related mirror neuron system. *Biological Cybernetics* 87: 116–140.

Papineau D. 1987. *Reality and Representation*. Oxford: Oxford University Press.

Papineau D. 2003. *The Roots of Reason: Philosophical Essays on Rationality, Evolution and Probability*. Oxford: Oxford University Press.

Peacocke C. 2004. Interrelations: concepts, knowledge, reference and structure. *Mind and Language* 19: 85–98.

Perner J. 1996. Simulation as explication of prediction-implicit knowledge about the mind: Arguments for a simulation-theory mix. In *Theories of Theories of Mind*, ed. P Carruthers, P Smith. Cambridge: Cambridge University Press.

Perner J, Howes D. 1992. "He thinks he knows": And more developmental evidence against the simulation (role taking) theory. *Mind and Language* 7(1–2): 72–86.

Perner J, Leekam S, Wimmer H. 1987. Three-year-olds' difficulty with false belief: The case for conceptual deficit. *British Journal of Developmental Psychology* 5: 125–137.

Perner J, Ruffman T, Leekam SR. 1994. Theory of Mind is contagious: You can catch it from your siblings. *Child Development* 65: 1228–1238.

Perner J, Sprung M, Zauner P, Haider H. 2003. Want that is understood well before say that, think that, and false belief: A test of de Villiers's linguistic determinism on German-speaking children. *Child Development* 74: 179–188.

Perner J, Wimmer H. 1983. Beliefs about beliefs: Representation and constraining function of wrong beliefs in young children's understanding of deception. *Cognition* 7: 333–362.

Peterson C, McCabe A. 1994. A social interactionist account of developing decontextualised narrative skill. *Developmental Psychology* 30: 937–948.

Peterson C, Siegal M. 2000. Insights into Theory of Mind from deafness and autism. *Mind and Language* 15: 123–145.

Pillow BH, Lovett SB. 1998. "He forgot": Young children's use of cognitive explanations for another person's mistakes. *Merril-Palmer Quarterly* 44: 378–403.

Pinker S. 1994. *The Language Instinct*. New York: Morrow.

Pinker S. 2003. Language as an adaptation to the cognitive niche. In *Language Evolution*, ed. MH Christiansen, S Kirby. Oxford: Oxford University Press.

Podgorny P, Shepard RN. 1978. Functional representations common to Visual Perception and Imagination. *Journal of Experimental Psychology* 4: 21–35.

Povinelli D. 1996. Chimpanzee Theory of Mind? The long road to strong inference. In *Theories of Theories of Mind*, ed. P Carruthers, P Smith. Cambridge: Cambridge University Press.

Povinelli D. 2003. *Folk Physics for Apes: The Chimpanzee's Theory of How the World Works*. Oxford: Oxford University Press.

Povinelli D, Eddy TJ. 1996a. Chimpanzee: Joint visual attention. *Psychological Science* 7: 129–135.

Povinelli D, Eddy TJ. 1996b. What young chimpanzees know about seeing. *Monographs of the Society for Research in Child Development* 61: 1–52.

Povinelli D, Giambrone S. 1999. Inferring other minds: Failure of the argument by analogy. *Philosophical Topics* 27: 167–201.

Povinelli DJ, Vonk J. 2003. Chimpanzee minds: Suspiciously human? *Trends in Cognitive Sciences* 7: 157–160.

Povinelli DJ, Vonk J. 2004. We don't need a microscope to explore the chimpanzee's mind. *Mind and Language* 19: 1–28.

Premack D. 1988. "Does the chimpanzee have a Theory of Mind?" Revisited. In *Machiavellian Intelligence: Social Expertise and the Evolution of Intellect in Monkeys, Apes and Humans*, ed. RW Byrne, A Whiten. Oxford: Oxford University Press.

Premack D, Dasser V. 1991. Perceptual origins and conceptual evidence for Theory of Mind in apes and children. In *Natural Theories of Mind*, ed. A Whiten. Oxford: Blackwell.

Premack D, Woodruff G. 1978. Does the chimpanzee have a Theory of Mind? *Behavioral and Brain Sciences* 4: 515–526.

Prinz J. 2002. *Furnishing the Mind: Concepts and Their Perceptual Basis*. Cambridge, MA: MIT Press.

Prinz J, Clark A. 2004. Putting concepts to work: Some thoughts for the twenty-first century. *Mind and Language* 19: 57–69.

Pust J. 1999. External accounts of Folk Psychology, eliminativism, and the simulation theory. *Mind and Language* 14(1): 113–130.

Putnam H. 1981. *Realism, Truth and History*. Cambridge: Cambridge University Press.

Putnam H. 1988. *Representation and Reality*. Cambridge, MA: MIT Press.

Putnam H. 1990. *Realism with a Human Face*. Cambridge, MA: Harvard University Press.

Quine WV. 1956. Quantifiers and propositional attitudes. *Journal of Philosophy* 53: 177–187.

Quine WV. 1960. *Word and Object*. Cambridge, MA: MIT Press.

Ramsey F. 1926/1990. Truth and probability. In *Philosophical Papers*, ed. DH Mellor. Cambridge: Cambridge University Press.

Ratcliffe, M. 2007a. From Folk Psychology to commonsense. In *Folk Psychology Reassessed*, ed. DD Hutto. Dordrecht: Springer.

Ratcliffe, M. 2007b. Rethinking commonsense psychology: A critique of Folk Psychology, Theory of Mind and simulation. Basingstoke: Palgrave Macmillan.

Ratcliffe M, Hutto DD. 2007. Introduction. In *Folk Psychology Reassessed*, ed. DD Hutto, M Ratcliffe. Dordrecht: Springer.

Rey G. 1996/2000. Concepts and stereotypes. In *Concepts: Core Readings*, ed. E Margolis, S Laurence. Cambridge, MA: MIT Press.

Richard M. 1990. *Propositional Attitudes: An Essay on Thoughts and How We Ascribe Them*. Cambridge: Cambridge University Press.

Richner ES, Nicolopoulou A. 2001. The narrative construction of differing conceptions of the person in the development of young children's social understanding. *Early Education and Development* 12: 393–432.

Rizzolatti G. 2005. The mirror neuron system and imitation. In *Perspectives on Imitation: From Neuroscience to Social Science: Volume 1: Mechanism of Imitation and Imitation in Animals*, ed. S Hurley, N Chater. Cambridge, MA: MIT Press.

Rizzolatti G, Arbib M. 1998. Language within our grasp. *Trends in Neuroscience* 21: 188–194.

Rizzolatti G, Graighero L, Fadiga L. 2002. The mirror neuron system in humans. In *Mirror Neurons and the Evolution of Brain and Language*, ed. M Stamenov, V Gallese. Amsterdam/Philadelphia: John Benjamins.

Rizzolatti G, Fadiga L, Fogassi L, Gallese V. 2002. From mirror neurons to imitation: Facts and speculations. In *The Imitative Mind: Development, Evolution, and Brain Bases*, ed. A Meltzoff, W Prinz. Cambridge: Cambridge University Press.

Rizzolatti G, Luppino G. 2001. The cortical motor system. *Neuron* 31: 889–901.

Rollins M. 1986. Mental imagery and methodology in cognitive science. *Logos* 7: 57–68.

Rollins M. 1994. Reinterpreting images. *Philosophical Psychology* 7: 345–358.

Root M. 1986. Davidson and social science. In *Truth and Interpretation: Perspectives on the Philosophy of Donald Davidson*, ed. E Lepore. Oxford: Blackwell.

Rosch E. 1973. Natural categories. *Cognitive Psychology* 4: 328–350.

Rosch E. 1975. Universals and cultural specifics in human categorization. In *Cross Cultural Perspectives on Learning*, ed. R Brislin, S Bochner, W Honner. New York: Halsted.

Rosenberg A. 1985. *The Structure of Biological Science*. Cambridge: Cambridge University Press.

Röska-Hardy L. 2000. Self-ascription and Simulation Theory. *Protosociology* 14: 115–144.

Röska-Hardy L. 2007. Understanding one's self: Narrative and autobiographical memory. In *Narrative and Understanding Persons*, ed. DD Hutto. Royal Institute of Philosophy Supplement. Cambridge: Cambridge University Press.

Roth PA. 1988. Narrative explanations: The case of history. *History and Theory* 27: 1–13.

Roth PA. 1991. Truth in interpretation: The case of psychoanalysis. *Philosophy of the Social Sciences* 21: 175–195.

Roth PA. 2000. The object of understanding. In *Empathy and Agency,* ed. H Kogler, K Stueber. Boulder: Westview Press.

Rowlands M. 1997. Teleological semantics. *Mind* 106: 279–303.

Rowlands M. 1999. *The Body in Mind*. Cambridge: Cambridge University Press.

Rowlands M. 2003. *Externalism: Putting the Mind and World Back Together*. Chesham: Acumen.

Russell B. 1912. *The Problems of Philosophy*. Oxford: Oxford University Press.

Ryle G. 1949. *The Concept of Mind*. London: Hutchinson.

Sabbagh MA, Baldwin DA. 2005. Understanding the role of communicative intentions in word learning. In *Joint Attention: Communication and Other Minds*, ed. N Eilan, C Horel, T McCormack, J Roessler. Oxford: Oxford University Press.

Sacks O. 1995. *An Anthropologist on Mars*. Sydney: Picador.

Savage-Rumbaugh S, McDonald K. 1988. Deception and social manipulation in symbol-using apes. In *Machiavellian Intelligence: Social Expertise and the Evolution of Intellect in Monkeys, Apes and Humans*, ed. RW Bryne, A Whiten. Oxford: Oxford University Press.

Scerif G, Gómez JC, Byrne RW. 2004. What do Diana monkeys know about the focus of attention of a conspecific? *Animal Behaviour* 68: 1239–1247.

Scholl BJ, Leslie A. 1999. Modularity, development and "Theory of Mind." *Mind and Language* 14: 131–153.

Segal G. 1996. The modularity of Theory of Mind. In *Theories of Theories of Mind*, ed. P Carruthers, P Smith. Cambridge: Cambridge University Press.

Segal G. 1998. Representing representations. In *Language and Thought: Interdisciplinary Themes*, ed. P Carruthers, J Boucher. Cambridge: Cambridge University Press.

Segal SJ, Fusella V. 1970. Influences of imagined pictures and sounds on detection of visual and auditory signals. *Journal of Experimental Psychology* 83: 458–464.

Sehon S. 2005. *Teleological Realism: Mind, Agency and Explanation*. Cambridge, MA: MIT Press.

Sellars W. 1956/1997. *Empiricism and the Philosophy of Mind*. Cambridge, MA: Harvard University Press.

Sheldrake R. 1999. "The sense of being stared at" confirmed by simple experiments. *Biology Forum* 93: 209–224.

Sheldrake R. 2005. The sense of being stared at: Part 1: Is it real or illusory? *Journal of Consciousness Studies* 12: 10–31.

Shelley M. 2003/1817. *Frankenstein or The Modern Prometheus*. Ann Arbor: Borders Classics.

Sigman MD, Yirmiya N, Capps L. 1995. Social and cognitive understanding in high functioning children with autism. In *Learning and Cognition in Autism*, ed. E Schopler, GB Mesibov. New York: Plenum Press.

Sinha C. 1988. *Language and Representation: A Socio-Naturalistic Approach to Human Development*. Hemel Hempstead: Harvester-Wheatsheaf.

Sinha C. 2004. The evolution of language: From signals to symbols to system. In *Evolution of Communication Systems: A Comparative Approach*, ed. DK Oller, U Griebel. Cambridge, MA: MIT Press.

Sinha C. 2005. Blending out of the background: Play, props and staging in the material world. *Journal of Pragmatics* 37: 1537–1554.

Slaughter V, Gopnik A. 1996. Conceptual coherence in the child's Theory of Mind: Training children to understand belief. *Child Development* 67: 2967–2988.

Smith B. 2002. Keeping emotions in mind. In *Understanding Emotions*, ed. P Goldie. Aldershot: Ashgate.

Smith M, Apperly I, White V. 2003. False belief reasoning and the acquisition of relative clause sentences. *Child Development* 74: 1709–1719.

Smith P. 1996. Language and the evolution of mind-reading. In *Theories of Theories of Mind*, ed. P Carruthers, P Smith. Cambridge: Cambridge University Press.

Sobel DM. 2004. Children's developing knowledge of the relationship between mental awareness and pretense. *Child Development* 75: 704–729.

Spelke E. 1990. Principles of object perception. *Cognitive Science* 14: 29–56.

Spelke E. 1994. Innate knowledge: Six suggestions. *Cognition* 50: 431–445.

Spelke E, Van de Walle GA. 1993. Perceiving and reasoning about object: Insight from infants. In *Spatial Representation: Problems in Philosophy and Psychology*, ed. N Eilan, R McCarthy, B Brewer. Oxford: Blackwell.

Sperber D. 1994. The modularity of thought and the epistemology of representations. In *Mapping the Mind: Domain Specificity in Cognition and Culture*, ed. LA Hirschfeld, SA Gelman. Cambridge: Cambridge University Press.

Sperber D. 1997. *Explaining Culture: A Naturalistic Approach*. Oxford: Blackwell.

Sperber D, Wilson D. 1998. The mapping between the mental and the public lexicon. In *Language and Thought: Interdisciplinary Themes*, ed. P Carruthers, J Boucher. Cambridge: Cambridge University Press.

Stamenov M, Gallese V, eds. 2002. *Mirror Neurons and the Evolution of Brain and Language*. Amsterdam/Philadelphia: John Benjamins.

Stawarska B. 2007. Persons, pronouns and perspectives. In *Folk Psychology Reassessed*, ed. DD Hutto, M Ratcliffe. Dordrecht: Springer.

Sterelny K. 1997. Navigating the social world: Simulation versus Theory. *Philosophical Books* 38(1): 11–29.

Sterelny K. 2003. *Thought in a Hostile World*. Oxford: Blackwell.

Stich S. 1979. Do Animals Have Beliefs? *Australasian Journal of Philosophy* 57: 15–28.

Stich S. 1982. On the ascription of content. In *Thought and Object*, ed. A Woodfield. Oxford: Oxford University Press.

Stich S. 1983. *From Folk Psychology to Cognitive Science*. Cambridge, MA: MIT Press.

Stich S. 1990. *The Fragmentation of Reason*. Cambridge, MA: MIT Press.

Stich S. 1996. *Deconstructing the Mind*. Oxford: Oxford University Press.

Stich S, Nichols S. 1992. Folk Psychology: Simulation or tacit theory? *Mind and Language* 7: 35–71.

Stich S, Nichols S. 1995. Second thoughts on simulation. In *Mental Simulation*, ed. M Davies. Oxford: Blackwell.

Stich S, Nichols S. 1997. Cognitive penetrability, rationality and restricted simulation. *Mind and Language* 12(3–4): 297–326.

Stich S, Nichols S. 1998. Theory Theory to the max. *Mind and Language* 13: 421–449.

Stich S, Ravenscroft I. 1996. What is folk psychology? In *Deconstructing the mind*. Oxford: University Press.

Stout R. 2004. Internalising practical reasons. *Proceedings of the Aristotelian Society* CIV: 229–243.

Strawson G. 2004. Against narrativity. *Ratio* 17: 428–542.

Stueber KR. 2000. Understanding other minds and the problem of rationality. In *Empathy and Agency*, eds. H Kogler, K Stueber. Boulder: Westview Press.

Stueber KR. 2006. Rediscovering empathy: Agency, folk psychology, and the human sciences. Cambridge, MA: MIT Press.

Stufflebeam R. 2003. Brain matters: A case against representations in the brain. In *Philosophy and the Neurosciences: A Reader*, ed. W Bechtel, P Mandik, J Mundale, S Stufflebeam. Oxford: Blackwell.

Surian L, Leslie AM. 1999. Competence and performance in false belief understanding: A comparison of austistic and normal 3-year-old children. *British Journal of Developmental Psychology* 17: 141–155.

Taylor AE. 1955. *Aristotle*. New York: Dover.

Taylor C. 1985. Self-interpreting animals. In *Human Agency and Language*. Cambridge: Cambridge University Press.

Taylor DM. 1982. Actions, reasons and causal explanation. *Analysis* 42: 216–219.

Tomasello M. 2003. On the different origins of symbols and grammar. In *Language Evolution*, ed. M Christiansen, S Kirby. Oxford: Oxford University Press.

Tomasello M, Call J. 1997. *Primate Cognition*. New York: Oxford University Press.

Tomasello M, Call J, Hare B. 2003a. Chimpanzees understand psychological states—The question is which ones and to what extent. *Trends in Cognitive Sciences* 7: 153–156.

Tomasello M, Call J, Hare B. 2003b. Chimpanzees versus humans: It's not that simple. *Trends in Cognitive Sciences* 7: 239–240.

Tooby J, Cosmides L. 1992. The psychological foundations of culture. In *The Adapted Mind: Evolutionary Psychology and the Generation of Culture*, ed. J Barkow, J Tooby, L Cosmides. New York: Oxford University Press.

Tye M. 1996. *Ten Problems of Consciousness: A Representational Theory of the Phenomenal Mind*. Cambridge, MA: MIT Press.

Vaccari O, Vaccari EE. 1961. *Pictorial Chinese-Japanese Characters: A New and Fascinating Method to Learn Ideographs*: Vaccari Language Institute.

Varela FJ, Thompson E, Rosch E. 2000. *The Embodied Mind: Cognitive Science and Human Experience*. Cambridge, MA: MIT Press.

Varely R. 1998. Aphasic language, aphasic thought. In *Language and Thought: Interdisciplinary Themes*, ed. P Carruthers, J Boucher. Cambridge: Cambridge University Press.

Velleman JD. 2004. The centred self. *Unpublished manuscript.*

Viger CD. 2001. Locking on to the Language of Thought. *Philosophical Psychology* 14: 203–215.

Vinden P. 1996. Junin Quechua children's understanding of mind. *Child Development* 67: 1707–1716.

Vinden P. 1999. Children's understanding of mind and emotion: A multi-culture study. *Cognition and Emotion* 13: 19–48.

Vinden P. 2002. Understanding minds and evidence for belief: A study of Mofu children in Cameroon. *International Journal of Behavioral Development* 26: 445–452.

Vinden P. 2004. In defense of enculturation. *Behavioral and Brain Sciences* 27: 127–128.

Von Eckardt B. 2003. The explanatory need for mental representations in cognitive science. *Mind and Language* 18: 427–439.

Walton MD, Brewer CL. 2001. The role of personal narrative in bringing children into the moral discourse of their culture. *Narrative Inquiry* 11: 307–334.

Watson A, Nixon CL, Wilson A, Capage L. 1999. Social interaction skills and Theory of Mind in young children. *Developmental Psychology* 35: 386–391.

Welch-Ross MK. 1997. Mother-child participation in conversation about the past: Relationship to preschooler's Theory of Mind. *Developmental Psychology* 33: 618–629.

Wellman HM. 1990. *The Child's Theory of Mind.* Cambridge, MA: MIT Press.

Wellman HM. 1991. From desires to belief: Acquisition of a Theory of Mind. In *Natural Theories of Mind,* ed. A Whiten. Oxford: Blackwell.

Wellman HM. 1998. Culture, variation, and levels of analysis in Folk Psychologies: Comment on Lillard. *Psychological Bulletin* 123: 33–36.

Wellman HM, Liu D. 2004. Scaling of Theory-of-Mind tasks. *Child Development* 75: 523–541.

Wellman HM, Phillips A. 2001. Developing intentional understandings. In *Intentions and Intentionality,* ed. B Malle, LJ Moses, DA Baldwin. Cambridge, MA: MIT Press.

Wellman HM, Wooley JD. 1990. From simple desires to ordinary beliefs: The early development of everyday psychology. *Cognition* 35: 245–275.

Whiten A. 1991. *Natural Theories of Mind: Evolution, Development, and Simulation of Everyday Mindreading.* Cambridge: Blackwell.

Whiten A. 1996. When does smart behaviour-reading become mind-reading? In *Theories of Theories of Mind,* ed. P Carruthers, P Smith. Cambridge: Cambridge University Press.

Whiten A. 1997. The Machiavellian mindreader. In *Machiavellian Intelligence II: Extensions and Evaluations*, ed. RW Bryne, A Whiten. Cambridge: Cambridge University Press.

Whiten A, Horner V, Marshal-Pescini S. 2005. Selective imitation in child and chimpanzee: A window on the construal of other's actions. In *Perspectives on Imitation: From Neuroscience to Social Science: Volume 1: Mechanisms of Imitation and Imitation in Animals*, ed. S Hurley, N Chater. Cambridge, MA: MIT Press.

Whyte J. 1990. Success semantics. *Analysis* 50: 149–157.

Wilkerson WS. 1999. From bodily motions to bodily intentions: The perception of bodily activity. *Philosophical Psychology* 12: 61–77.

Wilkerson WS. 2001. Simulation, theory, and the frame problem: The interpretive moment. *Philosophical Psychology* 14(2): 141–153.

Wimmer H, Perner J. 1983. Beliefs about beliefs: Representation and constraining function of wrong beliefs in young children's understanding of deception. *Cognition* 12: 103–128.

Wing L. 1996. *The Autistic Spectrum*. London: Robinson.

Wittgenstein L. 1953. *Philosophical Investigations*. Oxford: Blackwell.

Wittgenstein L. 1983. *Remarks on the Foundations of Mathematics*. Oxford: Blackwell.

Wittgenstein L. 1992. *Last writings on the philosophy of psychology. Volume 2: The inner and the outer*. Oxford: Blackwell.

Wohlschläger A, Bekkering H. 2002. The role of objects in imitation. In *Mirror Neurons and the Evolution of Brain and Language*, ed. M Stamenov, V Gallese. Amsterdam/Philadelphia: John Benjamins.

Woodward AL. 2005. Infants' understanding of the actions involved in joint attention. In *Joint Attention: Communication and Other Minds*, ed. N Eilan, C Horel, T McCormack, J Roessler. Oxford: Oxford University Press.

Woodward AL, Sommerville JA, Guajardo JJ. 2001. How infants make sense of intentional action. In *Intentions and Intentionality*, ed. B Malle, LJ Moses, DA Baldwin. Cambridge, MA: MIT Press.

Woodward J. 1984. A theory of singular causal explanation. *Erkenntnis* 21: 231–262.

Wynn T. 1991. Tools, grammar and the archeology of cognition. *Cambridge Archeological Journal* 1: 191–206.

Wynn T. 2000. Symmetry and the evolution of the modular linguistic mind. In *Evolution and the Human Mind: Modularity, Language and Meta-Cognition*, ed. P Carruthers, A Chamberlain. Cambridge: Cambridge University Press.

Wynn T. 2002. Archaeology and cognitive evolution. *Behavioral and Brain Sciences* 25: 389–438.

Zahavi D. 2007a. Expression and empathy. In *Folk Psychology Re-Assessed*, ed. DD Hutto, M Ratcliffe. Dordrecht: Springer.

Zahavi D. 2007b. Self and other: The limits of narrative understanding. In *Narrative and Understanding Persons*, ed. DD Hutto. Royal Institute of Philosophy Supplement. Cambridge: Cambridge University Press.

Zahavi D, Parnas J. 2003. Conceptual problems in infantile autism research: Why cognitive science needs phenomenology. *Journal of Consciousness Studies* 10: 53–71.

Zlatev J. 2005. What's in a schema? Bodily mimesis and the grounding of language. In *From Perception to Meaning: Image Schemas in Cognitive Linguistics*, ed. B Hampe. Berlin: Mouton.

Zlatev J. 2006. Language, embodiment and mimesis. In *Body, Language and Mind. Vol 1. Embodiment*, ed. T Ziemke, J Zlatev, R Roz Frank. Berlin: Mouton.

Zlatev J. 2007. Intersubjectivity, language and the mimesis hierarchy. In *The Shared Mind: Perspectives on Intersubjectivity*, ed. J Zlatev, T Racine, C Sinha, E Itkonen. Amsterdam/Philadelphia: John Benjamins.

Zlatev J, Persson T, Gärdenfors P. 2005. Bodily mimesis as "the missing link" in human cognitive evolution. Lund University Cognitive Studies 121.

Index